EDWARD LEAR

The Art of Poetry

Collected Poems 1955–75

Marko the Prince
(*Serbo-Croat translations*)

The Noise Made by Poems

Yevtushenko's Poems
(*translations*)

A History of Greek Literature

The Life and Times of William Shakespeare

Boris Pasternak: A Biography

Tennyson

PETER LEVI

EDWARD LEAR

A Biography

MACMILLAN

B/LEI

First published 1995 by Macmillan London

an imprint of Macmillan General Books
Cavaye Place London SW10 9PG
and Basingstoke

Associated companies throughout the world

ISBN 0-333-58804-5

1 3 5 7 9 8 6 4 2

A CIP catalogue record for this book is available from
the British Library

Typeset by CentraCet Limited, Cambridge
Printed by Mackays of Chatham plc,
Chatham, Kent

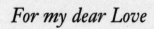

For my dear Love

Contents

CONTENTS

List of Illustrations

SECTION ONE

1. Ann Lear (National Portrait Gallery)
2. Edward Lear by W. H. Marstrand, 1840 (National Portrait Gallery)
3. Preliminary study of a parrot, 1830–32 (Department of Printing and Graphic Arts, Houghton Library, Harvard University)
4. Snowy owl (Linnean Society/E.T. Archive)
5. Hyrax, 1832 (Agnew and Sons/Bridgeman Art Library)
6. Civet, 1836 (private collection)
7. View of Florence, 1837 (British Museum)
8. Chichester Fortescue (Hulton Deutsch)
9. A. P. Stanley (National Portrait Gallery)
10. Crummock Water (Fotomas Index)
11. Letter from the *Nonsense Alphabet* (Victoria and Albert Museum)
12. Self-portrait
13. Sketch of Burpham, 1834
14. Sketch of Osborne by Queen Victoria (The Royal Collection © 1995 Her Majesty Queen Elizabeth II)
15. Subiaco, 1841 (British Museum)
16. Marathon, 1848 (Ashmolean Museum, Oxford)
17. Athens, 1848 (Ashmolean Museum, Oxford)
18. Bassae, 1854–5 (Fitzwilliam Museum, Cambridge)
19. Countess Waldegrave (Vivien Noakes)
20. William Holman Hunt (National Portrait Gallery)
21. Party at Strawberry Hill (Mary Evans Picture Library)
22. Villa Tennyson (Vivien Noakes)
23. 'Condé Terrace', Corfu (National Library of Scotland)

SECTION TWO

How Pleasant to Know Mr Lear

How pleasant to know Mr Lear!
  Who has written such volumes of stuff!
Some think him ill-tempered and queer,
  But a few think him pleasant enough.

His mind is concrete and fastidious,
  His nose is remarkably big;
His visage is more or less hideous,
  His beard it resembles a wig.

He has ears, and two eyes, and ten fingers,
  Leastways if you reckon two thumbs;
Long ago he was one of the singers,
  But now he is one of the dumbs.

He sits in a beautiful parlour,
  With hundreds of books on the wall;
He drinks a great deal of Marsala,
  But never gets tipsy at all.

He has many friends, laymen and clerical;
  Old Foss is the name of his cat;
His body is perfectly spherical,
  He weareth a runcible hat.

When he walks in a waterproof white,
  The children run after him so!
Calling out, 'He's come out in his night-
  Gown, that crazy old Englishman, oh!'

He weeps by the side of the ocean,
　　He weeps on the top of the hill;
He purchases pancakes and lotion,
　　And chocolate shrimps from the mill.

He reads but he cannot speak Spanish,
　　He cannot abide ginger-beer:
Ere the days of his pilgrimage vanish,
　　How pleasant to know Mr Lear!

INTRODUCTION

THIS BOOK arises not so much from childhood experience as from lifelong pleasure in the work of Edward Lear, and more immediately from an attempt to put together a lecture on Lear as a poet, a role in which I thought he was utterly under-estimated. The lecture was given at Oxford, and printed in 1991 by Yale University Press in *The Art of Poetry*, but it was unsatisfactory, because there was a great deal I did not know or had not considered, both about the paintings and about the context in life of the poems. I did not remember that Blake in his 'Milton' in 1808 had defined the extent of London, 'in immense labours and sorrows, ever building, ever falling', as stretching from Blackheath to Hounslow and Finchley to Norwood, though he puts Hampstead and Highgate outside it. What is worse, I had not grasped the importance of the thirty and more thick volumes of Edward Lear's diaries at Harvard, or of what is revealed in his vast and still largely unpublished correspondence. I had not understood how his poetry, varying in tone from the merest jokes to the most serious, was scattered. Some of it, a poem for Thomas Hanbury for example, is still being traced. Indeed, there is still no complete, reliable edition of it, so that any reader of the list of thirty-seven Nonsense publications of Lear's work in the Royal Academy Lear Exhibition Catalogue of 1985[1] will be amazed, and book collectors will despair. Those who consult the list of his various scientific engravings of birds and animals will be even more appalled at how scattered they are.

A great deal has been done, particularly on the occasion of that exhibition. I have relied on the unfailing generosity, the lifelong experience and the vast knowledge of Edward Lear of his biographer, who is the editor of his *Selected Letters* (1988), and the writer of by far the best book about his paintings (1991), Vivien Noakes. My debts to other people, such as the Gillies family, are really debts to and through her. They ramify to such an extent through every page of this book that it is likely I have not always acknowledged them in detail, though I am most deeply grateful for her help. I could not have done without the photocopies of Lear's letters which she has collected. To Kevin Van Anglen, to Eliot House, Harvard, to its Master and to the Houghton Library there, which owns thousands of Lear's paintings, boxes and volumes of his manuscripts, and the whole of what survives of his diary, I owe a debt almost as vast and as unrepayable. Thirdly, I was enormously helped and my work much speeded by photocopies made available to me by Dr Lee of the rare books collection of the University of Bristol, and by the Tennyson Research Centre at Lincoln, which has Lear's letters to the Tennyson family. It will be seen that reading all this material was in itself a formidable task, but one document illuminates another and in the end, because of his long diaries and his endless letter-writing, Edward Lear is a rewarding subject of historical study.

He was that from the beginning, of course. He was a rare or unique combination of charm and brilliance and hard intelligence, and a volcano of creativity; he was gregarious and clubbable and socially merry, but with a deep enough tinge of private melancholy to make him interesting. Some of the secrets of his friendships remain obscure: I do not really understand the gloom of the Lushington family for instance, and I wish I knew Fortescue better. I am not really sure why Gussie Bethell refused to marry him, but neither perhaps was he. She was the great-aunt of a close friend of mine, which fact gave me a sense of closeness to Edward Lear before I had ever read about his life. One gets that sense more strongly from the immediacy of his water-colours. It was those, I think, that first drew one's interest to him: both the way he painted and the thrilling places he had been. The easy days of the 1930s, when the Northbrook and Lushington collections of Lear came on the market at once, and you could buy a water-colour in Museum Street for 5s., were alas long over; the huge Harvard Lear archive had begun to be formed at that time by Philip Hofer and W. Osgood Field, his assistant and friend, and it has at least done Lear the enormous service of sheltering his water-colours from sunlight. But even in the 1950s it was still easy to buy an Edward Lear for £5 or £10.

It is mostly Lear's letters to private friends that reveal him as possibly the greatest caricaturist of his adult lifetime. This skill of his had been barely discernible in the illustrations of his Nonsense books, which are very much more wooden and less appealing than the pen and ink originals; those are often drawings of an exquisite subtlety. He became more widely known following the publication of his correspondence with Chichester Fortescue by Lady Strachey in a lavish edition in 1907, and a second volume in 1911. While she was doing this work her eyes were failing, and she was no longer young; furthermore, she seems to have imposed a kind of prudent censorship on some of the letters, although the originals are now luckily out of harm's way in the Taunton public records. They are there because Lady Strachey, formerly Constance Braham, a niece of Fortescue's wife Lady Waldegrave, had married a country neighbour at Sutton Court near Chew Magna in Somerset. Many of the families Lear knew, and for whom he drew his caricatures or self-portraits, married into one another, so that Lady Strachey was a cousin of the Beadons, the Bruces (Lord Aberdare), the Norths and Symonds, Sligger Urquhart of Balliol, Lytton Strachey, the Pattles, the Prinseps, the Lushingtons and the Tennysons. Anyone familiar with the lives of grand Victorians will recognize this as a usual phenomenon: I record this one case as typical of many.

In the midst of this entanglement prowls Lear, as lonely and as tigerish as his cat – or as his numerous cats, because in the twenty years between a stray kitten called the Froglodyte, which he picked up with John Proby in Sicily, and the twin brother and sister Lear and his servant called Fee and Foss, from *adelphi* and *adelphos*, there were a number of others. Lear's zoological drawing has a vast range: it seems that nothing was beyond him, and the care he took over the tiniest detail, on every hair of the hyrax, is still astounding. He might also have well become the most distinguished English painter of birds, had he persevered: if there had been money in it, that is to say, because he lived too late to have a rich and generous patron and too early to enjoy an organized commercial success. John Gould, who ruthlessly exploited Lear, and did carve himself out a success, was an extremely tough nut. It is not simply on the basis of Lear's spectacular parrots that I place him so high, but for those birds where just a pinch of caricature enters into his drawing: most of all the half-dozen or so owls in Gould's *Birds of Europe*, the Great Snowy Owl for example.

We all used to think of Lear as one of those extraordinary Victorians, like G. M. Hopkins, who contrive to be interesting in many different ways, and yet their whole is somehow greater than the sum of their parts. The whole of what Lear was, as of what Ruskin was or what Byron was, comes slowly to light in the course of reading their full life-stories and their letters as well as their more formal writings. In some ways Edward Lear has been very well served. Several of his friends wrote small memoirs of him, and in the next generation Angus Davidson, who was a minor member of Bloomsbury and the translator of Alberto Moravia, wrote a gentle life of Lear in 1933, which in its day was a revelation. It certainly was so to me as late as 1958, when I first came across it. Still, it was not a very deep book, and it did not by any means exhaust the available sources; all forty volumes of the diaries could have been bought for £5 in about 1930. With the first biography of Lear by Vivien Noakes in 1968, we are on much more solid ground. Indeed, with the latest edition of that book (1985), the Royal Academy Catalogue (1985), the *Selected Letters* (1988), and *The Painter Edward Lear* (1991), she has put down solid foundations for all future Lear scholarship. I have seldom or never discovered that she missed anything.

My first intention was to explore Lear's poetry, and I suppose that I thought a note on his travels would do no harm, since I had explored and loved many of the same places. I swiftly discovered (but a little too late) the magnitude of this task, and I have tried to do justice to every aspect of it, though it has sometimes been summary justice. The fascinating thing about the poems is that they developed so late in Lear's life, out of children's entertainments which clearly already contained autobiography in a kind of transformation scene. One is not certain whether he is laughing or weeping. The remote inspiration of this highly individual form of art is stranger still: it seems to have roots in the traditional mummers' plays, which were seldom written down and almost never seriously recorded until too late, about the 1900s; yet they go back to Shakespeare's day, and proliferate in the children's nursery rhymes collected by the Opies.[2] Lear's idea of Nonsense itself seems to derive from these rhymes. It can be found in Kele's *Christmas Carolles* (1550), or more conveniently in Herbert Read's 1939 anthology, *Knapsack*:[3]

> Tirlery lorpin, the laverock sang,
> So merrily pipes the sparrow,
> The cow broke loose, the rope ran home,
> Sir, God give you goodmorrow.

Things are out of hand in the kitchen, the crow goes to the water, the goose goes to the green, it is a kingdom of topsy-turvydom or escape beloved to children. 'Tirlery lorpin' is like 'Tirra lirra', the song of the lark, but the sparrow has a role closer to home. In his last poem, that is, in the one he intended to be his final statement, which he sent to fourteen or more friends at the end of his life, Lear pruned his material unmercifully, and the laconic result is indeed the most brilliant of self-caricatures, hiding and revealing its meaning by the same words: and it is beautiful as well as musical. It is in its way the essence of Alfred Tennyson's poetry. It is almost as if some urchin had picked the gold watch from the nineteenth century's waistcoat pocket and run off with it, while it played its intimate mechanical tune. The art form of Uncle Arly goes a long way beyond parody.

But Lear was professionally and, I think, essentially a painter. There is a passage at the end of Chesterton's *Man Who Was Thursday* that reminded me recently of his paintings: Chesterton, Maurice Baring, a nephew or cousin of Lear's friend Lord Northbrook, and Aldous Huxley all wrote interesting essays about Lear, but this is about dawn. 'Dawn was breaking over everything in colours at once clear and timid: as if Nature made a first attempt at yellow and a first attempt at rose. A breeze blew so clean and sweet, that one could not think it blew from the sky; it blew rather through some hole in the sky.' Give or take a little and this seems true of the crisp, airy quality of Lear's Cretan sketches, and the light cavalry dash of his sympathy with mountains to the very end of his life. It is as if some instrument, first confidently though very youthfully sounded in the Lake District 1830s, and coming to perfection in the 1860s and 1870s in spite of Lear's breakdown over his house, and over his Indian journey, could still be heard with that harshly mellow quality we associate with the old age of artists; and yet the instrument remains the same. The power of the black, final version of his Tennysonian paintings is very great, as is the richness of his unfinished *Enoch Arden*. Whichever way you look at Lear, and there are indeed many, he was an interesting and, within his limits, a great artist.

It is sometimes difficult to trace him. The *Journey to Petra* was published by Lushington in *Macmillan's Magazine*, April 1897, though it has luckily been reprinted in H. Van Thal's valuable selection from Lear's travel writings (1952). Granville Proby printed Lear's cartoon version of their Sicilian journey as *Lear in Sicily* (1938). Ray Murphy produced an abridged version of the *Indian Journal* in 1953, Rowena Fowler a very beautiful *Cretan Journal* (1984) and Denise Harvey and Philip Sherrard an equally beautiful *Lear in Corfu* (1988): these last two are the only thorough, well-produced and fully illustrated editions of any travel writings of Lear to appear, either in his lifetime or since. His earliest travel writings are hard to find. He used his diaries like his sketches, of which he left at least 10,000 to friends who had supported him with money. He kept them as a quarry, to be written up or painted up on winter evenings. He projected an *Egypt*, for example, which has never appeared, although he did write up his diaries.

He was never satisfied with the financial arrangements for his travel books, which were laborious to produce, and more so to distribute to the subscribers. He hesitated over the means of illustration, drawings on stone or on wood and, at the end of his life, various forms of photographic printing. Only the Tennyson produced after his death is in its way satisfactory: but Hallam Tennyson was not pleased even with that. The Bodleian Library has a fine copy (unsigned). The poems – 'To E. L.', 'On his Travels in Greece', 'The Palace of Art' and 'The Daisy' – were privately printed in 100 copies signed by the poet, by Boussod, Valadon, 1889. Beautiful as this posthumous book is, Hallam is to be found cajoling and badgering the publishers in a way that Lear was never in a position to do. 'I return the Lear reproductions. Can you possibly insert two small Goupilgravures of the divine Peneian Pass and of the Palms and Temples of the South. His Lordship would *much* like this.' There are six of these letters, including 'Why have Lord Tennyson's copies of the Lear book not been forwarded?' and 'Jan. 19, 1890. Send *me* at once to Osborne, Isle of Wight, where I shall be on Tuesday, a copy of Lear's Illustrated Book for Her Majesty.' On 30 January, 'The books arrived last night. My father likes them.' It is an august ending to a protracted agony; the letters are at Harvard.

It is possible to discover in libraries copies of the *Journal of a Landscape Painter in Albania* (1851), in *Southern Calabria* (1852), and in *Corsica* in 1868 (1870), and they were all three shortened and reprinted in the 1960s though not even the reprints are now easy to find in antiquarian bookshops, and of the old editions both Corsica and Albania would now cost four or five hundred pounds. But Lear's earliest travel books are more difficult still. *Views in Rome and its Environs* (1841) is a privately printed folio, as the *Parrots* had been, and an extremely rare book that very few libraries possess, although Harvard has acquired a copy in the last sixty years. That is not coloured, but some copies exist where the lithographs were coloured by hand, that is, where they are aquatints, like the *Parrots*. *Illustrated Excursions in Italy*, two volumes in quarto (1846), is a little easier to find; for example the Bodleian Library has both volumes. They were apparently issued in April and as 'Second Series' in August, but Volume 2 seems to be rarer, at least in public libraries. The *Views in Rome* and the *Excursions in Italy* offer little in the way of text. Even *Southern Calabria*, with its second part 'The Kingdom of Naples', makes a pleasantly youthful impression. *Albania*, where Lear is alone with his servant, and conscious perhaps of Colonel Leake as a great example, is more solemn and more professional.

The finest of Edward Lear's productions as a traveller is probably *Views in the Seven Ionian Islands*, because its chromolithographs are of such beauty and done with such care. There is a brief text, and we have the diary that covers this period (1863). Lear had planned the book for some time and it marks a high point in his career as an artist. No one was producing anything like it at the time, no one had done so in the past and certainly no one has done so since. It may be remembered that 1864 saw the British withdrawal not only from Corfu but from the entire province of the Ionian Islands, which were handed over to Greece, so that to this most unlikely of British dependencies Lear's book is a funeral monument. It marks an end of things in another way too, because when Lear first went out to Rome in the 1830s, and even when he settled in Corfu in the 1850s, it was still normal to buy a souvenir image of the place from a painter, but by 1865 it was perhaps more usual to buy photographs, and by 1885 picture postcards. Lear was most interested in photography, and kept an accurate eye on its usefulness to him as a painter. At the end of his life he was interested to find some of the same people he had known as technical staff in C. J. Hullmandel's lithographic studio when he was printing parrots from his own drawings on stone, not long after the death of Blake, at work for a photographic company called Autotype. The *Ionian Islands* prints are often found separately, but when they are bound the text is of course with them. They were reproduced in facsimile in 1000 copies in 1979 by Broadbent of Oldham, but I have never seen an example of that edition.

The reader of this book will draw many sad observations about the lives of artists in the nineteenth century. It was Lear's fate to fall in with the Pre-Raphaelites at a time when he was vulnerably open to bad advice. They were wonderfully decorative artists, of whom William Morris, whom Lear never knew, was the most serious, but Lear fell under the influence of Holman Hunt, an assured but quite irresponsible young man with his way to make, and much time and energy were wasted. The very idea of being exclusively a topographic artist, that is, a painter of places without much in the way of people, was hard for the public to swallow. Lear was not confident with faces, as Peter de Wint was not. Of course, his landscape painting goes back to an eighteenth-century and earlier tradition: to Poussin and to Claude. That is where Lear found and learnt it. But paintings of pure landscape did not make large sums of money. A gentleman might pay for a picture of the deer in his own park, as Lord Egremont paid Turner. A scene with a ruin might equally do well. But the obsession of Cézanne, who was nearly thirty years younger than Lear, with Mont Ste-Victoire, which means so much to us, would have appealed very weakly to the Victorians. Queen Victoria was taught drawing by Lear, yet we know that the Queen thought Turner was mad; what she really relished was Murillo.

If Lear had done nothing but his birds or his zoos, or nothing but his travel books illustrated with landscapes, or even if he had written only his letters and diaries, or nothing but his poetry, we would still surely respect and admire him today. At the time when I lectured on Lear in 1988 I had long since given up the idea of writing about him at greater length, since it was obviously desirable that Vivien Noakes, who already knew so much about Edward Lear after working on him for more than twenty years, should produce a full book, such as her then publisher refused to contemplate. My ambition was revived by her Academy catalogue and by the Lear exhibition. Ruth Pitman's *Edward Lear's Tennyson* (1988) and Philip Hofer's *Lear as a Landscape Draughtsman* (1967) sharpened my curiosity.

In writing Tennyson's biography I had put aside his relationship with Lear, as I felt it to be more part of Lear's life than the poet's, and the poet hardly seemed conscious of the intensity of Lear's feelings. I did not then know what was in Lear's diaries about the Tennysons. It will be a pleasure now to put that right. I have scarcely dealt with Lear's musical settings of Tennyson or of other poets. I have heard a few, but they are not very strong, they are the thin distillation of an essence of lyrics that we prefer as they are. Lear was not as great a composer as he was a painter, not as original in his music as he was in poetry. It is curious that the closest analogy to his parodies, his sadness and his humour is to be found in the work of John Betjeman, which has an equally musical component: they were both almost essentially performers. But nothing I have suggested can quite explain a single one of Edward Lear's innumerable gifts.

I am most grateful to the Houghton Library at Harvard and its staff; the Earl of Derby and his librarian; the London Library and its staff; the Gloucester and Quedgely public libraries; Dr Gordon, the Librarian of Newcastle University; Sue Gates of Lincoln; the Scottish National Library; the Liverpool Public Library; the Ashmolean Museum, Oxford; the Librarian of the Linnaean Society; the Bodleian Library, Oxford and its staff; Mr and Mrs Devitt; Matthew Connolly; Mr Harvey-Bathurst of

Eastnor Castle; the Headmaster of Rendcombe College; Christie's of Scotland; Agnew's; David Carritt Ltd; the Leger Gallery; Mrs Patrick Kavanagh; Mrs Lees-Milne; Mrs Mary Burn; Mrs Ross; the late Anne Jeffery; Mr Simon Hanbury of La Mortola; Mr Anthony Hobson of Whitsbury; Chris Hare of Southern Heritage, as well as to those I have thanked already. We all equally owe thanks to the late Philip Hofer and Mr Field of Harvard, through whom the mass of Lear's life's work has been preserved and can be studied. While I was awaiting proofs, a few new fragments came to light which should be recorded. A life of Parson Hawker of Morwenstow, a friend of the Bishop of Exeter of the day and so no friend to Canterbury, reveals that the Archbishop Lear loved had so few teeth that even his calls to prayer could not be understood. I have seen for sale in a Devitts catalogue an illustrated alphabet like Lear's with rhymes and cartoons in which the hero has a distinct resemblance to a thinner, wiry-whiskered Foss. The booklet is called *The Fan*. It should finally be noted that the method Lear was seeking in his last years for the reproduction of his paintings was in fact discovered and used by the son of Samuel Palmer (died 1881) in his edition of his father's drawings for Milton's *Minor Poems*, for which he certainly used both the techniques of photography and of etching, in a mysterious combination.

Peter Levi
Frampton on Severn

CHAPTER ONE

BOYHOOD

EDWARD LEAR was born a Londoner, his parents' twentieth child, on 12 May 1812, four months after Dickens, and 103 years after Dr Johnson. In 1812, George III was still king, you could shoot snipe in Conduit Street, and a flock of sheep might slow you down in Piccadilly. London must have looked much as Canaletto had painted it: all the same, it was just beginning to burst the boundaries of what we now call a country town. Soane's Bank of England was being built, but Hampstead and Chelsea were distant villages across the fields. Those who were born citizens of that astounding city were doomed to live out their time in a constant and catastrophic decline of the quality of life. By the mid-century coal had blackened every building, and the smell of the Thames and the smog were at their worst. Edward Lear was forced to spend most of his winters abroad because of his weak lungs.

Early in the century, the suburbs had become a prudent refuge, though each in turn was swallowed up as London spread beyond them. Edward Lear's home was in the village of Holloway, at the corner of Holloway Road and the Seven Sisters Road, just on the flank of Highgate Hill. The house was called Bowman's Lodge because it was said to stand on the site of an old archery field, where Bowman's Mews is now. In the 1843 *History of Islington* it belonged to Charles Mann. The house appears, from a print used to advertise the girls' school that it became, to have been built and stuccoed in the late eighteenth century. It was a capacious, unpretentious villa of two storeys protected from the road by iron railings, with two or three trees to give it some privacy. Other buildings crowded it from the sides. After it had been adapted to serve as a girls' school, it was pulled down in Edward Lear's lifetime. The print to

advertise the school shows only five bays, but Lear drew it in his diary
with seven, and he also remembered an attic which the print has tidied
out of existence. There were finer houses not far away, and gardens
designed or improved by Repton; Bowman's Lodge was just a suburban
dwelling-house for a minor professional man, not unlike some in the
area that still survive as doctors' surgeries or solicitors' offices.

The Lears had chosen it because it was convenient for the City. Mr
Lear was marked both by his successes and his failures in life, as part of
that swiftly increasing middle class which was socially mobile in both
directions. If one compares Edward's early life with the early chapters of
the comic novel *A Rogue's Life*, by his friend Wilkie Collins (1879), one
must concede that he might have gone either way. Still, to imagine
Holloway as it was, one must think away the grizzly, crowded accommodation of the last 170 years, above all the railways with the spread of
differences they have made. All the same, the Holloway Road and the
Seven Sisters Road were already busy and important highways. The
Great North Road through Holloway was a drovers' track as well as a
highway: Romney had lived and worked in a public house not far from
Bowman's.

Edward's first excursions were away from London, towards Highgate
and in Hornsey Fields. Later in life his memory flooded with sadness at
the sight of any beautiful landscape. He wrote in his diary for 1 June
1870:

> What a mingling of sadness and admiration of landscape botheringly will
> persist in existing. All the unsought morbid feelings – (certainly unsought
> for I knew not what even the meaning of morbid was in those days) – of
> past years crop up at once – such as the Hornsey Fields and Highgate
> archway, and the sad large thorn tree at Holloway about 1819 or 1820.

Hornsey Fields lay to the north, and Highgate Arch was an Elizabethan
tollgate; now the fields are gone and nothing remains of the arch except
the name Archway, where the A1 heads away towards Scotland. Once, it
must have marked the beginning of real country.

The house stood about a mile and a half from what is now King's
Cross Station, yet houses were pretty there and not very high; it was not
far away that Keats listened to his nightingale. For 200 years or more
Londoners had been moving out of London, step by step. As it became
busier and cast its shadow further, people like the Lears moved for
cheapness as well as amenity and rural peace. Their first child was born
in Pentonville, a mile or so closer to the centre. We know little about

their origins, though more than Edward knew, since he was brought up by his elder sisters and given only a cobweb of family mythology. George Lear, the son of a butcher from Gillingham in Dorset, came up to London in the seventeenth century and became an apprentice fruiterer. By 1692 he belonged to the Company of Fruiterers and was a freeman of the City. He was illiterate, but when he died in 1745 he left seven children and a sugar refinery. This was a profitable business based on West Indian sugar cane and therefore on the slave trade. One of his seven children was Edward's grandfather, Henry, who ran a refinery in Thames Street, close to London Bridge; his parish was St Benet's, Paul's Wharf. The year before his father died he married Margaret Lester; they had six children, the youngest of whom was called Jeremiah, born in 1757. He was Edward's father.

The whole family moved to Whitechapel, which was a solid suburb in those days, but there Henry died of a fever. His widow Margaret still carried on the family business, and Jeremiah was brought up as a sugar refiner. Edward knew nothing about all this; he knew more about his mother's side of the family, though even that somewhat cloudily. In 1788, Jeremiah married a Whitechapel girl called Ann Skerrett. The wedding was at Wanstead, and Edward's sisters told him it had been an elopement, but that was not exactly true, because the banns were called normally. The bride was an heiress in a small way. She and her mother both had long lives, and although Edward never knew his grandmother, who died in 1802, his sister Ann knew her quite well. She left money to Ann, either because she was the eldest surviving grandchild or because she had to look after the other children. This grandmother's memory went back to the 1745 rebellion. Her daughter married at nineteen when Jeremiah was thirty-one: they settled in Pentonville and their first child, Ann, was born there in 1790. She was twenty-two years older than Edward, and they were deeply dependent on one another; she never married and was like a mother to him.

Jeremiah prospered at first in his career. In 1790 he joined the Fruiterers, and in 1799 he was Master of that Company. At that height of success he became sworn in as a stockbroker, which in those days was a dangerous game, as he was to discover. When the new Stock Exchange was built he became a share-holder in it. He was not alone, of course, he had uncles and brothers of whom we know almost nothing, who supported him and apparently cushioned the blow when it came. We know more about his wife's family, because their memories were tenacious of grandeurs long ago. Edward's sister Sarah Street, who had married a bank manager and settled after his death in New Zealand, was the grandmother of Sir Harold Gillies (1882–1960), and it is through his family that we have a typescript of Edward's letters to Ann, and an assortment of other information. Edward's mother bore twenty-one children, though only three of his sisters married, and of those three only Sarah had children of her own.

Ann Skerrett's case is astonishing, but not unique. Indeed, in some ways it is similar to my own grandmother's, who also bore twenty-one children. As a result my father, who was one of the youngest, was largely brought up by unmarried elder sisters, his mother was often unwell, and although there was money while my grandfather was alive, my father did not inherit much, and his youth was adventurous. It is not uncommon in such families that by some mysterious compensation of nature a number of the children or grandchildren should be childless, and that is what happened in Edward's family. Two children were still-born or died at once, and two Henrys, two Sarahs and a Catherine died very young, so Edward cannot have known more than thirteen or so of his brothers and sisters, even as a tiny child, and we shall see that many of them, let alone most of his cousins, remained mysterious to him. His mother's family claimed descent through Florence Skerritt, Florence Usher and Eleanor Mason from the Brignalls of Durham. It is curious that this family tree is entirely matriarchal.

The important focus of the story is sister Ann. Edward destroyed twenty years or more of his own early diaries, but his letters to Ann were very full, like the chapters of an exuberant journal only slightly self-censored for publication, and the manuscript, which disappeared only in the 1930s when the typescript was made, may one day re-emerge. It was from Ann or Eleanor that he learned to draw, in that perfect and lucid style of flower-painting so common in the days of the *Botanical Magazine*, and apparently so unattainable in ours. He was taught the art by his sisters in what they called the painting room. They in turn had learnt it by copying, aided no doubt by one of the numerous text-books of the 1800s. Edward's earliest models of animal drawing were the illustrations to Buffon. It is not certain what edition he had, and these illustrations varied, but probably it was not luxurious. The whole work in French in its numerous volumes covered all natural history, including that of man, distinguished from other animals by the size of his calves and his habit of kissing, but by 1812 it had been edited in one volume for children with *jolies gravures en bois* (1809), and translated. Tennyson as a boy educated himself out of his father's copy, though that is not among the books in the Tennyson Library at Lincoln. The woodcuts in my 1809 copy are appealing, and it may be those he first painted, but the 1809 book is tiny, and his father might well have owned something more substantial.

The drawings Edward made as a boy, those in the album now in the National Library at Edinburgh, for example, are perfectly conventional, of parakeets and pretty little birds and butterflies, and of brilliant flowers. He grew up with a girl's accomplishments, as those were in 1812: natural history drawing of birds, flowers, and a few shells, slight, comic verses and parodies of poets like Collins, and singing and some original composition of song, though he was unable to write his songs down. At that stage he might have been a vicar's daughter. He was affectionate, he was devoted to children, and he cultivated intimate friendship wherever it was offered. Maybe he felt an unassuaged passion for the nursery with its happy games, but a nursery he had not known for long. In a way he was like the lady buried at Crewe who 'painted in watercolour, played upon the harp, and was an intimate friend of the Duchess of Bridgewater'. He grew up without knowing how to ride a horse or shoot a gun, or how to fish, and without classical languages until late in life. He was quite uneducated in any normal sense.

All the same he was happy. His worst suffering was what is often called temporal lobe epilepsy, which from early boyhood attacked him up to ten or fifteen times a month, sometimes several times a day. From about the age of six to eleven, when he went to school for a short time, Edward brooded over his epilepsy, suffered it continually, and feared it 'every morning in the little study when learning my lessons, all day long, and always in the evenings and at night. The strong will of sister Harriet put a short pause to the misery, but very short' (*Diary*, 15 August 1866). Although he became convinced that his disease could not really ever be controlled, and so had no need to blame himself for its persistence, Edward knew what was wrong because his sister Jane had the same disease. It is probable that he thought as most people did at the time that the spasms had some gruesome connection with sex, and maybe with madness, but whatever shame he felt about them seems to have vanished in middle age, after he had consulted doctors. Harriet taught him how to control the spasms, and he did so to such a degree that few or none of his friends guessed the secret until he was dead and it was found in his diaries. He seems to have taken up his active, outdoor landscape painter's life as a kind of therapy, and his achievement of a lifework on the scale and of the quality he did achieve was a victory beyond all expectation and praise.

We can enter into his early feelings only through his later memories.

> The earliest of all the morbidnesses I can recollect must have been somewhere about 1819 – when my father took me to a field near Highgate, where was a rural performance of gymnastic clowns etc – and a band. The music was good – at least it attracted me – and the sunset and twilight I remember as if yesterday. And I can recollect crying half the night after all the small gaiety broke up – and also suffering for days at the memory of the past scene. [*Diary*, 24 March 1877]

At some time in his childhood, Lear must have seen mummers' plays, with their comic, melancholy characters who are like village naturals or Shakespearean rustics. The plays are mostly lost now, but they were popular and traditional entertainments, made all the more poignant and mysterious by being handed down through centuries by the illiterate, with much resulting incomprehension. They lie behind much of Lear's lyric poetry and his style of humour, as we shall see. The feeling he came to call morbid appears to range from a childish wailing at loss to the Watteauesque melancholy of a sunset. It is the sadness of his limericks as well as their funniness that appeals so strongly to adults. The sadness he felt after his evening at Highgate and which he remembered for so long does not need explaining to anyone who remembers their own childhood. It has nothing to do with the pre-epileptic condition of trance that critics have attributed to Tennyson.

Edward was a nervous, short-sighted little boy. Once Ann took him to Margate: seaside resorts were booming in these years, and in 1848 he still remembered Mr Cox's hawk, 'and the colliers disembarking coal at the pier – and the windmills – and the chimneysweep you so *cruelly* MADE me walk round and round to see he was not smoking – shocking. My imperfect sight in those days – ante-spectacled – formed everything into a horror.'

In 1816, when Edward was four, Jeremiah seems to have gone bankrupt for a four-year period. The event is as mysterious as any in Edward's childhood, but in 1816 his father defaulted on the Exchange, owing £2150 11s. 1d. A friend called Smith enabled him to settle these debts at half a crown in the pound with £269 5s. 5d., but meanwhile tradesmen's bills came in that he was not able to meet. Jeremiah appears to have gone to a debtors' prison, perhaps King's Bench, and is said to have stayed there until 1820. Most of the daughters were pushed out to work as governesses, and it is not clear how many of them survived. The house at Holloway was let to Jews: Edward grew up believing that they 'always opened the windows in thunder-storms – for the easier entrance of the Messiah, but to greater spoiling of the furniture'. But at some point Jeremiah borrowed £1000 from his banker which he repaid, and it is not clear how long he really spent in prison. His attendances at the Fruiterers' Company were apparently uninterrupted. Vivien Noakes is sure he was never in the King's Bench.[1] The Islington Rate Book gives his name down to 1819–20, then Jh Lear and Josiah Lear until 1825 when Josiah is crossed out and Jeremiah reappears. This might be a kinsman, or it might be a clerical error. Jeremiah is not in the records of debtors' prisons at all, so far as they survive, and certainly not in the official bankruptcy lists in the *London Gazette*. The Gillies papers date his bankruptcy July–September 1818 and October–December 1819, and refer to the *Times* Index, F26a 2a and F402b. He is recorded only as a defaulter on the Stock Exchange but continues as a member.

Who knows what happened? What was Jeremiah doing in his room at the top of the house, which he kept locked? He worked there on Sundays, sometimes from four in the morning, and no women were ever allowed in. What is queerer still, there was no recorded visible product of his work. Working on Sunday combined with the registration of his children's baptisms in the Nonconformist register at Dr Williams' Library suggests he was not a conventional Christian, and the 'forge' he used suggests some kind of experiment. Dr Johnson once spent three days experimenting in secret at the Chelsea Pottery, though his idea turned out fruitless. Was Jeremiah, too, a scientific experimenter? Was it sugar-refining he thought he could improve? It appears to me probable that he was like Johnson's Sober, in the *Idler* essay (31, 18 November 1758), whose 'daily amusement was Chemistry. He has a small furnace, which he employs in distillation and which has long been the solace of his life. He draws oils and waters, and essences and spirits which he knows to be of no use; sits and counts the drops as they come from his retort, and forgets that while a drop is falling, a moment flies away.' It is possible to be such a man, to nourish such an obsession, and still to dress for dinner.

The circumstances were clearly dire, as his banker, whom Edward knew later in Roehampton, confirmed, but Jeremiah behaved honestly and appears to have avoided extreme penalties. When he was in prison the children believed his wife took him or sent him a six-course dinner every day 'with the delicacies of the season'. Edward felt his elder brothers had left his mother in the lurch at this stage, but the truth was that they were swiftly offloaded to the United States as forgers and deserters. Mrs Lear and the remains of her household went to New Street, which I well remember as a ravine of grimy brownish-yellow brick, draped in Dickensian shadows, near my father's warehouse in Houndsditch before the Blitz. Among a number of curious trades, I think it nurtured a button-hole maker. For a very long time that had been a Jewish area, and the Bevis Marks Synagogue was close by, but there is no evidence of a Jewish connection of blood with the Lears. Anyway, Edward Lear hated the place. When the trouble was over, and the remains of the family apparently back in Bowman's Lodge, Mr and Mrs Lear went away with their daughter Florence down-river to Gravesend. That was cheap and peaceful and a place of pleasure; it was what Margate became.

Before 1840 Gravesend was a small, quiet seaport and a traditional place of refuge, beyond the jurisdiction of London magistrates and convenient for a sudden flit to the Continent. The house where old Lear lived for his last four years, Parrock Place, has gone now, but it was in the parish of Milton. It might perhaps have been the Georgian house called Parrock Hall. The piers and libraries and pleasure-gardens were all in the future, and so was the railway. All the same, Jeremiah Lear was regular in attendance at the Company of Fruiterers until his dying day.[2]

It is possible that Gravesend was only the refuge of a sick old man, a retirement cottage. By the time Edward was fifteen his father was seventy; after 1827, when he may be said to have retired, Edward does not seem to have worried about him. Jeremiah died of a heart attack in 1833 at the age of seventy-six, and was buried on 5 September. Ann Lear lived on in south coast resorts until she died at Dover in 1844. Edward's letters to his mother show some concern for her, and anxiety that she should have enough money, but he never seems to have wanted to see her again. In 1837 when Edward was twenty-five, his sister Florence died at the age of thirty-one, and at roughly the same time two other sisters, the governesses Cordelia and little Catherine, also died. The grim and tough-minded Harriet went to Scotland, where she died unmarried; of Mary we know that she married a Mr Boswell in Sussex, went to New Zealand with him and died childless, but Edward was always conscious of them and kept in contact of a kind through Ann and Eleanor. The only members of his family he continued to see regularly after the age of fifteen were his sisters Ann, who was then thirty-six, who had refused at least one proposal of marriage and been in love with a major, Sarah Street, who was thirty-three, and Eleanor Newsom who was twenty-eight. Yet the Lears were tenacious of their family identity. In New Zealand in 1935 Robert Michell still treasured a panel of the wedding dress of Eleanor Mason, which must have dated from around 1700. Mary Boswell, to whom Edward used to send money when he could, kept a silhouette of him made when he was a boy, probably at Margate. It passed through her family to the National Portrait Gallery in 1915. All the perplexities of this account, and they are more numerous than I have underlined, and some of Edward's vagueness about his family and early years, are only typical of the myths and confusions that arise in enormous families.

One stray brother called Charles, born in 1808 and only four years older than Edward, does deserve notice, since he found his way to West Africa, where he became a kind of medical missionary. It is best to tell his story in the words of Sophie Street, who was married to Charles, son of Sarah Street; they were written down, with much other family lore, by Mrs Bowen, Sophie's grand-daughter, in 1907.

> [Charles Lear] was a great favourite of the Chiefs, and when he nearly died of malaria, was put on board a ship for England. The Captain would not take him without a nurse, so Adjouah the native girl who nursed him went too. Charles insisted on marrying her first. He took her to his sister Eleanor Newsome who had no children, and lived with her husband at Leatherhead, Surrey. The story goes that the first day after her arrival she poured the jug of water in her bedroom over her head. They became very fond of Adjouah, and sent her to school for three years, and Charles returned to the Mission field, where he died. Afterwards she became a Missionary and returned to work amongst her own people.

Interpretation of this unlikely tale is of course open to anyone, but Charles Lear certainly vanished again into Africa, probably in the 1840s.

The break-up of the Lear family was traumatic to the youngest, yet the handful of pictures we have of them all give a comforting, ordinary impression. Except for Mary and Harriet they were tall, and Jeremiah was on the handsome side. Ann probably painted in miniature on ivory; the painting she sent to Edward in 1847 by a Mrs Arundale is full of character and beautiful: Edward thought it perfect in every detail.

We know little more of his childhood. He could read and write and do sums, though his spelling was wild all his life. His accent was sufficiently normal that no one ever noticed it. At the age of ten he suffered a bad experience involving a brother and a wicked cousin which he always remembered, including the exact day when it occurred, which he checked as an old man. He said it was the worst thing ever done to him, yet we have no idea what it was. At eleven, he went to school, no one knows where or for how long. From these obscure and perhaps not extraordinary beginnings, he emerged into daylight at the age of thirteen as bright as a button. From 1826 to 1831 he wrote a series of verse letters that would not have disgraced the young Keats, who has left rather similar outpourings. The first went like this, for 111 lines all in the same rhyme.

To Miss Lear on her Birthday

Dear, and very dear relation,
Time, who flies without cessation,
Who ne'er allows procrastination, . . .
First then I wish thee, dear relation,
Many a sweet reduplication
Of this thy natal celebration:
And mayst thou from this first lunation
Until thy vital termination
Be free from every derogation
By fell disease's contamination,
Whose catalogic calculation
Completely thwarts enumeration, –
Emaciation, fomentation,
With dementation – deplumation
And many more in computation
For these are but an adumbration: –
– And may'st thou never have occasion
For any surgic operation
Or medical administration, –
Sanguification, – defalcation, –
Cauterization – amputation –
Rhubarbaration – scarification –
And more of various designation: – . . .

Edward had an early passion for Byron, like the rest of romantic, youthful England, and bitterly mourned his death, as did young Alfred Tennyson and John Clare. His own verse shows no trace of Byronic influence beyond a jaunty, devil-may-care tone. Indeed, the trouble with his kind of brilliant verse is that the better it gets, the worse it gets, because improvement of technique drags it towards plodding imitation. It is characteristic that the earliest, pre-adolescent attempts are thrown off at white heat, and show deliberate virtuosity, as Keats does. They are private letters, and it is natural that they embody the wish to be amusing, and to show off. Life with Ann gave Edward as a boy happy security and a source of fun, and the life and landscape of Sussex and the friends he made there offered a thrilling liberation just when he needed it. In 1821 Mary had married Mr Boswell, in 1822 Sarah married Mr Street, a Sussex bank manager, and in 1823 Eleanor married Mr Newsom and settled at Leatherhead. There is not a lot to be said for Mr Boswell, as we shall see, but the other two were good matches, and Sarah had settled at Arundel, so that by the time he was eleven, some three years before the surviving verse letters began, Edward began to visit Sussex.

It is curious how Lear's early experience of life coincided with that of Charles Dickens, who was born a few months earlier in the same year, and whose father went to the antique Marshalsea prison for a debt of £40 to a baker when Charles was twelve. For Dickens, who was shocked and humiliated by early encounters with the working class on equal terms, every detail was engraved on his memory, but for Lear, the whole of his miserable boyhood was obliterated. Yet they knew just the same London. They might easily have met as boys running around in the Marshalsea; statistics do not make it unlikely; there were some 30–40,000 cases of arrest for debt in 1837 alone. Peter Ackroyd[3] casts a terrible light on the affair. In fact the paths of Dickens and the Lears did cross soon afterwards. Angus Davidson in his life of Lear[4] tells a story he must have got from Sarah Street's descendants that Jeremiah Lear, wandering through London in his palmy days, came across his own name on a brass plate, went in and got to know his namesake: the second Jeremiah lived at Batworth Park, Lyminster, and it was in that house that Sarah met her future husband Charles Street. This second Jeremiah's youngest son George came to work in London in 1825 and in 1827 was articled as a clerk to lawyers called Ellis and Blackmore in Raymond Buildings, Holborn Court. Lear's close friend Husey Hunt worked there too. Also in 1827, Charles Dickens joined the small firm as a clerk, at 10s. 6d. a week rising to 15s. 'Having been in London two years,' George wrote later, 'I thought I knew something of town, but after a little talk with Dickens I found I knew nothing. He knew it all from Bow to Brentford.'[5] Dickens wrote of George Lear that he owned horses, went home to the country in the summer, had a few grand acquaintances and was an 'aristocrat of clerks'. Lyminster really was a paradise, with an Anglo-Saxon church and a fine view of Arundel across the watermeadows of the Arun, so Dickens was right, as always, to suspect a touch of class. He and Edward Lear were both close observers of class for the rest of their lives, both haunted by a despairing sadness which has little in common with the famous 'black blood' of the Tennysons, and which they learned to intermingle with the purest gaiety.

The gaiety was infectious. As a young man Edward was fond of jokes which were verbal and original and emerged in a swift, sparkling stream rather like soda-water from a syphon. They were part of his charm from the beginning. At a period when Charles Dickens and his fellow-clerks were bombarding the hats of those who passed by Raymond's Buildings with cherry-stones, Lear was arranging a visit for tea with a friend called Harry Hind (December 1830):

> ... if it won't suit
> I can bring up my flute,
> To skiggle and squeak,
> Any night in the week.
> – Dash, now I go to my dinner,
> For all day I've been a-
> way at the West End,
> Painting the best end
> Of some vast Parrots
> As red as new carrots, –
> (They are at the museum, –
> When you come you shall see 'em, –)
> I do the head and neck first;
> – And ever since breakfast,
> I've had one bun merely!
> So – yours quite sincerely.

He could write as easily, indeed all too easily, in the manner of Thomas Hood or Lord Byron. His 'Bard's Farewell'[6] begins: 'Farewell mother, tears are streaming Down the tender pallid cheek ... roses dreaming ... gleaming ... speak.' It continues with rhymes like 'grieve me ... deceive me'. A landscape poem called 'Bury Hill'[7] is just as mechanical but in its bad style very able. It holds out no promise that Lear will be a poet. It lies in its album, which might almost be a young girl's, side by side with pictures of pretty birds like kingfishers and a very few pencil landscapes framed between two trees[8] or seen across a fence.[9] There are pairs of ringdoves, pairs of swallows, and carefully balanced landscape compositions. One would not really imagine that Edward Lear was going to be any good as an artist either, though the conventional style of the day, and what instruction he had received, are certainly more impressive in his pictures than in his verses.

> When the light dies away in a calm summer's eve
> And the sunbeams grow faint and more faint in the west,
> How we love to look on till the last trace they leave
> Glows alone like a blush upon modesty's breast,
> Lovely streak! dearer far than the glories of day
> Seems thy beauty – and silence and shadow enshrined,
> More bright as its loneliness passes away –
> And leaves twilight in desolate grandeur behind! . . .

Edward is deadly serious, and the conventional language perfectly encloses his real feelings, just like a young man's evening clothes from a provincial tailor that enclose a real body. Indeed, his sunset feeling is the same here as it was at Highgate when he cried himself to sleep: 'some dream that will wake in a desolate heart Every chord into music . . . The joys which first woke it are long ago crushed.' His poem on the ruins of the temple at Aegina is in the same book: 'And the far off glorious clashing/Of thy cymbaled votary/Came through the soft air flashing/ Like the sound of years gone by'. That was written in October when Edward was seventeen, and it would be fair to say the whole composition might well have won a prize at a public school or even a university, in spite of the rhyme

> And oft in silence *o'er thee*
> The dark cloud passes on
> And it sheds a deeper *glory*
> O'er thy wild oblivion.

The Aegina poem is illustrated. It was published in the *Poetry Review* in the 1950s, and amongst the suburban verse in which that periodical then delighted it was scarcely distinguishable. There is another in the Catalogue of the Royal Academy Lear exhibition[10] which is pretty but no better, and there is a parody of the camel-driver's poem by Collins about the Lears' baggage leaving Holloway, which is clever rather than funny. Its importance is that it was clearly a parody. There was no time of life when Lear might not parody Thomas Moore or Tennyson or any chance author (such as Lady Agnes Gray) in pictures or in verses or both; his despair deeply underlay these performances, and his gaiety riotously invaded them.

CHAPTER TWO

THE PAINTER

OF BIRDS

EDWARD must always have been a swift learner, though his mind jumped like a firecracker, and the processes of his development are not always easy to follow. We know he learned drawing from Ann because an album has survived at Harvard[1] which contains their work side by side. Whatever is unsigned must be attributed by judgement, and to make matters worse, drawings were added at different times: a flower study is dated 1 May 1828, and a drawing of wheat is signed 'EL del. 9 Sep. 1834'. The lovely flower drawing which is titled *Eleanor's Geranium*, Twickenham, 18 June 1828,[2] is so extremely able one feels it could scarcely be by a boy of sixteen, and in its lightness, its subtlety of shade and colour, and its crispness it must surely be called more beautiful than conventional. Possibly his sister painted it: Edward could never spell her name and often wrote Ellen or Ellinor. All the same, he was learning to paint flowers, and in the style he was taught he swiftly became perfect. The notebook or album at Harvard has larkspur, columbine, wallflower, sea-shells, butterflies, some real feathers mounted, some butterflies with honesty and a note from some Linnaean text-book, 'Class 15 Tetradynamia, Order 1 Siticulosa'. The lessons in natural history and drawing evidently proceeded together. To provide one's own illustrations to Linnaeus had been a passion since the exquisite little pen drawings of Thomas Gray, but Gray was a bachelor, and there was still thought to be something old-maidish about natural history. The spirit of the enterprise is to be found in the flowers of the 1840s gathered in Richard

Mabey's *Frampton Flora* (1985). Edward's flowers were not scientific, though they were didactic, and became so vivid as to be dreamlike.

Sarah Hoare (1777–1856) gives full expression to the old-maidish aspect of Lear's occupation in her *Poems of Conchology and Botany*, which are not much read today, but Peter Pindar (1738–1819) put the matter more succinctly in a dialogue between Banks and Herschel.

> With novel specks on eggs to feast the eye,
> Or gaudy colours of a butterfly,
> Or new-found fibre of some grassy blade,
> Well suits the idle hours of an old maid . . .

Perhaps the quotation is unfair to Ann, because her years as Edward's tutor seem to have been idyllic. Pindar thinks men are better adapted

> To pepper a poor Indian like a duck;
> To hunt for days a lizard or a gnat,
> And run a dozen miles to catch a bat;
> To plunge in marshes, and to scale the rocks,
> Sublime, for scurvy-grass and lady-smocks.

Indeed, both Edward's training and his natural bent did lead him in that adventurous direction, but never quite as far as his friends Gould and Audubon. Whether his illness or (as I believe) his short sight was at fault, he was always just a little more timid than the wildest and hairiest explorers of his generation.

Ann painted some hideous pheasants on the sea-cliffs, and Edward worked hard at his backgrounds, though not always from life. Two amazing ornamental birds, probably drawn in London, are set against some palm trees improbably flourishing in the bald Sussex turf at the cliff's edge. Yet Edward's loganberries (I think they are his) are as well executed in their more obvious way as Eleanor's geranium: the fruit is fine but the leaves magnificent. One comes to recognize his hand, in hawkweed not from the life, in a finch on plums, in a mauve-pink moss rose with a caterpillar, in Linnaean notes and queer spellings like 'laburnam'. The striped shells have the cold look of reality, and they are all Sussex coast shells. The water-lily is surely Edward Lear, and so I think is the virtuoso morning glory in a loaded plum branch. Some of the queer birds are headed 'Zoo', and a Turk's-head lily is annotated 'Drawn from one gathered in the garden at Hackney by F. H.', and a purple variety of the same lily says 'Drawn from Nature, Holloway A. L.' Which of them painted the bee on a yellow tuft, or the yellow-headed narcissus with a cluster of five flowers on one stem? Whose is the white Skops owl pasted into the book? The extremely comic sick parrot on a perch must certainly be by Edward. Parrots had been owned and petted by women for 100 years, and still were in the 1870s. More than once in this series little birdies on their branch agree, and it is not without reason that Lear's serious career finally began with the Psittacidae, but as an observer of nature he was deeply and frequently amused from the beginning. What appears to be a mushroom of some kind carries the note 'This curious vegetable production I found May 1st 1828', the same date as the flower study.

Most of his field excursions were around Arundel, and he learned to walk long distances. In the end he knew the coastal villages from Chichester to Hastings and beyond, which is the whole extent of the Downs; indeed, with the exception of those of his hero, Turner, he has left records better than any we have of West Sussex. We are lucky to have an early account of a visit there in a verse journal written to Ann in 1829. It is not the original, only a copy, and either the month or the day of the week is wrongly copied out or (just as likely) wrongly written by Edward. The poem describes five days in January or November 1829; the editor of the *Letters* favours November, when the 2nd fell on a Monday, though it is a tempting thought that 7 January might make this fine, brisk five pages of verse a birthday present, Ann's birthday being on the 17th. It does not really matter, but the high spirits of the conception and the detail could as easily be a sixteen-year-old's as a seventeen-year-old's.

On the Monday evening Edward had bought a ticket for the coach and then gone to a dance; he got back to his lodgings at cock-crow and packed until half past four in the morning. At six he got up, 'Wished goodbye – took my hats and umbrella – And shivered and shook to the White Horse cellar.' The Arundel coach left the White Horse yard at eight every morning, but already so early in his life he seems to be lodging independently, and we do not know where Ann was unless the goodbyes were said to her, although in that case 'my lodgings' is a queer phrase. He took an outside seat, cheap but cold.

> Sat on the top of the stage and four –
> For Robinson half an hour or more, –
> W[e] rattled and rumbled down the Strand
> Where the mudscrapers stood in a dingy band
> And rode away from London smoke
> Or ever the light of day had broke.

Chelsea and Fulham and Putney Bridge, –
And Kingston on Thames with its banks of sedge, –
Esher and Cobham – how cold they were!
Oh! it was enough to make anyone swear!
– Thumped my feet till I made them ache, –
Took out provisions, a meal to make, –
Offered a sandwich, – (I had but three,) –
To my neighbour, who sat with a shaky knee,
'Sir' – said she with a glutinous grin,
'I'll thank you for *two*, as they seem but thin, –
And shall feel quite glad if you'll give one 'arter,
To this here young lady, what's my darter.'

They followed the Old Portsmouth Road by Ripley, Guildford and Godalming, Northchapel, Chittingfold gate and Petworth, by which time Edward was blue with cold. Here they turned towards Arundel.

Down Fittleworth Hill we made a dash
And walked on foot up Bury Hill side, –
Half hot – half cold – like a lukewarm hash,
And as stiff as a lobster's claw – wot's tied.
Arundel town at last reached we,
As early as ten minutes after three.
Went to the Bank; found no one there –
Wanted a dinner – the cupboard was bare, –
Set off to Peppering – Cloky and I –
Over the hard chalk merrily . . .

Bury Hill was the scene of Edward's earlier and gloomier adolescent poem about the sunset. The Bank was Mr Street's, and the Streets probably lived there. Peppering House was at Burpham, a village that leads nowhere except up on to the Downs. Edward often drew the outbuildings and sketched nearby at this time, and the Drewitts who lived there were family friends. Indeed on the way there he met Sarah with her children on her way back to Arundel. It was five before he got to 'the old Elmtree' and amazed his friends. (I do not know who Cloky was, not a pony because he was unable to ride, either a person therefore or a dog.) Edward seems to have been taken in by the Drewitts as a boy and added to a troop of children, some roughly his own age. The family mattered to him, he adored Peppering House, and was happy there. They may well have been kin of some kind to the Streets, but it is they, almost more than the Streets, who were the key to his Sussex excursions.

Gobbled enough to choke a Goliah –
Drank my tea – and sat by the fire;
Saw the baby – that unique child –
Who squeaked – and stared – and sniffed – and smiled; –
Then went to bed with a very good will . . .

On Wednesday he got up before sunrise, left a note, and ran to Arundel, where he arrived by eight. After breakfast he went up the hill with Sarah to Brookfield, 'White frost covering the country still, Just like a frozen syllabub froth,' ate some oysters, and saw the boys skating and sliding. He fixed to come and stay with Sarah the following Sunday, then went off again in a freezing cold wind to Jeremiah Lear's at Batworth Park, Lyminster. That house was another powerful influence on him. It was a cultured upper-middle-class establishment:

Found the wind blew vastly bitterly,
Called at Lyminster – John at home –
Looked at the plates of Rogers' Italy, –
Talked of reform and Chancellor Brougham: –
Back to Arundel made a run, –
And finished a lunch at half past one –
Out again, and called at Tower
House . . .

The illustrated edition of Rogers' *Italy* (1830) apparently became available late in 1829, which confirms the late date of this letter in the year. The book is a remarkable object, lavishly illustrated with engravings by Stothard and Rogers, and often found in amazing bindings of crushed mulberry morocco or green and gilt leather. In the previous ten years the poem had not sold, and this new illustrated edition was a device of Rogers, who was a rich man, to bring it to public attention. One of its publishers was Moxon, whom Rogers set up in business, and one of the first fish that business caught was Alfred Tennyson. Stothard did far less for the edition than Turner, whose dramatic energies filled the sky over Paestum with lightning and dashed water down the rocks of Tivoli like the beard of God, but Stothard had already captivated Edward as a boy with his memorable engravings for Robinson Crusoe. (He is said to have first interested Lear in drawing landscapes, but I can observe no trace or shadow of an influence.) As he grew up, Edward came to worship Turner. 'Copy first the works of God, and then the works of Turner.' There is a distant view of Florence from some poplar trees in Rogers' *Italy* that might almost be an early Edward Lear of Rome.

The distances are not long, Lyminster being only three or four miles to the south of Arundel, and Peppering not quite as far, though a worse road, north. All the same, Edward displays lively and remarkable energies and appetites. Since after one more walk with Sarah he dressed and 'Devoured a dinner with infinite zest' he must have kept clothes at their house. They then all went next door for tea with the Wardropers, one of whom was a subscriber to Lear's first Roman views, and the Blanches. One or other family may have lived at Tower House. He stayed the night with the Streets, having lost at chess and at backgammon to James Wardroper, eaten a supper of stewed oysters, and 'read original verses', which sound like someone's album or manuscript. He cannot have been alone in pouring out light verse: it was a normal part of the culture, and the Streets were civilized people. It was only by chance that no one played an instrument that evening.

The following morning he and Sarah walked to Hampton Beach, now alas Littlehampton, to look at the winter sea. At half past eleven, after a snack of bread and buns, they called at Brookfield but found no one, and at Calceto where they found Mrs George Coombe, formerly Fanny Drewitt. The names now become numerous, and only the most painstaking local antiquarian research could make any sense of them. They sat with Fanny until one in the afternoon, dined (at home?) on mutton and caper sauce, popped in next door for ten minutes or so, and called on Uncle Richard (Street) in order to see Miss Hurst, but found a crowd and stayed. Miss Bischoff fell over, they dined (again?) at Miss Upperton's

> And lastly setting off again
> Just as the day was on the wain [sic],
> We got to Arundel at last.

This social whirlwind is entirely typical of Edward Lear all his life, though he did have fits of revulsion from his own gregariousness, as most people like him do. He was a fat-faced, jolly youth; Ann called his brother Biffin, because he was as round as a Norfolk cooking-apple, and Edward when the time came for him to describe himself was 'perfectly spherical'. People in Sussex, in that tiny and consciously civilized society that gathered under the skirts of Arundel Castle, not far from the Trollopian Close and grand eighteenth-century buildings of Chichester, thought Edward an incurable eccentric, but they accepted him, and he was pleased with them. He was agile in provincial societies and happy at tea-time: that was one of his greatest assets. He does not mention going back to the Drewitts, but concludes for some reason

> . . . hoping that your wine may be
> As good to all infinity
> Of time, and that your pears mayn't spoil, –
> But multiply – like Widow's oil –
> I have the pleasure to sign here,
> Myself – Yours most obliged – E. Lear.

He wrote again in verse to Ann in April 1831, the day after leaving Sarah Street, who stuffed him with puddings, chops, cutlets and pies, and fussed over his health and the fog and his possible dizziness, so that he was not allowed to explore the river or the Castle. That does not seem overprudent, if the fog was as bad as Sussex fogs can be.

> So I stayed still at home and worked hard at my drawings,
> And looked at the rooks – and sat hearing their cawings.

He was endeavouring to put on weight, and claimed to have achieved it. The disease sounds like a nasty fit of asthmatic catarrh, which did afflict him. He had left London ill and pale and drawn, but now his face was looking plumper. He gave reports to Ann about Sarah's two sons, Charles who was good but dull, and Freddy who was a little monkey. He liked children or came to like them, almost on principle, but he never lost his severe eye for the ones who were nuisances. He saw much of life as a sort of extended nursery, and was stricken with nostalgia for an intimate warmth which perhaps he had never known or not known soon enough. It is curious that his memory, which was so good about adult life, was so faint and weak and practically non-existent about his early childhood. The only thing that he really remembered about it was being carried out as a baby to see London illuminated for the victory of Waterloo.

That April he was 'in my favourite abode' at Peppering where 'They are all just as kind as they ever have been'. He was drawing a pigeon, and going out to dinner with Fanny Coombe at Calceto. In this letter drawing has become a serious concern, and so far as we can tell he was already making his living at it, though with no thought for the serious economics of his future. About this time someone took him to Petworth where he met Lord Egremont, a very wealthy patron of modern art. He never forgot that brooding nobleman's awkward question: 'But where is all this going to lead to, Mr Lear?' Egremont was Turner's patron: there is a picture in the private apartments at Petworth of a herd of fallow deer coming close to the windows in snowy weather; if you look out of the window you sometimes see the same deer at the same spot in the park where their ancestors were painted. The experience might make anyone a landscape painter.

But Lear began to earn before he was perfect in his art, so that his contributions to album art, to the most ridiculous of ornamental postcards (as it were) cherished by young ladies, overlap with his earliest signs of real talent. His *Peppering House* of 1829 is a pleasant enough drawing, though the seagulls are rebarbative and the enormous balancing tree is derivative not only from nature.[3] The house is an ordinary, somewhat bleak villa like a vicarage, three windows long and three deep with a smaller wing built on to it. Sketches show he was more excited by the outbuildings. Lear himself says that he 'began to draw for bread and cheese about 1827, but only did uncommon queer shop-sketches – selling them for prices varying from ninepence to four shillings', in modern terms from £3–4 to about £20. We know he coloured prints and screens and fans, and made morbid disease drawings for hospitals and doctors. Daniel Fowler, a painter he knew at the time, recalls that his 'first attempts at earning money were made in offering his little drawings for anything he could get to stagecoach passengers in inn yards'. That is Fowler of Amherst Island, who was two years older than Lear and lived to be eighty-four: he has only recently been studied.[4] But like others of Lear's acquaintances of these days they seem to have drifted together and apart like atoms in a chaos.

He had certainly not got over his links with the Drewitts. He addressed a remarkable poem called 'Illustrations of Miss Maniac' 'for Miss Drewitt [probably Fanny, who became a lifelong friend] with EL's respects', which appears to have been pasted in an album. The illustrations are really remarkable, since they are cartoons drawn fully in the style of caricaturists then fashionable, quite unlike his own later style. All the same, that is a career and a direction he might have pursued. The text is sharper than usual and expresses a fear of madness which must surely be genuine. 'Sometimes I feel but know not why/A fire within me burn/And visions fierce and terrible/Pursue where'er I turn . . .' But 'reason overthrown' goes with a comic illustration of Indian passage by the North Pole, Perpetual Motion, Discovery of the Longitude, and Way to Pay the National Debt, so it is not easy to know how seriously to take the gloomy verses.

> Beyond those far blue hills I feel
> Was once my home of bliss,
> And there my father's cottage stood,

> A roof more blest than this.
> Ah now I think I see them come,
> The forms I used to love,
> And hear the evening shepherd bell
> Sound sweetly through our grove.
> But they are gone! . . .

There follows the complaint of a rejected lover, which is not convincing. The whole poem satirizes real feelings. His father in a temper is illustrated by a comic caricature saying, 'Go along do! – you hussey.' It is possible the poem is unfinished, but equally one feels it might go on for ever. It is a disturbing kind of joke, written around 1830.

About the same year, or in 1831, he sends a verse letter to Eliza Drewitt. The message is to keep the book and copy the verses, because Edward will not need them for some time. He has just seen Mrs Hopkins, a *Parrots* subscriber of Bank, Arundel.

> I saw you at Houghton – I stood on the ridge
> Upon Bury Hill side, – and ride over the bridge.
> I have sent you these numbers by Robert – they'll be
> An amusement perhaps to inspect after tea, –
> They are beautiful things and I think they're not dear –
> For both reading and pictures . . .

Robert was Eliza's brother. We do not know what periodical Edward had brought from London, but one gets the same impression as before of a busy little world of young people in the provinces, happily scurrying through their youth. We have also a joke 'Ode to the little China-man', of seven four-line stanzas; this comic foreigner, who sounds like a statue or a drawing, declares at the climax, 'In spite of my eyebrows – two feet long – I'm Miss Eliza's beau!!' It is a normal sort of tease, no doubt, but one is interested to confirm how deeply Edward had embedded himself in that small society. A single stanza gives some idea of the quality, but the varied refrain 'high diddledy dee' (or 'di' or 'da' or 'do') shows promise of metrical jokes to come.

> (But everyone – as the Frenchman said –
> Everyone to his way) –
> (When he boiled in a pipkin his grandmother's head) –
> With a high diddle – diddledy-da!

Lear's first really helpful patron was, as far as we know, a Mrs Wentworth, though Lord Egremont was interested enough in him to be another of the subscribers to his first volume of *Parrots* soon afterwards. But Mrs Wentworth was a sister of Walter Fawkes of Yorkshire, another of Turner's patrons, who owned that heron's head which is one of the most striking images in British bird painting. She lived at 49 Wilton Crescent, and it was she who introduced Lear to Prideaux Selby (1789–1867), who was the leading amateur ornithologist of his day. His *British Ornithology* began with a volume of plates in 1821, *Land Birds* followed in 1825 and a second volume of text in 1833. The whole work was complete in 1834 with 228 plates, twenty-six of them by his kinsman Admiral Mitford. From 1825 to 1843 *Illustrations of Ornithology* in numerous volumes by Jardine and Selby appeared, and in that work Lear had nineteen plates in two volumes in 1834 alone. He would draw for any scientist or any engraver or really anyone at all who would pay a minimum for his drawings. The financial rewards were not huge, but Prideaux needed pictures and Lear went on supplying them. In a letter of that same year he agreed to draw fifteen plates for £10 for Lizars, who was Jardine and Selby's excellent engraver. In his first *Parrots* volume he emerged with several distinguished scientists among his subscribers, and signed himself on the frontispiece 'A. L. S.' (Associate of the Linnaean Society). Years later that distinction was withdrawn from him because he became an inactive member, although his bird and animal drawings went on being pirated and copied all his life, with no monetary advantage to the artist. He would be proud to see how his books are venerated at Burlington House today. But cheerfulness kept breaking in. It does so in a pair of perky little parakeets on the frontispiece of *Illustrations of the Family of Psittacidae* by E. Lear A. L. S., to be completed in fourteen numbers (1830). Alas, it never was completed. Odder still, he gave Mrs Wentworth in April 1830 with an inscription recording his gratitude to her a collection of seventeen bird drawings, mostly of imaginary birds, such as a fire-crested, red-breasted, black-spotted, white-bellied, magpie-tailed, corvine-beaked, wood-pecking starling, in a lightly sketched realistic landscape with a fern. It is a very surprising creature.[5]

About the same year he gave a 'First Drawing Prize' to a Holloway or Highgate girl called Miss Fraser. The prize was an album of delights.

> My album's open; come and see; –
> What – won't you waste a thought on me;
> Write but a word, a word or two,
> And make me love to think on you . . .

As well as Lear's poem, the album came with a Rex Whistlerish drawing of the album itself open at a drawing of little birds, a lyre, a sprig of myrtle, a palette, and something that I fear must be a pipe, all on a mantelpiece, which is garlanded in colour with huge old roses and tiny daisies. Ornamental motifs of that kind and any ornamental flower-pieces are often copies at the time. The more delicate of the exotic imaginary birds are probably Ann's inventions. The head of a peasant woman shows a talent that came to nothing. A boss-eyed and uninten-tionally funny leopard might be shockingly bad, if it were not so much better than Blake's *Tyger*, which has a pleasing nursery aspect. The inheritance of uneducated or self-educated artists at that time was a mighty heady mixture. Blake died in 1827, the same year as Byron. Lear as a boy copied the ruins of Aigina more than once, and butterflies on a cross between a moss-rose and a peony on rice-paper, and imaginary birds in an amazing coastal scene with a lot of palms that otherwise resembles Rottingdean, and a formal composition of flowers of a vividness so terrifying as to resemble barge-painting.[6] All of these must have been intended for albums or for screens.

It has been suggested he went through a kind of apprenticeship to Selby, but if so it was not in any formal sense, and I do not feel that he owes a lot to Selby's drawing style. He made himself useful and taught himself by copying. Selby can only have suggested subjects and paid for them. He was a man of determination and enterprise, who engraved his own copper plates when he could find no engraver. He was a sportsman and an expert in British forest trees (1842) who led an expedition into Sutherland, but was largely self-taught. When Selby wrote the two volumes on *Pigeons* (1835) and *Parrots* (1836) for Jardine's Naturalist's Library, it was Lear who supplied the plates. Lear's flower painting dried up more or less completely: it survived only as extremely skilful foliage and grass in the backgrounds of his pictures, to recur in its full beauty only in his Indian journey and in the passionate gardening of his old age. He must have used the same handbooks as other people. He took an early lithograph he made of 'a rustic scene', an enormous tree with flourishing side-whiskers of foliage, from J. D. Harding, and he acquired a copy of *A Practical Treatise on Painting* by John Burnet, probably on the advice of another artist, in 1836. But he was conscious of being uneducated or self-educated, and was constantly exploring new tech-niques, not in the free spirit of a genius like Turner, yet at least with unceasing curiosity to his dying day.

He drew birds and also animals from life at the London Zoo, which had been opened in 1828 by Sir Humphry Davy as President of the Royal Society and Sir Stamford Raffles as posthumous patron. Popular exhibitions of animals had been common, of course, for years; at the Surrey Zoo, opened that same year, you could see lions and tigers and kangaroos, and take a ride on the back of a giant tortoise, but the new Zoological Gardens were supposed to be scientific; they were therefore a godsend to publishers and illustrators. Lear seems to have supplied a few of the drawings that were reproduced as woodcuts in an early guide to the collections (1830, quadrupeds and 1831, birds), some lemurs and some macaws. He had been living with Ann in the Grays Inn Road, and she must still have been subsidizing him to some extent. In 1831 they moved to 61 Albany Street to be nearer his work at the Zoo, because at the age of eighteen he had the confidence to undertake his *Parrots*.

That meant concentrating, and it produced in consequence that wonderful sharpening of focus that makes Lear a great zoological artist. But he was still committed in several directions. He helped Thomas Eyton with his *Ducks* (Anatidae) and Thomas Bell with his *Tortoises and Turtles* (Testudinata). One of those he was particularly fond of, a tortoise, turns up again and again in his life, as T stands for Tortoise, and clambering among the rocks in his temple of Bassae (in the FitzWilliam at Cambridge). Owls among ruins appear very early: they were not from life until he started working at the Zoo. But at almost any time in the 1830s he might produce his same heavenly sketches for the *Transactions* of the Zoological Society or the *Zoology of Captain Beechey's Voyage* or Gould's bird books. All the same, none of the brilliant animal sketches, not even the impertinently perfect Whiskered Yarke, can be dated with his first Zoo sketches: he appears to have begun with the parrots, and it was in preparing plates from them that he made the extraordinary progress as a painter that can still be charted, from the folio sketches and notes at Harvard to the final aquatinted lithographic plates.

But the *Hyrax capensis* at Harvard he sketched and annotated at 17 New Broad Street on 13 April 1832, which makes it the first datable animal sketch, with an added interest because an exquisitely perfected version came on to the market in 1993 at Agnew's, and one may compare them. The little beast is properly called a Rock Hyrax, and was one of the favourite creatures of the late Cyril Connolly. The first drawing says 'Long rough ochry hair' and 'ochry mottley hair falling soft over the toes', and 'a fringe of browner ochre line' and 'a crease'. Then Lear took it home and inked in his own pencil notes and filled out what had been pencil sketching with washes of colour. The perfect (Agnew's) hyrax is lighter, the toes are perfect, the shading subtle, the whiskers much more charming and the nose cocked at a lively angle. Being lighter (as hyrax fur in fact is), it shows up the ears and the pondering eyes better and permits a treatment of the fur in which every hair tells. It is a thing of extraordinary beauty and accuracy. The Harvard sketch is already wonderful and entertaining, but it is only by seeing the perfect version that one spots what is not quite right about its predecessor. Even the shadows the little beast sits in are improved beyond apparent possibility. Both of them are infinite improvements on pictures like the Javanese Peacock of 1931. It is care, veracity and intensity that make this animal so dignified and so very beautiful, as it was care and veracity and intensity that made the youth of Edward Lear the greatest age of natural history painting. It is symbolic that he made fifty plates at least for the *Voyage of the Beagle*.

I do not think what had altered was the great voyages, which had been going on since Drake and Raleigh, nor was it grand patronage which had been constantly available for more than a century. No doubt it was partly the creaking forward, the slow inching forward of science: first the herbals and the herbals from America and the new plants from China, then the monumentally useful achievement of Linnaeus, and now Davy following Banks as President of the Royal Society. Davy was President from 1820 until his death in 1829; it is true that he devoted his declining years, which started early since he died at fifty, to salmon-fishing and the tying of fishing flies. It appears that administration bored him, but whatever sadness he suffered as an elderly man, one would like to think of him cheered up by the Rock Hyrax.

The big change that came about in this period was surely in the methods of printing in colour. There had been glorious publications in the past, yet all the patronage of the French kings produced only, as it were, Redouté's roses, looking like the miracles of fairyland on vellum. Lithography, and the chromolithography that quite soon followed it, wrote a new chapter in the understanding of natural history.

The best bird book in the past was probably Dutch, unless it was James Bolton's *Harmonia Ruralis* (1794–6), intended as a prelude to his never-completed *Song Birds*: he died at twenty in 1795. The early bird book was undoubtedly a luxury product, because the only colouring was by hand. A trained work-force instructed by the artist added the exact colours to the printed images. In the same way, a trained work-force painted every flower and shell on every teapot and plate. The colourists were women and not well paid. Now that the images could be engraved on stone they could be used for printing in much greater quantities, because wood and copper wore out much sooner. That is how limited editions arose; the plate was destroyed so that you would not have blurred copies palmed off on you. The first coloured lithographs were hand-coloured, but being new the business was very well organized, and Edward Lear learned how to divide and subdivide his birds more or less feather by feather, so that the colouring could be perfectly simple. What is more, he learned to do this with extreme realism: in fact with veracity, intensity and humour as well. That is the triumph of his *Parrots* and of his *Owls*. His unit, as it were, was the bird's feather or a scale of the tortoise's shell. The other creatures such as the little hyrax were more difficult to reproduce in colour because they required subtler subdivisions of colouring: they could be perfect as a sketch or as a framed drawing like the *Common Shrew* and *Water Shrew* (1832), but they took less easily to coloured lithography; there was an obvious brilliance about the success of the birds.[7] At Knowsley, working for a private patron on and off from 1831 to 1837, Lear has left more than 100 pictures of birds and beasts, but only seventeen were printed in 1847. The book is extremely rare, though luckily the Linnaean Society has a copy since Lord Derby was its patron.

When Lear began to paint for money he was amateurish if no longer technically speaking an amateur; we do not know what he used to sell in the inn yards, but apparently small sketches in water-colour. He probably sold them in Arundel, not London, as small souvenirs, and they would therefore as likely as not have been conventional landscape sketches, like Harding's. He did not know yet how to use oils, nor was he yet taking part in that extraordinary and indeed wild and wonderful movement of British water-colourists that came to maturity with the work of Turner, Cozens, Cox and the rest, painters as different in their styles and as individualist as they were sudden and brilliant in the observation of light and shadow and colour. Lear was more specialized: his undertaking of the *Parrots* was scientifically a grand conception, because no one had ever fully published a single species of birds. His images had no weight of text to intersperse, but the plates were the biggest and best ever, except for Audubon's.

He ransacked London for obscure parrots and cockatoos, he worked in Bruton Street before the birds got their cages in the Zoological Gardens, and by the end of 1830 he was put up for the Linnaean Society, and at that time N. H. A. Vigors, Secretary of the Zoological Society, introduced him to Sir William Jardine, one of the sturdiest of gentleman

amateurs. But Audubon ransacked all America: he worked in the field
with a gun as well as a pencil, and painted his astonishing birds when he
had shot them and fixed them with wires, so that some of their poses are
unnatural. The difference of the last sixty-five plates which Audubon
painted, of birds newly discovered in the West that he had never seen
alive, makes it clear how closely his best work was tied to the observation
of nature. Lear had to seek out pictures of Latin American trees to copy,
but Audubon often employed boys to draw backgrounds, the first of
them being Joseph Mason, a boy genius who was his pupil and travelled
with him from 1820 to 1822, from the age of thirteen to fifteen, after
which nothing of him is known. Later Audubon used another boy for
four years, and his own two sons: John drew the bittern for him, and his
wife Lucy drew the swamp sparrow.

Audubon was in Britain from 1826 to 1829 looking for patrons or
subscribers and discovering engravers. Lizars of Edinburgh did ten plates
for him, and Robert Havell of London undertook the others. There
were 435 plates in 200 copies of his *Birds*. They were sold for 1000
dollars a copy; Audubon reckoned his expenses at 115,640 dollars, and
the plates did not begin to be resold at a profit for a good 100 years, but
he made a profit. There were other editions of course, including the
1840–4 octavo of 1200 copies, but of the original Elephant folios 134
copies survive, ninety-four of them in America and seventeen (at last
count) in Britain. It will be seen that the economics were daunting, and
called for a large capital sum which Lear never had. Audubon employed
no fewer than seventy colourists, although we know nothing about them
except their accuracy. Audubon's widow gave his entire collection of
water-colours – the originals, that is, of the Elephant folio plates, with
every bird life-size, to the New York Historical Society, where they may
still be seen.

Lear knew Audubon, and long cherished a dream of visiting America,
but finance debarred him from such a career, even if he had been
physically tough enough, as he was intellectually, to endure it. It is none
the less worth comparing their work. Audubon is more dramatic and in
many plates his backgrounds play a more interesting part. His images
are more startling, though their eyes are often not so lively, and the
humour which so subtly enters into Lear, as it does after all into the
character of parrots, though seldom of owls in real life, is absent in
Audubon, except in the cases of the Saw-whet Owl and the baby Snowy
owl. When they met, Lear had a lot to learn and nothing to teach, yet I
seem to see his influence in these owls, as something foreign to Audubon

and not quite digested: Lear was already drawing splendidly funny owls before 1829. It appears that it was Audubon's influence that drew him to the courageous enterprise of his *Parrots*. The English scientific establishment supported him and he began to have private patrons, but they were not enough, as he would discover. He taught in St James and Cavendish Square: he knew Richard Curzon, for example. But there was scarcely a living to be found in England by this way of life, only at best a niche. If Lear had been to school, and then to Cambridge, let us say Trinity, in 1829 or 1830, he could have been taken up by Whewell and passed a tranquil life as a scientist with theological doubt for a private hobby. That road being shut to him, it followed that in England all roads were similarly closed. America really was, as it still is, a bigger, wilder, more open country.

CHAPTER THREE

THE LITHOGRAPHER

EDWARD settled to work at the London Zoo with determination, but that was not the end of his Sussex connection, or of his youthful explorations of London, which was growing even faster than he was. Dickens gives a sense of what that was like. Years later one discovers with amazement and by chance, when a young Greek servant dying at San Remo of diseased lungs gets an attack of syphilis, that Edward had suffered an attack himself. 'Considering that I myself in 1833 had every sort of syphilitic disease, who am I to blame others who have had less education and more temptation?' It looks as if this bad experience occurred when he was wandering about with Bernard Senior, a lawyer's clerk in the same office as Dickens and George Lear, son of the Sussex Jeremiah. The only other friend he is known to have seen a lot of was William Nevill, a boy from Holloway. Senior inherited money and settled at Hastings, changing his name to Bernard Husey Hunt because of the inheritance; both he and Nevill were close to Lear as long as he lived, and so was the younger Fanny Coombe, daughter of George Coombe and Fanny Drewitt. With Eliza, young Fanny's aunt, Edward also seems to have been on intimate, teasing terms. His youth begins to look normal and clear enough, and the Dickens connection illuminates it. He might easily have been a younger and of course heterosexual member of Mr Pickwick's club: he was a warm, affectionate, somewhat frustrated man, who tried to marry but failed, and that is all – there is no evidence whatever of homosexuality in his life.

The *Parrots* enterprise was bound up with innovations in the technique of painting, and with the introduction of lithography into England by C. J. Hullmandel. Mystery and confusion surrounds the invention of this process; it was a closely guarded secret for some time. The process of printing with stone had been known in England for years, but it was used for imprinting patterns on cloth and as such so close a trade secret that little is known about it today. Lithography on paper was invented by Aloys Sennefelder in about 1796, in Munich, though numerous other claimants were working on similar lines, one as far away as Berlin. Still, it appears that Sennefelder has the precedence, and he patented his idea in 1799, and in London in 1801, though he was not a good businessman and so the spreading of the new process, which contained a whole cluster of secret details and crucial improvements, especially regarding the new ink, was almost more complex than its origins. His disciple among the English was Ackermann, who translated his handbook in 1819. In 1809 Sennefelder had issued an extra pamphlet called *An Important Communication* and in 1819 he added a supplement called *Essais en dessins et gravures*, with examples of the wonderful results that could be obtained.[1]

The basis of the original art was inscribing on hard stone instead of soft copper or wood: Sennefelder originally used Kelheim limestone, which he had for grinding his colours.[2] He first used his new method for printing a play he wrote as a law student, and for music. His French disciple André (1800), a music publisher, bought the process for 2000 florins. In 1801 Sennefelder visited London: the idea of cloth printing thrilled him but he did not persevere in that line, probably because of the numerous trade secrets involved. By 1807 his business was in trouble and in 1834 he died in Munich, but meanwhile Goya had discovered lithography in 1824, Géricault had used it for his *Boxers* in 1818 and Delacroix for his *Wild Horse* in 1828 and his *Tiger* the following year.[3] Artists were excited by its range of possibilities for black and white, though publishers preferred to colour the lithographs by hand. Chromolithography was still in the future: Newton's colour analysis had led to Le Blond's three-colour printing from copper, using three plates, by 1732, and something similar, with a fourth plate for black, resulted in coloured lithography, sometimes with eleven different plates, later in the 1800s.

All these new inventions were of the greatest interest to Edward Lear. He was conscious of what was going on in this area all his life; he was as we shall see a very early photographer, and experimented to the end of his life on different methods, none of them quite satisfactory, of reproducing his work. Had he lived another twenty years, it is certain he would have watched the technical difficulties being overcome. As it was, he was a perfectionist who was seldom or never satisfied.

What he learned and used for the *Parrots* was in the workshop of C. J. Hullmandel, born in London in 1789, the son of a German musician, who had learnt the lithographic process in Munich. In 1818 he produced some Italian views with it, and from 1821 to 1826 he worked for Engelmann and Coindet in Paris, but in 1827 he produced significant improvements, and set up his workshop in London, which was a labyrinth of rooms and mysterious processes. He was supported by the artist J. D. Harding and the scientist Edward Faraday, although he was attacked in 1829 by T. C. Croker, an Irishman who had worked in Paris and was recommended to the Admiralty by the famous J. Croker Wilson (no relation): there he introduced lithography, for the better printing of naval charts. Hullmandel wrote a lot of pamphlets, many of which are hard to track down. His lithographic work in London was triumphantly successful. It was in his studio that Edward Lear met Clarkson Stanfield, later an Academician, and probably J. D. Harding and David Roberts. It was certainly here that he heard Turner sing a comic song, 'And the world goes round a bound a bound'. He learned more about technique than he ever wrote down: the use of a touch of gum arabic for highlights and gleams for example, and the usefulness of scratchings when the water-colour is finished. He seems to have known all about the controversy over white body-colour. Turner once said to someone, 'You will be the death of water-colour painting, with your white body-colour.' Lear did not use it, but he does seem to know of Turner's way of hanging up sheets to dry or half-dry with different body-colour shades, blue, yellow or whatever, which was spotted once, like laundry-lines, in his bedroom in Yorkshire where he was a visitor.

One of the big excitements of the day was the collected edition of Byron that came out in seventeen volumes in 1832, with Moore's *Life*, some letters, and illustrations intended to rival those of Rogers' *Italy* (1830), which they certainly do. John Murray was the publisher, but the artists were Hullmandel himself (an Alpine lake left over from his Italian views), Clarkson Stanfield, J. D. Harding and Turner. There are two plates or vignettes at the beginning of each volume, often from sketches by W. Page, a few by T. Barry. Lear remembered being a boy of twelve when Byron died (though later he thought he had been fifteen), and often recalled how he had been grief-stricken. He was certainly a devoted fan, and the pictures, which are all from classical or romantic lands, must have excited him: Marathon, Chios, Athens, Troy, Corinth, Venice, the Walls of Rome (a brilliant study by Turner), Istanbul, the Hellespont, Parnassus, the field of Waterloo (a Turner as dark as Waterloo is in a

French lithograph of the Guard retreating) and 'the Castellated Rhine'. We know also that Lear was thrilled to read letters from a friend in Rome: he was not yet twenty.

Hullmandel had translated Raucourt's French *Manual of Lithography*, based on experiments done in the Paris School of Roads and Bridges (1820), and it must be said that the edge of foreign scientific eagerness had been vital to lithography, before the artists pounced on it in the nineteenth century. In fact the new invention would not have taken place, to judge from Sennefelder's autobiographical essay (Porzio), had the author not had a solid grounding in chemistry; he would not have known as much as an English schoolboy. One cannot but recall Shelley's interest in science at Eton, which amounted to no more than nearly electrocuting the headmaster. It is typical of the state of affairs in the 1800s that a French report on German lithography in 1814 was quite inadequate because the Germans kept their secrets to themselves, and the first two lithographic printers in Paris were furiously jealous of each other: Raucourt had to work out the method largely for himself, under the wing of what had become the Royal School of Roads and Bridges. Hullmandel translated him before composing a handbook of his own, too late to influence Edward Lear. Just how makeshift it all was may be judged from a note of Hullmandel that 'in Germany stones are often preserved with onion juice with the addition of a little brandy', or his advice to avoid scaling in summer by keeping the stone damp, the gum thin, and adding one-third part of sugar candy. The whole affair was between elementary, blow-your-head-off science and the highest development of European art, and Lear also was between the two, attracted by both.

Yet Hullmandel and Raucourt are already anxious to point out that 'in great cities, a number of persons are to be met with who give the greatest care and attention to those objects which concern the fine arts'. An artist need not make varnish or grind colours. It is just temporary that 'a lithographer is obliged to become a stone-mason, carpenter, shoemaker, etc., and to prepare his own black, his varnish, and his ink'. Hullmandel's rooms did go some way to removing this responsibility, and later in the century Raucourt's wish that there might be lithography shops did come true, but Lear worked at his parrots drawing on the stone himself, and learning the process as it was in 1830, acquiring a more intimate experience of the work involved than he would have got later. The ink was made of lamp black, with some two ounces each of tallow candle, virgin wax, 'shell-lac', and exactly two of common soap, to make the rest soluble in water. Raucourt's manual is practical, but also extremely experimental, so that without Hullmandel's refinements and advice, and his staff, Lear would not have turned out his masterly plates so swiftly. Again, it must be remembered that the mastery was largely in the colouring, in the last details of his practical execution. He made only 175 copies. His plates must sell as a luxury and therefore be valued for their rarity. This is a queer inversion of the natural possibilities of lithography; Lear probably took it up as a method because it was the latest scientific device. He never could find the mass audience for which he could have worked: if it did indeed exist so early in the nineteenth century, then there was no money in it for the artist. But this tactical mistake (as it appears to me by hindsight), or at least this limitation of scope, crippled his whole career.

Still, one must admit that even in France, 'where the drawings and plans of the public works had hitherto, from the great expense of engraving, remained buried in portfolios: thus a number of ingenious and useful inventions were lost', the remedy developed by Roads and Bridges of circulating in lithographs every important invention was still on a pathetically small scale. 'This plan has succeeded beyond all expectation ... 150 impressions of each drawing are required.' One should compare the sad little association of 150 engineers of which Raucourt was so proud with the fact that a child in India in the 1920s could learn the best engineering drawing in the world just from the *Encyclopaedia Britannica*, as Mr Chaudhuri remembers. Lithography in itself was only the first step. The price per drawing, which is explained in detail, was in 1820 computed at £2 18s. 8d. for an engraving on copper and 7s. 9d. for a lithograph. That does not of course allow for Hullmandel's profit, for the artist or scientist, or for the cost of colouring. The cost of printing when everything was ready was also less for a lithograph than for an etching.

Engraving on copper had another severe disadvantage which lithography inherited. It was impossible to combine the plates with the printing process for words so the text had become an appendage that ceased to interest makers of fine plates. The plates therefore tended to become the property of connoisseurs rather than scientists or doctors. The old herbals had circulated very widely with their woodcuts, but what Redouté produced was not intended to be seen by most people. There were effectively no public libraries. The patches of text in Audubon's birds were introduced by his friend Professor MacGillivray of Edinburgh for £50 or £60 a volume (there being five), just to vary the very long series of pictures. The makers of the great bird books included amateurs like Lear and technicians like John Gould, who was the taxidermist to the Zoological Society when Lear first met him.

So the parrots were entitled 'Illustrations': on the engraved black and white frontispiece to Part 12 the dedication read: 'Under the patronage of and dedicated by permission to the Queen's Most Excellent Majesty, Illustrations of the Family of the Psittacidae by E. Lear A. L. S.' and the word PARROTS was boldly printed. A list of subscribers was also printed, and the plates were issued in small sections, advertised as 'To be completed in fourteen Numbers'. They never were completed, because of a certain reluctance of some subscribers to pay up, and probably because Lear had underpriced the whole undertaking. He finally got rid of the rights he had in it to Gould the taxidermist. What Lear did produce came out quickly: twelve parts between 1830 and 1832. They were large folios, and no book as big of this kind had ever been lithographed in England. The variety which keeps one gasping lay in the plumage: in other bird books like Bewick's and Audubon's there was a variety of species, but Lear chose to concentrate on one, either for scientific reasons or because he lacked confidence.

A young Zoo keeper would hold the bird while Lear measured it in various directions, then he would sketch it once or twice in different poses in pencil. Some of these sketches contain very funny caricatures of the British public who came to goggle. He got his formal permission to work in the Zoo in June 1830, signed by Lord Stanley as its President. My own memory of the parrot house is of the most terribly loud noises of squawking and screeching, but at that time not so many birds were immured together. The public clearly irritated Lear far more than the birds did; the way people stare at an artist at work or a caged animal was something he never got used to.

One can see from the Harvard parrot sketches that he planned the next stage very exactly. His pencil drawing was annotated, and that was worked up into a water-colour, of which the colours were precisely analysed, and a black and white drawing was produced with feathers outlined in black lines like the scales of a fish. This model version was redrawn on stone by Lear himself in the queer ink that was necessary, and his finished water-colour with all its subtle touches, with the ruffled feathers of the bird's outline as fine as hairs, the ready tongue and the gleaming eye, was handed over to the colourists with a colour chart. It was of course an advantage to him that you could choose your own style and make your own drawings on the stone: you did not have to hire an engraver or a woodcutter.

The Harvard and also the Montreal water-colours are done in ink and pencil over original pencil sketches which include doodles or caricatures of birds and their poses. It is possible to see several versions of the same bird done with increasing confidence; experimental, thin colours become the assured and full-blooded coloration of the final bird. They are majestically perfect in their folio size, crisply drawn, gleaming with white of egg, lively and curiously beautiful. They breathe personality, as parrots often do in real life. The only drawing of a parrot I have ever seen to match them is by Ruskin, a sulphur-crested cockatoo that he drew from life at the Zoo when it was asleep, one day in 1877. It is almost more like a Lear than like the original parrot. Lear not only worked at the perfect version of each bird, but he ran off experimental proof versions, using the stone for them, which he then annotated. The Victoria and Albert Museum has some of these rejected versions. The most compelling feature to the eye is his coloration, but what he never forgot, once learnt, was his impeccable draughtsmanship. In the backgrounds of his parrots and all his creatures, and in the *Parrots* frontispieces, the vegetation is most gently indicated and subdued: unlike Audubon, he does not colour it. But in it one may see the subtle possibilities of black and white lithography which so excited Hullmandel.

Forty-two plates were published in the end. When the first two came out, as mentioned in the previous chapter, Edward was put up for the Linnaean Society the following day by N. A. Vigors of the Zoo, Thomas Bell and E. T. Bennett who wrote the 1831 Zoo Guide, and when the ninth section appeared William Swainson the American zoologist, writing from St Albans, acknowledged the huge importance and orig-inality of his contribution: 'The red and yellow macaw is in my estimation equal to any figure ever painted by Barraband or Audubon, for grace of design, perspective, or anatomical accuracy.' He wanted extra copies of two plates. He wanted to exchange proofs, his own, I take it, being the bird lithographs for Part 2 of Richardson's *North American Fauna* (1831); he really longed to be helpful. He felt the background vegetation to white birds should be coloured: 'the cold, "drawing" aspect which the plates have would then be removed.' In January 1834 Lear wrote to Sir William Jardine that he had decided against letterpress and stopped the series. 'Their publication was a speculation which so far as it made me known procured me employment, but in the matter of money occasionally caused loss.' He wrote to the Newcastle bookseller Mr Empson:

> I was obliged to limit the work – in order to get more subscribers – and to erase the drawings – because the expense is considerable for keeping them on, and I have pretty great difficulty in paying my monthly charge – for to pay colourer and printer monthly I am obstinately prepossessed – since I had rather be at the bottom of the River Thames than be one week in debt – be it ever so small.

On 15 April 1832 he wrote in a copy for Ann, with the proud dedication to Queen Adelaide. The copies left over he sold to John Gould who wrote in his turn to Sir William Jardine: 'If you are not complete as far as published I can make them so – I have some idea of finishing them myself.'

Gould was a man whose ambition came close to effrontery, and since Edward Lear came under his influence at this time and was ruthlessly exploited by him, it is important to understand his position. He was a self-made, practical ornithologist of astonishing energies, and his various enterprises entitle him to a high place among Victorian entrepreneurs. He was a gardener's son, born in 1804 at Lyme Regis, which makes him an all-important eight years older than Lear. His father moved to the royal gardens at Windsor in 1818 when he was a gardener's boy of fourteen; he held a gardener's post for a while at Ripley Castle on the River Nidd, between Harrogate and Ripon. In 1827, at twenty-three, he applied for the job of taxidermist, to stuff the dead birds left by Sir Stamford Raffles' widow to the Zoological Society, and got it. Stuffing birds was already his hobby, but the contact with great men which London and his new post brought him fired his ambition further. In 1829 he married an able and talented governess, who drew all the plates for his first book. He called the book, for which he had a load of Indian bird-skins to stuff, *A Century of Himalayan Birds*: published in 1832, it was highly praised. But from then on he modelled his productions on Lear's. 'But who will do the drawing on stone?' asked his wife Edith. 'Who? Why, you of course.' He employed Lear, he scratched out Lear's name from the plates he reproduced, and for a few years until Lear was grown up (he was not twenty until 1832), he dominated him. But he did so almost casually, because for his *Birds of Europe* (1832–7) he amassed and published almost 3000 plates. He must have treated many artists in the same way, but so far as I know no full study exists of the vast anonymous industry that must underlie his bird books. The solution to this problem may perhaps lie unrecognized in the Natural History Museum's collection of prints and drawings. Mrs Gould died in 1841 and for his later work, the *Birds of Great Britain* (1862–73, five volumes with 367 plates in all, weighing twenty pounds), Gould co-operated with Hart and Richter, whose productions are 'like portraits in cosmetic, lacking the fine bones of Lear's draughtsmanship' as Brian Reade put it in *Lear's Parrots* (1949). Gould was a remarkable and persistent workman, lacking only in taste, where Lear's is perfect.

Edward Lear did not drop everything to draw birds. He taught drawing to the children of a Madam Zieltszke in Tavistock Square and to anyone else who asked him. He drew for the woodcutters to illustrate E. T. Bennett's *Gardens of the Zoo Delineated*, perhaps for the quadrupeds (1830) but certainly for the birds (1831). The artist chiefly credited was William Harvey. Where did Harvey get the drawings, on which he must have noticed the EL monogram? It is probable enough that they met. Harvey was trained by Bewick himself and, Brian Reade tells us, received his first puff from Wainewright the poisoner. Drawing animals from life was a rather new idea, and Harvey was an enthusiast. Lear told Empson that he contemplated an expedition to the north with excitement, if only because of his family connection with Durham: it is a pity that he never met Bewick; as far as I know, he did not read his autobiography either. Nor is any influence of Harvey to be found in Lear's drawing style.

Lear was busy at this time on many projects. He went bird-chasing after parrots belonging to Lady Mountcharles, Lord Stanley (of course), a dealer called Leadbeater, N. A. Vigors of Chester Terrace, Sir Henry Halford, the King's doctor, described by an enemy as 'the eel-backed baronet' for his social manoeuvres, and of course Gould. He helped Gould in turn with some of the backgrounds for his Himalayan book although he was still producing parrot after parrot, in 1830 and 1831. Edith Gould drew the birds from her husband's sketches and Edward touched them up.

'About 1830 I think or earlier, perhaps 1828 – I went with him [Gould] to Rotterdam, Berne, Berlin and other places – but it was not a satisfactory journey; – and at Amsterdam we layed the foundation of many subsequent years of misery to me.' This was Lear's first journey out of England, and it remains a little mysterious. They were evidently in pursuit of lithographers and publishers of bird books, or of natural history of some kind, which is all they had in common. Amsterdam perhaps attracted them because of the brilliant Dutch bird books which Sacheverell Sitwell so admired. But what failed to satisfy we do not know. The journey itself, particularly to Berlin, would not have been an easy one, since they must have used public stage coaches. The mistake made at Amsterdam must have been a loosely or, on Lear's part, foolishly drawn-up agreement that he would work for Gould's *Birds of Europe*, 'drawn from nature and on stone by J. and E. Gould', though Lear had done a substantial amount of the work. 'He was one I never liked really,' he wrote at Gould's death in 1880,

> for in spite of a certain jollity and Bonhommie he was a harsh and violent man. At the Zoological G. at 33 Bruton St at Hullmandels – at Broad St ever the same, persevering, hard-working toiler in his own line, but ever as unfeeling for those about him. In this earliest phase of his bird drawing, he owed everything to his excellent wife, – and to myself, without whose help in drawing he had done nothing.

Drawings Lear made might surface long after he had abandoned zoology. His ducks done for T. C. Eyton appeared in 1838 and his lithographs of tortoises for a monograph by Bell only in 1872. But at least he was acknowledged. Sir William Jardine, using his birds for ordinary small-scale engravings in the late 1830s, refers in print to his 'accurate pencil' and his 'known talents'. He made all but one of the plates that Lizars engraved for Selby's *Pigeons* (1835) and most of his *Parrots* (1836) and was duly complimented in both volumes, although we have seen how little money he made. Some of his work was simply looted. Reade gives an example[4] and there are so many others that the subject is an entangled one. What is clear is that in the 1830s Lear was ready for anything. His parrot-feathers are most carefully delineated, they are constructed and not drawn in the mass: that is for the benefit of the colourist. But with animals like the little hyrax, an early drawing not perfected for years (not until someone wanted it), or like a queer and charming kangarooish creature painted with water-colour and gum on body-colour (1835), or the peculiar snub-nosed civet *Viverra binotata* (1836), he conveys the softest of fur by something like stippling. These are all water-colours, not prints, and he will cheerfully take up any appropriate technique. One feels that by now he could have conveyed the blush on Redouté's roses, had he chosen to do so, and his civet with her tiny eyes and paws and her long, curling cat-tail is so vivid you can smell her.[5]

But the best drawings Lear ever did were probably his lithographs for other people. The brilliance of his toucans with their enormous beaks and absurdly gleeful and naughty expressions has never been bettered or rivalled. He was painting them by 1834, when he made the ten best plates in Gould's first book on a single species, a fashion Lear's Psittacidae had set: *A Monograph of the Ramphastidae, or Family of Toucans.* He was not credited, and in the second (1854) edition his name was obliterated from the plates: 'Drawn from Life by J. and E. Gould' was substituted. Lear's best work – owls, cranes, vultures and pelicans, and some of his eagles – was in the *Birds of Europe.* Mrs Gould did the warblers and finches and so on, of which Susan Hyman unkindly remarks that 'they are easily identifiable by the fact that they manage to look like stuffed specimens even when copied from living animals'.[6] Lear drew the monstrous, the sinister and the eccentric, the heron, the owls, the black stork and the sympathetic flamingo. Audubon boasted of drawing every bird life-size: hence the huge size of his folios and the curious and often most beautiful though unlikely poses in which he has wired up his bigger birds. Lear does not need to contort his and they look natural, but the flamingo of course goes into extraordinary contortions naturally. He likes birds looking so queer.

The pelican was one of the passionate loves of his life, and he drew a Dalmatian pelican for Gould with the cliffs of Dover behind it. The pair of birds is masterly and utterly convincing in detail. Even his ostrich-like *Rhea americana* is convincing, and one can see at a glance why, as Lord Stanley complained, it refused to mate in Lancashire. These big birds are a kind of wonderland. The Great Auk, the Great Egret and the Solan Gannet are vast and mysterious, much more so than they are on nature films, but as if they were free and standing on the carpet; there is no sense of taxidermy or of a cage; they might suddenly give a squawk. The most impressive of all are the charming Snowy Owl, though in life it is more terrifying, and the fearful Eagle Owl, though in fact the bird was stuffed, and the water-colour of a Spectacled Owl just like an elderly Lancashire cobbler, which Lear drew in 1836 for Lord Stanley. Teng-malm's Owl, which Vivien Noakes reproduces in *The Painter Edward Lear*,[7] is perhaps more attractive than any of these, but it is Lear's secret that he conveys terror and wildness as much as Géricault. My own absolute favourite is one of those owls to be found among the half-dozen or so I believe he first did for Bell, the Great Snowy Owl. The most reliable list is by R. D. Wise, including an exact bibliographic description of the *Parrots*, in the Royal Academy Catalogue.[8] It includes a list of the three birds named after him, Lear's Macaw which turns up as *Macrocercus hyacinthus* in the Harvard sketches and on plate 9 of the *Parrots*, Lear's Cockatoo and the Tabuan Parrot from Fiji, *Platycercus leari*. A number of the birds are still apparently unpublished: an upside-down lory and a Sandwich Island parakeet at Harvard, for example. Sometimes the colouring is so intense that the paint comes through the paper. The 'Hyacinthine Macaw', his own bird, is a more brilliant blue than any reproduction has been able to make it. In October 1867 Lear wrote to his friend Lord Northbrook, who later bought these water-colours from Quaritch in 1892, that a copy of the lithographs had been bought at a sale for £6, 'the first lithography of its kind of the size in England and led to Gould's improvements ... many of which the said foolish artist drew'.[9]

In these very active years even his letters were full of zoology, and the queerer the animal the more it arrested him. He wrote to the Coombes in July 1832, addressing himself to their baby Fanny Jane. 'I write by candlelight – and in a hurry. – My letter indeed is addressed to you – solely from a staunch belief that your whole kindred – friends – connections and acquaintances are dead and departed.' She is to tell her Aunt Eliza that he was taken ill in London and could not meet her coach, and to tell Robert that he asks for beasts or birds only to have them from friends. 'I have a rather Zoological connection – and being about to publish British Quadrupeds – I have now living – two Hedgehogs, – all the sorts of mice, weasels, Bats etc. – and every beast requisite except a Pine Marten.' There follow another animal joke for W. Wardroper about a cure for dropsy in chickens, a tease for Mrs Street about her misfortunes and illnesses, messages to the extended family, and his signature 'Your three parts crazy and wholly affectionate Uncle Edward'. Lear was one of the world's natural uncles.

Already in October 1831 he had proudly listed his zoological friends to Mr Empson, promising Landseer's autograph, noting that three sets of *Parrots* had gone to Russia, and begging for help with South American trees because 'I often want them to put birds upon when I draw for Lord Stanley – which is very frequently.' He promises at the same time to draw Empson some flowers which had been sent by parcel. In 1834 he acknowledged a payment from Sir William Jardine that seems to have been on the late side, £5 for some drawings and £3 for the last six issues of the separately issued parts of *Parrots*. He will draw Humboldt's Lagothriae 'as soon as my health will allow of my riding to the Surrey Gardens'. The journey must have been a difficult one; the gardens are now Chessington Zoo, and fog made Lear ill every January. He would supply parrot pictures (apart from his *Parrots* to which Gould now owned the rights) for £1 each 'because Parrots are my favourites, and I can do them with greater facility than any other class of animal'.

His letter[10] was that of a professional man and an expert, in spite of its boyish modesty. He found some of the sub-species of parrots obscure and hoped Sir William would clear them up. A glance at the bibliography of the parrots named after Lear makes it plain that this situation persisted into modern times. He criticized Sir William's Naturalist's Library series for the unevenness of colour in copies of the same book. 'The Sabaeus (Green Monkey) is in some copies a bright green – in others *nearly wholly* gamboge.' He is alarmed by the disproportionate size of creatures too, *Simia sciureus* being shown bigger than the orang-outan. Certainly as he went on he gathered confidence in the curious world of zoologists into which he had strayed, and he surely gained facility in smooth-haired quadrupeds. His great patron was Lord Stanley, who summoned him in 1832 to record the rarities of his private menageries at Knowsley.

Knowsley deserves a book to itself. When Edward Lear arrived it was a smaller but rambling pre-Victorian castellated house like an Oxford college: it was about the size of Mycenae, and its regime was eighteenth-century or earlier. The Earl of Derby was at this time nearly eighty (he reigned at Knowsley for fifty-eight years, dying in 1834) and his house in principle thirteenth-century, acquired by marriage in the fourteenth. It had seen many alterations. The Earl had thought of pulling the old place down and starting again, but in the end all he had done was to build a huge new hall for entertainment, with an impressive entrance door. His entertainments were on a most generous scale: on Mondays he entertained the neighbours, up to 100 of them at a time, and on every day from June to November places were set for forty, who would range from house guests and poor relations to casual visitors. This Earl had founded the Derby on Epsom Downs and was extremely proud of his horses. He had married an actress *en deuxième noces* with whom he was cherubically happy, being far from London and king of his distant province. Greater and lesser houses in Lancashire used to be suddenly visited, and Lord Derby's visiting card was a fine print of his favourite racehorse, which had won the Derby. These must be valuable now, but they are still to be spotted here and there, hanging in dark corridors in their dark frames. The Earl did not know everyone who dined with him: indeed some old officer whom the Earl had never met and never heard of is said by Osbert Sitwell to have reserved rooms at Knowsley for many years in one of the obscurest and most rambling wings. There is another time-honoured story told of a Lord Derby, that as the guests sat down to dine, one was seen to pick up his silver in wonderment, and turn over his plate to gasp at its grandeur, and the Earl happened to notice him. He rapped the table and called out in a loud voice, 'Mr So-and-so has called for his carriage.' The offender was shown out, and in the nervous silence that followed the Earl was heard to remark, 'Funny kind of fella, talkin' about a fella's things.'

It was into this daunting human showground of rare specimens that the young Edward Lear was introduced in the summer of his twentieth year. Lady Derby, a former actress, was younger than her husband but had died in 1829. It had been a love match, even though she was about forty when they married. Her father was a Cork apothecary and her mother the daughter of a Liverpool publican, but for years Lady Derby had been the rage of London; Charles James Fox and the Duke of Richmond were among her followers. Her stage career had begun with roles in *Columbine* and *Love in a Village*, and went on to include the erotic – Almeida in *The Fair Circassian* – but she was personally respectable. When the Dowager Countess died on 14 March, Elizabeth Farren, as she then was, bade adieu to the stage on 8 April, bursting into tears during her farewell speech, and married Lord Derby, who had been Earl since 1776, on 1 May. Her sister, Margaret Knight, was another actress whose family Edward Lear encountered later.

It is useful to notice at once that Lord Derby's sister Lucy had married the Rev. Geoffrey Hornby of Winwick, because his grandson, who was born in 1799, married the same Mr Hornby's second daughter, who was his first cousin. Thus the Hornby and Stanley families became deeply entangled for a time. At that date the fact of Mr Hornby being a clergyman did not of course preclude him from being a gentleman of lineage. The Hornby clan was more numerous and perhaps held more land in Lancashire than even the Stanley clan. Edward Lear became their devoted friend; he was closer to the Hornbys than to the Stanleys. He was terrified of Knowsley and depressed by its strange machinery. Although he was always most respectful with the Derbys, I see no evidence that he liked them, except for that splendid old man the twelfth Earl, whom he worshipped. None the less he cultivated a long relationship with them, warmer on his part than on theirs, and liked to feel he was an old retainer, but that surely was because he lacked a home of his own. When he first came to Knowsley, feeling rather like a new boy at an ancient public school, the Earl's son, Lord Stanley, was there, and the next after him in line of succession, the Earl's grandson, who had already married his first cousin with the Earl's consent in 1825. He was in politics, where his deadly enemy in the early 1830s was Daniel O'Connell, with whom he tried to fight a duel. Edward was probably influenced by Stanley loyalty in conceiving a passionate hatred for the Irishman. The old Earl's great-grandson, the fourth in line to succeed, was at that time a child of three (he was born in 1829). His father, being on the earnest side (he translated the entire *Iliad* into leaden English verse), sent him to Rugby under Dr Arnold, which luckily had little effect. There is no doubt that the family had brains, although their politics, and the almost royal ugliness of Knowsley as it was by 1845, are another matter. When the boy left Rugby he went to Trinity, Cambridge and there became an Apostle, like Tennyson. But the line of earnestness was on the increase, and when Edward Lear was at his wits' end for money and finally dared to ask for some, this nobleman, with the idiocy of the really rich, assured Lord Northbrook that a direct loan would be a terrible mistake.

There was no intention to exploit, it would not have occurred to any member of that grand and interesting family that they were being mean. But although Lear was paid and had his keep for the work he did at Knowsley, it was not perhaps as much as a middle-class living wage. We have one of his bills for finished work. Only the most fashionable painters of portraits in oils could make a good living: it was the faces that brought in the guineas. As late as the 1840s when Clarkson Stanfield painted a boat with no people in it, just a hulk wallowing, that was thought revolutionary. Stanfield had been trained in heraldic painting and then pressed into the Navy. His early jobs were all at painting stage scenery, a task he was happy to perform for Dickens. He did not become an Academician until the second half of the century began. As for water-colourists, they were casually employed as drawing masters, at Eton and in country houses: Lear taught the young Stanleys of Alderley, which was not far from Knowsley, in this way. Since pupils learned by copying, there has often been confusion about the work of a great-aunt and that of some great and famous artist like David Cox or Peter de Wint, though never about Lear. Knowsley still has a collection of Lear's fine water-colours, and Lord Stanley must have been pleased with them, as well he might be. Lear wrote to him for years about zoology, the sweetest letters, but inevitably his true friends in that home of crumbling grandeur were younger sons and cousins.

The Bishop of Norwich, for example, a cousin of the Derbys, was appointed in 1837. Before that he had the family living of Alderley, his father was the first Lord Stanley of Alderley and his brother the second. His connection with Edward Lear must have been birds, because in 1836 he produced two volumes called *The Familiar History of Birds*. They had tried earlier to make him Bishop of Manchester but one can sympathize with his ducking out of that. Norwich, on the other hand, was a quite unreformed diocese, and he went through it like a dose of salts, demanding regularity and importing an Irish Catholic priest to advocate temperance. That approach would have appealed to Edward Lear. One of his great friends was Arthur Penrhyn Stanley, who was later Dean of Westminster; they went to Ireland together, to which journey a handful of drawings is the monument.

At Knowsley Edward got to work quite quickly on his commissions, rather like an upper gardener. The animals were kept in paddocks – the rhea must have had a field – or indoors: there was plenty of room for the tree-rats, eagles, various cranes and tortoises. Today, Knowsley has quite a big herd of elephants. Lear seems to have drawn every species that was new to him. The beautifully demure jaguar looks as dangerous as any Hellenistic lady sphinx. The unidentified tree-rat does not look as if he relishes captivity. One of his most peculiar drawings is the sun-grebe which has a salmon-like sheen on the belly and neck. It is called *Heliornis senegalensis*, but I do not think I have ever seen one in real life. Lear drew this fish-like, thin-headed, delicate-necked bird in gum mixed with water-colour and Chinese white, which must be the secret of his glimmering appearance. The tree-rat (1834) is unidentified to this day: his tail is coiled two or three times tightly round a branch, but he is all watchfulness: will he scuttle or spring? The final versions of these mesmerizing water-colours were apparently made in London. They are less spectacular than the parrots but more perfect. They are as good and as humorous as the letters of Jane Austen.

Giraffes were a real novelty. One wonders how Lear would have drawn them. We have his reaction, because he wrote to Lord Derby (as he was by then) in June 1836 from 28 Southampton Row, London.

Zaida (female), Yabulla, Selim, Mabrook (male) are the Giraffes names. Of the giraffes – I dare say your Lordship has been already written to by Mr Sabine [Vice-President of the Zoo and FRS] . . . I do not for my own part know which is the most picturesque party – the animals themselves or their Keepers the Nubians. I have enclosed the signatures of the three, Abdallah, Carbass and Omar – that your Lordship may see their writing. All of them are very good-tempered men – but the *extreme* crowds of people who flock to see them discompose them now and then. As for the

Giraffes, I never imagined anything living of such extreme elegance, and I much wish your Lordship could see them.

He was still extremely busy. He was making lithographs (now lost) for his old friend Mrs Greville-Howard and awaited her return to London. 'I grumble at London more and more.' When she died nearly forty years later, she left him £100. He contrived to be allowed to draw the heads of the four Nubians, but then had no time to do it 'or I should have sent some sketches to your Lordship'. He had been at the Zoo with the future Lord Stanley of Alderley and his wife, and had spent a day or two at East Sheen with Mr Edward Penrhyn who was married to Charlotte, Lord Derby's daughter. He was off to see Mr Baker with whom he imagined he might go to the Himalayas, but he was only invited for a day or two in Hertfordshire. Perhaps it was Sabine's idea to send him to India, but Sabine, who took him to see Baker, died the following year. Lear also reported that Cross's garden, which was a menagerie at Redcar, had acquired a four-horned antelope, but no new birds. Cross had a son, John, who married Elizabeth Hornby, Lord Derby's first cousin, and John became one of Edward's closest friends. It will be seen that the Lancashire connection was extensive, and that Edward Lear in London was in touch with many parts of the spider's web. As soon as he had done Mrs Greville-Howard's lithographs, he would be off to Knowsley for his annual working visit.

Yet he did not enjoy that life, and in a month or two his whole career would take a new direction; Lancashire is unkind to asthmatics, and zoology was going to be dropped. Lord Derby published seventeen of Lear's drawings in *Gleanings from the Menagerie and Aviary at Knowsley Hall*, privately printed in 1846, with some very complimentary remarks by J. E. Gray of the British Museum. But by then Lear had been living in Rome for nearly ten years.

CHAPTER FOUR

INTIMATE
INTERLUDES

EDWARD LEAR'S LIFE, like most young men's, developed in more than one direction at once. Sussex and the jokes with Eliza Drewitt, and zoology, and a course he took at Dr Sass's drawing school in London, and the Zoo and the birds and the tour with Gould, and one must add the dose of clap and explorations of Dickensian London and choking nearly to death in its increasing fogs, and the strange, distant half-world of Knowsley were all crammed together into a few years. People were found and lost quite casually: he never saw Mrs Wentworth from 1828 to 1863, and he ceased to visit Peppering although the Drewitts went on living there in the same house into this century: Ruskin was a visitor there. Mrs Powell, née Dawtrey-Drewitt, sent a comic poem by Lear about the bad road to the *Sussex County Magazine* not long ago.

Lear's technical tricks were sharply observed and precisely applied, but as he knew, Turner was already dissolving the great rivers of Europe in coloured mist like swathes of the finest satin, and as he probably also knew, Gainsborough before his death in 1788 had already exploded the English landscape into a mixed imaginative storm of oils and chalks and, at that fine point of exactitude, there were suddenly in a new way no rules. The Academy might tell Constable to 'take away that green thing,' but it is the boldness, novelty and simplicity of the new painting now vaguely labelled Romantic that take one's breath away.

On 3 October 1834, two years before his formal landscape attempts in the Lakes, Lear signed a drawing at Burpham which has been entitled *Boy Reclining by a Thatched Mill, Burkham*; Field reproduced it in his sumptuous, private catalogue, *Lear on my Shelves*; it is now at Harvard. The boy in his tall, shady hat, and indeed the whole vignette, might almost be by some member of Samuel Palmer's circle at the time. The only work of Lear's even remotely like it is his drawing of an old barn at Peppering with a tumbledown fence and some hens and young turkeys, done on the same day.[1] A fine drawing of Peppering church among trees against the Downs, of which a fainter, feebler, early version is in the Edinburgh album, has the same date. The reclining boy has no ancestors in Lear's work, and no progeny. He is a local farm boy, younger than Edward, who was twenty-two by then and through with his parrots. What Field calls a mill is just a ruinous, roughly thatched hut containing a cask of some kind, and the boy lies on grass outside it in his smock. The scene has a miraculous clarity, as if it were observed by G. M. Hopkins. Compared to this, the *Rustic Scene* he lithographed and the *Sugarloaf Hill* he drew in Ireland in 1835 are terribly stiff, though *Wicklow Head*[2] is a fine drawing. Perhaps it was the uselessness and informality of the Burpham sketch that set him free. Later on he valued it, because he gave or sold it to his great friend Lord Northbrook. His letters tell us little about his Irish tour except that he went to Glendalough with A. P. Stanley and his Uncle Penrhyn. They climbed a difficult ledge bare-footed, though Lear had to be helped round by an old woman who popped the pair of them into St Kevin's bath.

In 1836 his summer expedition had a Knowsley background again, since Knowsley is close to the Lakes, where poets and artists had visited or settled ever since Thomas Gray and Wright of Derby, seventy years ago or more, and which had become fashionable as a result. It was on this year's visit to the Lakes that Lear decided to become a professional landscape painter. He wrote to Gould in October:

I left Knowsley (only half my work done) on the 12 August for a sketching tour, and really it is impossible to tell you *how, and how enormously* I have enjoyed the whole Autumn. The counties of Cumberland and Westmorland are superb indeed, and though the weather has been miserable, I have contrived to walk pretty well over the whole ground, and to sketch a good deal besides. I hope too, I have improved somewhat – (hard if I haven't after slaving as I have done) but you will judge when I get back ... I could not go on to Scotland ... I am staying to finish what I promised Lord Derby before I went away ... Nothing particularly new here – Weasel headed Armadillo etc. etc.

Lear used his Lakes sketches to make some finished water-colours – the coloured *Wastwater* is dated 1837 – but luckily a number of the drawings that first gave him confidence have survived. He painted Wastwater, and perhaps Crummock (1836) for the Rev. J. J. Hornby, whose nephew travelled with him. The nephew had exactly the same name as his uncle, but differed from him in becoming headmaster and Provost at Eton. It is a long connection, but it seems to throw light on the Warre family's devotion to Lear and to their parrot, whose epitaph in Dulverton Woods (1907) Belloc translated from Warre's Latin into his stiff monumental English: E. L. Warre quotes it in the foreword to Edward Lear's *Parrots* by Brian Reade. In one of his late and reminiscent letters in 1884 Lear says: 'He and I – (the Provost) – used to run races all over that part of the country – and perhaps you don't know that I know every corner of Westmorland; Scawfell Pike is my cousin, and Skiddaw is my mother-in-law.'

Sometimes even earlier sketches survive in a later form as water-colours, as illustrations of Tennyson: the churchyard yews of the Kingly Valley near Chichester or the real mill at Arundel, for example. But the sketch called *Umbellifera*, of which only the title shows high spirits, since it represents umbrellas on a wet day at Kendal,[3] the marvellous and careful sketch called *Rydal Water*, dated 7 October 1836 and therefore certainly finished at Knowsley, and the beautiful, less solemn or grand *Brathay near Ambleside* (11 July 1836), sold in 1966 for £120, might persuade any young painter that he had a genius for landscape. The British Museum has a few more of these important lakeland sketches; Mr H. V. Day of Dorchester used to have a number, including water-colours (September–October 1836) and it was from his collection that those in the Museum came.[4] *Rydal Water* is taken from the top, north end of the lake, which spreads out between hillsides into the distance. It is a tranquil pencil sketch with reflections in the water and deer grazing by the lake. The peculiar thing about it is the two long-legged water-birds who are so perfectly placed in the foreground water. They are white, they show their heads and necks as they crane towards each other, though they have their backs to the painter. What on earth are they doing in Rydal Water? They look exactly like big white egrets, and they are certainly not English herons which Lear well knew how to draw. Egrets have been recorded as exotic vagrants that far north – there are two near the Severn now, and a flotilla on the Exe – but Lear would surely have mentioned them to Gould? Can they have escaped from some reverend gentleman's aviary? Were they added at Knowsley? They are a mystery.

Lear visited Colonel Howard at Levens on the way to the Lakes and on the way back, and the Stanniforths and Bradylls, all three subscribers to Gould's books, but his principal hosts were the Hornbys. He did not like Levens, though he drew it respectfully: he preferred the mountains. He was, as he remained all his life, prodigally generous to his hosts: it is hard to tell his friends from his clients, and the amateur conventions of the water-colour make it harder still. Many years later, at least one lady of his own generation was shocked and disgusted that he dared to *sell* his water-colours. He painted *Wastwater* in 1837 for the Hornbys as a present, with golden autumnal trees and two cattle bathed in a Cuyp-like golden haze that consumes rocks and withers the blue mountains. The whole thing is too golden: it is like those shaggy Highland cattle that gloom about large canvases in hotel dining-rooms, paddling on the dark edge of lochs. But Windermere from the road from Kendal to Bowness holds all the promise of the Greek mountains Lear was born to paint. It was done on 10 July 1836, in pencil with the silhouettes of hill-tops clarified, I think, with ink, and the wonderful wash-like use of water-colour that makes him the inheritor of the eighteenth century. The hills in this picture are so exactly analysed that they are almost Towne-like in their clarity: there really are such days, and topographic exactness was Lear's true north, for better or for worse.[5] He scribbled notes on his pictures as he had done on his early parrots, like 'all heathy green', 'misty', and 'yellowish grey'. It is probably important that he thought his eyes were going: the fear haunted him all his life until it became a fact. 'I have had such a cold as to be half-blind . . . my eyes are so sadly worse, that no bird under an Ostrich shall I soon be able to see to do.'

In 1837, Lord Derby and Robert Hornby combined to pay for Lear to go to Rome. Ariel was set free from the menagerie, and he was for ever grateful. Nor was he then unkindly cast off, since Derby corresponded with him and he was always welcome to stay at Knowsley. His position there must be further clarified. We know that he expected to dine and have his being in the housekeeper's dining-room or servants' hall or whatever, but it is not clear how he was promoted. Probably his first visit was a brief one, as a guest, I imagine, to see the work and decide whether he would undertake it. The second was a working visit, and he told a painter he met at Hullmandel's that he was not sure whether he was to live above or below stairs. This was in the days of the old widower Earl, who was as we have seen an extremely jolly man. Shelley's mother said of him in her memoirs (1787–1817), 'Dear old man! His joyous temperament, and his love of society and good cheer, made his guests as happy and merry as himself. He constantly bantered the young ladies on their good looks, and about their lovers . . .'[6] So it may be simply as the artist recalls, that the Earl's voice called at once down the stairs, 'Mr Lear, Mr Lear, come up here!' But Angus Davidson says what happened was that the children kept making excuses to vanish from table, and the Earl discovered it was because of their friend the funny man. The Earl had him up at once to dine, and from then on he was a beloved guest. That has the ring of truth, and probably derives from Lear's friend Lord Carlingford through Lady Strachey. Lear was crazy about children and held many generations of them enthralled. He really was a very funny man, impromptu and in his impromptu drawings. He may claim to be the funniest caricaturist there has ever been, mostly of animals, particularly cats. His human beings and self-portraits took longer to take off, though in the end they were the best.

How Lear came to find himself among 'half the great men of the day' at Knowsley, was obscure and a little magical to a later generation. Lady Strachey, introducing the first volume of his letters says that Lord Stanley, already thinking of his *Gleanings* (1856) [sic], went to the London Zoo, was much struck by Lear's drawing, and engaged him on the spot to do his birds.[7] She imagines Lear was employed then and there. But she does cast light on his position at Knowsley through a letter he wrote late in life to Lord Carlingford. He had found in his sister Ann's papers a letter, one of those which stood in for the journal he burnt in 1840.

> The Earl of Wilton [son of Westminster] has been here for some days . . . married Lady Mary Stanley. He is extremely picturesque if not handsome, and dresses in crimson and a black velvet waistcoat, when he looks like a portrait of Vandyke. Miss —— says and so does Mrs —— that he is a very bad man, tho he looks so nicely. But what I like about him, is that he always seeks me to drink a glass of champagne with him at dinner. I wonder why he does. But I don't much care as I like the champagne.

> Lear asked Miss —— why it was a little later and 'she began to laugh and said, "Because he knows you are a clever artist and he sees you always look at him and admire him: and he is a very vain man and this pleases him, and so he asks you to take wine as a reward." Ha! Ha! Ha!'

There is at least no doubt about it being the cheerful Lord Derby who promoted Lear. But it is not absolutely certain which of the Lords Derby suggested to Lear or challenged him to write limericks. It does sound much more like the same old man than any of the others: if so, it was when Lear had not been long at Knowsley and that fits in too, because the Earl picked up a book called *Anecdotes and Adventures of Fifteen Gentlemen*,[8] which is not likely to have been lying about more than ten years after its publication. Although Lear did not produce his limericks publicly until 1846, he was fertile in fantasy, and we will never be quite certain when he wrote his first limericks. He himself never uses that word, and his examples have rules of their own that no one else follows: he called them *A Book of Nonsense*, by Old Derry down Derry, with two volumes of thirty-six poems each. The name Old Derry down Derry appears to have come from a character in a mummers' play, and, as we shall see, several other elements in his nonsense verse throughout his life come from the mummers. It would appear that if he ever actually saw such a play it lay deeply buried in his subconscious memory. The fact that where he is most original and memorable he is also blatantly derivative does not affect the use and value of what he produced. There is, if I may say so, a certain analogy with the works of Shakespeare. The *Anecdotes of the Fifteen Gentlemen*, and the *History of Sixteen Wonderful Old Women* (1820), had already established the rhythm, which is very close to the works of Thomas Moore and a hundred childish songs, but the limerick certainly has a metrical perfection of its own.

John Newbery was one of the most important publishers of children's books in the eighteenth century: *Mother Goose's Melody or Songs for the Cradle* was his.[9] Newbery first came to London in 1744, but it was only in the 1760s that he spotted the commercial possibilities of nursery rhyme. Oliver Goldsmith did the necessary hackwork, since he adored children as Lear did. He sang to Dr Johnson and the Literary Club 'his favourite song about An Old Woman tossed in a blanket seventeen times as high as the Moon'. Newbery's firm was somehow bought or inherited by John Harris, the general manager, and Harris and John Marshall, the publisher of *Anecdotes of Fifteen Gentlemen*, were rivals. It was Harris who had just produced the *History of Sixteen Wonderful Old Women*, and both books were successful. J. O. Halliwell included the old men of Tobago and Bombay and the old women of Surrey, Leeds and Norwich in a collection of orally transmitted nursery rhymes in 1846. The plot of the limerick as Lord Derby noticed it and as Lear inherited it was simple enough. In its classic state it goes back to a prehistoric form of the anecdote which is older than the Greeks: a man from so and so did such and such, this or that happened or was said, and he said or did so and so.

The *Fifteen Gentlemen* may have been written by R. S. Sharpe, a grocer who composed children's verse, but the all-important illustrations were by Robert Cruikshank. They are forceful and funny and brightly coloured. When Lear produced illustrations to his own limericks they appear at first to approximate to this style, but that is because they were sent to London to be copied, and no one took comic drawings for children seriously, at any rate Lear's printers did not. But the interesting thing is that he began by doing his own illustrations of some existing limericks and then embarked on his own. A Knowsley album with an 1854 watermark has poems from a numbered series stuck into it: 'There was a sick man of Tobago', 'There was an old soldier of Bicester', both from Marshall's book and probably by Sharpe, and 'There was an old person of Sparta', which is Lear's composition, funnier than his predecessors'.[10] In 1981 Ada Duncan of Naughton House, Fife, brought to light two albums, one with drawings and verses which appear to date from the early 1840s: Edward met the Lady Duncan of the day at Rome in the late 1830s. The little book was published in facsimile as *Bosh and Nonsense* in 1982. The drawing of the Old Lady of Prague is certainly brilliant in its comic brio and more amusing than the usual version.

But it was not only limericks that he illustrated. Many of his comic drawings are hard to date, but it is important to bear in mind that he did all the events of 'Hey diddle diddle the cat and the fiddle, the cow jumped over the moon, the little dog laughed to see such fun, and the dish ran away with the spoon'. That was later, for the daughter of J. A. Symonds, though he may first have devised it for any child at any time. It was quoted by Byron in derision of Wordsworth in 1804, so :t was well known. We have his 'Sing a song of sixpence', which differs a little from the canonical version, with the same remarkable and by then perfected mastery of line and comic brio.[11] (In the illustrations, Lear's 'Hey diddle diddle' has got into the middle of 'I sing a song of sixpence'.) If it were true, as I used to think, that genius is the survival of the powers of childhood into an adult world of technique and criticism, then Edward Lear would be the exemplary genius. He is more complex than that, however, and one must not abstract his funny side from all the rest of his qualities.

The song that Lewis Carroll uses, 'Humpty Dumpty', first occurs in English in a manuscript of 1803, though in the seventeenth century it apparently meant a drink made with heated ale and brandy, and in the late eighteenth century it could be 'a little humpty dumpty man or woman'. The rhyme itself is oddly close to a limerick. Lear noticed it and drew the story in three stages before *Alice*. It is in Mrs Beadon's scrapbook at Harvard, put together between 1852 and 1858. She was a vicar's wife and an old friend of Lear; the manuscript has the 'Song of sixpence' and much else; I have never before heard the old rhyme (as it must be):

> Three red roses all of a row,
> See how they grow,
> See how they blow,
> O, O! nor did I know
> 1, 2, 3, 4 and 5,
> I caught a hare alive,
> 6, 7, 8, 9 and 10,
> I let her go again. Why did you let her go?
> Because she bit my finger so.

My typist knew it though, as 1, 2, 3, 4, 5/Once I caught a fish alive ... Many illustrations follow that, from a Calabrian hurdy-gurdy man, thistles, a hedgehog and a paddle-steamer. Lear draws a sleepy, slightly drunk-looking owl and a furiously disgruntled parrot, a fine pen sketch of a cyclamen, then an owl, a grasshopper, a peacock, a tortoise, a rat, a butterfly, a dragonfly, a parrot and a frog. There are letters and jokes and little caricatures of Orther of Nonsense. There are qualities of warmth indicating confidence and mirth and children about this album, that must in some way reflect his first acceptance in the children's world at Knowsley.

The limericks are so famous that one is tempted to say nothing more about them. They are best read in the original size, twice as big as they are in Holbrook Jackson's edition, and with crudely coloured illustrations. The personality of the author is never far distant, and they are probably best of all with fresh drawings which someone draws for you when you cannot quite read for yourself. At that stage the connivance and giggling that can take place between reader and listener are a necessary part of the magic. But they are fascinating for adults also. The pathos or sadness of some of them is very touching. I am particularly fond of the Old Person of Sparta, who had twenty-five sons and one daughter; he fed them on snails and weighed them on scales, that wonderful person of Sparta. But where had Lear observed him? The likeness to an early-nineteenth-century Greek is startling, and so are the row of his children and the number of them. It seems to me that Lear must have seen some ancestor of Kavafis in the family shipping business in Liverpool. The Old Man of Corfu, on the other hand, is a sailor, maybe a skipper but still a mariner. He never knew what he could do; so he rushed up and down till the sun made him brown, that bewildered old man of Corfu. The Old Person of Tring who embellished his nose with a ring has the air of a Rothschild, but he may not be one: long noses are common in comic drawing, the *Anecdotes* have one on the Old Man of Tobago. Lear was sensitive about his own nose, admittedly, and I count five huge ones in the book as Jackson prints it, and one huge sharp nose with an equally huge sharp chin. But the Rothschilds did not own Tring or settle there before 1870, so the Old Person of Tring must be quite innocent. He is just strangely prophetic, as the very first limerick of all prophesies the size and shape and look of Lear's beard in later life: yet it was drawn at a time when he was beardless. This old man has a long nose too.

> There was an Old Man with a beard,
> Who said, 'It is just as I feared!
> Two Owls and a Hen,
> Four Larks and a Wren,
> Have all built their nest in my beard!'

Lear has often been blamed for a certain inbuilt feebleness or lack of punch in his limericks, because of the rhyme-word of the first line, which is usually a place-name, being repeated in the last. That is something he inherited from the anonymous creator of the histories of the old women, and even so he did not adopt it as an absolute rule. He used it very often with subtlety: 'And frequently walked about Ryde'; 'It's a regular brute of a Bee'; 'Which agreed with that person of Leeds' (note the internal rhyme); 'That amiable Man of the Isles'. Each poem has its own rhythm, and within the severity of form they vary on their smaller scale, as unexpectedly as Shakespeare's sonnets. The alternative pattern of a third and quite fresh rhyme-word for the last line creates a completely new form. In Lear's form the last line is a diminuendo or a casual or throwaway line, but in the other, later form, which was used for hilarious obscenities collected by Norman Douglas and often falsely ascribed to Lord Tennyson, the final line is a sudden crescendo with a rhyme like a stone from a catapult: nothing satisfies that form as well as an obscenity. It is the taste for these strong verses in adolescence that destroys the childish enjoyment of Lear's weak-looking limericks, and that is a pity.

Tennyson, in the only limerick he really did write, maintained the diminuendo even in the new form.

Consider the Old Man of Madras, a rhyme Lear uses for one who rode on a cream-coloured ass, but the length of its ears so promoted his fears that it killed him, a charming rhyme with a sad, ritual diminuendo. In the style of the 1890s, that becomes an Old Man of Madras whose balls were made of brass, they clashed together in windy weather, and sparks flew ... The new form expects a powerful ending, and its final rhyming word must crack through some barrier of inhibition. Even the Old Man of Nantucket introduces a certain naughtiness reinforced by the repeated rhyme: he kept all his cash in a bucket, but his daughter called Nan ran away with a man, and as for the bucket Nan tucket. Few of these later limericks give the mild, fantastic amusement of the Learian originals. Still, it is a tribute to him as well as to the form, which was popular and widespread, so that Dickens like Halliwell thought it was purely traditional nursery rhyme, that limericks did so proliferate. Alfred Tennyson wrote one when his last publisher asked him whether he had ever written a limerick. 'No,' he said, 'but I could'; and after a pause,

> There are people who live down in Erith
> Whom nobody seeth nor heareth,
> And there by the marge
> Of the river a barge
> Which nobody guideth or steereth.

It has an admirable because unexpected metaphysical quality and an interesting similarity to 'The Lady of Shalott'. The climax is like that of some ghostly short story of exactly the period of Tennyson's old age. It was as impromptu rhymes that limericks became popular and still are so today. A battle of limericks in the clubs arose over the case of Bishop Colenso, between Soapy Sam, Bishop of Oxford, and Thackeray of the Reform. Auden composed the epilogue to the *Rake's Progress* (1951) in a series of slightly uncanonical limericks for each character.

> ANNE: Not every rake is rescued
> At the last by Love and Beauty;
> Not every man
> Is given an Anne
> To take the place of Duty.

Lawrence Durrell wrote an unforgettably sad and elegiac lyric about the island of Delos, which has circulated for many years by word of

mouth, but for one reason or another, like many modern limericks, it
has never been published. George Seferis wrote the most admirable
children's limericks in Greek: a whole book of them for a grandchild.
There is life in the old form yet, and it easily permits variations: the
slightest alteration of its rhythm can set it off on a new course. But Lear
was content with what he found. He perfected his comic drawing, he hit
on new ideas, that was all. He was not by nature a destroyer and re-
maker of forms.

He did hate loud or discordant noises, the bee's buzz, the unanswered
bell, and the gong, he derided the Lady of Welling who played on the
harp and caught several carp, he feared cows that might be bulls, he
wrote mostly about animals. Nearly every single one of this first book of
limericks is about an animal or a fish or a bird, and their scale is often
part of the joke, a gigantic robin or the huge, fat dog of Kamchatka
(where dogs were used by the Russians for transport and eaten, alas, by
the Chinese) and the large dancing raven. The whole list seems to
consist of horses, birds, pigs, dogs, fish, bees, rabbits and rats, cats,
donkeys, snakes, bears, flies, an owl and an ape. The people are harder
to categorize, but there is among them a fat-faced, comic figure who is
traditional, who was pelted to death with stones and put into stocks by
the beadle and sat placidly on a post in the sea. That is one of Lear's
limericks with a new rhyme-word in the last line.

> There was an Old Man of the Coast,
> Who placidly sat on a post;
> But when it was cold
> He relinquished his hold,
> And called for some hot buttered toast.

This character is the traditional Fool in any mummers' play, the
peasant, the anti-hero, almost the village natural who took refuge under
the protection of the squire's wife, the Russian natural fool who may be
a Holy Fool: this is, as we shall see later, a form of the Yonghy Bonghy
Bo, Edward Lear's image of himself, even at a time when he was not fat
(except maybe in the face) but 'tall, rather ungainly in figure, very
agreeable and genial in manner'. His limericks are full of eccentricity,
they are based on that, and on the loneliness underlying it. 'She twirled
round and round till she sunk underground.' 'He said if you choose to
suppose that my nose is too long, you are certainly wrong.' 'She said I
don't care, all the birds in the air are welcome to sit on my bonnet.'
'When they said How d'ye do, he replied Who are you?' 'When they

said You'll grow fatter, he answered What matter?' Terrible things may occur to a person in a Lear limerick, they drown or they are stoned or cut up, or a sarpint runs into their boot. Very few are perfectly, beatifically happy. One who is so is the Irish peasant who appears to be another form of the Fool. He has the sweetest smile.

> There was an Old Man of Kilkenny
> Who never had more than a penny;
> He spent all that money
> In onions and honey,
> That wayward Old Man of Kilkenny.

He is booted and spurred with a pigtail tied in a bow, and dressed in a most old-fashioned, eighteenth-century style with a peculiar high collar. Probably he is a caricature of somebody real Edward remembered, and no doubt the transactions in the limerick are a parody of some remembered conversation in which the habit of the Irish of spending their negligible money on honey and onions was being deplored. The visit there in 1835 made Arthur Stanley more tolerant for ever, and Edward Lear's main wish in all the limericks seems to be to escape from the awful conventions of the places and people where he found himself or imagined himself. His hero apparently is the Old Person of Basing, who is like him also in a distinct lack of skill in equitation. All the same:

> There was an Old Person of Basing
> Whose presence of mind was amazing;
> He purchased a steed,
> Which he rode at full speed,
> And escaped from the people of Basing.

The loneliness, the need to escape, the fear of awful fates from insects or dogs or from the whole population rising up to smash you, combine to say something worrying about Edward. We know from his earliest Sussex days that he was well known for never being able to do things in the same way as other people, in fact for his inbred eccentricity, and we know that he was conscious of that. Sweet sister Ann calmly accepted whatever he did or was. She was more like the Young Lady of Portugal whose ideas were excessively nautical: she climbed up a tree to examine the sea, but declared she would never leave Portugal. She did go to France admittedly, to help the Protestant Mission in Normandy: that was her most exotic holiday. Most of her life she just sat at home in London, treasuring Edward's regular letters, which by now had begun to flow once a fortnight, and passing them on to her sister. Whenever he wanted to marry, it was usually to someone much like Ann.

She is a comforting presence somewhere behind the gleeful and alarming fantasies of these little poems. She gleefully wards off a formidable bull with a small seaside spade, or a number of happy sisters carry off the pieces of John Bull's torn-up blue spotted waistcoat. Even when she sinks into the ground from dancing she does so with a satisfied expression. The Young Lady of Tyre may not attract us, but she enraptures the deep, and the one who plays tunes with her chin on the harp-strings is gleeful rather than malicious. When they bake the Old Man of Berlin whose form was uncommonly thin they do so with a determined, cheerful look, and the classical goddess who carries off trophies of dead flies to Troy is a dignified beauty; the point must be that she is one of the Ionians with billowing skirts mentioned by Homer (*helkechitones*) and much discussed in the nineteenth century. Tennyson as a boy imagined them at Maplethorpe and thought their dresses billowed on the windy battlements of the sand dunes. The cousins who caught toads in Rhodes enjoyed themselves, and the Majorcan aunt walked seventeen miles and leaped fifteen stiles with good humour; the Lady of Tartary fussed sweetly over her husband, even the Young Lady of Clare died happy enough, when she found she was tired she abruptly expired. Among Lear's women only the Old Lady of Parma is disagreeable, and the Young Person of Smyrna's grandfather is a bit fierce, but one feels she will get over her bad mood. There was trade between Liverpool and Smyrna then, though I doubt if Lear had seen these imaginary Turkish ladies.

The places of the limericks are mostly exotic. There is no Norwich, no Bicester, but Buda and Tyre and Kamchatka delight him. English places are well known or northern – Dover and Cromer or the Wrekin and Hurst and Mold – but Tring is unexplained, and Weedon, which is in Northamptonshire, is queerer still. The railway must have passed through it, and the picture of a train, which must surely be about 1835 with so tall a chimney and such grim carriages, confirms the early date of these illustrations. From Liverpool to Manchester was the earliest of routes and dates from 1830. As he grew older, Lear became an experienced railway traveller, more so even than Alfred Tennyson, because he was constantly dashing from one country house to another and from one friend or client to another. He came to dislike travelling in the badly sprung or unsprung dogcarts and similar vehicles he was offered on back-breaking country roads; he preferred a walk, which he performed uncomplainingly for many miles. He took a particular dislike to leaving the train at Cirencester (now it would be Kemble), and to the carriage journey that followed along the Roman road to Rendcombe. He went there a number of times because it was built for Sir Francis Goldsmid, whose family were his clients. The place now has the look of some enormous spa hotel, eight by ten bays, three storeys and a preposterous great tower, designed by Hardwick. Its terraces sweep down in formal gardens to a deep wooded valley: today it has become a school, and you can hear the traffic between Cirencester and Cheltenham. It was not yet built in the 1830s. But then in those days Ryde, where the woman bought her fashionable clogs, was a very small place indeed, and so was Chertsey. As for Poole, one of my uncles flew the Turkish flag there, in front of his house by the waterside, but not until the 1880s; in the 1830s his parents were still in Istanbul. One would be pleased to live in a place with a limerick by Lear about it.

People sometimes wonder why there are no limericks in other European languages, and no nonsense verse. The answer is that there are limericks in French:

> Il y avait un jeune homme de Dijon,
> qui disait je m'en fous de religion,
> je proteste par ma foi je déteste tous les trois,
> et le Père, et le Fils, et le pigeon.

There is plenty of nonsense verse traditional among children in German, some of it by excellent poets who are to be found (though not their nonsense verse) in anthologies. There is a tradition of it in Russian which needs to be explored. In most countries children's verse has simply not been collected; it may never have been written down. I doubt if Lear would have started to print his had printing itself not been a particular interest of his. Now the first editions are so rare as to be unfindable, because as anyone knows who remembers an early Lear in the nursery, they fall apart from overuse, they get torn to pieces, they get loved to death. One does hear welcome news of German nursery rhymes in the footnotes to the Opies' *Dictionary*, but one is lucky if anything like that survives into a nursery. It appears from a number of extraordinary analogies between English and German rhymes that traditional children's nonsense is medieval or earlier. There are traces of it in Latin and in Greek.

It is important to establish that point because a rich, undefinable waterfall of orally transmitted poetry and nonsense certainly reached

Edward Lear in his infancy, and it crops up in his life in many forms. Can one say that his public contribution to nonsense begins with the Stanley and Hornby children at Knowsley? One cannot, because the verse he circulated privately is comic, he wrote comic verses into his journal simply as they came into his head. And it is impossible to date the exact point where these things began: his alphabets for instance. The great lyrics are late, but by 1841 he was writing parody history, and by 1842 his comic drawings for 'Sing a song of sixpence'. Either may have begun at Knowsley or in Sussex, or who knows where? In his own nursery, possibly. The history is that of Caius Marius, it is a wonderful manuscript[12] made for the family of Edward Penrhyn at East Sheen. Marius marries Julia Caesar, wins some wars and quarrels with Mrs Sulla. He hides among the bull-frogs in some rushes: they are horned bull-headed frogs or frog-legged bulls. He escapes to Carthage where he broods among ruins, returns to cut off his enemies' heads with a very rude gesture, drinks too much and expires. Was it written for a schoolboy? Or was it the memorial, the written version, of some old light-hearted joke?

Lear's visual humour is prolific. It extends to nearly every subject that seriously interested him: to the exploration of landscape, to birds and all zoology, to botany, gastronomy and of course to stories. In 1838 Gould went to Australia to gather material for the *Birds of Australia*. Edward Lear drew a page of comic drawings, probably then but no one knows for whom, labelled *Portraites of the inditchenous beestes of New Olland*. It looks to me like a parody of a seventeenth-century travel book, doubtless imaginary. The first kangaroos seem perfectly serious, but after that the page riots. Ye common nature Catte is particularly attractive, and so are the duck-billed platypus and the possum up his gum tree. The queerest is Ye peculiar or prickly porkyoupine. At the same time or earlier he drew Ye Hippopotamous or Gigantic Rabbitte and a charming frieze of animals going into the Ark, for the Coombe children, with the elephant inscribed 'efelant'.[13] The sheet of New Holland creatures is now in the Pierpont Morgan Library, and the Coombe children's animals are in private hands. The Coombe drawings were very likely done for little Fanny to whom Edward started writing when she was six months old. For jokes like these she must have been three or four or so, which would date the drawings to 1835 or 1836. The big rabbit is inscribed with a long joke about it belonging to George Coombe, and eating lettuce and living in a box, and 'Alle day longe he moveth his nose up and down, but in other respects he is a harmless beaste'. It is clear enough that Edward relished all these jokes and lavished time on them.

It is curious that none of the alphabets he made for a number of children which were shown in the Academy can be dated before 1860. The 1958 Arts Council exhibition catalogue, which is introduced by Brian Reade, speaks of alphabets done 'at various times since the eighteen-forties';[14] one of them, which is now at Harvard, was done for the Tattons around 1849. Lear did not publish any until 1871; the Tatton alphabet was issued by Warne, apparently in the 1890s and then in 1926, when it belonged to J. D. Hughes, a famous Manchester bookseller. This manuscript is still the earliest Lear alphabet known. Mr Hughes sold it to W. B. Osgood Field, a young collector of Lear manuscripts under the influence of Philip Hofer at Harvard, where both their collections came to rest.

Thomas Tatton was already an old friend of Lear's in 1837; he was a cousin of the Penrhyns of East Sheen, so his son T. E. Tatton would be an obvious recipient of an early alphabet. T. E. Tatton of Wythenshawe was born in 1846; his father, T. W. Tatton, did not die until 1885. The boy with the alphabet had a normal upper-class career as his father did: Eton, Christ Church, the Cheshire Yeomanry, and an appointment as JP. It is perhaps worth tracing the history of the little book in detail, since if one were to judge the dates of all Lear's alphabets by the criterion of style, this one would be twenty years or more later. The fact of its being so undoubtedly early, and inscribed 'Drawn and Written for T. E. Tatton by Edward Lear', means that the line of development I am about to suggest is not a reliable criterion of date.

Drawings to illustrate alphabets so that children learn the names of the letters and the spelling of the pictures are certainly older than the nineteenth century and may be found on samplers 200 years earlier. The *Golden Primer* (1819) in the Opie collection at the Bodleian Library is a closer example because of its careful finish. It cost threepence plain and sixpence coloured. It is not perfectly skilful in its colours, which are often too dark, but the goat is splendid and wild and Welsh-looking, and the fox has fine whiskers. What they all lack is the text that Lear would supply, and this varied. The style of his rhymes seems to me a genuine nursery style and not an invention, but just as the dates of his rhymed alphabets are hard to pin down, the text, like the pictures for each letter, may vary a lot or a little: writing them must surely have been a frequent task. In 1860 he performed it for the Prescotts.

A was an ant
Who seldom stood still
And who made a nice house
In the side of a hill
a!
Nice little Ant!

C was a cat
Who ran after a rat
But his courage did fail
When she seized on his tail.
c!
Crafty Old Cat!

These really are children's rhymes with the simplest verses and the simplest drawings. The Goat is a farmyard animal, the Light burned all night, the Pig's tail was too curly (indeed rococo) and that made him surly. V for Villa sounds like Peppering or Arundel: it stood on a hill by the side of a river and close to a mill. V! Nice little Villa! X looks like a member of the House of Lords in Turkish slippers and a furious temper, but he is Xerxes, and Z is a mineral specimen of Zinc. All this is close to other people's books, it is so cool and tame it is all but insipid. One might have advised Lear not to publish it, but his point is deliberate variety, and the next is more elaborate.

F was once a little fish
Fishy
Wishy
Squishy
Fishy
In a Dishy
Little Fish!

H was once a little hen,
Henny
Chenny
Tenny
Henny
Eggsy-any
Little Hen?

The Owl and the crested Lark are charming but the reader may feel that the rhymes cloy. The Jam is Jammy, Mammy, Clammy, Sweety-Swammy, and the Rose is Rosy Posy Nose Rosy Blowsy-growsy Little

Rose. But Q is a Quail, U is a tea-Urn, and X is Xerxes as usual: Xerxy Perxy Turxy Xerxy Linxy Lurxy . . . and Z is still Zinc.

It was the words that improved more than the images, because in these alphabets Lear was operating within a convention, as he was up to a point in his birds and animals: only in the alphabets it was a nursery convention and he felt the warmest affection for it. In the next alphabet the big improvement is Xerxes, whose image is a fifteenth-century sultan with a huge striped turban, a cross expression, sword in one hand, spear in the other. He is almost heraldic, and indeed the animals have just the same stiffness, like Noah's Ark figures: Ape, Bat, Camel, Dove, Eagle, Fan (made of beautiful stuff and when it was used it went Puffy-puff-puff), a perfectly red Gooseberry, Heron, Kingfisher, Yak and (at last) Zebra.

> H was a heron
> Who stood in a stream
> The length of his neck
> And his legs was extreme
> >   h!
> Long-legged Heron!
>
> Y was a yak
> From the land of Thibet,
> Except his white tail
> He was all black as jet
> >   y!
> Look at the Yak!

All these alphabets are to be found in Holbrook Jackson's *Complete Nonsense of Edward Lear*; they were published by their author in 1871 and 1872. Lear's next attempt was a set of fully drawn cartoons without the childish stiffness he had apparently been imitating: the words are jokes in prose: the Comfortable Confidential Cow, who sate in her Red Morocco Arm Chair and toasted her own Bread at the parlour fire, the Fizzgiggious Fish on stilts (because he had no legs), the Enthusiastic Elephant rowing with a kitchen poker, the Goodnatured Grey Gull carrying the Old Owl and his Crimson Carpet-bag across the River, the Jay doing up her back hair with a Wreath of Roses, Three feathers, and a Gold Pin, a Lobster mending his own clothes, a charming Newt with a Christmas pudding for his grand-daughter, a Parrot reading the paper through glasses and eating parsnip pie, a quail smoking a pipe on the handle of a Tin Tea-kettle, a Tortoise (as at Bassae) playing a drum, a

Vulture writing Verses to a Veal-cutlet in a Volume bound in Vellum, Xerxes drinking XX, the moon-faced Yonghy-Bonghy-Bo, and the *chef d'œuvre*, five monkeys riding a Zebra. All the animals except the zebra are anthropomorphized, like Beatrix Potter's. This masterpiece was done in 1870 for a child met by chance in a hotel, and the Yonghy-Bonghy-Bo was a name for chestnut husks when they walked together in the woods. The lyric was not written until December 1871, so it is interesting to see the creature's image so early: it reappears on the 1871 manuscript of the lyric[15] which is at Harvard.

The last alphabets to be published before Lear's death are earlier than this fine and grown-up example, made for a child of five or six, one would assume. But the later ones slide back into the children's convention, as I am sure Edward Lear could do at any time, as if he had never left it. The A of the first of these is extraordinary because A was an Area Arch, where washerwomen sat; they made a lot of lovely starch to starch Papa's cravat. The vignette is fascinating, like an illustration to Dickens or Mayhew. Every letter contains a reference to Papa, from B was a bottle blue Which was not very small; Papa he filled it full of beer, and then he drank it all, to Papa's new Hat, a regency-looking topper lined with red inside. R was a Railway Rug Extremely large and warm; Papa he wrapped it round his head in a most dreadful storm. S was Papa's new thumping Stick, T was a tumbler of Punch which Papa for some reason drank in the middle of a wood.

Last of all in Jackson's collection comes an alphabet in rhymes without illustrations, a new but much less memorable formula: it is odd to what a degree the simplest drawing of an egg or a fish and the childish rhymes enliven one another. A has fallen over and hurt his Arm, and the rest of the couplets attempt unlikely remedies: V said I'll stand upon a chair, and play the Violin, W proposes Whisky-Whizzgigs, and X some XX ale, R some Rats, T a Turnip, G Green Gooseberry fool, and so on until we come to the alarming conclusion.

> Y said, Some Yeast mixed up with salt would make a perfect plaster!
> Z said, Here is a box of Zinc! Get in, my little master!
> We'll shut you up! We'll nail you down! We will, my little master!
> We think we've all heard quite enough of this your sad disaster.

But perhaps one of the best is the last to be published: T. E. Tatton's little manuscript book. Its form is what in the context of all Lear's alphabets one may call classical, and the drawings are often very well observed.

A was an Ass
Who fed upon grass
And sometimes on Hay,
Which caused him to bray,
A!
What a good Ass.

The drawing of a Bee is some two inches long but very convincing. C is some Coal, which is proper for Lancashire, E one of Lear's fiercest and most magnificent Eagles, dashed off in pen, who sate on a rock and stole lambs from the flock. G, rather surprisingly, since the geography seems to be dictated by rhymes, is a Gull who flew over from Hull, but crossing to Jersey was drowned in the Mersey: it does at least demonstrate that Lear's use of local names was deliberate. J for Jug held barley water 'for my son and my daughter'. The Lark is Shelleyan and in full voice, and the Mill looks like a Sussex mill, but the Needle is more surprising: it was used by a beadle to sew on a ruffle torn off in a scuffle, needful old Needle. The Owl is a simplified, attractive creature with eyes like suns. The Punch is a bowl of cold punch in a glass pot, which nobody tasted, observed at Knowsley no doubt. The Quail and the Thrush (who whistled a song that was rather too long) are lyrical and beautiful drawings. Of all these little pen sketches, the Thrush is my favourite. U is an Ukase which the Czar keeps in a book-case, and X for Xerxes looks like a Turkish infantryman with a scimitar like a rainbow, and sure enough, he is Old Xerxes, who the first of all Turks is. It is this nice rhyme and not the coincidence of territory that so often makes Lear's Xerxes a Turk. Edward Lear saw Turkish soldiers for the first time in 1848 when he went to Istanbul at a time when T. E. Tatton was two years old: he was not back in England until July 1849. As for Z, it was a plate made of Zinc, which sounds unlikely; the mineral sample that supplanted it was an increase in realism, I suppose. Was a zinc plate used in printing?

In contrast to that, one of the latest of all his alphabets was done day by day in Italy for a sick child called Charles Pirouet, with a letter on a card produced every morning and placed on his breakfast table. Each card began with four different ways of doing the letter, then came the illustration, and a verse scribbled underneath. C was a brilliant cartoon of Lear's cat, old Foss, which he was always drawing in his correspondence at that time. There are touches of humour in the verses as well as the drawings, but charm predominates, as for children it should.

I was a little old Inn
By the side of a dusty road,
But very few travellers ever came
To that not very nice abode.

It is oddly like Tennyson's limerick about Erith. The Pirouet alphabet is now in the Victoria and Albert Museum, and it was reproduced in 1953, indeed the C for Cat is now sold as a greetings card; it is oddly like the card of Foss you can buy at Harvard. I have the impression that I have not described all the alphabets I ever saw. I do not think I ever saw Gertrude Lushington's (c. 1860) mounted in a rag-book, though it is at Harvard, but I do recollect one published by Rota in 1968 which I have lost or given away.

In all these various productions for children I have not yet mentioned music. It was music that led Lear to parody the idiotic drawing-room after-dinner songs which afflicted that age, and were driven out only by the wireless and the gramophone. My mother remembered them performed in the 1900s, and parodied them for us. It was the music that permitted the exaggerated sentiments of the songs, some of them by Moore and later by Tennyson. Lear used to sing them dead seriously, and constantly recalled them if the words had touched him, but he also parodied them, sometimes switching from one mode to the other in mid-performance. Lear's voice in singing had a queer high-pitched chanting tone as Belloc's had, but when he composed songs he could not write them down because he could not read music, so many are lost. Luckily some of his comic lyrics survive. It was only towards the end of his life that he wrote those and they were not really meant for children. All the same, he produced a gleeful series of caricature illustrations to the ballad 'Auld Robin Gray' in about 1836, when he seems to have been visiting the home of its author, Lady Anne Lindsay, at Haigh Hall, Wigan, which is within calling distance of Knowsley. She wrote it about 1770, but Edward was mercilessly comic: perhaps the Lindsays egged him on, because they have treasured his manuscript ever since. He drives her away in a two-wheeled chaise drawn by a nondescript horse in spectacles; she simpers with a gin bottle, he grasps a glass, they have a beer barrel too and bottles of whisky, rum and brandy dangling behind. 'I'll try with all my heart a gude wife to be, for old Robin Gray is very kind to me.' He is a bearded man with spectacles and loud plus-fours, much like Edward Lear in thirty years' time, but not at all like Edward then.[16] His sense of the musical absurd was alive, even if it had not yet burst out to complete self-expression.

CHAPTER FIVE

ITALY

EDWARD became happy from the time he decided to be a landscape painter, not only in the Lakes, as one can see from his sketches, which are still visionary water-colours of the pale lilac mountains or swift and vivid details snatched in pencil, but in what he remembers from that time. Apart from childhood memories, 'unsought morbid feelings of past years', that flooded his mind at the sight of the Greek landscape in 1849, were 'the heights above Plymouth in 1836–7 – the Godesburg 1837 – Civitella 1839 and Nemi'. He relegates the thrill of 'the Mill at Arundel, or Peppering' to early boyhood, to 1824 or 1825: perhaps the second since the Drewitts built their house at Peppering in 1824, when he was twelve. The heights above Plymouth are the small hill to the west of the city, which overlook the harbour, though they are scarcely higher than Plymouth Hoe. In June and July 1837 he must have climbed plenty of breezy hilltops on a tour of Devon and Cornwall, which was his goodbye inspection of English landscape. He stayed at Bovisand with Captain Hornby, who became Admiral Sir Phipps Hornby; it lies close to Mount Edgcumbe, handy for the fleet, and it was there that he made *The Book of Bovisand from Edward Lear to Capn and Mrs Hornby and their Family*. The collection contained a series of landscapes, figure studies and so on: in fact it was an advanced version of the albums he had made as a boy. A fine view of Plymouth Sound seen through an arch at Mount Edgcumbe (3 July 1837), which the Arts Council showed in 1958, [1] is with the rest of the group in the Victoria and Albert Museum.

A little further west along the coast lies a village beyond Portwrinkle called Downderry, which could, I suppose, have brought back into Lear's mind, since he liked absurdity in place-names, the *nom de plume* of the merry old Derry down derry. The Hornbys and their faimily were his friends for life; this small group of drawings does not mark any great technical advance, but that was a time of great happiness.

He set out with Ann in late July (and wrote on 3 November as if they were making their experiments together), but he left her in Brussels. The subsequent journey had scarcely altered since the pioneer English travellers of the eighteenth century; the path to Rome was well trodden enough, and from the beginning Lear not only followed a procession of the English upper classes, but he mostly mixed with them. That meant he was slow to pick up foreign languages, though he worked at several and in the end achieved all his targets. He largely ignored French and Italian society, because he had no point of entry there, no equivalent of Knowsley. Rome, which was his destination, was an extremely backward but more extremely glamorous city. Its Jacobite connection was not forgotten during the Regency. Keats was buried there, its baroque architecture was sophisticated and unsurpassed in all Europe. It was a goal of artists and of young men who aspired to be civilized, although Edward Lear did not quite know what to do when he got there. Victoria was a very young Queen and newly crowned: the neoclassic age was not over, but the ruins of Rome were still a romantic muddle, water-buffalo grazed in malarial marshes around Paestum, and Greece was far too wild and perhaps too expensive for Edward at twenty-five. Scientific archae-ology was scarcely in its infancy; it may be dated from the political crisis of 1848, when Mommsen was deprived of his Chair at Berlin, and set to work in Switzerland and in the Kingdom of Naples and the Two Sicilies, collecting and verifying Roman inscriptions. But archaeology came too late for Edward: it never touched his heart, and anyway he was a landscape painter, devoted to things as they are, to the flying moment. He adored the Alps and the great lakes.

At first we must trace his progress in sketches. His work at the time resembled that of Prout, who had been a predecessor in the field of topographic lithography; other contemporary artists cast some flickering light on it, but Edward's sense of composition was quite classical, his usual viewpoint of a worm's-eye view with a foreground of botanic minutiae could have been learnt from the early-seventeenth-century Dutch, though no doubt it was instinctive, but his passion for Claude and after him Turner, although it does not tell us anything immediately valuable about Lear's early work, persisted and in the long run led to fruitful developments in his style which would otherwise be unexplained. For example, Lear enormously admired the American sublime landscape painter Frederic Church's *Heart of the Andes* (1859), an eagle soaring among peaks. That has little enough to do with Claude and more with the idea of exact records of topography, and Lear's own *Windermere* of 1836, but Turner had been working in Lear's mind for a lifetime, and he liked that picture, painted when Church was thirty-three, because of its physical wildness; he compared it with 'Arctic scenes, South American magnificences',[2] and if he cooled about Claude, whom Turner recommended, it was a slow process of cooling. It is probable that as a young man he idolized Gaspard Poussin and Salvator Rosa's wonderfully romantic trees, but from that position he moved painlessly on. He was an autodidact in painting as in everything, and almost too conscientious, but from quite an early stage, in bursts at first but steadily later, he was also utterly original and free. It was topographical exactness that turned him away from Claude: 'Of course there are many who think that trees should never be painted green (because they *are* so), and that all Landscapes should be filled up with trees like Claudes (because they *ain't* so)'.[3] It was truth that set him against Poussin and Salvator Rosa. His art was topographic, and he relied on finding any exciting or exotic touches it may have in the external world: hence his journeys.

The first record of his passage south is his *Castle of Elz, Mosel* (18 August 1837), a dramatic study of an impressive hilltop Schloss which unluckily for us is a perfect model of the Scottish Baronial style of architecture, which of course was still to come.[4] There is a sketch dated a few days later of a half-timbered street in Frankfurt called *The Jews' Quarter*. The street is grim and dark, and the people look extemely conventional yet mysterious also, but that is because most of their faces are hidden, because Edward could not trust himself to draw faces. The sketch is at Harvard, but the finished drawing (1838) in black chalk heightened with white on blue paper, is in the Victoria and Albert Museum. It is Proutesque, no doubt, and severely dramatic, but it is nothing to the fizzing melodrama of what was to come in Italy, nothing to the Amalfi in grey and brown washes and white body-colour, where the light is like a lightning flash, based on a sketch of July 1838,[5] or the *Paliano* of the same year, with its wreathing ten-foot roots of a chestnut tree and its Claudean calm distance.

He wrote from Milan, and then from Florence. Meanwhile, Ann had written to him from Brussels where she stayed until May 1838. It appears to have been her first Continental expedition as well as his. 'I am so glad to find you are comfortable and well,' he replied. 'Your accounts of Bruxelles and its people very much amuse me, and though by your praises of the Beer there, I fear you have taken to drinking, I rejoice to hear you like the place so much.' He had five English pupils in Florence and intended to stay on for a month. His old friend Sir William Knighton, who used to draw beside him at Sass's art school with Egg and Frith, the Russells and the Tattons were all in Florence in various hotels near his lodgings, which, alas, he does not name. 'Just after I last wrote I left Milan with only knapsack and sketchbook and off I set.' He met Knighton and his family by chance at Como, 'and a famous holiday we had on the beautiful lake'. Sir William was brought up as a painter under Sir David Wilkie but he is said to have lacked talent. He seems to have married money, what Lear called 'a fooly Scotchwoman' who put an end to his bohemian days. He was all the more pleased to see Edward, and used him as a drawing tutor for the children.

Edward left by steamer on 7 October, 'and rushed into the uttermost parts of the lake, fifty miles off – at Domaso . . . nothing can give you an idea of the horror one first feels at Italian village inns . . .' He hated the huge cold rooms, the stone floors, and the open windows: but these were early days, and he was going to get used to far worse conditions than those. As he remarks, 'You soon get used to the bare-footed people who wait on you.' What he came for was the scenery.

> *It was quite beyond anything I have seen*; the dark blue lake reflects the white houses of Domaso – and over them enormous Alps, Jiggy-Jaggy – shut out the Italians from Switzerland. Being resolved to see all the district, I took a boat quite to the top of the Lake where it is awfully grand – and then walked to Chiavenna beyond which Switzerland begins. Chiavenna is just by the Pass of Splugen, and is awfully grand: some time ago (1680) part of the mountain under which it stands fell down plump and killed 500 persons – a whole village. After getting some sketches of it, I was glad to proceed Southward again.

He walked down the east side of the lake to Colico.

> I tried to stop at Novate but could not, as all they had to eat was mutton and goat's flesh, half putrid, garlic – and dreadfully sour wine, and although Colico was not over comfortable, it was a good deal better. At Bellano there was a better inn and I stayed three days. All this part of the Lake is magnificent – it is as narrow as a wide river, so you can see the hundreds of spires and villages on the opposite side, while the Alps always form the background.

At Lecco Edward saw his first olive trees. 'I think they are very beautiful, more like a huge lavender bush, or a fine grey willow than anything else, and all over little shiny green olives.' The boats had red or blue or white sails, and at sunset the Alps were pink. He explored Cadenabbia, Dongo, Musso and Rezzonico, in a trance of enjoyment. He got to Lugano by water, past cliffs crowned with autumnal crimson and yellow. The quay revealed huge wine barrels drawn by milk-white oxen, rows of women with baskets of enormous logs, and numerous Capuchins, always a thrill to the English, even at Calais. 'Back I trotted to Como which had now become a sort of old friend', through woods of olive and chestnut ('you cannot fancy anything as wonderfully beautiful'), where he discovered a bright green mantis. The truth is that here on the edge of the Swiss Alps, long before he got to Rome, Edward Lear had discovered his Grail and his deep vocation.

He took a cab with friends from Milan to Florence for about £5 each, going at walking pace. He mostly walked, peering through the vines and poplars for Alpine glimpses; he noticed the airs of past grandeur in Italian towns and the tall bell-towers in the market-places. They were behind two other carriages, one with a zoologist and his family bound for Naples. There had been a cholera scare, but now the roads were free again. Five days brought them to Modena, which was the first of innumerable independent duchies requiring passports, and the same evening to Bologna and the Papal States, 'as full of beggars as Russell Square used to be'. There they overtook the Knightons who had started two days earlier, and the following morning they all got up together at four for the crossing of the Apennines. The carriages had to be pulled by oxen. There were eight coaches in the convoy, with all their passengers walking; all thirty-two of them were English. At the top they were in Tuscany, where they spent the night at 'a vile little inn at Pietramala, for the real inn was of course crammed by the sudden deluge of arrivals'. November 1st was the last day of the week's journey. Edward walked twenty miles while the *vetturino* crawled, and there at his feet lay Florence, in a landscape he thought just like a Claude.

The trees and villages were a sudden change, and the city was far more magnificent than he had expected. No one in England, to be fair, knew very much about Renaissance art or architecture. The Piazza Granduca overwhelmed him: that was the Piazza of the Signoria, where the statues thrilled him. He stuck close to Knighton, 'who knows Arts so well', and to Lady Knighton, his mother. He liked elderly ladies, if they were of some sophistication and kindness, as we shall see. 'It is all a hurly-burly of beauty and wonder. The Grand Duke rides about everywhere, and the whole place is like an English watering-place, with so many strangers.' He was thrilled by being able to buy hot roasted chestnuts for forty a halfpenny, but the cold soon set in. On Sunday there were 300 tourists and their servants at the English church, so it is not surprising that Lear taught every evening and thought of staying for six weeks on the pretext of letting the cholera clear. Mrs Tatton's family, the Russells and the Knightons were all nearby and various other Penrhyn cousins were coming next week. It all sounds like a shooting party in Lancashire; Robert Hornby had just written to him as well. The Florentines encouraged everyone to linger, with rumours of cholera and highwaymen further south. But December found Edward at Rome: Florence can be bitterly cold and foggy, and once that endless late autumn comes to an end, it will snow. All the same, he regretted the medieval picturesque, and the bed of 'lilac coloured mountains', the Zebra Cathedral and the towers and spires. One can understand his imagining the mountains were lilac, like the ones he painted in the Lakes, but the queer thing about all this is that he never mentions the Florentine Duomo. He reserved his wonder for the dome of St Peter's.

Edward arrived in Rome in another cab with Dennew, an artist who has sunk without trace, and Theed, a sculptor who not only made the Africa figure on the Albert Memorial but tried to float in England the idea of coloured statues. He carved the Duchess of Kent attired in her full grandeur for afternoon tea at what her daughter Victoria intended as a tea pavilion at Frogmore, containing her mother's grave. When the time came, Tennyson wrote the Queen's mother's epitaph.

Theed brought Lear another precious letter from Lancashire. He and Dennew were old Romans who had done the journey a dozen times. By the short route via Siena, they took five days all the same, travelling from three or four in the morning until five at night, with the travellers walking much of the way. Mount Radicofani was the boundary of the Papal States. Beyond it you saw 'lines and lines of blue mountains stretching into the sky, and plains that look as if they extended to Jerusalem', which bring you at last to 'the waste, dreary desert of the Roman Campagna'. Until Mussolini drained the Pontine marshes and the modern world caught up with the papacy, connoisseurs of Rome were always great connoisseurs of the Campagna, because it was ageless and seeded with ruins. A little later Edward would be drawn into it and become addicted, but in 1837 it was certainly flat, and a natural waste infested with disease that had swallowed plenty of Roman ruins. The Popes were not progressive monarchs in the nineteenth century. 'The effect is very wild and melancholy, for you see no towns, only the Dome

Ann Lear.

Edward Lear by his friend
W. H. Marstrand, 1840.

Caricatures of visitors made while
sketching parrots at the Zoo.

Lear's snowy owl (lithograph).

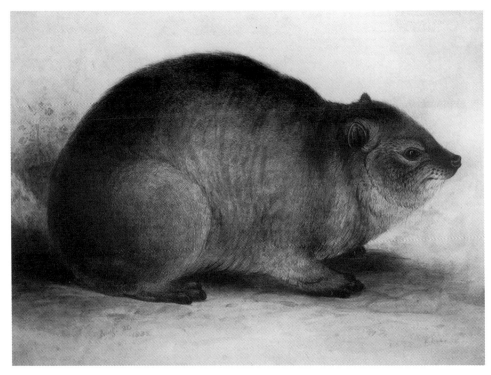

Lear's finished drawing of the rock hyrax.

Lear's civet, 1846 (lithograph).

Florence, 1837 (pencil).

Chichester Fortescue,
Lord Carlingford.

Dean Stanley.

Crummock Water,
Cumberland
(an early drawing).

The Letter C,
one of a long series
of caricatures of Foss,
Lear's last cat.

C was a lovely Pussy Cat; its eyes were large & pale;
And on its back it had some stripes,
and several on his tail.

There was an old man with a beard,
Who said "It is just as I feared!
Two Owls and a Wren, four Larks and a Hen,
Have all built their nests in my beard!"

Self-portrait in
caricature with
bird drawings.

Sussex, 1834
(pencil sketch).

The Queen's sketch
made under Lear's
tuition when Osborne
was half built.

Subiaco, 1841 (pencil).

Opposite, top: The mountains look on Marathon, and Marathon looks on the sea. Marathon, 1848 (finished watercolour).

Opposite, centre: Akropolis of Athens, 1848, from Lykabettos (finished watercolour).

Opposite, bottom: Bassae, 1854–5 (oil painting) bought for Cambridge by subscription by seventy of Lear's friends.

Frances, Countess Waldegrave, 1850 (lithograph after Swinton).

William Holman Hunt, about 1860, painted by D. W. Wynfield.

Party at Lady Waldegrave's home, Strawberry Hill (from the *Graphic*).

Villa Tennyson, Lear's last house, San Remo.

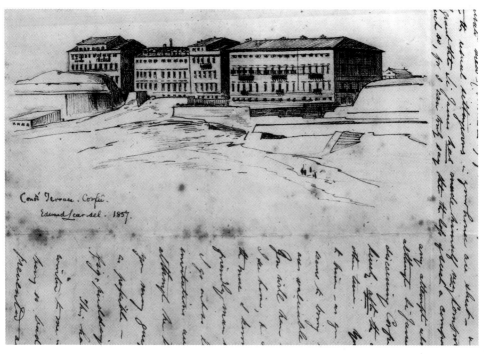

'Condé Terrace', where Lear lived at Corfu, with Napoleonic gun emplacements
in the foreground (from a letter to Lady Reid, drawing in pen by Lear).

of St Peter's, and you wonder at such a vast tract of unpeopled waste.' At least the peasants pleased him, with their high-crowned hats and their blue or red cloaks, just as he had seen them in pictures. The shepherds wore goatskins and the women red bodices, pea-green skirts and square white headdresses. He came back and drew one in the Campagna as soon as he could, and the distant view of St Peter's as well, from Arco Oscuro and the Pincian Hill.[6] Better still, the Campagna turned out to contain large and magnificently horned and shaggy goats.

In Rome with Theed's help, he settled in Via del Babuino (Baboon Street), near the Spanish Steps and the English church, the Academy, the restaurants and coffee-houses, 'all the English and all the artists'. Baboon Street leads from the Piazza del Popolo and the gate in the walls of Rome straight to the Piazza di Spagna, and it had been a foreign quarter for hundreds of years. Behind it is the artier alley of the Via Margutta, but Baboon Street has fine seventeenth- and eighteenth-century houses, many of them now antique shops. The Pincian Gardens are a stone's throw away. The Anglican church is now, alas, a curiosity, since it was rebuilt by G. E. Street, but the Greek café, Caffè del Greco, is one of many reminders that this was a Greek Catholic refugee quarter in the 1500s; the café is where Goethe and in the twenties Thorwaldsen had stayed. The Baboon of the street-name is the popular term for a Greek Silenus who belonged to a fountain beside St Athanasius; he was broken up long before: Lear never saw him, still less his modern replacement. The whole quarter is about as far as it could be within the walls of Rome from the ancient centre: indeed, the Popolo of the Piazza indicates a separate parish community that formed around a church built on some imperial tombs in the eleventh century to suppress their wicked ghosts. All the same, for Papal Rome, and for St Peter's across the Tiber, it was not at all badly placed.

Here Edward was happy enough to remain for years, starting with two rooms on the second floor for a couple of pounds a month; they were better than the ones he used to share with Ann at 28 Southampton Row. He would go to the same café as the other artists at eight in the morning and meet them again in the evening in the Pincian Gardens; at five they all dined together in a *trattoria*, then Edward went off with Sir William Knighton for two hours at the Academy. By 14 December he already had two or three commissions for water-colours, and he was giving painting lessons to Mr Tatton. In 1881, when he was old, he looked back on those years with happy nostalgia: 'the charm of early artist life ... The calm and brightness of the view, and the lovely sweetness of the air, bring back infinite days and years of outdoor delight; and I am thankful for this blessing, though it can only last a few minutes.' He was inclined to think by then that the only purpose of a topographic painter was 'converting memories into tangible facts'. One is tempted to say that he was driven out of business by the camera and the picture postcard; that consideration is certainly relevant to his career, but the dates do not fit, and the crisis does not enter deeply into what, if anything, went wrong; the change is more than an episode in the history of public taste, because of its profound consequences, but Edward always had the keenest interest in what photography and every new form of printing might accomplish, and that experimental interest was in a sense his tragedy.

It was close to Christmas, the streets were full and the atmosphere was gay. Cardinals in sedan chairs with three footmen, priests in white, black, piebald, scarlet, cinnamon and purple, friars in masks, bishops and monsignori in purple or red stockings amazed him. And it was the season of the *Pifferari*, bagpipers in tall black hats with peacock feathers from the Kingdom of Naples, who traditionally passed through Rome every year with their migrating sheep and goats, and were still doing so in the 1930s. 'I have drawn two or three, and they are most picturesque.' There were cattle too, grey, sleek monsters with enormous horns, tied around with ribbons and bells, pulling their numerous carts; there were mules and columns of soldiers. More important still, Edward felt well. 'I sit and draw all day long in the sun, among the ruins, and often find a cloak too hot.' There were bits and pieces of ancient Rome everywhere, columns joined together with bricks to make walls, antique walls with modern roofs, a Roman amphitheatre built into the walls of a palace, a medieval castle built on an antique arch, and everywhere tombs and fallen columns. Before 1939 you could still see the tip of Soracte from the centre of Rome, glittering white in the winter: a mountain immortalized by Horace. Edward wandered right across the city from where the zoo is today to the Pantheon and the arches of Titus and Severus and the Coliseum and the wilderness of ancient baths: but already he was more intrigued by 'the long lines of aqueducts and tombs on the desolate and beautiful Campagna'. Considering this whole intoxicating mixture, the cloudless skies and the golden sunsets, it is surprising that his surviving sketches are so comparatively sober.

What of the other artists whom he saw in the cafés and the Pincian Gardens, though he hardly names them? Some of them we know because years later he meets an old friend from his first Roman days. One in particular fascinates me because his style and Lear's are so near and yet so far. At the end of October 1837, Samuel Palmer married Linnell's daughter and they took their honeymoon in Italy. By the end of the month they were in Milan, by early November in Florence, then in Rome. In June the following year, the Palmers got to Naples, and we know that Samuel and Edward met on their summer expeditions. The Palmers exhibited in Rome but almost no one came, and Samuel sold only one picture, to John Baring, the only client to whom he had been introduced. The Barings were to become Lear's friends and patrons later; it is clear that no pictures could be sold until one knew the client personally. One suspects this in the case of Lear, and Palmer confirms it. A letter to Linnell when he set off for Naples establishes that he was frustrated by knowing *none* of the English gentry. He left Rome in June 1839, spent autumn in Florence, and came home. Later on he did illustrate *Pictures from Italy* for Charles Dickens (1846), but that was his only commission. As for his Italian painting style, one could reasonably class him as a Pre-Raphaelite at Pompeii fifteen years early, except that he was better than they were. The Pompeian picture is reproduced in colour on the jacket of Clay's *Gell in Italy* (1976) and is in the Victoria and Albert Museum. Late in life, Palmer struggled for a long time with his illustrations of Milton, as Lear did with his equally dark illustrations of Tennyson. Their paths crossed physically only once, but they were both too dazed by Italy to notice one another; it is curious how much they had in common.

Lear had many more introductions: 'Calls and cards are already as tiresome as in London.' He took Christmas dinner with a Mr Hatfield, perhaps a friend of Theed, and dined every Sunday with Sir William Knighton. He communicated with Lord Derby about the zoologist Prince Musignano of Corsica, whom he failed to meet; the only purpose of seeing the Prince was for Lear to act as Derby's agent for rareties, and he found none. In Italy small birds were slaughtered in numbers for food; he found himself eating jay, and saw jackdaws for sale in food shops. At Milan he discovered a bird shop, with some Amazon parrots and canaries, but the only bird there that interested him was an owl in poor condition. Switzerland yielded no chamois and no marmots. Searches down holes in the Campagna revealed neither porcupine nor tortoise. All he could report was how frogs were skinned in Milan, how cats had their tails cut to keep them faithful, or at Chiavenna their ears pierced to hold ribbons, news of the gloomy Florentine Zoo and of the last few hundred camels at Leghorn and at Pisa. He might do better with botany, so he promised dried flowers from the Coliseum. He went on working at his art which he hoped might continue to improve, but even that was in a rut. Possibly the light floored him, as they say it did Palmer. He sometimes felt one of his old bird drawings was worth two of his new landscapes. Still, the views excited him. He liked the cyclamen at the Coliseum and the violets and wallflowers on the 'palace of Augustus', meaning the Palatine, I suppose, unless he means the emperor's tomb near the Tiber.

No doubt it would be long before he shook off his appealing sobriety: no doubt, as Palmer went home after Italy and painted Surrey in an Italian light, Lear's temptation would be to paint Italy in an English light. He sought out what appealed to him and all his life he often found it by working in the very early morning, in the few moments when the light in Italy is most English. But one can see him break out. At first it is into melodrama, at Amalfi and at a grey nameless ruin on a hilltop,[7] and in his splendidly eighteenth-century-looking Temple of the Sybil[8] at Tivoli, with its beetling cliff and its trees like stage scenery. The washes are the same in texture: black chalk heightened with white at Amalfi, ink, water-colour and Chinese white on the hilltop, both on blue paper, and pencil and Chinese white on buff paper at Tivoli. Plainly he was experimenting with what could be done with meagre resources, and what he used depended on what he had with him. But his painting of *Virgilian Narni* (1839) is a thrilling construction of yellows and ochres and darkness.[9] The sky may be English but the architecture on the hilltop is not. The tower seems to lean, straining in the wind, and the dark trees make pools of luxurious shade, as they would in a poem by Horace. *Val Montone* (1839) in the British Museum is a fine study in more purely English taste. In different pictures at this time he used water-colour and body-colour and wash, he experimented in colour without drawing, and from the journey to Naples in 1838 onwards, when he and his group had shared a hotel with the Palmers, he began to paint in oil. He treated it quite freely, as if it had been water-colour.

Water-colour painting began in England with the military school in the Tower of London, from which Thomas and Paul Sandby emerged at the time of the 1745 rebellion and were employed by Cumberland's expedition into Scotland. Paul recorded the fortifications of Scotland, that is, he drew the fine romantic ruined castles of the country. But the whole point of the art as it was then conceived was to dash down swiftly a truthful sketch that might be useful to a general officer. The emphasis on travelling, on castles and antiquities and landscape arose in the wake of that. Oil goes back to the Renaissance; it was taken more seriously by patrons for that reason, and regarded as something of a mystery. Edward had intended to learn at the Roman Academy, but in fact he learned mostly from his friends. Many of those were Dutch, and W. Marstrand, his inseparable friend for a year or two, has left a portrait of him: serious, quizzical and nearly thirty. Another friend was Thomas Uwins, the nephew of a famous figure in the world of painters in the last generation who became an official of the English Royal Academy. With young Uwins Edward went on down the coast beyond Naples. It is possible that Palmer taught him oils, or it could have been Uwins, since they were together when he tried them out, or it could have been an old friend to whom he was devoted, whose method he said he followed so that it separated him from the crowd of English painters – Penry Williams. But the works of Williams are as far as I can see not very good: at best his influence, since he had been in Italy since 1820, must have been on getting to know the country; Williams was a truthful documentary painter of the Picturesque. The overwhelming vote of that generation was to ignore ancient Rome except as scenery. Palmer painted Pompeii as if it were a flock of goats catching the light. He painted a 'modern Rome', but never the 'ancient Rome' that was meant to go with it.

In Naples Lear just missed knowing two interesting English residents of an earlier generation who were best friends. One of them, Sir William Gell, had died in February 1836 at the age of fifty-nine, and the other, Keppel Craven, who was two years younger, had moved out of the city to La Penta near Salerno, where he bought a convent in 1834. They had both been attached to the court of Queen Caroline of England, who at one stage of her unhappy marriage to the Regent took refuge in Italy like a Jacobite. Edward Lear had stared at the empty d'Este palace which once contained her, when he was at Lake Como. She died indeed in 1823 in the Thames-side house of Craven's stepfather, the Marquis of Brandenburg. The friendship of Gell and Craven was lifelong, their way of life was aristocratic, and their knowledge of Italy – Gell of its antiquities, Craven of the entire wild region of the Kingdom of Naples, and both of its upper class – was unparalleled. Now Gell rested in the Craven family tomb, which was in the form of an Ionic temple, but in 1821 Craven had published the southern, and in 1837 the northern provinces of Naples. Lear quoted that book voluminously and with deference, and it appears to have inspired him to do something like it, only illustrated with lithographs.

Gell of course did not influence him, yet some of that deplorable and feline old gentleman's knowledge of the terrain was passed on to him, and then through him, because a letter of Lear's now at Edinburgh advises another English traveller about Paestum. The information is banal: to get to Salerno 'a diligence used to go every afternoon at two from Naples'. But when he mentions Paestum he lights up.

> See Paestum from Salerno (these expeditions require *early rising*). If you could return by the longer road – cioe Eboli – the better, as it is more beautiful. There is also an Inn at Eboli (an old Benedictine convent) and you might possibly reach that straight from Naples – about 40 to 42 miles I think.

This was addressed from his new lodgings in the Via Felice (now vanished) in January 1840, but the beginning of the letter is lost; the other advice was about more northerly expeditions from Rome. It becomes clear enough, then, that Lear had been to Paestum and seen the temples there. This first expedition of his south of Rome sounds magically happy. Hazlitt dismissed English artists in Rome as loungers and loafers, and even bohemian Haydon thought them a dirty lot, but Edward did not like the urban version of Mediterranean life; he felt he had more in common with the elements, he always worked conscientiously and he enjoyed exercise. He did not feel tempted by the upperclass life either. He left for Naples in May with Thomas Uwins.

After four days of that amazingly noisy place, with its 'sheep, goats, monks, priests, processions, cars, mules, naked children and bare legged mariners', they moved on. They tried Pozzuoli but the fumes of Vesuvius affected Edward's breathing so badly that he spat blood.

> The volcano's smoking, groanings, bumpings, thumpings, vomitings, earthquakings and other eccentricities always annoyed me from morn to night. I was however most fortunate in witnessing one of the finest eruptions known for many years – a midnight scene I can never forget.

They sought out a cool, quiet place uphill and inland. They found Capo di Cava, a village with no noise but birdsong, where they could eat and drink abundant and delicious food and wine for 2s. 8d. a day. It was from this lyrical spot, through woods full of cuckoos and nightingales in full season, that they visited Pompeii and Paestum. But at the end of August they were in Rome again. Although his lodgings in Via Babuino were cheap because the landlady was an old acquaintance of Theed, now she wanted to double his rent; so he moved on to the Via Felice, which I

do not know, somewhere further from the Piazza di Spagna but still
close to the Pincian Gardens. Evelyn Waugh talks about the Cardinals
taking their exercise there, sidesaddle on mules, but Edward Lear never
noticed them, and if Waugh's vignette came from the Carnarvons, then
it was a little later.

Lear exploded with pleasure over Tivoli. The Sibyl's temple stood in
an inn yard on a precipice, and the ruins of the villa of Maecenas were as
unreal to him as the palace of Aladdin: it was 'a pile of beautiful arches,
and over these are numerous cascades. In this Paradise of a valley you
may wander for days, and every hour see a new view ... The only
objection is the incessant uproar of waterfalls.' Never had he seen such
grandeur of enormous cypresses as he saw at Cardinal d'Este's palace.
He fills the margins of his letter with tiny squared pictures. They are
wonderfully classic, precisely chosen views, and some of them are
reminiscent of his first book of drawings of Rome. The illumination of
St Peter's excited him too. Four hundred men were slung on ropes all
over the dome and the facade. They planted small paper lamps until the
whole church seemed transparent, it seemed to be leaking light through
thousands of pin-pricks. At about nine in the evening, hundreds of
torches and oil lamps suddenly blazed up. That was done with fuses; the
same system was still in use in the chapel at my school, forty or fifty
years ago, to make all the candles spring alight with one flash. In Rome
it really must have looked like the most beautiful thing in the world. 'I
can only compare it to a tremendous diamond crown in the dark night.'
There is a childlike side to Edward revealed only in letters to Ann: he
hints that he would like her to come out and live in Rome with him.

In May 1839 he set out for Florence, a few weeks before Samuel
Palmer maybe, but Edward and his party stopped on the way, at Civitella
di Subiaco, and he stayed there until mid-October. This expedition
repaid him abundantly, because then and later Civitella became a focus
for his landscape collection. Influences are hard to trace: we have a
painting by him based on a Claude or a Turner copy of a Claude in the
Liber Veritatis, as beautiful as it is mysterious; it cannot be exactly dated.
His Neapolitan contemporary (1806–76), Giacinto Gigante of the
'school of Posilippo', knew Craven and Gell, and some of his landscapes
have a striking resemblance to mature Lears, the subjects being alike,
and the rocky foreground with the asphodels, the light on a pair of stone
pines, the distant cliff: but Gigante is not as meticulous as Lear became.
Tom Uwins probably knew him, since one or other Uwins had drawn
Gell in 1830. Lear's painting became brilliant in 1839. There is a

landscape of San Cosmato done at the end of August 1844, 'painfully on an aqueduct top in a high wind' as a mere sketch of warm autumnal cliff and dark foreground trees, with a monastery high on the precipice and a water-mill below, which is as dashing as anything scribbled in the face of the enemy a hundred years before, wonderfully accurate and intensely beautiful. That is all that one needs from a painting, but for Lear this was only a record, not intended for sale. It is the cover picture of Vivien Noakes's *The Painter Edward Lear*.

The tiny sketch he did for Ann of the slumbrous cypresses at the Villa d'Este became a formal oil painting[10] and so did the ruins of the temple of Venus and of Rome, an empty apse that caught the light nicely with the church tower of S. Maria Nova behind it; it still stands beside the Arch of Constantine, although an attempt to patch up its antique grandeur in the 1930s has left it less bare and less attractive than it was 150 years ago. Paul Mellon gave the picture to Yale. Since it was painted in 1840, the year that Mommsen first came to Rome, it may stand for a monument to the neoclassic age which was closing. It is a solid construction full of strong, even light, with only the distance hazy because of Lear's poor eyesight. It is now never possible to see any classical city with quite the clarity of those days: in the 1930s and as recently as the war, the older generation of archaeologists would speak of the astounding clarity of the sky of Athens which had not been utterly obscured until the 1970s, but today the light in these neoclassic pictures is as irrecoverable as antiquity itself must have seemed to be in 1840. The art of painting had begun to alter in that year. Constable had died in 1837, and by 1840 Cézanne had just been born in Provence. Egg and Dadd and Frith had formed their alliance, David Roberts was home from the Levant, and old Wilkie died on the way back from Istanbul. By 1845 the first regular paddle-steamers ran from England all over the eastern Mediterranean, and Thackeray described the voyage in his *From Cornhill to Grand Cairo*. Lear was not the most adventurous of men; wherever he went someone had been before him. But in 1841 he published a folio volume of lithographs, *Views of Rome and its Environs*, and in 1842 he began to explore the Abruzzi, the northern province of the Kingdom of Naples, which started not far east of the gates of Rome.

Lear's first Rome book is extremely rare now: it was privately printed for him by Hullmandel, 'E.L. del. et lith.', and could be bought from T. McLean in Haymarket. One of its finest plates is of some tall trees and a wild hilltop near Civitella di Subiaco. The plates are black and white, but wonderful and mysterious; they give one as strong a sense of another world as the Temple of Venus and of Rome does of a vividly present, available world. He had worked hard at variety: a castle at the mouth of the Tiber was his frontispiece, he went north as far as Bracciano, and in other directions to Nemi and Frascati and Rocca Giovane. He braved oxen treading straw at Roiato, and the Tiber water-buffaloes, which were kept for making mozzarella cheese, but he avoided people, except for the wizard cloaks and hats that still excited him, and which he showed in *The Gate of Alatri*. He could manage a Gothic colonnaded monastery with statues, but he was nervous of great architecture. If he drew it he felt more at home with a bit of wilderness as foreground. Of course he included Rome from the Pincio and the Via Porta Pinciana. He drew the 'picturesque' fair of S. Anatolia with folkloristic baskets and bagpipes, and a goatherd at Sambuci with a Welsh witch's hat at a broken bridge. He drew the botanical profusion of Valmontone more carefully than Gigante could have done. It is reasonable to call this lovely book an exercise in the picturesque as Penry Williams would have understood it. But being in the drabbest of lithography, not aquatinted, it could scarcely advance his cause in England: the most it could do was to advertise him as a painter, yet it was as a colourist, particularly in water-colour, that he was so brilliant. And one or two weaker or absurd images might have deterred a person from commissioning a coloured Lear unless they had seen one.

The book was published with the young Queen's name at the head of the list of subscribers. We must think of our great-grandparents, bewhiskered and bewildered, poring over it when they had not been beyond Dover. For six years from 1838 we have none of Lear's letters to Ann and few to anyone, although we know he revisited England in 1841: 'I think of publishing some Lithography on coming to England to pay expenses etc but I am not yet certain.' He worked at the lithographs at Knowsley in August. 'My life here is monotonous enough, but such as pleases me more than all the gaiety in the world. Dear Lord Derby is surrounded by his children, grandchildren, nephews and nieces, and is really happy.' The affectionate tone of this remark might suggest that it was now and in this nest that he laid the eggs of his limericks, and yet I do not believe so, because the lithography kept him so busy. He cannot have been drawing on the stone so far from London, because it would be difficult to transport twenty-six prepared stones; he must therefore have been reducing his sketches and finished pictures to the linear and shaded images that lithography could reproduce. The same grading of lighter and lighter distances with a dramatic figure or two in the middle ground, and botanical interest in the foreground, occurs with deliberate variations in every picture, as if the School of Posilippo and not the conventions set by Hullmandel had him in their grip. It is astonishing what he could do within the form. The book was sold to subscribers only, so that Lear could be sure of getting his money back: a mistake, surely, but one he could scarcely avoid.

He loved Rome, 'the unbustling, ancient, dead sort of atmosphere over all persons and streets'. By now he was on intimate terms with Prince Musignano, and used to spend days at his country house. He told Gould that the Prince was at Pisa, on his way back from a great scientific meeting that few English attended, and from which Pio Nono banned the subjects of his state. Meanwhile, Edward worked at his oils in the summers though not in the winters, perhaps for lack of the light he wanted, or (let us hope) because of the press of his pupils. We know that some time in the 1840s he became friendly with a merry widow, a rich and well-connected lady, the same Jane Apreece, cousin of Scott, who had married Humphry Davy three days after his knighthood, and was to be found in Rome after his death in 1829. She was a blue-stocking with leisure and a carriage, and she and Lear had a hilarious time exploring the Campagna together. Many years afterwards when his diaries were burnt he thought that relationship might have made the core of a book, the jokes of that dead time had been so funny.

Still, jokes are no way to pay and promotion. In 1841 'my plans depend partly on those of some of Lord Derby's family who are here this winter'. He would come to England (as we have seen he did) to 'run about upon railroads, and eat beefsteaks'. He was pleased with landscape, on the whole, and he was getting on extremely well. 'The wish of my life at present is quiet, to live in the country, and paint landscapes, the pencil-cutting, pudding-making lady [a wife] included.' In September he was in Scotland with Lord Breadalbane at Kilchurn. Breadalbane was President of the Scottish Antiquaries, but Lear took the journey light-heartedly; he travelled with Phipps Hornby, and illustrated their adventures with a set of thirty-six cartoons which have never been published and, I think, seldom seen. This set is the earliest survivor of a number of small travel souvenirs of the same kind. From Rome he wrote to Lord Derby rather desperately about how his loyalties were English, and how only the letters from Stanleys and Hornbys, particularly Robert Hornby's letters, kept him going. In 1842 he went to Sicily with two pupils, one of them Leopold Acland, son of Sir Thomas, and the other a nephew of Sir Stamford Raffles. He found the Greek temples there made Roman ruins look vulgar and modern, and he identified what he wanted to draw, but a tour of a month is not a serious period for that surprising island. He reported in a brilliant letter to Lord Derby which foreshadows the best of his travel narratives, yet to him Sicily would always remain a sideshow: which seems a pity. It was not frequented by enough wealthy English people to furnish him with pupils or patrons, even on the small scale on which he attracted patrons.

Lear's biggest success in the 1840s was one which might have been the foundation of a career, had he lived permanently in England. In the summer of 1846 he was invited to give drawing lessons to Queen Victoria. He seems to have behaved with his usual frankness and friendliness. When she showed him some treasures he burst out, 'I say, where did you get these?' She replied, 'I inherited them, Mr Lear.' He never quite understood why, whenever he went to the hearthrug in front of the fire after dinner, suave silver-haired courtiers lured him away from it on excuse after excuse; it was reserved for the Royal Family, though they were not so rude as to tell him so. But a relationship based on benevolent familiarity on the Queen's part, and a kind of awestruck intimacy on his, was somehow set up. He took to heart the warning he must have been given by somebody not to boast, and was always a bit secretive about his dealings with the Royal Family thereafter. All the same, they descended on him now and again, and none of them ever forgot him. Although he came to hate the fuss and fume of having anything to do with royalty, he always adored Victoria, and the Royal Family even bought some inexpensive water-colours from him. The reason for his being summoned to Osborne House, which was being built then, as an alternative seaside place to Brighton Pavilion, was that the Queen was impressed by Lear's second and much fuller travel book, *Illustrated Excursions in Italy*. This time he had the formula exactly right.

There is not much doubt about the usefulness of Lear's influence on the Queen's style, although he seems to have had none on her taste. The lithographs that impressed her were dramatic treatments of excitingly foreign subjects, and her own favourite painter was Murillo: she liked Landseer, but she thought Turner was crazy. It is unclear how she formed that view, whether through Lord Egremont or from gossip or having viewed with alarm some billowing naval canvas, but it would not have pleased Edward Lear. What he did influence was her water-colour technique, making it more robust and sharpening her eyesight. On the Queen's British journeys and in the Highlands she spent hours sketching, and the result is a record that still fascinates.

Was it that Lear fitted the sobriety and the modesty of her manner in painting? One might expect her style to have been somehow imperial, but it was not in the least like that. She wanted to record, and did so more accurately and perhaps with more humour after Lear had given her his course of lessons. The style was much like that of Prince Charles, her descendant. It expresses that essential core of bourgeois feeling I have heard called 'power-defended intimacy', and is of course no worse for that. However, it is not a phrase one could use of Lear's personal style, and it is possible that in teaching her he was swayed back towards the orthodoxies of his first drawing text-books and Sass's drawing school. She remembered him at Mount Edgcumbe, and his eye for what was paintable somehow entered into hers.

The Queen had a sketch by Lear of the tower at Osborne when the house was still unfinished engraved and offered to the artist as a present. It is an excellent but wholly unmemorable or unimportant image, which he treasured for the rest of his life. It is sad that he never had the financial benefits royal patronage might have brought him. Had he painted earlier in oils on a generous scale, one may guess that the Queen would have been pleased with his pictures whatever the Academy thought. Alas, as a career step, the Queen's drawing classes did not lead anywhere at all, and Edward was too modest and too correct to make the most of them. When the engraving arrived, he told nobody but Ann.

CHAPTER SIX

SOUTHERN ITALY

LEAR brought out his lovely book, *Excursions in Italy*, in 1846, first one volume of thirty plates of lithography drawn on the stone by himself, forty smaller woodcuts, mostly drawn on the wood by himself, but the architectural ones done by R. Branston, and a splendid text, describing a journey he took with Charles Knight, who taught him to ride and to shoot. He included a map, a bibliography of the Kingdom of Naples, and some peasant music; that is, he disported himself over the whole range of lithography, except that he did not use colours. The second volume came out in August of the same year. It had been promised for the indefinite future if the first was a success, and I imagine planned on the same scale, but Edward was so excited by how well he did with the first volume, that he swiftly produced his second with fifteen plates, notes to the plates, thirteen woodcuts and no more travelling.

There is no doubt that Lear had intended to cover all the provinces of Naples, although practical difficulties got in the way, first over passports and permissions in the north of the Kingdom, where he was at the mercy of every isolated and tyrannical official and learned useful lessons for dealing with the Albanians and the Turks a little later, then because the disturbances of 1848 made his Roman base unsafe. He had intended, with his unique, lithographic witness, to outdo Keppel Craven. At the same time, from 1840 to 1845, Richard Ford was producing his invaluable *Handbook for Travellers in Spain* for John Murray. Everywhere in Europe there were now far more tourists than travellers, but a travel book must lead them on to a viewpoint which is hardier, better instructed, and more advanced intellectually than the safer routes would induce. The Abruzzi really were extremely wild; they were also a long way from Naples. The shepherds drove their flocks homeward to the south in early winter, but they also flooded Rome towards Christmas, because it was closer to their grazing grounds and offered an easier route. Frontiers they largely ignored; that has always been the privilege of transhumant wanderers: as recently as 1970 the same herdsmen moved tranquilly to and fro from bases in Pakistan, across Afghanistan and in and out of Russia. Edward Lear was thrilled to discover the routes and tracks through the Abruzzi. Travelling for the *Excursions in Italy* took up the autumns of 1842 and 1843, and over the next two years he prepared them for publication. After the English success of 1846 he travelled in the south the very next year, intending to return again and again.

What interrupted him was the revelation of Greece, and the beginning of the three deepest friendships of his life: the first with Chichester Fortescue, first met in the spring of Edward's thirty-third year, the second with T. G. Baring, whom he met early in 1848 – both Fortescue and Baring were fresh out of Christ Church, Oxford, and both were gentlemen of means due to attain political peerages as Liberals – and the third, as from 1849, with Franklin Lushington, with whom Edward became particularly deeply entangled and whom he followed to Corfu after the death of his brother. Lushington was a younger son who was passionate in his youth and published poems, but death after death depressed him until he turned as dry as dust. There was a strong legal element in his family make-up, but his eldest brother was a Professor of Greek who married one of Alfred Tennyson's more eccentric sisters, and translated 'Oenone' into lovely Greek verse, and 'Crossing the Bar' into sapphics which are charming but seem never to have been published.

So Edward's travels from 1848 onwards took him east of Italy; in 1851 he produced *Journals of a Landscape Painter in Albania*, his best title and best book so far, and attracted the friendship of Alfred Tennyson. His journals in Southern Calabria did not appear until 1852. But in July 1849 he had returned to England after more than a year of Greek and oriental travelling: he had been to Malta, the Ionian Islands, Greece, Constantinople, Albania, Cairo and Sinai. He mounted his assault on money and position by two towering mistakes: in 1850 he decided to start again as a painter and joined the Academy Schools, and having withdrawn from that false position, in 1852 he conceived a fit of defenceless adoration for William Holman Hunt.

None of these friendships was remotely sexual, though they were all deeply affectionate, and all lifelong. Whenever one of Lear's friends married, he would entertain the same affection for his wife, and cultivate an intimacy which was what he craved and needed most. Of all his friends' wives, the one he loved most was Emily Tennyson, who took over from Ann as his surrogate mother. Nothing could break these friendships, though he might brood a bit now and then about how one or another friend might have altered. When Fortescue became Lord Carlingford, Edward had withdrawn somewhat, as he knew how occupied his friend was with politics, but his outbursts of high spirits and his letters are most moving. They are the substance of his *Letters* and *Later Letters* edited by Lady Strachey, Carlingford's niece by marriage, and some of his funniest drawings are in them. When Baring became Lord Northbrook, he and Lear went on whenever possible in just the same way. When Northbrook ruled India as Governor-General and Viceroy, Edward toddled around that entire sub-continent, bemused by the Viceregal splendours but quite secure as a friend. Frank Lushington got a London stipendiary magistracy through Lear – they were on more equal terms – and was always willing to advise, and when the time came to act as executor.

The only friendship that faded was Hunt's: he was, alas, no Cézanne, and an element of envy and of calculation enters into his memoirs, though that was not visible in the 1850s. It is really the weight and idiocy of the illustrations that sinks his book, and the thought of his influence on Edward as a painter is terrifying. Edward enjoyed with Hunt the sense of a youthful band of brothers, the parody of a family, the bond of a group of outsiders who would defy the world. But his best, his freshest vein as a painter was his water-colour sketches, and those at least were unaffected by the Pre-Raphaelites. His big, heavy canvases of oil painting were a device to raise money, a parody of the tasteless taste of Victoria's middle years, a device that by and large failed. There are few exceptions: the small oils on the other hand are equivalent to his 'finished' water-colours. All these complications arose from his long stay in Rome, the ten years 1838–48, from the age of twenty-six to thirty-six.

The mass of water-colours that document Lear's journeys in the Abruzzi and in Calabria are in the Liverpool Public Library, where they are mounted as an extra-illustrated seven-volume edition of the 1846 and the 1852 books. This was done by Lord Northbrook, to whom Lear gave a snowdrift of his paintings. He did the same with the Indian journal now at Harvard, which Lear prepared but never published. The binding was done by Bayntun of Bath and is remarkably handsome. But one small relic of the Abruzzi has escaped this grander equivalent of a many-volumed photograph album: it is a cartoon version of the adventures with Charles Knight. Edward had known the Knights since 1838 and was on intimate terms with them. Charles's sister Margaret was the Duchess of Sermoneta, whose ragged keep Edward drew; his sister Isabella kept a few stray Lear drawings and poems in an album. One of these, called *Scene in the Campagna* (1842), shows a cheerful old fish in spectacles smoking a pipe and drinking at a café table alone in a plain, observed by an owl. A small grove of pine trees in the distance, an abbey, a faraway mountain, deepen the mystery. Had someone told Lear, to whom the fish bears a suspicious resemblance, that he just sat there drinking like a fish? The adventures are with the album in the British Museum. 'L. declares that he considers his horse far from tame. K. enquires amiably if his stirrups are short enough. He affectionately induces L. to perceive that a thornbush has attached itself to his repugnant horse. L. is besought to sit back in his saddle. They visit a Temple by moonlight. They are attacked by venomous dogs.' I particularly like 'L. politely requested by K. to stop his horse at Mondragone, Frascati'. Lear was taught to ride along the track that ran outside the walls of Rome, then for the first part of their journey he borrowed an Arab called Gridiron, which was Knight's, though later he reverted to an old plodder, and Charles took Gridiron home. As for the cartoons, they are only pen and ink, but Lear is very good at his own alarmed look and the wicked or disapproving expression of Gridiron.

He remembered their adventures for the rest of his life. On his deathbed he lay dreaming of the rides around Rome. The book was bound in a greyish sage, much like Leake's *Peloponnese*, but the title is wreathed in passion-flowers, roses, convolvulus and carnations. The epigraph is a respectful gesture to Sir Richard Colt Hoare, an authority (1819) even older than Keppel. The dedication is to the Earl of Derby, the bibliography included Mazzella's *Regno di Napoli* (1586) and Alberti's *Descrizione di tutte l'Italia* (1596), and the whole affair is most serious and solemn. Lear claimed to offer the first drawings ever published of 'a part of central Italy as romantic as it is unfrequented', which was surely true. The work was carried out as before, although several artists engraved the vignettes, including Hannah Fussell, with Branston doing eighteen of the forty-one. There were thirty lithographs. It must be said that most of the thirty-two authorities were small Italian guide-books: Lear was not precisely an explorer, nor did he penetrate the provinces of Naples any more deeply than Mommsen. Frascati of the cartoon is very close to Rome, but Subiaco is near the border of the 'further' or western Abruzzi (Ulteriore Secondo), east of that lies Teranco and the eastern region

(Ulteriore Primo) to the north, and Citeriore with the River Sangro to the south. These two provinces divide at Chieti, and at Pescara on the coast: movement between any of the three provinces produced bureaucratic obstacles. Beyond this part of the Kingdom of Naples to the north lay Monte Sibilla and Ascoli. The entrance furthest north of Rome was at Rieti and in the middle of the two 'further' provinces of the Abruzzi rose the giant bulk of Monte Carno and the Gran Sasso d'Italia; the third 'nearer' province was divided from the first by Monte Marrone.

From the start, which was 26 July 1843, 'a solemn feeling of antiquity impresses you' as you pass along the Via Praenestina under rock walls seventy feet high. Lear discovered 'something exceedingly grand and *Poussinesque* in the rock of Guadagnolo as seen from this shady fount; and yet often as I have been there, I was always too hot and too tired to sketch it'. The honesty is charming and adds a touch of informality to the text which it was lacking. They got into Naples after three days and Lear started annotating the flocks. He reckoned (using Del Re, 1830) that there were 700,000 head moving up after the May shearing and down in September, by three drovers' tracks. Some descended by Rieti or Arsoli in October. He notes Keppel Craven on the pipes 'whose longdrawn notes you may hear hour after hour in the summer days', a sentence oddly recalling a poem of 1910 by Mandelstam. When the shepherds get to the Campagna, Lear notes that they knit socks or read works of devotion. 'A more inoffensive and contented race of beings I never met with.' He came on a wine little worse than Marsala, and a wild confusion of misty mountains, the haunts of the wolf and the bear, and he came to Tagliacozzo, made famous by a footnote in Samuel Butler's *Hudibras* about a plastic surgeon who repaired noses ravaged with syphilis with slices from porters' bums; when the porter died the nose dropped off. He tells us the joke primly, with only a learned reference, and an account in Latin that leaves out Butler's reference to the porter's bum. They galloped to Lake Fucino through 'an indescribable quiet' and suddenly the roads died out.

At Avezzano he was pleased to observe a torrent of black and active pigs rushing down from the hills into the piazza, and vanish squealing up every lane. His bedroom had chickens and women's clothes in it, and dead fleas squashed on the walls. But the lakeside country was quiet lanes and poplars and low vines, with horses, sheep and goats in the shallow water. At Celano he sought for the grave of the author of the *Dies Irae*, but found little certainty about who had written it. They passed 'a herd of white goats, blinking and sneezing in the early sun, their goatherd piping on a little reed, two or three large falcons soaring above the lake'. At Avezzano, in drenching rain, they first had passport trouble, because every district required a visa of its own. They passed Sulmona without thinking of Ovid who was born there: they did not even see the ruined temple baptized as his birthplace. He noted the universality of omelettes with tomato or artichoke or garlic. By the end of the month they were at Chieti, with more passport trouble to amuse them while a horse was shod. Charles took a carriage to Pescara, Edward walked, and they swam in the Adriatic, then came back to Chieti and bought straw hats. They passed Loretto where the Virgin's house landed having travelled by air, conveyed by angels, from Bethlehem, but they ignored it. Less prejudiced readers will like to know that the Blessed Virgin of Loretto was appointed by a recent Pope to be Patron of Aviators.

Startled hens put out their candles that night and the bed collapsed, Charles slept on the table. Rocca S. Stefano meant biscuits and lemonade, Aquila meant nothing much but melancholy magnificence: empty palaces, deserted quarters, harsh line of mountains, but at least an inn. Edward thought Rocca di Corno greatly inferior to many passes in Cumberland. Really it is all as one supposed; this might be a long letter from Russia in the 1900s or Greece in the 1930s or Afghanistan in the early 1970s. And today? Somewhere on the Danube, perhaps.

But the travel jogs along and the lithographs are thrilling and unlooked for. As a formula for a book, this one is perfect, and one soon learns the trick of disregarding the severe and formal bits. In August they dine simply on eggs and talk simply about the Thames Tunnel, the subject that preoccupies the entire Kingdom. A boy tells Lear that fox is *cibo squisito*. Mostly he copes alone as best he may with 'poetical and sullen grandeur', and his excitements are a newly caught wild boar raging, or a lake 'like Wastwater but grander'. In grand houses he notes the absence of books or needlework, or any least sign of mental activity; only the snow shines on the crests in deepening blue skies at nightfall, and 'the night grasshopper begins her one low note'. He found some Greeks, at Abadessa, which does have an uncanny Greek look. A blind young man came *per veder l'Inglese*, and sang him 'twenty interminable verses' of a ballad about Navarino. He could not understand any of it, and an old and hideous lady offered to undress him. These Greeks were refugees of 1744. At Lanciano the opera *Sappho* was well performed at a fair. He met a Baron 'who with the Baroness and a large poodle were the equally uninteresting inhabitants of a prodigiously grand palazzo'. The following day he saw turkeys everywhere, and the Cardinal of York's Stuart portraits, left to a lady-in-waiting by the Countess of Albany. It rained, and at Atri 'age and damp have obliterated the greater part' of the frescoes. At Mopelino was a house with Thorwaldsen prints where they praised the Duchess of Hamilton's singing. The forests were unfelled and hawks abounded in them for some reason to do with Roman customs dues on wood. 'I was rather tired of wandering about alone.' But his drawing is thrilling and thrillingly true to Italy, *Sulmona* being perhaps my own favourite.

He tried again in 1844, when he did some wonderful drawings, but essentially bad weather put an end to the long string of his adventures. This is summed up by his arrest at Civita Ducale, where he showed his passport, signed by Palmerston in 1837, only to set off the policeman whooping with glee: *Ho preso Palmerstone*! I have taken Palmerston!

The journey he took with a chance-met friend in 1847 has left a tiny and fragile memorial which in its published form (1938) looks as frail as it must have done when it was discovered lurking in the back of a book. John Joshua Proby was not well at the time, but he was determined to get to Sicily; he died in 1858. His father inherited the title Lord Carysfort in 1853 on the death of a brother insane for the previous forty-six years, but Lear knew nothing about that. Proby was probably a Roman pupil, since he was born in 1823; they certainly drew together in the series of cartoons that commented on their Sicilian journey. He was an Irishman and his father was MP for Wicklow; in 1841 Proby went to Balliol, where his friends were Clough, Shairp and, I suppose, Matthew Arnold; in 1843 he was one of a reading party in the Lakes. He got a second in 1844, though Jenkyns of Balliol did not want him to sit for an honours degree, possibly because his old tutor W. G. Ward (deprived in 1842) was thought a bad influence. Alas, by February 1847 his life was despaired of. Proby was a friend, or might have ripened into one, much like Lushington and Baring; Carlingford was his kinsman. But his importance here is not the comparatively feeble set of jokes and drawings, the best of which is about Froglodytes at Ipsica, which lived in the caves of that prehistoric place, and one of which Lear wanted to adopt; it is just the flavour of his company, and the small, casual journey on which Edward happened to draw Syracuse and Agrigento. 'Nothing of earth can be so beautiful as Girgenti with its six Temples – I speak of the old town – and the flowers and birds are beyond imagination lovely. I must however need say that the gnats, fleas, wasps etc. etc. require much philosophy to bear.' In June they were at Syracuse where he found the quarries 'now used as gardens, being sheltered are really quite like

Paradise. Every kind of tree and flower grows luxuriantly in them, and they are as full as possible of nightingales.' That is a letter to Ann, more charming and less realistic than the journals in the Abruzzi, but both styles are true to his nature. It is at Agrigento that he catches the warm colour of the stone better in water-colour than ever in oil; at Syracuse he catches only the cold ghostlike dance of the grey forms in the quarry. It would yield him an oil painting, but I prefer his sketch in pencil and sepia and the wateriest washlike colour.[1] Edward Lear had come a long way. His technique had settled and solidified in a way that most of his lithographs fail to reveal. In some inner sense, he was ready for Greece now, in a way he had not been in 1837.

When he wrote to Ann from Rome in February 1847, he was immersed in his painting. Two small views in the Campagna for the Tattons were nearly ready, 'one was half done in England'. The other paintings were for Mrs Earl, Dr Henry and (it appears) Mr Bonham Carter, who was a friend, an MP married to T. G. Baring's elder sister. Edward expected to make £120 that season, but his pockets were empty, and it was all he could do to give ten dollars to a fund for the Irish poor and three to the Anglican church. As the days lengthened he gave up eggs for breakfast and lunched at twelve instead, though life was still cheaper in Italy than in England. His 'yellow cat whose face was like a frog' had deserted him, he was pleased to say, but he had a tabby kitten who tore his window curtains to tatters.

The friends who meant so much to him were all tried as travelling companions. He had known Chichester Fortescue two years in 1847, though the first letter to survive is from Via Felice in October 1847, after he had been round Calabria with Proby (the P. referred to in the book when it came to be written). But Fortescue had been on one summer expedition, and also with another friend to Greece. He intended to join Lear somewhere, but suddenly found himself an Irish county MP for Louth, and had to race home, leaving the friend, who was Sir F. Scott, to call on Edward alone. Edward was not best pleased at the time, but

> I will forget for a space that you are a British senator, and write to that
> Chichester Fortescue whose shirt I cribbed at Palestrina ... Proby, my
> constant companion (and few there be better), agrees with me about your
> view of the road to Aviano ... Avellino is exquisite, and so is Monte
> Vergine when not in a fog, – But of Apulia we saw little, only from hills
> apart, because why? the atmosphere was pisonous in Septbr ... We saw
> the tree that Horace slept under at Monte Volture ...

This travel letter, written long before the book, makes an interesting contrast. It is more breathless, more forthright and not quite as funny. In Sicily, 'the only break to the utter monotony of life and scenery occurred by a little dog biting the calf of my leg very unpleasantly as I walked unsuspectingly in a vineyard'. The joke about Froglodytes at Ipseica, which are 'good creatures, mostly sitting on their hams, and eating lettuces and honey', is more charming than its cartoon version. He hated the heat and the cold equally, and abominated the north coast of Sicily. Scott met them at Naples 'and to my disgust – no Fortescue'. Edward came to like Scott, as he liked most people, though he was conscious of a lack of courtesy to him on that occasion, because Scott had sent up Fortescue's card and not his own. However things happened, Edward returned from Naples to Palermo, and so from Messina at the north-eastern tip of Sicily, he crossed the straits to Reggio and plunged at once into what excited him most in Italy. His book is very well constructed, but it does let out some unexpected things about how he planned his invasion of the southernmost Neapolitan province. He sounds far more like a landscape painter and an aesthete than anything else. He is scholarly, but only in marshalling all resources for the most frivolously aesthetic purposes. He is very like a modern traveller, in fact.

He begins with an outburst of feeling that he would never have allowed himself in his Italian excursions and Roman tours.

July 25, 1847. The very name of Calabria has in it no little romance. No other province of the kingdom of Naples holds out such promise of interest, or so inspires us before we have set foot within it, for what do we care for Molise or Principato? or what visions are conjured up by the names of Terra di Lavoro, or Capitanata? But – Calabria! – no sooner is the word uttered than a new world arises before the mind's eye, – torrents, fastnesses, all the prodigality of mountain scenery – caves, brigands, and pointed hats – Mrs Radcliffe and Salvator Rosa, – costumes and character – horrors and magnificence without end. Even Messina derives its chief charm from the blue range of mountains and the scattered villages on the opposite shore – Reggio glittering on the water's edge ... the lofty cloud-topped Aspromonte, and the pearl-pale cliffs of Bagnara.

It had few explorers, fewer published records, and the scenery beyond the main road had been 'little portrayed, at least by our countrymen'. Apart from Keppel Craven there was Henry Swinburne on the *Two Sicilies* (1785), and there was Arthur Strutt's *Pedestrian Tour* (1842). Lear and Proby would tackle it together, each of them with his own painting and drawing gear. When he published in 1852, Lear presented twenty lithographic plates, some of them splendidly dramatic, but *Calabria* was an illustrated travel book rather than a book of lithographic plates with a text, and by 1852 not only colour but also photography had come a long way. Proby's paintings are not known to have survived. All the same, of all Lear's travel writings this book is the most carefree and amusing to read, perhaps because it has the least scholarly pretensions.

They found decent rooms at an inn for about 1s. 6d. a day, and the *Direttore* of the police, to whom they showed a Duke's letter of introduction. He was a charming old Frenchman 'who was playing at whist, double dummy'. The following morning life began in earnest.

> If you wish for milk at breakfast-time in these parts of the world, you ought to sit in the middle of the road with a jug at early dawn, for unless you seize the critical moment of the goats passing through the town, you may wish in vain. If you have any excursion to make and require to start early, you may as well give up the idea, for the 'Crapi' are 'not yet come': and if you delay but a little while, you hear the tinkle of their bells, and perceive the last tails of the receding flock in vexatious perspective at the end of the street.

Edward Lear writes now as an old hand. He is more relaxed than he was, but the rise of the Victorian funny book has just touched his style as if with plague. Still, he found the best views 'among its endless cactus and aloe lanes, fig gardens and orange groves'. He found a snow-capped mountain, a pretty castle, the blue straits, and whatever today would make a postcard.

But suddenly he is off, because the fruit really interests him.

> Below the castle walls are spread wide groves of orange, lemon, citron, bergamot, and all kinds of such fruit as are called by the Italians *Agrumi*; their thick verdure stretched from hill to shore as far as the eye can see on either side, and only divided by the broad white lines of occasional torrent courses. All the fullness of Sicilian vegetation awaits you in your fore-ground; almond, olive, cactus, palm-tree, aloe and fig . . .

They visited the botanic gardens of the Villa Musitano. 'Strange fruits are hanging on every side (though none of them particularly eatable).' In the course of the next day or two, a Musitano nephew found them a guide and a mule. Meanwhile, they finished their drawings and negotiated to share a cab to a certain sanctuary. 'A man must be guided pretty much by hazard in arranging a tour through a country so little visited as this: the general rule of keeping near the mountains is perhaps the best, and if you hear of a town, or costume, or piece of antiquity anywise remarkable, to make a dash at it as inclination may devise.' At noon four days after their arrival they got a guide. He was grave, tall, and over fifty, and his name was Ciccio (for Francesco). When he understood their intentions, Ciccio said 'Dogo; dighi, doghi, daghi, da.' This formula recurred frequently in Calabrese speech, but they never could understand it. Ciccio carried a gun and wore a long blue cap like a Sicilian.

So off they went. At the first halt for the night in a little hill village they were assured that Bagaladi, where they were headed, was not worth a visit, and Ciccio explained to the villagers that the English are a kind of French; still, the wine was reasonable and the general standard of things was (already) like that of the remotest Abruzzi. 'July 30. How like a vast opal was Etna as the sun rose and lighted up the immense prospect from our southern window. But alas, a world of cloud arose also, and soon threatened rain.' They started at six, past picturesque groups of houses, and

> many scraps of Poussinesque landscape which I fain would have lingered
> to draw, but a drizzling rain, augmenting rapidly, forbade delay; so we
> followed Dighi Doghi Da along lanes and paths, over the slope of bare
> hills, and up a long ravine, till the weather cleared, and we arrived at an
> elevated plateau, when the whole Toe of Italy is finely discernible.

They could see the wild range of *Pentedatelo*, and Bova, their objective, on a peak. That mountain is one of Edward Lear's finest lithographs; it is so melodramatic, so exact, and simply so beautiful. The name is the corruption of the Greek 'Five Fingers', which is still the popular name for Taygetos, the mountain of the Spartans and of the Mani. Perhaps both mountains were named as seamarks by Greek sailors. Lear is much exercised by the survival of Greek colonies in south Italy, maybe from ancient times, but none of them is so old: the Greek language has survived there only since the fall of Byzantium and the heroic exploits of Skanderbeg. That admirable Italian scholar Comparetti cleared the matter up in the 1890s.

They arrived at last at the village of Bagaladi during the siesta, but when their hosts had woken up, they were immediately given 'a substantial meal of maccaroni etc., good wine, and sparkling snow'. The next village was several hours distant, so they agreed to stay the night. They had walked far more than seven hours after all, under a hot sun. Siesta came upon them. When they woke it was nearly sunset, so Lear rushed out to draw.

It is a wild scene, the shattered houses still hang ruinously over the shivered clay sides of the mighty torrent-track, a broad sweeping line of white stone, for, far winding through the valley below; above rise the high hills we have to cross tomorrow, half in golden light, half in purplest shadow; and among the topmost furrows and chasms sparkles the little village of San Lorenzo – atom signs of human life made more striking by their contrast with the solitude around. We returned to our humble but very clean home, and sat us down at a little table to pen out some of our sketches.

The lady of their house, who was particularly civilized though she was married to a village policeman, turned out to come from Livorno, and to have lived in Malta, Constantinople and elsewhere with her father, who had 'a little bit of trouble', *una piccola disgrazia*, that is, he had killed someone. 'At night the moon was full; the wide valley was all still, save for the twitter of its million hosts of grasshoppers.'

Lear annotates these as *Cicada Pleboeia*, but he goes on to note that they never utter except after sunrise and then until sunset. Children tie them to their own ears by twos and threes, and the noise they make like that is 'like scissor-grinders' wheels'. Both ancient and modern authors, he remarks, maintain that cicadas are silent on the western edge of Calabria, and he tells a silly story on which a scholar had cleverly poured scorn, about the reason being that the cicadas once interrupted a sermon by St Paul. With this feeble jest he leaves the subject: all the same, there remain some queer problems about these noisy creatures. Lear was a good bug-hunter; he had been interested in the subject since childhood. His Linnaean identification by the Latin name is likely to be right. The modern theory, which seems to me madder than most, is that the noisy insect is a beetle-shaped creature and not a cricket or grasshopper at all, a view adopted by classicists which mightily confuses scholars of Theocritus and Virgil. The truth may well be that numerous small creatures make furious noises all over the landscape, but why those around Reggio should be silent while those around Locri rave from dawn to dusk would then become a multiple, not a single, mystery.

All the last day of July, as they climbed towards Bova, 'said to be the last remnant of Magna Graecia', the cicadas 'buzzed and fizzed, shivered and shuddered, and ground knives on every branch above and around'. The travellers picked their way along inadequate paths through lovely oak woods, towards Condufori, of the people of which Ciccio would say only, 'They're Turks.' They had done well, he said, to sleep at Bagaladi, dighi, doghi, da. They had an introduction at Condufori, but the man was away, and his sister ran about squawking with panic: all they could get out of her was 'I am a woman and I don't know nothing.' Ciccio lit his pipe and said, 'They're Turks, dighi doghi da.' There was a bad inn, where they had a meal of eggs, wine and snow. The room was dark and so full of things that Lear sat down on a pig, which removed itself disturbing a dozen or more hens. A large crowd of villagers discussed them in impenetrable dialect. Out again in the furnace heat they crossed another dry and stony river-bed to enter the district of Gerace (a place-name meaning, I think, *hierax*, a hawk, or the Hawk's Nest). Lear offers a charming note on a village he never saw, further down the torrent bed, which produces honey, mushrooms and asparagus all the year round and may be where Praxiteles was born.

The view was extensive, the peasants were picturesque, and Lear and Proby sat and drew the outline of Etna in the distance, beyond the sea. It is this sort of distant view that most profits by the penning or outlining of silhouettes, which can of course be done later; it occupied Lear's evenings for most of his life. The initial sketch was in pencil with some dashes of swift colour and a few scribbled notes, then the outlines were marked in pen in the evening. We know he kept notebooks always with him, but they do not survive; they may have recorded the exact viewpoint or the same kind of note he often scribbles on a sketch, usually in jokey spelling. If and when one of the sketches was chosen by Lear or a client to be worked up into a finished water-colour painting, there would be no notes visible except maybe the brief title (always topographic) and date and signature. The process taken as a whole was elaborate and thoroughly deliberate: it is equivalent to the writing of a poem, first a few lines scribbled down or remembered, then a working copy, then corrections, then a fair copy, and finally a revised copy fit to be printed. But it is up to us whether we prefer the first swift sketch, penned in and washed, or the final and most perfect painting. At present there is some confusion in Lear's case, since it is true that the revival of interest in him since the 1939 war was first in his freshest and wildest sketches (which were still very cheap), and it is only now that the finished water-colours, which are masterly and beginning to be very expensive, are distinguished by the cleverer dealers from the mass of the 10,000 or so water-colours that he left in this world. One of which is the view of Etna on the last day of July, 1847.

They arrived exhausted, fainting for sleep and famished for supper, which took its time; that, as Lear remarks, is 'the greatest penance of this roving life'. But the greatest pleasure of it is surely the early morning in a new place, when one wakes in the eagle's nest. At Bova they were in the Palazzo Marzano, a homely, unornamented building that 'stands on its brown crag, looking over worlds of blue wood, and Sicily floating on the horizon's edge . . . just where a painter would have put it'. Their host assured them Fox had been to Bova to study geology: he had the vague idea that Fox and Pitt had governed England together. The truth is that it was an uncle of Edward H. Bunbury MP, in 1829 (Bunbury's uncle was Charles James Fox's nephew). Bova as a town claimed ancient Greek origin, and after much shuffling among dictionaries Edward became convinced that as a Greek colony Bova was at least pre-Norman, as Keppel Craven had suggested. His argument was largely that since 1600 learned Italian writers had left Bova out of account. It is a pity one cannot believe him. Even in Greece the survival of the ancient language into the modern has been quasi-miraculous; it is an adventurous story full of ups and downs; the people of Bova and its villages were refugees, not lineal survivors of the ancient Italian Greeks, who died out.

The tour jogs on very happily, but the question arises how Lear's prose compares with his painting, and the answer surely is not at all. The brown rock and the blue woods are slightly unusual, and yet deeply conventional. Have you ever seen a blue wood? One must discriminate between fine shades of colour, particularly when dealing with the peacock's neck hues of the sea seen from a mountain. Language is impossibly imprecise, and Lear deals with it best in the rough and comic notes he addresses to himself on sketches. But what about this? 'A pergola-walk, tangled with grass below and fig-bushes hanging above over walls of grey rock, commands vistas, among the vine-branches, of the long, graceful form of Etna, with clear lines of rock and river creeping down to the far sea . . . hives . . . cactus in immense luxuriance.' The phrases are effective if you know such places, but not otherwise, because the words are not individuated. The description does give a clear if general idea, though I am not quite sure where the figs are planted, and I merely assume the rivers to be wet. But all this expenditure of prose does what an atlas can do for a detailed map: it furnishes a context for the paintings. And the part of the book which is mere travel journal furnishes a new and thrilling dimension to the excitement of the sketches.

'Our days passed quietly away,' as he says. The cactus that covers the mountainsides is the barbary fig, or in Greek the frankish fig (frangosy-kia), imported once from the Americas as an effective cattle fence and poor man's rampart. It has a fruit which in Greece only children or the very poor will eat, though they do say it is delicious. Lear says:

The fruit, which at its best may be compared to a very insipid apricot, is greatly valued by the Calabrians, and seems to form no small proportion of the food of the poorer classes. From the precipices which frown among the numerous dry rivers towards the shore, this extraordinary vegetable hangs downward in grotesque festoons and chains of great length, and in many places forms a thickly matted surface, which to any fortress on the cliff above would be a complete defence. In early summer the bright yellow blossoms add a charm to its strange and wild appearance.

They left early, when the earliest sun had coloured Etna pale pink. Descending the steep steps, they passed the prison, where the one-eyed, malevolent-looking servant woman who attended them at Condufori glared out from behind bars, having murdered someone the previous night. The broad dark shades of morning filled the valley with delicious coolness. By climbing down a sort of rock ladder they got to Palizzi, another crag town. 'No wilder, more extraordinary place than Palizzi can well meet artist's eye.' Edward left Proby to draw while he adventured into a ruined castle 'full of incidental picturesqueness – namely a cottage, a pergola, seven large pigs, a blind man, and a baby', where the squealing of the pigs summoned a fine, Greek-looking girl who directed him by streets 'swarming with perfectly naked, berry-brown children ... astonished mahogany Cupids' to the village inn. He reckoned himself the first Englishman to tread down these streets. He sets out with some accuracy the conversation of the villagers, their tedious insistence and innocent amazement, but it is too long to copy down. Their most reasonable question is, Have you no rocks, no towns, no trees in your own country? The same conversation may be sampled fresh to this day by any traveller in remote lands.

But drawing was difficult: the stream was full of soaking hemp, and stank, the rocks were full of cactus and the naked children gathered everywhere to watch. So off they went, climbing Pietrapennata (the Flying Rock) to a view so extensive, Poussinesque and beautiful that it relieved all Edward's worries. 'What detached and strange crags! What overhanging ilex and oak! What middle-distance of densest wood! What remote and graceful lines, with the blue expanse of the eastern sea, and the long plains of the eastern side of Italy.' The village, when they came to it at sunset, was crowded with peasants coming home for the night, bagpipes were playing, and the women's dress was more colourful. The headman, fat and silent, was seated in the market-place: he took them to his house, which was disgusting, being wholly devoted to the silk-worm, full of yellow cocoons and foul with the sickly smell of thousands of caterpillars. From this evil hole they emerged with the horrors about boiled worms, stewed chrysalis, moth tart, warm sherbet and nasty wine cut with snow.

S. Agata, on the other hand, was a humble place, half of which seemed merged in 'the Baron's huge old dirty Poussinesque Palazzo', but beyond it lay shady groves of chestnuts and beyond them the shrine of S. Maria di Polsi, which stood on a hill above a terrific torrent coming down from Montalto. He makes the monastery sound like a painting by Magnasco, a painter who would surely have amused but not inspired him. As it was, they painted in the cloister, where the Superior exclaimed over the bizarre idea of an Archbishop's wife, or on little peaks of rock in a violent wind, where the woodmen gaped at them. When they left in search of Gerace, they were given a medal and a print of the Madonna di Polsi, 'the original picture having been discovered by a devout ox, who inveigled one of the early Norman Conquerors of Sicily all the way from Reggio to this place', whereupon the ox knelt down and dug up the picture with its horns. By oleanders, ferny glens and ravines of ilex, they threaded their way downhill to San Luca, where their horse needed shoeing. Ciccio also lost a shoe, so with much grumbling over the weight he added himself to the animal's load, as they trailed along the level coastal plain. At Bovalino they found an antiquarian Count who 'bustled about like an armadillo in a cage', Count Garrolo.

His conversation was exhausting in a Dickensian strain of dottiness. 'He had read the Countess an ode to ancient Locris all along the road, it had amused her, a Latin ode.' She had borne six children, all now dead, and was near her latest confinement. 'He would read us a page, two pages, three – Locri Opuntii, Locri Epizephyrii, Normans, Saracens – Indian figs and Indian corn – Julius Caesar and the Druids, Dante, Shakespeare – silkworms and mulberries – rents and taxes, antediluvians, American republics, astronomy and shellfish.' This was at least a change from the brutal lethargy they had got used to in Calabria, but when the pregnant Countess was produced after dinner, she could not get a word in but '*Nirr si*' and '*Nirr no*' (*nirr* meaning *signor*). That night the Count himself provided a vast silver basin and jug for washing, but the following morning he shook hands fifteen times each with his guests and rushed away, 'to make a note of some poetic reflections, give orders to the (two) servants, sell a horse, buy some grain, pick some flowers, cheer up the Countess'. In the distance beyond the mountain called Kondoianni they could see Gerace, the successor to ancient Locris. It was a big cathedral town on a narrow ridge of rock much split and stricken by earthquakes.

On 10 August they got there. It was civilized both for the better (the luxury of an afternoon ice) and for the worse (deadly readings by a learned antiquary until he fortunately fell asleep), and Edward enjoyed the colours, 'its white or delicate fawn-hued cliffs, and grey or dove-coloured buildings coming beautifully off the purple mountains'. He seems dazed by colours beyond what words will contain, his lithographs are black on a creamy, yellowish ground, allowing the odd wisp of white cloud, they convey nothing of what he means; his water-colours are magical but in a world of their own. Peter Quennell conveys something in his 'burning white stones' of Lear's Calabrian riverbeds, 'where great black swine wallow in the dull pools', but it is not colour that he conveys. One can at least say that the crags of Gerace, apart from the delicacy of their colour, were to Lear like the crags of Suli, that monument of Greek independence and of death: they were abrupt, melodramatic and intolerably steep. The weather he describes is earthquake weather. In 1851, in August, Melfi which was one of his towns was ruined in six seconds: 163 houses were levelled, ninety-eight partly levelled, five monasteries and seven churches (including the Cathedral) collapsed. It was about two-thirty in the afternoon, and the water was coming up hot from the wells.

On the 13th they started for Roccella, a fortified rock about twice the height of a palm tree. They got lost and benighted, but these adventures occur so regularly they are hardly worth much detail: they always end well, as this one did. The worst they suffered that night was a conversation about the lack of fruit in England, much scorn being poured on the feeble gooseberry and the weak greengage. 'It is probable that no stranger had ever visited these wild and unfrequented nooks of a province.' The reader who wants to get an idea of just how wild it then was, should take a look at the wooden columns from a ruined Calabrian monastery in the Victoria and Albert Museum. The grandeur of gorges, the painful tracks, the utter isolation of the country are poised on the paradox that these things seemed normal. It was Proby, who did not take sugar in coffee, and Lear, who stopped to draw bee-eaters near Gioiosa, who appeared abnormal. It was abnormal to be travelling at all. At Canalo, which lay among amazing rocks, they encountered recent memories of a royal visit by steamer, with a royal excursion inland on a vast crowd of donkeys; it sounded like a fabulous event. They ate roasted squirrels and mushrooms of queer shapes and colours; 'my former ornithological studies caused me to recognize a few corvine mandibles'.

From Canalo they turned to western Italy, by the Passo del Mercante. At the top was a broad green plain surrounded by beechwoods, with cattle and herdsmen; they walked downhill in a morning breeze over fresh young fern, into forest with glimpses of the western sea. It is a pity in a way that they never got to Otranto; I wonder what Edward would have made of the elephant column-bases, or the vast, brilliant mosaic like a figured carpet in the nave of the Cathedral. But down they came to Castelnuovo: Lear had the distinct idea that some political change was brewing, his hosts were oddly taciturn and he encountered suspicion. Still, he pondered the views. 'This is not easy; studies of tall graceful olives, and Claude-like richness of distance, are innumerable, but the choice among such scenes is difficult.' One can see he has dropped into a different landscape. At Polistena he searched for and discovered the house where young Morani, a Neapolitan painter only three years older than himself, had been born. They had met, presumably at Naples, in 1838. The painter's two sisters proudly showed the only two paintings they had, one of Walter Scott when he came to Naples for the winter of 1831–2, the last ever painted of him, though Edward thought it neither beautiful nor truthful, and the other of Pio Nono. Morani painted a country picnic in the Italian National Gallery, but he was not an influence on Lear so far as I know.

Earthquakes disturbed Edward, particularly the terrible one of 1782 of which he now saw the relics for himself. His pages are impregnated with the smell of water-melons, which the locals thought would be fatal to him, and of Indian corn, and of malarial swamps. He scorned the carriage road from Reggio to Naples, but they did enjoy its few luxuries, such as a real breakfast on 26 August, a piazza to draw in, the oranges and olives and feathery palm-trees, 'the town of Scilla sparkling at the foot of its cliff'. Finally, by a road he calls 'Silent in its dusty vines', a quotation from Byron perhaps, which I cannot place, they got home to Reggio. There they made small expeditions to places like Calanna, but the end of the month saw them in Messina. Lear recrossed the strait at once, while Proby was to follow. There at last revolution, which had been long expected, overtook them. Edward was at Melito, under Pentedatilo, in the southernmost town of all Italy. A few guns fired in the air and women wept and men became frantic with hunger for news. That night Edward was awoken by the strangest of queer noises, but they came from a very big, very dirty sheep under his bed.

At Reggio, which he and Ciccio reached at one in the morning, every house was lit up, and troops of armed men paraded here and there with music and banners that said 'Viva Pio IX', or 'Viva La Costituzione'. Ciccio groaned, 'Can't you see what it is? It's a revolution! Dighi doghi da.'

No one took the least notice of us as we passed along, and we soon arrived at Giordano's Hotel. The doors were barred, nor could I readily gain admittance; at length the waiter appeared, but he was uproariously drunk.

'Is Signor Proby arrived by the boat from Messina?' said I.

'O che barca! O che Messina! O che bella rivoluzione! Ai! ao! Orra birra burra-ba!' was the reply.

'Fetch me the keys of my room,' said I, 'I want to get at my *roba* (things).'

'O che chiavi! O che camera! O che roba! ai, ai!'

'But where are the keys?' I repeated.

'Non ci sono piu chiavi,' screamed the excited camariere, 'non ci sono piu passaporti, no ci sono piu Re – piu legge – piu giudici – piu niente – non x'e altro che l'amore la liberta – l'amicizia, e la costituzione – eccovi le chiavi – ai! o-o-o-o-o-orra birra ba!'

After a remarkable night Lear got some unwilling boatmen to carry him over to Messina to rejoin Proby. They heard naval gunfire off Reggio and in a day or two took ship for Naples, neither of them having the least idea what had happened. As the end of a travel book this is somewhat alarming. But they had seen Venosa where Horace was born, and they saw Paestum too. They had climbed among some remarkable rocks and lived on familiar terms with some extraordinary human beings. They could reasonably call themselves experienced travellers, and in the last few weeks Edward had become addicted to travelling, both as a painter and as a person. He was thirty-five years old.

CHAPTER SEVEN

A TASTE OF
GREEK LANDS

PROBY had been a substitute. The idea or half-formed plan Lear was forced to abandon when he went to Calabria had apparently been to travel with Chichester Fortescue on a wilder appendix to the grand tour. Greece was certainly attainable, since Tennyson's friend Richard Monkton Milnes had been there in 1832 and 1842 as well. Thackeray's *Notes of a Journey from Cornhill to Grand Cairo*, by the new paddle-steamer route, had been written in 1845 and widely read. It had not occurred to Lear to explore unknown lands before it was too late; it would scarcely be too late for another 100 years. But he was enthusiastic enough to use the first easy means he could afford, for Mediterranean travel at least, and he was anxious to get a stock of sketches where very few artists had been before him. There were always some who had been, because not only had Greece attracted artists (since the 1760s), and in fact altered British architecture by introducing genuine Doric, but also Palestine, and by extension the whole eastern Mediterranean, had produced a new class of affluent patrons prepared to pay for the religious picturesque. Roberts had tapped them and he was not the first. Even the remote fortified monastery of Sinai, under more or less permanent siege by the Bedouin of the desert, and the remote valley of Petra, with the insatiable and turbulent rabble that controlled it, had been visited and recorded. All the same, to Edward Lear the dew was still fresh on the grass.

By entering the House of Commons, Fortescue and T. G. Baring in turn were lost to him as travelling companions. Proby had been exhausted, and soon (though Lear did not know it at the time) became ill. The next friend he found for company was the young C. M. Church, nephew of the great Philhellene, General Sir Richard Church, who was still alive in Athens. Church carried the stamp of all Lear's friends at this time. He was a scholar and destined to settle as a Canon of Wells; his friendship, like Fortescue's and Baring's and A. P. Stanley's, lasted for a lifetime. He is mentioned in a letter to Fortescue in a list of friends in February 1848 at Rome,[1] with Baring and 'Lord Eastnor', who must be the future Lord Somers, for whose father Smirke built the amazing grandeurs of Eastnor Castle (1810–24) on the edge of Herefordshire. Lord Somers was a patron on a vast scale, and married to Virginia Pattle, who was a sister of Julia Cameron the photographer and an aunt of Virginia Woolf. He or perhaps his wife collected paintings by Watts, but his tastes were mostly antiquarian and he is not known to have had any Lears. All the same, he was one of the few men approached to lend money to Lear in his old age; they must always have been friends.

Travel arrangements with Church did not go well: the two friends appear to have missed each other more than once. But Church as his uncle's nephew was a valuable ally. Edward wrote home to Ann from Athens in early June 1848 that he 'will probably go to Constantinople and return with me. He tells me all the reports of disturbances in Greece are nonsense, as he has *just been all round it*.' It is possible that we attach too much weight to Lear's friendship with Fortescue simply because their correspondence has so largely survived, but to Fortescue he opens his heart from this time on as he does to no one else. When Fortescue became a Cabinet Minister, then a peer (he was already an Irish peer's brother), and married the very grand, very rich Lady Waldegrave after years of being her attendant cavalier, the friendship became less close, but it did not cool. Lear had still to meet the last of his very close friends, Lushington, a silent self-consumer of woes with a useful legal and practical brain, who appears closest of all, and yet I sense was in fact less close than Fortescue, only closer as a legal adviser. Church was never quite as close: the three friends to whom he gave his uncounted thousands of remaining pictures at his death were Fortescue, Baring and Lushington. Lord Somers, who succeeded in 1852, was just a rich friend and a man of taste.

Edward met Baring through an introduction from Fortescue: they had both been at Christ Church, Oxford, not long after Gladstone. They were never as close again, but they thought well of each other, and turn up in the same exclusive clubs later in life. 'Thankyou for your introduction to Baring,' writes Lear,

> he is an extremely luminous and amiable brick, and I like him very much – and I suppose he likes me or he wouldn't take the trouble of knocking me up as he does considering the lot of people he might take to instead – We have been out once or twice on the Campagna, and go to Mrs Sartori's [a kinswoman of Lord Barrington] or other evening popular approximations together. He would draw very well – and indeed does, – but has little practice. Altogether he is one of the best specimens of young English here this winter . . .

The Clives were in Rome in 1848 and he liked both of them, but they were patrons rather than intimates, maybe because when Edward met them they were already married, and George Clive was a barrister, an MP, and soon to be a junior minister. Their house was Perrystone, in Herefordshire, which sadly burnt down a few years ago with all its contents, including Lear oils and water-colours. And about 1844 in Rome Lear had met another of his most important patrons, Henry Bruce (1815–95), who as a politician passed painlessly from the Cabinet to the peerage in 1873 as Lord Aberdare, Lord President of the Council, but when Edward met him was a young barrister spending the last two years of his twenties in Rome and in Sicily for his health. His father had inherited a wild estate in the Aberdare Valley which luckily turned out to be rich in coal, so rich that in the seventies the peer pulled down his old house, which was genuinely baronial and dated from Edward II, to build a new one. That did, however, mean that he commissioned Lear's finest and perhaps largest oil painting, which now belongs to the City of Cardiff. Bruce went home in 1845 and married Arabella Beadon; he became an MP only in 1852. T. G. Baring inherited a wonderful collection of paintings accumulated by his old Uncle Tom, but he was personally interested in Lear's work and a true friend to him. Landscape was one of his pleasures in life, and he enjoyed the same kind of walking tours as the painter. Lear was always gregarious, partly out of curiosity and partly because in the small world of the English abroad he liked to meet whoever was 'spoken of as well worth knowing'. He liked anyone who 'seems a sensible fellow and don't talk watering-place rot', but as he sagely observed to Fortescue in January 1859, 'these people go squittering after sights, and are no more themselves seen'.[2] Whatever terms he was on with his rather numerous friends, he was still an outsider to

English society at its stiffest; if he were ever invited to a new Knowsley it would still be to draw the menagerie, and he would not dine upstairs. In Calabria he overheard two young English sprigs discussing him in an inn.

'I say, Dick, do you know who that fellow is who we were talking to last night?'

'No.'

'Why, he's nothing but a damned, dirty landscape painter.'

This story has not been placed, but he recurred to it and harped on it, and on his own title of 'dirty landscape painter', for many years, so the insult had nettled him. The same cannot have been said of the future Lord John Proby, whose father was to be Earl of Carysfort, so Edward must have been alone, probably at Messina or Naples if not at Rome. It was not perhaps a standard reaction to him, though the sprigs thought it was, and it was one he feared. But one should remember that at any time down to 1918 or later, Europe echoed to opinions of the kind.

Meanwhile Lear was restless. The revolution left him three weeks to waste, which he spent with Proby messing around Paestum and other loved places, not getting back to Rome until 14 October. He did not know how or where or whether to improve his figure drawing. He wanted to take off to Apulia and Calabria again,

or wherever I Archipelago (Archipelawent, Archipelagone) or whatever I do – I strongly long to go to Egypt for the next winter as ever is . . . a strong wish to see Syria and Asia Minor . . . Yet this is clear – the days of possible Lotus-eating are diminishing – and by the time I am forty I would fain be in England once more.

That would be by 1852. He began to pack things for home. Then in early spring he jumped at the chance offer of a Mr Bowen, who ran the University of the Ionian Islands on Corfu, to come and use it for a base to explore Greece. Italy was in an untidy, smouldering condition which threatened revolution. At Reggio it was suppressed but now it had broken out in Lombardy. The port of Ancona was shut, there was serious trouble at Venice and at Milan. It was not good news for travellers: on the way to Naples for a ship Edward encountered columns of marching men. But from Naples one could get to Malta, and so by a British paddle-steamer to Corfu. At Malta he disliked the landscape: 'hot sandstone, bright white houses, stupid little trees like rubbishy tufts of black worsted'. He was not trained to draw ships, and no doubt the thought of Turner terrified him. Considering the number of British sailors of that time who did draw them, stiffly perhaps but with a beautiful accuracy, one can understand his diffidence, yet it seems a pity. Thackeray was thrilled by Malta,[3] reserving his spleen for Athens, which he claimed was spoiled for him in advance by a classical education: that at least Edward Lear had not suffered. But in Malta let Thackeray speak for him, in 1844.

'On the 5th to the inexpressible joy of us all, we reached Valetta, the entrance to the harbour of which is one of the most stately and agreeable scenes ever admired by sea-sick traveller. The small basin was busy with a hundred ships, from the huge guard ship, which lies there a city in itself; – merchantmen loading and crews cheering, under all the flags of the world flaunting in the sunshine; a half-score of busy, black steamers perpetually coming and going, coaling and painting, and puffing and hissing in and out of harbour; slim men-of-war's barges shooting to and fro, with long shining oars flashing like wings over the water; hundreds of painted town-boats, with high heads and white awnings, – down to the little tubs in which some naked, tawny young beggars came paddling up to the steamer, entreating us to let them dive for halfpence. Round this busy blue water rise rocks, blazing in sunshine, and covered with every imaginable device of fortification: to the right, St Elmo, with flag and lighthouse; and opposite, the Military Hospital, looking like a palace; and all round, the houses of the city, for its size the handsomest and most stately in the world.

Thackeray had come from London and Lear had come from Rome, but Thackeray could paint in words, in a way that Lear could seldom or never achieve. Yet one swift sketch by Lear that summer of the Acropolis of Athens at sunset, melting away like a snowflake, is what Thackeray could not attempt and Turner could only have rivalled. If you can say it in words you do not need to paint it, Thackeray must have thought.

Edward wrote to Ann from Corfu, where he arrived by the mail packet, which had left Malta in a high wind on 15 April: it seems that the mail travelled by a 'War steamer' called *Volcano*, which was comfortable enough in spite of a heavy swell. She arrived among the Ionian Islands under the huge full moon of spring. He saw Cephalonia and Zante (Zakynthos), Missolonghi, Ithaca and Leucadia (Levkas), and about three in the morning *Volcano* anchored 'in the beautiful Paradise of Corfu bay'. The small and sea-scattered province of the Ionian Islands had come into British governorship with the collapse of Napoleon, who in his brief turn had taken the islands from Venice. The archives of

Italian Corfu (Kerkyra) stretch back through a labyrinth of dusty cellars and forgotten centuries, but the British occupation did little for the good of the island, indeed it would not last another twenty years. Meanwhile the British marched up and down the new esplanade with military bands, and little boys turned cartwheels of delight. Still, the French left a library and reading room of great beauty, the *Leschi Anagnoston*, and the British the game of cricket, and (of all surprises) a university, which alas did not outlive them. Bowen, who was an acquaintance of Fortescue, and of a certain Wynne who later became a Jesuit, was to turn out an ambitious man and a tricky character, though at the moment all was peace and pleasure. Richard Monkton Milnes had been ecstatic about Corfu, particularly about the size and age of the olive trees, and Edward Lear felt the same as he looked down from his bedroom at the calmest of seas, the villas and the cypresses. The bedroom was

> like one at Knowsley, or anywhere ... Nothing can be more lovely than the views; I never saw any more enchanting. The extreme gardeny verdure – the fine olives, cypresses, almonds, and oranges, make the landscape so rich – and the Albanian mountains are wonderfully fine ... Here and there you see an Albanian all red and white – with a full white pettycoat like a doll's, and a sheepskin over his shoulder.

The ordinary Greeks wore red capes and white, very full Turkish trousers; the women black or blue with a red kerchief.

Before he started his Greek travels, Edward dined with Lord Seaton, a sweet, domestic old man who was a Waterloo veteran, and now the Governor. He had been Sir John Coleford: now he resembled some slightly shabby old Ruritanian monarch in a comedy. But Edward was anxious to move on, to explore exactly those islands that are the most famous of his prints. Zante was probably the most populous and certainly the most beautiful of the Ionian Islands, close enough to the Greek mainland for its lights to be seen twinkling in the distance on a clear night from Katakolo, the nearest port to ancient Olympia. It had a culture of its own, deeply Greek and fed by exiles from Crete when Crete fell to the Turks. In its popular theatre, actors and audience within living memory exchanged impromptu remarks in rhyming couplets: a custom even more skilful than that of cricket played on gravel at Corfu. Harvard has a magnificent sketch of Zante that Lear made at this time; it is both the stormiest and calmest of images, with olive trees like breaking waves, white churches and houses like pebbles, a stricken sky and in the foreground some oblivious goats. It is the cover of Hofer's

Lear as a Landscape Draughtsman (1967). Seeing its insomniac spires is to feel the thrill of what that little island town still was in the 1840s, *Zante, Zante, fior di Levante*. The first great poet of modern Greece, Solomos, grew up there, trusting more to Italian at first than he did to Greek: he learned his Greek as a poet from blind Cretan ballad-singers who sat outside the wine-shops of Corfu. Lord Seaton knew him as Count Solomos. Edward Lear could easily have met him, but he never did; yet his painting expressed much that Solomos loved, particularly in these island sketches where 'the sea is sleeping in the arms of earth'.

He had only £150, yet he was already longing for someone to pay his expenses to Jerusalem. We know that he set off among the islands, but the next we hear of him is in another letter to Ann, from Athens. He had been touring the southern end of Corfu, and waiting for Somers of Eastnor to tour with him, since he was expected on the next Malta steamer, 'or perhaps Wilmot-Horton would by then have been able to go somewhere – or if not, I should then have decided to go alone for a little while, as I already know enough Greek'. But his good luck continued: he suddenly ran into the Seatons with Sir Stratford Canning and his entourage who were on their way to Constantinople. Lady Canning had been pressing him to visit her in Turkey for the last eight years, and he was swept off in her train by private steamer, the *Antelope* man-of-war, as the British guns banged away at the royal salute from the citadel. They steamed into the Gulf of Corinth to Vostitza (Aigion) and then Loutraki, to cross the isthmus. With two carriages and eight horses they contrived a seven-mile journey to another war steamer which took them to Athens; Lear had only one stirrup and Lord Augustus Loftus two of rope, and the steamer took five hours to get from the isthmus to the Piraeus.

'Poor old scrubby Rome sinks into nothing by the side of such beautiful magnificence. No words can give any idea of the appearance of such a vast mass of gigantic ruins all of dazzling white marble, of the most exquisite proportions – and overlooking such splendid tracts of landscape.' Here he met Church, who reassured him about the rumours of Greek disturbances. Greece was remote enough from the rest of Europe to be out of phase with it: the Greeks had their revolution in the early 1840s. It must have seemed like a piece of the moon in 1848. 'There is *no* shade whatever, no, not a bush, near Athens . . . the roads are very dusty . . . The King wears the full Greek dress and rides about often with the Queen.' He reports on the Acropolis at sunset:

Most of the columns being rusty with age the whole mass becomes like
gold and ivory – and the polished white marble pavement is literally blue
from the reflection of the sky . . . Owls are extremely common, and come
and sit very near me when I draw . . . All the little comforts of dear old
Italy – ice, fruits etc. are quite unknown . . . The Areopagus is now only
inhabited by sheep and goats.

It appears he could not tear himself away. He rode around Greece
with Church, had a fall, and then got ill, so that he did not reach the
Embassy at Therapia before the very end of July.

The illness was 'partly a fever . . . partly a regular want of cleaning out
and doctoring', and it struck at Thebes; in addition to stomach trouble
and heat stroke (he had lost his umbrella) Lear was bitten by some
venomous insect, and came home to Athens on an air-bed rigged between
four horses. He was looked after by Sir Edmund and Lady Lyons in
Athens, and by the Churches: he might easily have died. The two young
men had travelled by way of Marathon and its unexcavated mound, with
food, beds, cooking-pots and a servant who looked after all arrangements
for a fixed sum per day, and a column of seven horses. *Marathon* is one
of his most Byronic paintings: it is now at Oxford. They would halt for
three or four hours at ten in the morning, and then push on until dusk.
Their route took them by Rhamnous and Oropo to Chalkis, which was
still a fine Turkish town with palm trees and minarets sprouting above
its walls, as they do in a sketch in the Benaki Museum, then up Euboea
to cross over again to Lamia, where Edward was captivated by the storks,
from one to eight or ten nests to a house, the ruined minarets and
deserted houses having even more. 'The clatter they make with their
bills is most curious, and make you fancy all the town are playing at
backgammon.' The last of them were slaughtered as a Turkish relic, only
in the 1960s.

He had seen the mountains near Thermopylae and Kithairon from
the Theban plain, and the huge opportunity that Greece still presented
afflicted him like his fever and his infected blood. He had not been ill
for eleven years, but this malady took two months and some kind nursing
at Therapia, where he had to be carried up from the harbour in a sedan
chair, from which he would poke his head to vomit, to the fury of passing
Turks, out of travel-sickness. He told Fortescue late in August that he
planned 'a huge work (if I can *do* all Greece –) of the Morea and all
together. But my main object in seeing Greece was improvement in
sheer pure Landscape – (hang Ruskin) – and some of that I feel I have

got already.' The prospect of settling down in London, either socially to *petit maître* praises, or to terribly hard work in which he risked everything, terrified him. Still, he had not lost that wildly exciting impetus of youthful confidence which was so well merited in his case: if only he lived another ten years, '*wouldn't* the Lears sell in your grandchildren's time'. Alas, that time when it came was the lowest point of his reputation: it is only now, nearly 150 years after he wrote that letter, and more than 100 after his death, that he is beginning to be recognized. At the time, Edward was beginning to think thoughts he did not directly voice, about marriage and children: Baring was about to marry Elizabeth Sturt, a squire's daughter from Crichel. He was the first of these friends to marry, surely because his career and his finances were already secure.

Meanwhile, Edward recommended Ann to explore Dartmoor or the Wye Valley, and he wrote her a long, fascinating account of a private ceremony of the Sultan, which he attended with the Cannings.[4] And he sketched incessantly. One of the most remarkable of his Turkish scenes is his *Sweet Waters of Asia*; he was better on the whole and more tranquil than he usually had been in Athens, where he tried out dramas of colour and shadow, not always successfully: his *Hagia Sofia* as a mosque with a galley passing is an amazing image, and so is *Beybek on the Bosphorus* with its undisturbed reflections.[5]

Gallipoli, 10 Sept. 1848, Salonica Steamer is another marine sketch, not only beautiful in itself, and astonishing because its subject is so peacefully ignorant of any future, but fascinating because it so successfully disregards the circumstances of Lear's creating so full a record of an idle hour. The *Sweet Waters of Asia* are scarcely lazier; it is only by hindsight that one can spot a certain urgency in the movement of the small boats. We have the story in the *Journals of a Landscape Painter in Greece and Albania* (1851). Charles Church had gone to visit Troy, and the two of them were meant to meet at Athos to explore the monasteries. Edward was on an Austrian steamer called the *Ferdinando*, with its lower deck crammed with Turks, Jews, Greeks and Bulgarians, who were sailing to Saloniki in order to get to Thessaly, Bosnia, Wallachia or (I assume) Bulgaria. The overcrowding was due to engine trouble in another steamer. Edward was thrilled by Constantinople as they left it, 'the towers of wonderful Stamboul first pale and distinct in the light of the rising moon, and then glittering and lessening on the calm horizon', but for half the following morning they stuck at Gallipoli, 'taking in merchandise, and indulging in eccentric casualties – demolishing the bowsprit of one vessel and injuring divers others, for which we are

condemned to three hours of clamour, and arrangement of compensation'. He does not even mention making a sketch, only some premonitory
twinges of fever off the Dardanelles, and dosing himself with quinine.

Worse was to come. He was thrilled by the sight of Athos, 'a mountain
pile of awful form' looming against a clear amber sky, but at Saloniki,
which was swarming with Jewish porters in black turbans, he discovered
Athos was shut and Church was cut off by fear of cholera. Edward and
his luggage were fought over by the infuriated mob, who were subdued
only by a dozen or so policemen with long sticks. He stayed at a sort of
hotel he called 'the last dim ghost of European "accommodation"
between Stamboul and Cattaro: it is kept by the politest of Tuscans, and
the hostess is the most corpulent and blackest of negresses'. He and his
servant Giorgio, who was a Smyrna man, not to be confused with Giorgis
Kokalis, whom he found later in Corfu and who died in his service, were
barred from the east and from the south-west, so that only a move
north-west into Albania was possible. They could not return to Istanbul
without at least a fortnight's delay in a city that was plainly alive with
cholera, so Edward sensibly decided to set out at once, not knowing how
far he might get. It was his bravest and most exciting journey. W. M.
Leake had covered the same ground forty years before, and so had a
dozen others, but for Edward to undertake such a journey through wild
mountains and almost alone showed some courage. It is also probable
that undertaking it saved his life. The drawings and paintings that came
of it were numerous and excellent and of a marvellous variety. In the
end, as usual, he heard that the panic had been much exaggerated, but at
the time it was the most important factor in his planning, and somehow
or other, when the plodding started, the last rags and tatters of his fever
dissolved.

They left at seven in the morning with a mounted Turkish post-boy,
a baggage-horse, and their own two, for the ten-hour journey to Yenidje.
The plain of the Vardar (Axios) was fenced with thick haze, and only the
birds consoled him: kestrels rocking on tall thistles, hoopoes, rollers,
jackdaws, broad-winged falcons hovering and grey-headed ones sitting
composedly by the roadside. He did not enjoy his short, bucket stirrups
or his tall, peaked wooden saddle. At noon he drew the bridge on the
Axios and noted water-buffaloes, sheep and a Turk hawking. They
crossed and then for three hours galloped or trotted across the plain, and
he found himself at Yenidje, once a depot for the most delicious Turkish
tobacco. It was a wonderland of the picturesque that he drew unforgettably. 'It would not do to let a day pass without making a large drawing.'

He was as unable to sit cross-legged as his unhappy horse would have been, but when he lay down to drink tea the Turks pleased him greatly by preserving their habitual incuriosity. What with 'mountains of grandest form' appearing above the dark trees, and the cleanliness of everything compared to the filth of the Abruzzi, he was in good spirits. He assures his reader that 'the elaborate northern meal of breakfast may well be omitted'. At Arnaoutlik, a village of Greek and Bulgarian Christian peasants, he tells you at some length how to plan a picture. 'Blocks of old stone – squared and cut long ago in other ages – overgrown with very long grass, clustering lentisk, and glossy leaves of arum, form your nearest foreground.' Then post-boys, sheep, shepherd-boys with a reed flute, and finally houses: 'a mere village landscape in a classic land'. To sketch at his best he needed to be less patronizing and more excited, until ten or twenty years later, when he took to gardening and a quiet life, and the splendid late phase of painting that went with that, when there would seem something false, because repetitive, about the greater excitements of his youth. Now, the mountains were all before him.

He got easily enough to Vodhena (Aegae, Edessa), which guards the first mountain pass towards the district of Monastir and Lake Okhrida. They had come a serious distance from Saloniki in just three days, and although he still drew far better than he describes, we must be grateful for what drawing could not convey: the masked ladies with guards and rearguard, the outhouse abounding with cats and cobwebs, the saint's tomb with a view 'in which a solitary elder sits, in the enjoyment of tobacco and serenity'. Then they were into the rainy mountains, steaming their wet clothes over a fire and eating the salmon-trout of Ostrovo. Next morning the mountains were bright with snow, but as the day went on the rain fell again, and they were stuck for the night in a small mountain village, Edward in a pigeon loft that swayed and creaked in the wind, writing letters. The following day, as they came close to the city of Monastir, two post-boys met and got drunk together: one left the other embogged in a quagmire, then repented and went back to rescue him, all of which took time. Edward Lear's lithographed drawing of the centre of Monastir with a mountain behind it is almost too charming to be beautiful, but it conveys to perfection the mountain sun after mountain rain, and the shy, provincial atmosphere of the place. The feeling is neither wild nor remote; he might be sitting in a café with the paper in some city in France, except that he mildly looks up, and records in his journal eighty or 100 wolf-life dogs, snarling and howling over a dead horse in the next square. He visited the Pasha, who had been at

Cambridge and sent him a present of a basket of pears, and a letter to the Bey of Akhrida (a locust: now spelt Okhrida). In less than a day out of Monastir, Lear was out of the region that took its name, and into the new world of the Albanian language: 'At the edge of the western face of this high ridge, the beautiful plain and lake of Okhrida burst, as it were, into existence; gilded in the setting sun, and slumbering below hills, forest and snow, piled up and mingled with cloud midway in heaven.'

The journey becomes more and more magical and unlikely, less and less Greek. Indeed it would be fair to say that apart from three or four identifications of place-names by W. M. Leake, there was nothing Greek about it except the idea, the name, the excitement of modern Greece, which was still an image of revolutionary liberty and pure mountains. He liked the magnificent clothes of Albania north of the Apsus, or Ghegheria, Illyrian Albania, whose capital was Skhoder and whose western limit was Lake Okhrida. It was like stumbling into paradise by the back door. The happy inhabitants wore a long cloak of purple, crimson or scarlet, trimmed with fur or bordered with gold thread or braiding. Whenever he could, Edward collected picturesque garments for painting purposes, to dress his models if ever he should manage figure painting. As he walked down a street lined by geese in kennels, with a central stream crossed by stepping-stones, he was bombarded with little stones and bits of muck because of his white fur hat. Giorgio warned him to invest in a fez. But the Bey gave him a guard, and the pelting ceased. Only at night he was persecuted, by the squalling of cats on one side of his bed, and the quacking of ducks on the other.

He wrote again to Ann from Skhoder (Scutari, Podgoritsa), and makes it clear that he did take to the fez (who shall blame him?) and confirms how enthralled he was by the millions of tame water-fowl on the lake at Okhrida, white cranes and grey falcons you could all but pat, and the water-buffalo too tame to move out of your way. On the 25th they came down into a plain of olive trees ringed by olive-coloured mountains, with white minarets standing above the trees. The place was Elbassan, but he hated it. The streets were picturesquely roofed in with old mats or vines to make them dark, the inn windowless and the whole place tumbledown and deserted. This did not stop him drawing it most beautifully, however; often as one reads a travel book one wants to be elsewhere, sometimes in the past to make things worse, but with Lear one wants to enter into a work of art, something that is not ever possible, even for the artist. To draw undisturbed, idyllic and innocent pictures, Lear had to pay to be guarded by a policeman. 'The people of Elbassan were odious, and the town most unclean and horrible – so we left it unregretted.' The following day, the 27th, he came in sight of Tomarit or Tomohr, the mountain that bewitched Tennyson when the journal was published. That may have been because of the entry under 16 October. 'As this day was to be passed on the banks of the Apsus, for the purpose of sketching Tomohr, I awoke and rose at three, and by daylight the mountain sparkled like clear crystal.'

To the north he could see Tiranna (Tyrana), and there he slept in a room with a mad dervish armed with bells and a brass hook, who fortunately did him no harm. Armed with a letter from the Bey, they went by way of Croia, the mountain fastness of Scanderbeg, to Scutari. The Bey of Croia was only a boy, who showed Lear the contents of a writing-desk as a box of wonders. Edward liked him, so he drew him a train and a paddle-steamer, saying tiktoktik, tokkatokkatok and wish-washsquishsquash, to the young man's extreme delight. He gave him a pencil too, and some needles for his mother.

One can sense that the end of this arduous journey is now in sight. In the coastal towns he meets Franciscans and he plans his descent to Avlona as if he were taking a train; he is clearly not going to need all those needles any more. The important thing is, as he writes to Ann, that if only he can get his sketches safely home, he now has a complete new book of great originality. That must be the explanation of his further travels, because his £150 in 1847 could scarcely have stretched much further. It is possible Lady Canning gave him something even above his expenses for seven weeks and his steamer ticket home, but his Albanian book (1851) and his Calabrian book (1852) generated confidence, his *Book of Nonsense* (1846) had done well, and he had serious paintings in oils to exhibit from 1850 onwards. At the job of fitting words with pictures, he had become so urbanely skilful (because he was alone?) that one would have said the even flow of pleasures from his drawings, and the cheerful succession of misadventures and brief lyric moments in his journal, were almost too smooth: yet how dare one say that, when this is the book and these the lithographs that so moved Alfred Tennyson?

In fact the style varies enough to break the even flow. Lear was sensible not to try to return across those formidable mountains, which are dressed in snow like candy-floss well before Christmas; but from the literary point of view, that makes the good-humoured Acroceraunian romp, and the happy descent to the crowds of pelicans at Avlona, prefigured by the storks of Zeitun (Lamia), a warmer ending which is all but anti-climax. Most travel books have such problems. It is the biographer who should be most grateful for the ending, because the difference of mood shows so plainly. After all, the events, murders, thefts and wildness of Dukhades and the other Greek villages are objectively just as strong medicine as being pelted in the mountains and acquiring a fez. But either because the people in Epirus are so familiar to modern travellers, or because Lear feels himself at home among them, there is a warmth in this part of his narrative. How could that be, or why should it be, after such a brief time in Greece, mostly in bad health, and a week or so in Corfu?

I can only remark that among Greeks, almost any Greeks anywhere, Edward Lear found himself suddenly at home. They appealed to his sense of humour, like the pelicans.[6] The lithograph of pelicans is based on the hastiest of sketches made on 29 October. He saw them again in Egypt more than once, and it was the Nile pelicans which inspired the 'Pelican Chorus', written maybe in 1867, ten years before it was published. By then of course he was a middle-aged gentleman, composing an after-dinner song, and the collection of birds who come to the pelicans' daughter's feast will convey a certain heaviness, a sense of sadness at the zoo, to those who thirst for the pure mountain water of this book, with its sparkling, understated jokes, and young Edward Lear at the height of all his powers.

That last scene at Avlona was at the very end of October, but by January 1849 he was in Cairo with John Cross, an old friend from Redcar, a firm Christian and amateur zoologist whom he first met in his Knowsley days, and who was now paying for him as a travelling companion in Bible lands. We know a little of his movements meanwhile from a letter of thanks he sent Lord Derby from Cairo on 12 January: his fine skeletal drawing of the city,[7] not unlike his *Jerusalem* in the Benaki, is dated two days earlier: he had landed in Egypt soon after the New Year (4 January), got to Cairo in two days and met Cross there. Thackeray says the journey took thirty hours in a P&O boat like a canal barge, towed by a small steamer: the inside of a day by canal, and the rest of the journey on the Nile. It is just like the boats that take the intrepid traveller to Ballinasloe, he says. He was bored, but embarrassed to be bored: Edward Lear was less refined in his feelings. He used Lane's *Egypt* for a guide (as I did with equal pleasure 120 years later). 'The camels amuse and amaze me: I rode on one – a rehearsal ride, yesterday, and was not uncomfortable: only I wish they would not roar and snarl so.'

This letter to Derby makes an interesting tailpiece to Albania. It is here we discover that fire-arms were forbidden to the Albanians, which explains the pleasant multiplication of fauna, and here that we hear of the white egrets as numerous as coots in England on Lake Ochrida, the thousands of pelicans that looked like white stones until they suddenly flew away, and the plovers, ducks, sandpipers, herons and storks of the Albanian coast. By 7 November Lear had been at Iannina, not very far inland, though his best Iannina drawings date from 1857; there he encountered a letter from Lord Derby that had chased him from Constantinople, and a letter from Cross inviting him to meet at Malta. He set out at once, but 'many mishaps' on the way delayed him until 1848 was over. Since this was not the cholera season but the storm season it is likely that the attempt of the P&O to run a reliable service for passengers was disrupted. This Egyptian expedition would not produce another book: he already had material for two. It was just an opportunity he would not let slip. We must thank Cross for some brilliant sketches and paintings, above all the *Sinai*:[8] the sketch of the monastery in the wilderness with a veiled lady in the bottom left-hand corner seems to me far more exciting, and its pencilled rocks more awe-inspiring, than the elaborate mountain and camel caravan, around which hangs the gloomy air of Victorian hotel dining-rooms. Not that it is less than beautiful: but even Mount Tomohrit in oils, four feet by six, which is a fine academic study of 1872, based on a sketch twenty or twenty-five years old, lays a deadly weight on the imagination compared to the heavenly fresh sketch of the bridge at Scutari (1848), just lightly touched with sepia ink and water-colour.[9] Noakes offers another and better, more dramatic version of the Sinai camel caravan, in which the mountain is like an illustration from the geological museum,[10] a 'finished' water-colour of a little less than twelve inches by twenty, yet the same heaviness remains. The Harvard example is smaller still, so size is not the trouble, but ponderousness.

He sent Ann a letter so long it was a series of notices strung together. There was not a lot to do on the camel-journey to Sinai, Cross did a good deal of Bible-reading, and in the evenings Lear had leisure to write. One feels that he had got used to his traveller's life, and he might easily have gone on for ever, taking his camels through Turkey and Persia and China, and merely changing to a dog-sled at Kamchatka. He has time in this letter to be severe about modernist topographers, who put Sinai somewhere else, because how could Moses have climbed that fearsome rock or ever got down again? Lear and Cross agree that 'if the miraculous nature of the whole transaction be granted', Leipsius and Lord Lindsay and other unnamed scoundrels were fools to quibble about the steepness of the mountain. They had started on 13 January; by the 17th, Ann's birthday, they were at Suez: they stayed at Sinai three days and went back to Suez again, then in about eight days more they hoped to make Gaza, quarantine, and the Holy Land. But the weather turned bad and Lear suddenly became miserable and gave up. From Alexandria, he took ship for Malta.

There he met the two Lushington brothers, Henry and Franklin, for the first time. A distinct glory haloed them, because they were friends of Alfred Tennyson, the greatest English poet alive, with the possible exception of Wordsworth; their elder brother Edmund had married Tennyson's sister in 1842, and *The Princess*, since its second edition in 1848, had been dedicated to Henry. The Lushingtons were close in age, but Henry was Lear's exact contemporary. They had been at Charterhouse with Thackeray and Trinity, Cambridge with the Tennysons. It would soon be made public, and they must have known already, that Alfred's great series of elegies for Arthur Hallam, which would soon appear as *In Memoriam*, had turned towards hope with a poem about their brother Edmund's wedding to Celia Tennyson in 1842, and *The Princess* was set at their family house, Park Hall in Kent. Edmund was one of the best Greek scholars of the day and a professor in Glasgow, Henry and Franklin were both enthusiastic poets, though not much better than middling, but Henry had repeated some of Edmund's meteoric success at Trinity; he was a barrister, and Grey had appointed him secretary to the government of Malta. He was in the last stages of preparing to introduce a new code of laws to the legislative assembly. Franklin was in Malta on a visit; it is obscure to me whether he was really talented, though he had been a Fellow of Trinity; he was certainly a competent lawyer though a taciturn, difficult man, and Lear thought at first he was talented as an artist: I suspect he was Lear's pupil for a time and may have paid for the Greek adventure which swiftly followed. Whatever else one may think about him as his life unrolled, they were certainly lifelong friends.

The Greek journey can be traced by letters as usual, but far better by the most amazing series of sketches. It is now some months since I saw the mass of them at Harvard, but their effect is quite undiminished. They can be regarded as a continuous series with Albanian images like the *Bridge at Scutari*, but they are uniquely alive and powerful. They show a new concentration of Lear's powers more intense and more structural than he had shown at Calatafini in Sicily, for example, or the previous year in Corfu, where by comparison his pencil strokes appear to dawdle, to be puzzled,[11] lovely and willowy as his olive trees had already become. It was the mountains and rocks that stirred him so deeply,[12] and all his wonderful achievements of the 1850s were made possible by his Greek journey with Frank Lushington. He had in the end spent more than a year at intense practical work as a landscape artist, and with a serious intellectual disturbance about the theory of art. He had, as it were, got his eye in.

They arrived in Patras by 9 March, perhaps a month after his arrival in Malta, perhaps less. They went straight along the Gulf of Corinth to Vostitza (Aigion) by the old seashore road, then followed the ravine that lures you inland to Megaspelion, 'a wondrous place containing two or three hundred monks in a large cave'. Lear notes with some relief, 'My fellow traveller draws as much as I do, and we only complain that the days are too short.' From Megaspelion they got easily enough to Kalavryta, a medieval fortress in the most amazing country of crags, by which Lear was wonderstruck: he shows it not in his letter home but in his drawings. They wound through black pines and snowy mountains past Lake Phonia, sleeping in shepherds' huts with 'lambs poking about one's bed all night'. From Tripolitsa they made for Karytaina and Andritsaina in Arcadia, a mountain town where twenty years ago you could still buy the furs of hill foxes, and at last the remotest of Greek ruins, the Temple of Bassae. One need have no doubt that this was an extremely gruelling route, but 'the beauty of this part of Greece can hardly be imagined; – all the exquisite plains of the coast are seen through magnificent forests of ilex and oak ... Bassae ... I never saw so beautiful a landscape as it forms part of'. On their way south to Messene they had a day of rain, then from 21 March they were back on the mountains. It must be noted that Lear seems to have chosen the most mountainous of routes quite deliberately. He climbed down into Sparta (a slightly confusing drawing) and then saw Mistra, and in three days reached the plain of Argos, which was a dense carpet of wild flowers. 'Sometimes it is quite pink with Hepaticas – scarlet and blue Anemones, yellow Euphorbia, Cistus, and several hundred kinds of flowers I never saw before make the whole country a garden.' Today that part of it is mostly orange trees and lemon trees, but there are still flowers.

They visited Nauplion and the ruins of Mycenae, Nemea (a perfunctory sketch with a shepherd in it), Corinth and at last Athens. He next intended a trip by boat to Aigina and Sounion (which was still called

Colonna), and an expedition to Delphi. We know he went there by a small oil painting of enchanting interest of the olive trees in the valley below the classical site, painted from above and towards the sea. After that he becomes vague. He hoped to be at Patras for 22 April, 'and as then I must lay out my plan for returning home, I shall be able to tell you about when to expect me'. Piedmont was at war with Austria, so the Corfu route looked disagreeable because of trouble at Trieste. 'So I rather think of spending May in Epirus and Thessaly, and crossing to the Dardanelles sometime in June.' Then he could get to Malta and go home: it would appear that no regular service visited Corfu. In the end the two young men took a small ship from Delphi to Patras, and parted there with a pang on Lear's side that he never forgot, probably because he was alone again. His memory of the last six weeks was intensified by the thrill of Delphi, clinging to the rocks above its sea of olive trees. 'As for Lushington and I, equally fond of flowers, we gather them all day like children, and when we have stuck our hats and coats and horses all over with them – it is time to throw them away, and get a new set.' I do not think the key to all this is precisely sexual attraction, but the spring in Greece at full blast. Lear went on his own back to Iannina, over the Metsovo Pass to Tempe and the country round Olympus. His intention was to see the monasteries on Mount Athos, but the Holy Mountain was shut yet again, so he went home to England. Perhaps it was as well, because his sketches of those monasteries, and even the finished pictures when they came, were absolutely thrilling, but they are in another, sadder style. Like all true aesthetes he teetered between extreme happiness because things were so beautiful and sadness because the sun will set. But nearly twenty years later he recorded his journey in his diary (10 May 1862).

> There is everywhere a flood of gold and green and blue. This and the breeze, blowing freshly now and then, remind me of days in many lands before that knowledge came which tells us we have so little, and so much conjecture. On Swiss and Como hills in 1837, in the first years of Roman and Amalfi life 38–9, the long Civitella sojourns 1839–40, Abruzzi 43–4, Sicily and Greece 47, 48–9. I do not suppose now that kind of happiness can ever come back but by unexpected and unsought snatches; so I do not strive after it, nor mourn that I cannot have it.

Those were the years between the ages of twenty-five and thirty-seven, and the times in those years when he was working out of doors, and could say as Picasso said of painting, 'Je ne cherche pas, je trouve.'

CHAPTER EIGHT

LEAR AT FORTY

ENGLAND in the 1850s was very different from what it had been in the 1830s. The smell of London was thick enough to cut with a knife, Thackeray and Dickens and *The Times* and imperial politics were all at full blast, public taste was going downhill fast, and railway trains rattled over moors and grumbled and hooted through valleys, louder and faster than ever before. It was time for Wordsworth to die, and he did so in 1850, Turner followed him in 1851, and even David Cox did not last beyond 1859. The stalk of British painting was withered dry, and it was not to revive for a long time. What was wrong with the younger men? The visions of Palmer, Calvert and Linnell had run into the shallow water of nostalgia: Calvert (1799–1883), whose Virgilian landscapes were at least extremely pretty, felt 'a yearning to see the glades and nooks receding like vistas into the gardens of heaven'. Linnell (1792–1882) was a heavier and more slumberous painter, and perhaps those qualities are what the public liked, since in 1852 he moved to a big country house near Redhill and when he died there left £200,000 which he had largely made by landscape painting. He was West's and John Varley's pupil, but he represents the solemn and gloomy conventions that were stifling British art, and one may wish to add British life and British religion. Whatever is the truth about that, his canvases of trees in fullest leaf seem to encompass one like a mass of used green tea-leaves, his art is the direct opposite of Lear's brilliant sketches.

In the early 1840s, Lear had thought of illustrating the seventh book of Virgil, in which Aeneas discovers and the poet reveals Italy. His painting of Nar suggests his book would have been splendid. Then he played with the thought of illustrating W. M. Leake's travels in Greece, but that immense task soon deterred him, and anyway it would not have suited him, because Leake's eye was archaeological and precise, his journeys had been long ago, and his records were comprehensively full: he could not easily be mingled with the picturesque. In June 1849 Lear heard that an old family friend, Mrs Warner of Bath, had left him £500: the rest of her fortune of nearly £50,000 went to widows. 'I thought directly I heard of this matter that I would instantly marry one of the 30 viddies only then it occurred to me that she would not be a viddy any more if I married her.' In early autumn 1849, soon after his arrival in England, Lear collected this money; he therefore took the decision to go back to the beginning as a painter, because he believed that 'the root of the matter' was figure painting and without that key he could never unlock 'the landscapes that are in me'. Fifty years earlier he could have hired another artist to paint his figures, 100 years later he would have known that no key can unlock works of art from inside the artist but a random or a lucky one. His decision was, so far as one can see, a crashing blunder, not just a waste of time and energy, but the entry to a long labyrinth of mistakes he need never have made.

He began by re-enrolling at Sass's drawing school, the same private establishment he attended earlier, that acted as a filter for the Academy Schools, and there he prepared a folio of drawings from the antique. Uwins, his friend Tom's uncle, was the Academy's librarian, and sponsored him. Meanwhile Edward worked away at the finished versions of his sketches, which in themselves he did not think 'substantial' (that is, academic) enough, and began copying the beech trees at Uppark to make his oil painting of Tomohrit, which remained unfinished until 1877, though an earlier version for Louisa Lady Ashburton was delivered in 1851. The mountain is like a bright blue iceberg under a patch of clear sky with Constable clouds, which are really fine. It has been called 'the most sublimely picturesque' of his oils, recalling John Martin, and Lear himself wrote of the scene 'realizing the fondest fancies of artist imagination ... with tufted trees which recalled Stothard's graceful forms', yet personally it fills me with gloom, its darkness is deadly and its lights are unreal to me, and I do not follow where the waterfall comes from or where the river is going. It is the underworld posing as heaven.

Edward had been in England by June or July. He wrote to his friend Fortescue from Tabley House, Knutsford, on 1 August.

On leaving town I came to the James Hornbys at Winwick, and then migrated with them to Knowsley. After a week at each place and a day or two in Manchester, I came for four days to Tatton's of Wythenshawe and now am here for as many more . . . I have been living in a constant state of happiness. My dear old friends Mr Hornby and Lord Derby I found just as ever, though 72 and 75, and every day has caused fresh shaking of hands with old friends.

He had sixty-eight visits to pay, but hoped to get through fifteen or sixteen of them before 20 September, when he was due to move into 17 Stratford Place, and to get to work at Sass's. Part of his light-heartedness was surely relief that Mrs Warner's £500 enabled him to settle all his debts.

What do you think of my having *nearly, all but* become possessor of 40 or 50,000 £? Fact, I assure you, it makes me laugh to think what I could possibly have done with such a statistic heap of ore! However I have never it seems been attentive enough to the old Lady who always said she would enrich me, so she has died and left all to thirty poor widows for ever and ever, and much better too that she left it thus, for I should not have made as good use of it.

The Academy Schools offered a course ten years long: three years of drawing and anatomy and 'the antique', that is, plaster casts, and only then the Preliminary School of Painting revealed the mysterious qualities of oil paint, and the Upper School introduced real live models. History painting, of which poor old Haydon must have been the last living serious practitioner until his suicide, allowed Biblical scenes as well as classical, but that was all. Anyone interested in what this queer institution produced may find a historical subject in Turner's *Field of Waterloo* (very dark indeed) which appears as an illustration to Byron, and there is a fine Biblical scene on the stairs to the balcony in the parish church at Dartmouth. But the whole system was set up not without pedantry by Reynolds: Blake was one of the first of his critics, but by no means the last. Ruskin's *Modern Painters* was now in vogue (Volume 1 had been published in 1843). It was in the 1849 Summer Exhibition of the Academy that paintings first appeared signed 'PRB'. Edward Lear therefore stepped straight into the considerable disturbance created by the Pre-Raphaelite Brotherhood, which burst out in the late spring of 1850. This redoubled his disaster. He was thirty-eight, but the conversation of the talented young intoxicated him, he took sides with them and thought, as my father used to say, that the sun shone out of their ears. Holman Hunt, who was haughtily shrugging off the Academy and its Schools at the time, was twenty-three. Lear became for a time a late-born member of the Brotherhood; probably he was delighted to belong to something so up to date, and to something a little resembling a secret society. He loved the Brethren dearly and was loyal to them. The first one he met, I believe, was the sculptor Thomas Woolner.

He submitted his drawings from the antique to the Academy in January, and three more that were looked at in April after he had been three months a probationer. In January he was one of nineteen pupils admitted out of fifty-one candidates, 'and now I go with a large book and a piece of chalk to school every day like a good little boy'. He was accepted again in April, after which silence falls. The Keeper was a person called Jones who had served without great distinction in the Peninsula against Napoleon, and later in the occupation of Paris in 1815: he had emerged a fervent painter of battles. He had also been a friend of Turner's. The passing-out test in the Antique School was three drawings of sculptures or groups of them, drawings of a head, a hand, and a foot, and a timed drawing of an antique figure for which twelve hours were allowed. So far as I can discover, none of the class came to any good; Vivien Noakes thinks Lear took his leave of the establishment after one term, in the summer of 1850, perhaps because he ran out of money. That is quite likely, since he reckoned it cost him £300 a year to live in London. He did exhibit, though, in the Summer Exhibition, which used to be held in those days in the National Gallery; his picture was Claude Lorrain's *House on the Tiber*, a monument much visited by painters, though it has not survived.

The worst explosion over the Pre-Raphaelite pictures in that exhibition was a misdirected roar of rage from Dickens. He appears to have confused the Brethren with the Young England movement, the Eglinton Tournament, Disraeli, and whatever else he abominated. He was not precisely a philistine, indeed he followed Maclise in berating British art for its respectability and solemn dullness compared to the Italians; but his friends in three years' time or so, as soon as the magazine was founded, would be the self-made, satirical men who sat round the table of *Punch*. The values of *Punch* really did become to a fearsome degree the values of England. The worst of Dickens' wrath was directed against young Millais, whose *Christ in the House of his Parents* offended him because the male figures in it were not by Victorian British standards fully dressed. Dickens hated nudes, and above all male nudes: but the complaint about this picture (unless it was secretly directed against a rumour of the artist's long hair and beauty?) was dotty in the extreme, as Dickens himself showed when he first met Millais five years later, at dinner with Wilkie Collins in Paris, and sent him a note of grovelling admiration the following morning. Wilkie Collins' brother Charles was one of the Brethren. Dickens was equally aberrant at first about Wilkie, who was later his right-hand man: he found *The Moonstone* 'wearisome beyond endurance'. His violent reaction to Millais' painting may have been to the extreme realism of the naked body; it is conceivable that his old friend Clarkson Stanfield the Academician was at the bottom of it.[1]

But at this early stage the Lushingtons meant more to Edward Lear than the Pre-Raphaelites. Frank Lushington, for some reason of temperament or circumstance it is hard to penetrate at this fairly early date in his career, seems to have been an introspective, silent and perhaps embittered man. We know he was passionately patriotic and a mediocre poet; he may have been depressed by his brother Henry's absence in Malta. Was his trouble lack of advancement in his career, or the shadow of his two very successful brothers, or worry about women? No one offers a suggestion, and it is hard to escape the sensation that under normal circumstances he was cold and dull. Certainly both Edward Lear and Alfred Tennyson's wife Emily, whom he married in May 1850, commented on Frank's habitual sadness and silence. Edward visited the Lushingtons at Park Hall, it is said, in June 1849, and there he must have met Alfred Tennyson, during the build-up to that poet's marriage.

Certainly when Alfred took Emily to the Lakes for a honeymoon, Thomas Woolner, who already knew Alfred and had worked on a relief of his head, and Edward Lear were among the friends who called on them. Edward sent his belated wedding present, both volumes of his 1848 *Italy*, to them on 2 December. Earlier, perhaps, or soon afterwards he sent his new *Albania*, which was out early in 1851. It thrilled Alfred not only with the oriental exotic but because it fulfilled vicariously his own long-standing wish to travel in Greece. So at once their acquaintance became intimate friendship. Edward had always vaguely longed to make some equivalent in art to the early poetry of Tennyson, and now Tennyson sent him a poem of extraordinary beauty, 'To E.L., on His Travels in Greece'.

> Illyrian woodlands, echoing falls
> Of water, sheets of summer glass,
> The long divine Penlian pass
> The vast Akrokeraurian walls,
>
> Tomohrit, Athos, all things fair,
> With such a pencil, such a pen,

You shadow forth to distant men,
I read and felt that I was there:

And trust me while I turned the page,
And tracked you still on classic ground,
I grew in gladness till I found
My spirits in the golden age.

For me the torrent ever poured
And glistened – here and there alone
The broad-limbed gods at random thrown
By fountain-urns; – and Naiads oared

A glimmering shoulder under gloom
Of cavern pillars; on the swell
The silver lily heaved and fell;
And many a slope was rich in bloom,

From him that on the mountain lea
By dancing rivulets fed his flocks
To him who sat upon the rocks,
And fluted to the morning sea.

This remarkable poem reached Lear in 1851 and was published in 1853. Its metre is that of *In Memoriam*, which he could not get out of his head, and its tone Horatian, in Tennyson's matured vein in which friendship and much more are so fully expressed. The picture is one Lear might have longed to paint, but not one he did paint: only the tone was true. It was the tone he had used for the Queen in March 1851 in his first publication as Poet Laureate.

Then – while a sweeter music wakes,
And through wild March the throstle calls,
Where all about your palace-walls
The sun-lit almond-blossom shakes – . . .

That little lyric cost the Laureate fearful pains and crossings-out, whereas Lear's flows naturally, with wonderful improvements in the second version over 'Illyrian olives, foaming falls Of water, lakes of summer glass . . . The broad-browed gods at random thrown . . .' The gods seem to depend on a memory of Samson Agonistes, though from their relaxed attitude beside fountain-urns they recall the sculptures from the pediment of the Parthenon. The shepherds or goatherds at the end of the poem are as enchanting and as sad as Tennyson meant them to be: they are all that was left, after all, of the classical world in Lear's time: today they are as irrecoverable as the nightingale that sang to Keats.

The exchange of letters that marked Edward Lear's huge scheme to produce a visual analogy to Tennyson's poems had begun before this poem was finished. 'I intended long ago to have done a series of little landscapes illustrative of some of the Poems,' he wrote to Mrs Tennyson with her wedding present, '. . . There have been but few weeks or days within the last eight years, that I have not been more or less in the habit of reading Tennyson's poetry, and the amount of pleasure derived by me from them is quite beyond reckoning' (2 December 1851). That appears to date the beginning of his craze to the end of 1843, when he was thirty-one, and still exploring the Abruzzi, before he had met Chichester Fortescue or read Ruskin. In fact it dates from the enormous popularity and wide diffusion of Tennyson's two-volume 1842 *Poems*, which certainly established his reputation. Probably someone had brought a copy out to Rome that winter. Lear's idea is all the more interesting because it was so vague. In a Yale manuscript he calls his offerings 'Painting-Sympathisations'. The poet's grandson, Sir Charles Tennyson, remarks severely that they 'seem to throw a diaphanous veil over the words, nothing more', and Alfred detested his illustrators, mostly Pre-Raphaelites of a decorative and fantastical tendency. The only one to whom he was polite was Doré, but the letter is in French and no doubt diplomacy had entered into it. When Alfred went round London a few years after Lear's suggestion, to meet the painters Moxon had chosen for the (delayed) illustrated Tennyson of 1859, Lear was away in Corfu, and anyway he was not one of those chosen.

The débâcle at the Academy Schools must have done Lear's reputation a lot of harm, and the other Pre-Raphaelites to whom he adhered out of genuine enthusiasm could do little to help. Holman Hunt, whom he adored, gave him advice that was both patronizing and bad, and cultivated his own relationship with Tennyson as if he, and not Lear, were the original poetry-lover and the artist the Laureate needed. And yet there was something of great value in the equivalence Edward was seeking, even though he could never encompass it in his lifetime, because his scheme was too vast, and the means of reproduction, as they altered more and more feverishly, always failed to convey his drawings. I do not mean really what he had in mind, but what he had on paper. In the end the Tennyson scheme became a kind of card-index for the cream of his 10,000 or more sketches. He did not prosper. Settings of Tennyson to his own music were not popular, and his suggestion that Alfred should write him another poem about them met with a grim silence. He tired of Tennyson and became furious with him, and flung himself like a hurt child at Mrs Tennyson. It did no good, of course. Alfred hated his puns, and I am sure, if he knew them, abominated his parodies. They were two larger-than-life personalities who were better apart, but Edward was more naïve about this than numerous other larger-than-life persons who knew how to manage Alfred, or whom Alfred knew how to manage, like Carlyle and Gladstone and Dickens.

In the late summer of 1850, Lord Derby had commissioned a painting for £100, and Edward thought of Athens or Iannina. Then Hullmandel died, and Edward caught a bad cold at his funeral. In late November he told Derby that he now intended an Athens in harvest-time (to cheer up the empty plain of Attica). 'The groups of figures are as natural as they are picturesque in themselves, and indispensable to a good foreground in a large subject. Of course I cannot get this done for the next Exhibition . . .' In March he had still not forwarded his sketch to Knowsley. 'Regular darkness and fog-succeeding-fog' had undone him, he had bronchitis, and he had been working at his book. He designed the *Athens* with Hymettus and Mons Pentelicus (Pendeli) behind it, in the early morning light, as he really preferred mountains to groups of harvesters, and sent it off with the lithograph of his Avlona pelicans. Derby remarked in reply that there was little detail, and the simplicity of the subject would be hard to convey in a large picture. Still, Lear stuck to his guns for the time being, though what was finally exhibited, in 1852 at the British Institute, was *The Acropolis of Athens, Sunrise, People Assembling on the Road to the Piraeus*.

In that year he was forty, and at last published his *Calabria*. He went on exhibiting at the Academy until 1856, then again for a few years between 1870 and 1876, and very occasionally at the Institute or out of London. But the career of a successful oil painter eluded him, and he relied on what he could sell from his own studio. It is worth pointing out that he did not equal the number of pictures he listed as painted in 1847 and sold, which was thirteen, until 1858, when he managed seventeen. His travels and the preparation of his books, his illness and his social life all made inroads into his time; even so, his habit of work at oil paintings was terribly slow, and the Pre-Raphaelites made it worse.

The summer was his happiest time. In 1851 he spent most of it at Lydford (5s. a week and 1s. 6d. for three meals a day); his drawings there are charming but very unlike the dashing style he had attained in the Mediterranean. He was in Devon instead of at Knowsley because it was cheap; then on 13 June, just at the moment he had finished his *Athens*, Lord Derby died. Edward was in a gloomy mood, knowing that only constant hard work prevented his painting from sliding backwards. 'I certainly did improve last year a little – but I ain't sure if Lydford and the rain and the cows won't have made me go back this year.' All the same this letter to Fortescue was extremely cheerful.

> 'Mary, has the boy come back from the post with the letters yet?'
> 'Noa zur, hiss be drewndid!'
> 'He's what, Mary?'
> 'Hiss be drewndid zur, in the pewerfil rain.' (Later) 'Here be tew letters zur: – the boy is all queet drewndid zur as ever you see!'

He was finishing some water-colours and planning some paintings for the winter, and on the last stages of work on his *Syracuse*, presumably the splendid *Quarries of Syracuse* that Alfred Tennyson bought in 1852, or the version that won a prize the same year and was bought by Lord Beauchamp. All the same, when Lear went for a tour in Cornwall with Lushington he was not at all exhilarated, and as he wrote in a letter of consolation to Fortescue in August, 'There is only one fine day out of fifteen, and all the rest are beyond expression demoralising and filthy . . . Experience teaches, and a village summer in Italy *is* another thing to this.' The consolation was because Fortescue had met the love of his life. He was twenty-five and she was twenty-seven, but three times married already. Lear had seen her once, driving in a carriage down Piccadilly. She was rich, titled and of extraordinary beauty.

When Lear got back to London he intended to go to some Academy or other to draw from the life. In 1852, following the publication of *Calabria* and the deservedly extremely good reviews of *Albania*, he must have been something of a celebrity. He had a friend called Robert Martineau who lived down at Hastings, and who was a good middling sort of painter and fellow-traveller with the Pre-Raphaelites, and it was Martineau who brought W. Holman Hunt to see Lear in his studio at Stratford Place. Hunt's account is unreliable: in his memoirs he set Edward up as a buffoon, a droll eccentric scarcely worth mentioning as a painter except for his reverence for Holman Hunt. In fact his incense might have turned the head of an older and wiser man. (It did not turn Alfred Tennyson's.) Holman Hunt was young enough to be deeply impressed even by Little Holland House, which Lear thought of as the centre of 'Pattledom': Hunt had probably never before met a Pattle.

'Aristocrats there were of ministerial dignity,' he says, 'and generals fresh from flood and field.' But he is at least amusing about Tennyson: 'Mr Tennyson is delighted to make your acquaintance.' 'What made you say that? I never said I was ... Your voice sounds like the piping of a little bird in the storm.'² It is on Tennyson, of course, not on Lear, that Hunt focuses; in 1860 he catches the poet rather well (in Woolner's words) on his expedition to the south-west. 'We would watch Tennyson in his slouch hat, his rusty black suit, and his clinging coat, wandering away among the rocks.'

Hunt came to Stratford Place to see Lear's 'numberless drawings, which were in outline, with little to indicate light or shade. Lear overflowed with geniality', but he was anxious because he could not carry them out in oils. He had written in 'what outlines wouldn't explain – rox, korn, ski, indulging his love of fun with these vagaries'. How could he make pictures of them, because when he set himself down to try, he often broke down in despair? Hunt replied severely that he himself could not and would not attempt an oil painting from 'such mere skeleton outlines'. Over the *Syracuse* sketches, which it will be remembered had been extremely successful, Hunt expounded his own extraordinary view: 'These you could easily paint in the open air without leaving England.' He claims that Lear, like a mesmerized rabbit, replied, 'Oh! I will do this at once! But I will want you to direct me!' That does look like what happened. Lear found a spot beyond Hastings 'with abundance of fig branches rooted in the fissures of the rock, with rooks in hundreds' which he used for Lord Beauchamp's *Syracuse*.

Hunt had found Clive Vale Farm, at Fairlight in conventional painter's country east of Hastings, and there Lear was invited to join him and Rossetti. Joshuah Cristall had made Hastings the Mecca of painters in 1807, as Farington records: 'a Host of Artists are preparing to go to Hastings'.³ William Collins (1788–1847) had spent a summer painting at Hastings in the autumn of 1816, and George IV ordered his *Hastings Prawn Fishers* in the 1820s. By 1827 he could offer *Ventnor*, *Niton* and *Freshwater Bay*: southern England was laid open by landscape painters some years before the convenient railway trains of the mid-century. Indeed Lear and Collins must have known each other already, since Collins was at Ischia and Naples in 1837–8.⁴ There was a moment of panic about privacy and pet dogs before Lear arrived in Clive Vale, but he laughed it off. Martineau did turn out to own a formidable Newfoundland, but Edward seems to have enjoyed the bohemian and youthful way of life, and spent his evenings happily 'penning out' and chatting away in Italian to Rossetti. Holman Hunt's main object was to finish his *Strayed Sheep*.

Hunt wrote that Edward 'exercised me in Italian and beat out new nonsense rhymes'. The older man was an enigma to him: at first sight he showed 'no sign of delicacy', yet he had only saved his health by living in Rome for thirteen years. Hunt agreed with Augustus Egg that travel was a mistake for painters, except for short trips *à la* Roberts, yet in the end he was the death of his first wife by insisting on a foreign expedition, and the story of his sad, ridiculous *Scapegoat* can be read at length in his memoirs. It was sketches worked up in studios he disliked, for dogmatic reasons. He wrote of David Wilkie that had he lived, his sketches would have turned out no use. He felt personally about Lear that on the one hand nothing daunted him, and on the other no man could be more fearful. 'He would rather be killed than fire a pistol or gun.' As for Lear's painting, he despised it. 'Lear is a very nice fellow, but much to live with always,' he wrote to a friend at the time, 'he is about forty. I am being drilled in Italian by him, and in return I am letting him see me paint, which from his productions I confess myself unable to feel is a very great advantage.' In the evenings Hunt would pontificate about technique, and Lear would take notes in a book he called *Ye Booke of Hunte*. He must have been embarrassed by it later, or else lost interest, because it has never been found. Hunt contributed his conspiracy theory of the Academy, where he came to feel for example that Millais was only elected in order to split up the Brethren, and some of this distrust rubbed off on Edward. Yet in 1855, the Life School included Egg, Frith, Leighton and Val Prinsep. One cannot quite dismiss even Victorian painting or the Academy itself with a generalization.

The worst thing Hunt did for Lear technically was to encourage his use of an astonishing blue colour for hills in the distance: the same obnoxious shade of blue may be seen in the *Scapegoat*'s mountains. He seems also to have slowed Lear down, and condemned him to awful drudgery painting cedar trees in the gardens of hotels in winter. They spoke with respect of Turner 'with his unpolished exterior and his direct and piquant speech'[5] but they had not seen his Folkestone notebook,[6] which would have blown Hunt's small portion of brains perhaps, and shown Lear exactly what he needed to be shown. One must assume that Pre-Raphaelite technique, based on the German Nazarenes, a lugubrious fellowship, satisfied a sense of guilt: painting must not be easy, it must be drudgery and intricate in detail, so that one comes to hate doing it.

Turner and Claude had painted light: but sunlight was generally attenuated and distant in the new style. Painters like Constable had said in the 1830s that art in England would die out: Uwins, who spoke of a 'radical' plot against the Academy,[7] recorded that 'Art in England (1833) has said its last dying speech. The sailor-king, the Reform Bill, and the real distress of the country have finished it.' In the same year people felt the same thing about poetry: Tennyson was a great poet of an unexpected kind, as Lear was an unexpected painter; one cannot blame the young Pre-Raphaelites for not recognizing him, because his modesty and his longing to be conventional deceived them.

One night the Pre-Raphaelites recorded how many stars they would award to the immortals, the greatest of the great. They gave four only to Christ. Why did Hunt, who had abandoned hope in immortality, persist in painting 'spiritual' subjects? Why did Dickens get so cross about a painting by Millais of the dove returning to the Ark? After Christ came Shakespeare and the author of the Book of Job, with three stars each, then a crowded two-star class of Homer, Dante, Chaucer, Leonardo, Goethe, Keats, Shelley, Alfred Tennyson, Landor, Thackeray, Washington and Browning. One can spot Rossetti's Italian liberal contributions, but Landor and Chaucer are surprises. Single stars went to Boccaccio, Fra Angelico, Mrs Browning, Patmore, Raphael and Longfellow: a list that makes little sense, into which people seem to have been relegated. The unstarred immortals are much funnier: they are Isaiah, Byron, Wordsworth, Haydon, Cervantes, Titian, Poussin, Milton, Poe, Hood and Leigh Hunt. The entire exercise is amazing chiefly for who was left out, including all Dutch and French painters whatsoever, Turner and all poets except those of the present or last generation, apart from Shakespeare and Chaucer. Holman Hunt and Edward Lear were both uneducated, of course, but this list recalls the ardours and daftness of the Sixth Form; its serious deficiency is not its omission of the entire art of music, since these are young painters, or of nearly the entire female sex, but their apparent ignorance of those painters who could have been of any use to them. Uwins had at least been conscious of Etty.

They were visited by Millais, by Thackeray and by Leech, and William Rossetti came to stay: he helped correct the proofs of the *Journal of a Landscape Painter in Southern Calabria*. Edward wrote in October to Mrs Tennyson, thanking her for an invitation to Twickenham that had misfired: he was too far away and detained by a friend's visit, but it meant he missed Hallam's christening. His letter[8] explains that he had been on the verge of writing anyway, about the Tennyson illustrations of which he had spoken to her. He stuttered and stammered about his scheme, which he divided into 124 'Suggestive and Positive' subjects in the two-volume 1842 *Poems*. He left out *In Memoriam* and *The Princess*. By suggestive he meant mood pictures like 'hateful is the dark blue sky', and by positive he meant the moated grange and so on. He wanted to send a list of the 124 lines. Later the number of these constantly varied, but it stuck in the end at roughly 200. He did not want to be a literal illustrator, as he was quick to point out later, probably in answer to some gruff remark of Alfred's. In January he was still at Hastings, 'but the fall of the ceiling of my lodgings put out all my calculations'. He wanted to show *Venosa*, *Reggio* and *Thermopylae* to W. Rossetti as paintings influenced by Holman Hunt. The *Thermopylae*, which is now at Bristol, has an intolerable bright blue range of mountains which I have disliked since I first saw it thirty years ago. The *Reggio* is in the Tate Gallery. Lear thought Holman Hunt's *Our English Coasts* (*Strayed Sheep*) was 'in its Way absolute perfection'. Those interested must consult it for themselves in the Tate: it appears to me terribly literal-minded as an ideal of painting, and to have led Edward Lear a long dance. He adds, still to Rossetti, his deepening disenchantment with the English weather. To Hunt he observes that the weather prevents one even seeing Nature, let alone painting it. The sheep in the foreground of his *Windsor Castle* had moved, and he thought he would be forced to buy a flock of them. Still, he had sold *Syracuse* for £250 and won Lord Beauchamp's Art Union Prize. 'I dare say that ninety-nine out of a hundred will blame and not praise the colour [of *Thermopylae*], 'how green! how blue! how queer!' but that pleased him, because it meant he was a Holman Hunt man.

Two hundred and fifty pounds for a picture might please Edward at forty-one, in June 1853, but there were higher prizes to be won. Old Collins, born of a mad mother and an Irish dealer, had first made sums like that at thirty-six, 200 guineas from Sir George Beaumont and 150 from George IV, but they were only a sign that his income would accelerate sharply, and within a few years he made 500 from Peel, and at forty-six in 1829 a sum total of £1233, the highest point his annual income ever reached. He was an averagely successful painter, 'not quick in perceiving a joke although always anxious to do so'. He was collected by three of the Baring family, Fuseli was his Keeper of the Academy Schools and Wilkie his fellow-student, and he was an RA. Edward must have hoped for an analogous success.

Once we have his diary, from 1858 on, we shall be able to monitor his income more exactly, but already it appears that in spite of his doubts and occasional fits of desperation, Edward was a not unsuccessful painter. His trouble was that he did not produce enough of his oil paintings, or did not do them quickly enough, to make a lot of money, and for that, as already mentioned, the Pre-Raphaelites were to blame. Water-colours made very little in comparison, and the pictures that are most valued today, the brilliant, immediate sketches, were probably not saleable in his lifetime; at any rate, they were not sold. His finished water-colours, worked up in the studio from these sketches, do sometimes fetch a lot of money today, as much as £18–20,000, but never more in his lifetime than £50 or so at the most. No doubt he would have said of this as of the deeper woes of man, 'By the time I am 42 I shall regard the matter with 42de I hope.'

He wandered about England searching for the exact equivalent to the background details his sketches had recorded in the more clement Mediterranean. He favoured some rocks in Leicestershire, some cedars in a hotel garden near London by the Thames, and so on, and incredible as it seems, little by little his paintings came together. At times he carted his own seven-foot canvases home to his lodgings when it rained, which it did twelve days out of fifteen. 'If I could only get the leaves done, and one little bit of fern, I could get the branches and rocks easily. But the leaves are falling fast. Meanwhile I pen out: and colour old sketches.' He remained affectionate with Holman Hunt, whom he would call Daddy, because he was twenty years younger but the father of the Brethren. Meanwhile Charles Church, who was tired of studying, invited Edward to come up the Blue Nile. *Bassae* was exhibited, and his musical setting of 'Tears, Idle Tears' and other songs by Tennyson went to the publisher. He referred to it as 'Tiers, idle tiers': parody was beginning to take over. He did go to Egypt, but the final plan was to go with Hunt and his young friend Seddon. At the last moment they were delayed, so Edward went on his own, in December 1853, but just before he left Cramer's had published 'Flow down, cold rivulet', 'Edward Gray', 'Tears, idle tears' and 'Wind of the western sea'.

They are all too effectively pathetic. Lear had composed them at the piano that summer, and from then on performed them constantly. Tait, the future Archbishop, heard them in a room full of grandees copiously weeping, and said, 'Sir! You should have half the Laureateship!' Even Alfred rather liked them, because they did not distort. Marianne North, the eccentric botanical painter whose *Recollections of a Happy Life* (1892) is one of the memorable pleasures of writing about Lear, recalls the summer of 1853; her father was a local MP, and Edward, who was there in search of fig trees,

> would wander into our sitting room through the windows at dusk when his work was over, sit down to the piano, and sing Tennyson's songs for hours, composing as he went on, and picking out the accompaniments by ear, putting the greatest expression and passion into the most sentimental words. He often set me laughing; then he would say I was not worthy of them, and would continue with intense pathos of expression and gravity of face, while he substituted Hey Diddle Diddle, the Cat and the Fiddle, or some other nonsensical words to the same air.

In 1858 he published five more, and, it is said, three in 1860: at least nine more appear to have been lost, and he set one Shelley song, 'O world O life O time'.[9] In a way all this musical material is part of his courtship ritual in pursuit of Tennyson. But the element of parody led to lyrics of his own, and the music led to music of his own: to the nonsense songs.

Although I have portrayed 1853 as a frustrating time, much of it had been happy. Frederick North, Marianne's father and owner of the fig tree in favour, had an elder daughter called Catherine who married J. A. Symonds, the son of a Clifton doctor. Symonds was homosexual, but his wife and daughters seem to have known and not cared much. He was the founder of the English colony at Davos, which he loved for the beauty of its Swiss guides. Mrs North, the MP's wife, had once been married to a Mr Shuttleworth of Gawthorpe Hall, Lancashire, and their daughter had married Sir James Kay (Shuttleworth). All three ladies were to play important parts in Edward's life. He loved Marianne and her eccentric and untaught pictures, Catherine was a kind of Sibyl to him, though they were both children when he met them, and Miss Kay Shuttleworth played a diabolical role in his old age. Yet that summer went by happily enough. Edward possessed a stuffed rook, which he would wire to the fig tree in a variety of positions and draw. No doubt, had he owned one, he would have done something similar with a Southdown sheep for the foreground of Windsor Castle.

By 1853 the life of Baring and still more of Chichester Fortescue differed widely from Edward Lear's. Fortescue's diary shows he was moving in more glamorous society, where he met Matthew Arnold, 'happy man going to be married' (May 1851) and in June, on stage, 'saw Montijo shewing her ancles' who would marry Napoleon III. He shared rooms with Lear's client Henry Grenfell, a Christ Church man and another MP. At Nuneham in August two men who were house guests dressed up as women and made mock of the Warden of All Souls, whom they deceived. In 1853 Fortescue noted that Lear was angry at a picture being badly hung at the Academy, 'nice fellow, and good company he is'. In June Fortescue first saw Tennyson: 'Shaggy looking fellow, smoked a clay pipe'. He duly recorded the separation of the Ruskins, young Lord Ribblesdale's elopement with Polly Fleming, an equestrienne at Astley's nine years Fortescue's junior, in whom he had an interest, and his own sister's engagement to the eccentric orientalist Urquhart.

Lear wrote in 1853 to Fortescue, who was in gloom over what he felt could never be a love affair, '*I* don't mean to marry, never, – *you* should – but there's time enough yet for you – six or eight years perhaps.' He was wrong about Fortescue, who after many years in the humiliating position of constant attendant knight to a dazzling but slightly older Jewish lady, finally contrived to marry her and was happy ever after, and wrong about himself, since he proposed twice to the same girl, only she refused him. His rationalization was:

> In my case I should paint less and less well, and the thought of annual infants would drive me wild. If I attain to 65, and have an 'establishment' with lots of spoons etc. to offer, I *may* chain myself, but surely not before. And alas! and seriously, when I look around my acquaintance, and few men have more, or know more intimately, do I see a majority of happy pairs? No, I don't. Single, I may have few pleasures, but married, many risks and miseries are semi-certainly in waiting . . .

However that may have been, *Thermopylae* had been widely praised at the spring exhibition at the British Institution, and what tormented Lear about the rooks or jackdaws and the rocks was only how the shadows fell. In spring he was out of the lodgings where the ceiling had fallen, and in 65 Oxford Terrace. Richard Bethell, later Lord Westbury, an ambitious, abrasively dogmatic man, had bought a picture from him. Bethell became Lord Westbury as Lord Chancellor, but Lear's interest seems to have focused on his daughter Augusta or Gussie. When she grew up it was to her that he proposed, but she was not born until 1858, and the gap of forty-six years between them was never overcome. She was the great-aunt of one of my dearest friends. Edward suffered a good deal from Lord Westbury, and so, among others, did Jowett of Balliol, but this vignette fixes him.

'Speaking of Undique sequaces, and sequax,' he said, 'Let us remember the line and go and look for the translation,' but Lear said, 'My Lord, I can remember it easily by thinking of wild ducks.' 'How of wild ducks, Lear?' 'Because they are sea-quacks,' said I. 'Lear,' said his lordship, 'I abominate the forcible introduction of ridiculous images, calculated to distract the mind from what it is contemplating.'

He squashed Jowett by rolling out some early Byron from his forensic breast and saying 'Match *that* if you can, from your Miss Alfred Tennyson'.

Lear had tried and failed to lure Alfred down to Clive Vale Farm for Sunday lunch. The expedition to Cornwall with Frank Lushington was supposed to forward the illustrations, and he sent a cartoon of some brilliance of Seaford and the White Cliffs of Eastbourne with Napoleon III swimming crossly towards England. Apart from all his other talents, he was the best and funniest cartoonist of his generation. But his reports of progress with *Venosa* and *Reggio* were weary. 'Thermopylae stands still and Syracuse is shut up in a barn.' This is addressed to Emily Tennyson as usual, because she answered nearly all Alfred's letters and Edward's intimacy grew with her proportionately. In 1852 he was planning a visit, but the route was not obvious. He was told to try Alfriston (which is inland) or Lullington, and drew himself with an umbrella parachute crossing the coast. It was Leicester in October that finished him. He had been away from London, he said, 'shut up in a filthy wet valley – too swampy even for a postman'. He missed an invitation which would have included meeting Charles Tennyson.

> Stay here I *won't*, to be demoralized by years of mud and fog and gnats and rheumatism and small beer and stupid boors and coal fires and cholera morbusses and income taxes and Calvinists and steel forks and humbugs and midnight atmospheres all the year round. I have had enough of it, and forthwith I am growing moustaches, the sign of going elsewhere. I mean (seriously) to go with any liberal minded and liberally paying traveller who will take me as Artist abroad – Nanking, Hobart Town, Spain, or Timbuctoo.

What oft was felt, but ne'er so well expressed.
He sent the songs before he left, by Frank Lushington, whose appearance at Leicester sessions had been one small relief of his weeks among the rocks. 'You will be sorry to hear that my lungs and throat are so much worse that I am going off at once to see the Palms and Temples of the South.' The quotation from Alfred tactfully leaves out 'see before

I die', but I think death was in Edward's mind. 'I wish I could see you, but I shall wait to see my friends with comfort in heaven, for in England is none for me.' He had to go whether he could afford it or not, whether it served his career or not. That is how he got stuck with young Seddon in Cairo, and went up the Nile on his own. Seddon waited for Holman Hunt, but they are another story. Luckily, being abroad, Edward wrote to Ann regularly. He so identifies with her that he writes as if he were for a moment her elder sister. One may well ask why they never lived together, but there is no clear answer, except a hint that 'it would not have done', and the fact that a brief experiment put them both off it.

This time Lear took a steam-boat called the *Indus* by way of Gibraltar. From time to time a mist appears to swirl around him. In January 1854 he reported to his sister from the Nile:

> Girgeh ... a tumbly down place and so dusty ... Bellianeh is charming! such exquisite palms, such curious towers, built for pigeons! ... The sky was all in broad stripes of lilac, green, rose, and amber ... at times the ground was almost blue and grey with clouds of pigeons; the most beautiful little plovers and kingfishers hop just before my feet ... Did you go to see the panorama of Mexico in Leicester Square? – do if you didn't.

He loved Kasr el Saad, which years later became one of his most thrilling pictures. 'Imagine immense cliffs, quite perpendicular, about as high as St Paul's, of yellow stone – rising from the most exquisite meadows all along the river, while below them are villages almost hidden in palms ... It is one of the most beautiful spots in the world.' He got as far as Philae, where he stayed a week, 'more like a real *fairy island* than anything else', and the river buzzed with English boats. He did not like the Nubians, though, because they stank of castor oil and had rings in their noses. He wrote to Ann again, from Zermatt in August, on holiday with Husey Hunt, and finding the landscape very demanding and laborious (like a good Pre-Raphaelite). He wrote a dutiful pathetic letter to Lord Derby saying he was obliged to stay and die quietly in England, since an annual trip to Egypt was too expensive. Mary Howitt remembers that he advised poor Seddon where to find English equivalents of exotic rocks and trees. A few years later there would be photographs. A few years earlier, before there were railways, you could make a living as an itinerant drawing master. By February 1855 London had made him ill again.

'I have not cut off my beard, and now that half London wears moustaches it is not remarkable ... Oh my, ain't it cold. I think I will shortly cut off my legs and die like a disastrous old caterpillar.' This to Henry Bruce, with a fetching cartoon of himself doing so. The winter had not been profitable either: in June he wrote to Edmund Lushington that he had £157 10s., 'only think of that! So I shall spend the seven pounds ten in larx'. He house-hunted for the Tennysons in Sussex, because they wanted to buy their house, Farringford, in the Isle of Wight, but feared they could not. Emily wrote bursting with love and gratitude for Alfred, 'a love tried by all the changes and chances of a five years' marriage, and tried only to prove its unimagined worth more and more'. She sent Edward a private copy of the still unpublished 'Courage, poor heart of stone'. He complained to Alfred of his own waste of time and talent. He could not stay in country houses and not be idle. 'Do you think there is a Pharmouse or a Nin somewhere near you, where there would be a big room looking to the North? So that I could paint a pipkin or a mackerel?' There are numerous notes about failures to meet, far commoner before the age of telephones, and an account of a London cab being smashed into by a brewer's dray. But they did meet, of course, and Lear's letter of thanks to Emily for 16–20 October 1855 still exists. He recalled Farringford day and night, 'even to the plate of mushrooms, then Hallam and Lionel come in, and when they are gone, you and Alfred and Frank begin to talk like the gods together careless of mankind'. She recommended a thick plaster of flour and honey on the chest, which did her and Alfred a lot of good.

He felt he might take a room in Boxley near the Lushingtons in his old age. He compared the boat from Yarmouth to Lymington to his last with Frank, from Lepanto to Patras: 'F went on to the Bouchiers, – I homeward, – or, more truly to speak, to my empty lodgings where 3 chairs the coalscuttle and a table are the prevailing furniture'. Is there not an undertone of the Yonghy-Bonghy-Bo? His affection was more pressing and therefore more burdensome than he intended, and his loneliness was apparent. Still, by the time he wrote that, he was off to Corfu: 'a new beginning of life, but is made much pleasanter than I had believed it possible by help from others, as to commissions for drawings'. Frank was going out as a judge, and Edward was to keep him company. Frank's nephew (and Mrs Tennyson's) had just died at the age of thirteen, and in August his brother Henry had died in Paris, on the way home with a fever from his job in Malta. Their Cambridge friend G. S. Venables was with him, but Frank had arrived too late. There was a question now of Ellen Lushington going out to keep house for Frank, but she did not go in the end. It sounds as if Edward had agreed to go with Frank and look after him, although if so it is not clear with whom he had negotiated. No doubt the answer may be Emily Tennyson, or Frank himself. When the pair of bachelors found themselves alone on the island of Corfu, Edward gave evidence of hurt feelings to his diary of a kind he never otherwise admitted to having. They include some sense of an undertaking on his part which must now be gone through with, and a sense of a broken agreement.

We are lucky that he felt at ease to explode to Emily Tennyson. He did so at full length over an experience that often happened but which he does not usually recall with such freedom. He had been to church at Stoke Newington with the Nevills. It was a full dress parade of Victorian hypocrisy at its worst, and he foamed with fury. His cartoons of the congregation are more envenomed and funnier than the ones he used to draw of the people in the parrot house at the Zoo. The organ was out of tune and ill-played, the hymns sixteen verses long, all beginning with 'Jesus', the clerk snuffled, the church was draughty, the sermon was three-quarters of an hour on the Athanasian Creed. That Creed was one of Lear's pet hates, and anyone who thinks this is eccentric of him should read the shocking document. It is a relief to know that he could rely on Emily Tennyson's agreement. After dinner the family went to church again, while Edward walked alone beside the reservoir: 'and going too near those rabid swans they pursued me until I was fain to jump a ditch and of course jumped in.'

On 16 September 1855 at Dudbrook, one of his friend Lady Walde-grave's houses, Fortescue recorded Lear in low spirits,

> but sang some of his Tennyson songs. It is curious to see how much Lady Waldegrave likes him. He said how much he liked her and spoke of her utter naturalness, her truthfulness, her kindness. He spoke to me more of himself, his secret feelings, than he has ever done, showed me a good deal of his great and self-tormenting sensitiveness. We got upon women. I said I knew nothing of women for the last four years and more, literally nothing, which interested him very much. I told him something of my feelings. He was most affectionate and understood my devotion. I asked him if he understood her incredible fascination. He said, 'Yes I do. I find when I look at her myself sometimes that I can't speak.'

Then on 9 October, 'Sat some time with Lear, very delicate, going to Corfu. Lent him £50, poor old fellow.' Fortescue belonged to another world from Lear's, decent as he was, and the diaries show the contrast. He was active in politics, cheerful and cool; his rival in love was Lord

Newcastle, whom they went to visit by water from Strawberry Hill to Pembroke Lodge, Richmond: 'Harcourt steered, I pulled.' It was a world Lear could enter and in which people would be pleased to see him, in their relaxed way, but he could not live in it, and in the end it frightened him, or he was too poor, or he preferred his work. Fortescue was a good friend to him all the same, and so was he to Fortescue: they both wrote charming letters.[10]

Some time that autumn, when the wind was in the east and Lear had lost his singing voice, he dined in London with Lady Waldegrave, for years the beacon star of Fortescue's existence. He hastened to report to his friend how much he had enjoyed it. Her 'perfectly natural and kind manner' delighted him. She was a great hostess by this time, having become a Countess by her second marriage (first to a bastard Waldegrave, then to the Earl), and acquired some ruinous houses including Horace Walpole's Strawberry Hill, but then a large amount of money by her third marriage to the elderly, socially acceptable George Harcourt, son of the Archbishop of York, who made her mistress of Nuneham Park near Oxford, was a liberal, complaisant husband, and let her entertain and redecorate, which she did with verve. After thirteen years she married Fortescue, just as the Tennysons had married after thirteen years; her father had been a Jewish musician, famous in his day, her brother was a singer, her niece became Lady Strachey (later Strachie), but she and Fortescue and all her other husbands were childless. Few of the letters between Edward Lear and Chichester Fortescue have survived from the early 1850s, though they were certainly writing to each other. In February 1855, Fortescue paid £23 for a small water-colour of Civitella di Subiaco, where all in all one may say that Lear first found himself as a painter. 'I think your room looks extremely pretty – and the Pigchr is stunning as it hangs now.' Edward's letter ends[11] with an extraordinary series of childish jokes including the one every child knows as Why need you never starve at the seaside? Because of the *sand which is there*, and the limerick of the old man who said, 'How shall I flee from this terrible cow? I will sit on this stile and continue to smile – which may soften the heart of that cow'. That summer, Lear published the second edition of his limericks, this time all in one volume, but they did not make him much, and he gave a lot of copies away.

CHAPTER NINE

CORFU

IN A SENSE it was only now that Lear came into his own, since it was only now that he was living or at least lodging in a magical Greek island. But he was better at travelling, and happier moving, than he was at lodging: and then Corfu was far to the north, opposite modern Albania, and its winter was severe. It was Philae in Nubia or Upper Egypt he had called a 'fairy island': it was sunshine rather than antique, buried architecture that excited him. Corfu was a British dependency, and he took an imperial line about the local Greeks, as he would have done about the Maltese in Malta. He did not really think the British had done anything much for Corfu, as he confessed to Leake in a letter, they had let it lie fallow or run backwards. Still, he was there because he might sell his works to the British colony, as he had done in Rome and as others did in Malta, and came home to do the same in the summer. It would be a base for further expeditions, and he could usefully offer his company to Frank Lushington. His residence in Corfu from 1855 until the Ionian Islands were handed over to the independent Greek government in 1864 entered deeply and subtly into him all the same, and marked him as what he was, as his years in Italy and Switzerland did not; the fruit of those nine or ten years in his painting was abundant and beautiful.

His *Bassae*, which had been in the Academy Exhibition in 1855, dated back to his first journey with Fortescue, and his next Greek subject there, *Megaspelion*, which was not hung until 1873, dated from that same time. His Corfu subjects began to appear in numbers as soon as he had settled down, from 1856 onwards. The first four were sold to Lady Reid, the Governor's wife, to Robert Drewitt, his childhood friend from Sussex who was in Corfu for a time, and two to a general. Next year eight out of nine pictures were Greek, and in 1858 nine out of seventeen were Greek or Albanian, their rivals being Palestinian. His contentment in the scenery and light of Corfu is visible in the way he luxuriates in the olive groves, in his more contented, less dramatic mountains and cliffs, and in the way what had been exotic becomes to him familiar and domestic. The lithographic and tremendously fearsome cliffs of Suli seem now to belong to another, demonic world. Whenever he revisited England, Pre-Raphaelitism would be an influence, not just in the white ground of his paintings but in the stultifying search for equivalent details to decorate his foreign scenes, as the Leicestershire rocks and the tortoise from the Zoo decorated his *Bassae*, but in Corfu he was free. Lear and Lushington travelled out through Trieste together. In Prague the snow began to fall; in Vienna, which Alfred Tennyson would never visit because his friend Hallam had died there, it had already fallen, and the city lay white under the moonlight. All the same, the crossing of the Alps was easier by the railway over Semmering than it would be for 100 years by any other route. 'Nothing can be so kind and thoughtful as my dear friend all the way,' Edward wrote to Ann, 'making me take food when I did not care to leave the carriage, by buying cakes or bread and bringing them to me, and saving me all the trouble possible, although he, from being my mere travelling-companion in 1848–9, has now risen to one of the very highest places in the land at the age of thirty-three.' Lushington's position was indeed highly responsible, since the Greeks are not only good natural arguers and by temperant habitual litigants, but in Corfu had long enjoyed the subtleties of Italian justice, and remembered the French system as well. Lear arrived in Corfu when the coinage had Queen Victoria on one side and what looked like the lion of St Mark, only with a British crown, on the other. The governing city of the Ionian Islands was a small, provincial place bustling with provincial politics and all the intrigues that sprouted from a Governor's court.

Edward wrote to Ann on 13 December: 'At the beginning of June I expect you will see me back in England: and, excepting that my health is so much better already, you will be surprised to hear that I have even now several times wished myself back again, or rather that I had never come.' Corfu had altered utterly, because the Crimean War meant it had to be garrisoned with militia regiments instead of regulars, and since the new officers were county gentlemen, and the men often their tenants, all the available houses in Corfu were full of wives and families, whereas regulars would have lived in barracks. Lear had been lucky to get something at £24 for the six months. He felt utterly alone, and begged for letters, because he already knew that he would see very little of Lushington, who was going to be extremely busy. He rode out only for an hour in the afternoon, his house was unsatisfactory, so he was lodging in Bowen's palace. The reader of letters and memoirs of these days can trace Bowen's irresistible rise in status and position in a series of Byzantine moves, which Edward finally understood too late; at this point it is enough to notice that every move surrounding Bowen, who appeared to be all smiles, was exactly weighed and calculated. His intention at the time was to be Governor. 'In the evenings they go out to various official parties, and would gladly introduce me anywhere, but in the rainy weather one must have a carriage, and that costs a dollar each time.' Lear did not like balls, of which there were three a week, and felt shy of the etiquette of the Lord High Commissioner's (Governor's) court. There were no (English) newspapers or daily post and no one dropped in casually. 'I sit at home all day, almost unable to paint for very dejection.' This strange relapse into the infantile did not last, of course, but it underlies much of his gloom: he simply could not bear to feel so out of things.

The expense of sending out all his possessions and of furnishing his rooms also depressed him deeply. 'I suffered much from loneliness in Egypt, but then I had a never ending fund of novelty and excitement which kept such distress at bay ... If Ellen Lushington had come out and if they had a home, my days would have gone by in hopes of having someone to speak to in the evening.' He thought of nipping across to Brindisi and going to Rome after Christmas. He describes his way of life on the other hand as rather attractive. His servant made him toast and coffee, he had started three 'small subjects' at which he painted, at twelve he was taught Greek for an hour by a tutor who called, then sometimes he went for lonely walks among the lovely olives, and at dusk he had a half-crown dinner sent 'from the Mess', he ate alone and went to bed early. Then he suddenly adds,

> Today is so lovely and bright that I hope to go out to Chinopiastes and draw the view thence from among some immense orange trees, COVERED with golden fruit ... The beauty of the villages here is something not to be described, and I should certainly like to do one or two large paintings of Corfu – for no place in all the world is so lovely I think. The whole island is in undulations from the plain where the city is,

to the higher hills on the west side; and all the space is covered with one immense grove of olive trees – so that you see over a carpet of wood wherever you look . . .

But he must turn his thoughts to a painting of Philae; no doubt it was the one commissioned by Tennyson's neighbour, Sir John Simeon.

In February 1856 he wrote to Fortescue, apologizing for the grumbles and gloom of earlier letters, now lost. 'I still think of making Corfu my headquarters, and of painting a large picture here of the Ascension *festa* in June, for 1857 Exhibition, and of going over to Yannina and other Albanian abstractions.' It must be more than chance that neither of these indicates precisely a pure landscape. The *festa* would be a popular subject and it was the sort of scene many English painters had done in Italy; with figures perhaps he felt there was safety in numbers. It was the best winter for weather for nearly thirty years. 'When I get a house you *must* come out and have a run, and I'll put you up: I'll feed you with Olives and wild pig; and we'll start off to Mount Athos.' Balls were nearly over because of Lent; dinners persisted 'though I am soon going to back out of all'. He wished he could see Holman Hunt, who he heard was going to see Tennyson; he needed the company of an artist. Lushington would more or less do, but 'his work is tremendously heavy, and when he gets any leisure, he rides or yachts or shoots . . . I *did* ride all last Saturday for a wonder, and wish I had tin to keep a horse'. He asks for any message there may be for Lady Kozziris, whose husband had been an official in Smyrna. The name is a first indication of an intimacy Lear came to feel with that family's daughters, particularly Helen, to whom he all but proposed. Perhaps he really did so. Fortescue had commissioned another picture, but over that Lear dithered. In the end he painted a copy of Sir John Simeon's *Philae* at sunset.

He was now treating Emily Tennyson rather than Ann like his mother; he even attempted through her to get Frank Lushington a place in which that sternly intellectual man might be happier. He was frightfully busy, he could barely take two hours a day for exercise, he had six cases to read between nine and five, and of course he felt lonely. As Lear justly put it, 'he has become 70 and I have stuck at twenty'. Lushington said of Lear that he had 'a face partly of Socrates, partly of Sir John Falstaff'. Edward reported to Emily quite fully, even about the standard of food, and about Bowen's cunning marriage to the President's daughter, which made him kin to other grand Levantine families. In October he wrote from quarantine in Corfu on his return from Athos.

He had been two months on the mountain and at Troy on the mainland opposite, from which Athos is visible at sunset. Quarantine was only a five days' sentence, because of a rumour of cholera at Istanbul. He knew, though, that he had brought back drawings of unique value. To Emily he burst out about the wickedness and perversity of monasteries, which he found he hated, as a liberal humanist and equally as a Protestant Christian. The Sultan had recently confirmed the privileges and immunities of the monks for £1500 a year. Lear saw twenty big monasteries 'and perhaps 5 or 600 small hermitages or chapel-cottages holding one or two or more of the fish and water-melon eating prayer muttering old creatures who vegetate there'. He had brought away for Emily one of the little wooden crosses they carved. His servant was Giorgis Kokalis, from a refugee family from Souli from before Byron's time, one of many in Corfu. Giorgis had previously been years in service with a General Conyers and luckily knew Albanian as well as Greek and a little English, which made him specially useful to Lear. He had been very ill and nearly died on the expedition.

Lear was conscious of his opportunity in the landscape of Athos, and the precise delineation of its topography. His series of drawings exist in many versions, some extremely beautiful, but the series that impressed me most deeply was that of the black sketches made when he was dying, all of which are at Harvard. They are like a complete lifework, and they include an ingredient of desperation or of terror. Some of the places he drew are now ruins, none of them can ever be recaptured as they were then in their full vigour, yet they have never been reproduced.

> I never saw any more striking scenes than those forest screens and terrible crags, all lonely, lonely, lonely: paths through them leading to hermitages where these dead men abide, -- or to the immense monasteries where many hundred of these living corpses chant prayers nightly and daily: the blue sea dash against the hard iron rocks below -- and the oak fringed or chestnut covered height above, with always the great peak of Athos towering over all things, and beyond all the island edged horizon of wide ocean.

The invective gathers force: 'Many of these men are more than half foolish: they murmur and mutter and mop and mow.' It turns out from a letter to Fortescue that Lear had fallen down a flight of nineteen steps just before leaving for Athos and hurt his back, and was in considerable pain the whole time. Once he has warmed up he lets loose with a fine sentence about 'these muttering, miserable, mutton-hating, man-avoiding, misogynic, morose and merriment-marring, monotoning, many-mule-making, mocking, mournful, minced-fish and marmalade masticating Monx. Poor old pigs! Yet one or two were kind enough in their way, dirty as they were . . .' Fortescue answered with encouragement, but it is feeble stuff after Lear on Athos. His temper was sorely tried by old Lady Ormonde saying that she wondered how an old man could write such nonsense as *Maud*. And after the volcanic eruption over the holy mountain, in which landscape washes over into morals and then into humour, Edward also reverted to his everyday annoyances, which can at times be as irritating to the readers as the anxieties of an invalid with whom one lives too closely, and yet which are somehow a part of the matrix of his humour, his deep sadness and his lyrical leaps of heart: a part, that is, of what makes him one of the most brilliant and most rewarding of his generation at this time.

There was an earthquake while he was in quarantine, so he left the Palazzo Curcumelli, where his rooms became uninhabitable, and moved in next door to Frank. 'I never saw him so well, and could he but be married this would after all be the right place for him.' His feelings about Frank had a second wind, because Frank had at last been able to express himself (by letter) about his own state and about his brother Edmund's health, matters on which Edward had complained he was notably tight-lipped. Meanwhile, Edward wrote eight closely written folio pages to Ann. He needed the replies and he needed to write his letters, sometimes twenty of them a day. The 'if he could be married' about Frank Lushington may well refer back to conversations about him with Mrs Tennyson, and surely interprets something said in the rare letter of self-expression. It also fits Edward's thoughts about himself. On 9 August 1857, at Nuneham, Fortescue recorded, 'I have sat with old Lear both nights, he in low spirits, longing for sympathy which means a woman. As we drove away Lear said (of Lady Waldegrave), "Well, I can understand a man raving about her."' In 1856 he had been raving to Emily Tennyson about Helen Cortazzis as the perfect Tennyson scholar, but meaning all that phrase could imply in emotion about a Tennysonian heroine.

He spent the winter of 1856 working to seven evening after evening at his *Athos* drawings. He seems always to have known that they were in a way his masterpiece. He left Corfu on 19 May for Trieste, skating over a sea like a looking-glass under a cloudless sky. 'If the coals had been better and not so small – which made everything very dirty – the whole voyage would have been faultless. Notwithstanding all that, however, you know I always suffer from the shaking of a steam vessel, and I sometimes think, all the more so when it is calm.' All the same, he was calmly proposing to adventure in another ship to Venice, then to Milan, and over the St Gothard to Lucerne, and by railway to Basle and Paris. He found Trieste a fine great bustling modern city compared to Corfu. He had lived in Condi Terrace which, to judge from a drawing he made later for Lady Reid, was a fine building, but inside it was horribly noisy. When he got to Venice he hated that for its filthy smells and its unstable gondolas. Somehow the cult of art there annoyed him too. He took a vehemently Protestant attitude to the *Presentation of Christ in the Temple*, with Italian buildings and Doges' and senators' dresses: 'fibs is fibs – wrapped up in pretty colour or not'. Then, just as one is losing one's temper with him, he says, 'Ma'am, if this paper hath a crinkly and antique appearance, it fell into the water yesterday', and worries about a two-inch baby tortoise which has hidden itself in the candle-snuff. The water has, I suppose, made him think of Caliban, who had 'a most antique and fish-like smell'. The two little tortoises got safely to England in spite of many adventures; one was for his godson Allen Nevill. In that year Lear could first read the Bible in Greek, and first sold a painting to Sir John Potter of Manchester, a rich man who pondered openly on whether to 'take up' pictures or to 'take up' orchids.

It was the letter to Fortescue of January 1857 that tells us of Lear's arrangements in Condi Terrace ('or more properly, Bastione'), for which he paid £6 a month to a certain Scarpa. He had a studio thirty feet long with three windows looking north-north-east, and a smaller library or sitting-room behind it. A room half that size and a third of the studio size was his exhibition room, and his bedroom was like his sitting-room. The rest of the space was his servant's room, spare room, and so on. A Major Shakespeare, who in the end bought the camera Lear had been using experimentally at this time, lived overhead. Lushington lived next door, then the Cortazzi, and the Parson on one side, and Colonel Gage and Sir James Reid, the other Justice, on the other. Members of the Council of the Ionian Isles held this position of Chief Justice in rotation. Lear hoped for 100 guineas for a big picture of Corfu, which he would sell in England (to an MP called Evans), but meanwhile Lord Drogheda and various other peers had visited his exhibition room in Corfu. The Governor, Sir John Young, knew Fortescue, and wrote to him how he liked his friend Lear, and how Lady Young was taking up painting in his wake. She is memorable for her old-fashioned pronunciation, awnges (her friend Lady Reid called them oinges).

In London, Lear took a Stew-jew, as he called it, at 15 Stratford Place with the Hansens as usual. As he left for Trieste he felt his big picture needed Holman Hunt's advice, and 'two months of cropping and thought'. He had been going east, apparently, but 'Clive did not come, he stood for Derbyshire and failed.' It is only on stray occasions that one catches a glimpse of his entangled journeys, his dependence on friends as patrons of each one, and his unrelenting, labyrinthine ambition to cover at least the whole Mediterranean.

In England he fulfilled an old ambition to visit Fortescue at home in Ardee. Fortescue was Under-Secretary for the Colonies from 1857 to 1858, and again from 1859 to 1865, and only later Chief Secretary for Ireland, but Ireland was always his real home. His aunt, Mrs Ruxton of the Red House, Ardee, loved him greatly, his brother was a peer and a power in the land. Lear adored Mrs Ruxton, and 'never saw a better house than Lord Clermont's'. He knew this brother and his wife in Rome before he ever met Chichester Fortescue. Now he was delighted with Irish turns of speech, about whether the Scientific Association meeting was over, for example, 'Indeed and it isn't, but the strength of it is pretty well broken,' and the old lady who was told she ought not to grumble against God, being so well off, 'Sure and doesn't he take it out of me in Corns.' He loved the habit of calling after his friend in the street, 'Mimber!', which Lear adopted. He would paint all day until six and then walk for an hour with his friend before dinner. Looking back on this happy house in October, he could not remember being so happy himself for a long time. The only faint shadow was worry over a brother-in-law serving in India, near Benares, during the Mutiny. He died the following year.

It was while Lear was at Ardee, so contentedly observing the old aunt of eighty-five at her county business and country business and parish business, so cheerfully painting, and so pleased with Chichester Fortescue for company, that his old friend Robert Hornby died; it had been a friendship too intimate to explain, too strong and longstanding to do without or to replace. Edward found himself reduced to reading his favourite bits of *In Memoriam*, and one night he and Fortescue read the whole poem through together. All the same, Edward was thrilled by Ireland on this visit, with Newcastle, County Down, and Captain Finch's Tullamore, 'full of beautiful ruins and bridges and trees and roads and mills and hills and lawns and laurels'. He sent a stream of letters afterwards, one in Greek which, whether it is Lear's spelling (I suspect) or Lady Strachey's transcription that was faulty, makes extremely queer reading. To judge by Lear's diary, one would be inclined to blame him, and Lady Strachey does so. He has such difficult habits as writing upside down. But Lady Strachey reads *Kyrios* (Mister) as Son of Cyrus: so between them the letter is even queerer and funnier than Edward could have intended.

On the way back to Corfu, he got a wrong ticket and also his train smashed into another one. The pain in his back went on right across Europe. Lady Somers told him on the boat that she and Coutts Lindsay had landed on Athos, and lived there for two months in tents, 'various mucilaginous monks coming now and then to see them'. From Paris Edward went to Heidelberg, where he stopped to see the Bunsens (former ambassador) and then read his way through Frankfurt, Dresden and Prague ('Have you read Charlotte Brontë? It is very curious and interesting') and so to Vienna. German railways were already far better than English ones. Lear spent time at Vienna with young Robert Morier (ambassador to Russia 1884–93) and 'talked of Tennyson, Pattledom, Strawberry Hill and all kinds of things; nor was a very good dinner and wine an item of my visit to be left unnotified'. In this letter, Edward has taken on a sophisticated tone, he is at home internationally, Pattledom is his washpot, and over Strawberry Hill, in its amazing Victorian revival of grandeur, he has cast his shoe. He sailed from Trieste on the *Jupiter*, 'my man Giorgio' came down to meet him, Lushington had him to dinner that night, Sir James Reid the next, the 46th Mess for the next, the Youngs for the next. He complained, of course, most bitterly. He could not stand the pianos on each side, one above and one below, 'and you can neither study nor think, nor even swear properly by reason of the proximity of the neighbours'. The Cortazzi had gone and the officers were mostly new. He missed a drawing friend who had disappeared. 'I vow I never felt more shockingly alone than the two or three nights I have stayed in.' He was forty-five and sleeping badly with painful indigestion.

> I think I *must* have a piano: that may do me good. But then I remember Miss Hendon over my head has one, and plays jocular jigs continually. Then what the devil can I do? Buy a baboon and parrot and let them rush around the room? I know nothing. I still hold to going to Palestine if possible . . . If Helen Cortazzi had been here it would have been useless to think of not asking her to marry me.

His 1857 letter to Lady Reid,[1] to 13 Royal Parade, Cheltenham, was to console her for absence from her husband, and Lear treats her with careful charm: it is obvious that he had a strong feeling for the wives and daughters of his friends. Perhaps Lady Waldegrave, and Mrs Ruxton, and Lady Davy and his sister Ann had taught him more than we expect of a bachelor of his age. He writes now only to soothe her, and to assure her that all Corfu sees her husband's happiness when her letters come, to tell her how highly he thinks of her husband, and how they all miss her. 'Although he talks about Bachelor's fare, you may guess that the dinners are as nice as possible – not to speak of Leek soup, fig-puddings and other delicacies.' He complains of his own life only in general terms; he hopes to see an old friend for a month, 'which will make Corfu seem less a prison perhaps than it often does'. On Sundays he goes for long walks with Lushington and then dines with him: he says the same about him he has said to others except that his health is so much better he is now unrecognizable. Had Lushington had some kind of breakdown at the time of his leaving England? As for Lear, he is now tied to remaining in Corfu by his big canvases. In this letter he goes over the whole ground of Corfu from every point of view but a painter's, including how he now sees through the appalling Bowen. Even when he does write visual letters, as under pressure of fine weather he may, it does not sound like what he would paint: '. . . cloudless glory, for seven long days and nights. Anything like the splendour of olive-grove and orange-green, the blue of sky and ivory of church and chapel, the violet of mountain, rising from peacock wing-hued sea, and tipped with lines of silver snow, can hardly be imagined.'[2]

It may be that the New Year of 1858 was particularly terrible for Edward Lear because of his age both as a man and as an artist. One is not usually conscious of such a crisis – the male menopause as it is called – in one's own case, at least until it is over. But Edward was perfectly conscious of himself, indeed he was so to an unnatural degree, if only because he kept an introspective and absolutely honest diary. In 1858, when its surviving volumes begin, whatever happened is going on at full blast, but it may much more likely be that only the diary makes us think so. And then, which is the true picture, Edward in low spirits chatting at night with Fortescue, Edward at work, perhaps out of doors, Edward making friends happy for a few hours they never forget, or planning his journeys and recording their comedy, or is it this despairing man in the diary, showing by what titanic efforts he survives and improves? I do not hazard an answer, although Mrs Tennyson or maybe his sister Ann could have given one. The difficulty for a biographer is that it is very hard to record what Lear writes in the diaries without giving it really too much weight, as if a diary were the judgment of God or a final truth. But we know that it is not, and indeed his mood varies.

Jan. 1. The same perfectly clear and very cold weather. Rose at 5.30. Papadopoulos (tutor) came at 6. 8 breakfast. Pasting together the bits of the big Corfu picture . . . Lushington in for a moment. A little later came a wholesome and delightful letter from C. F., a vast and unexpected comfort . . . Perhaps the happiest New Year's day passed for a long time. The more every moment can be occupied the better. The Hendersons above me had a dance, but I was not much annoyed by it, only a sort of earthquaky bustly movement one was conscious of until sleep came.

Jan. 2. Pasting the Cartoon of the Corfu picture. But I had somehow resolved to go to S. Demetrios and draw a bit of rock with Mount S. Giorgio behind. So at 11, – I could not get out before, – off I set. What lots of turkeys come in at this time. There was some cloud today, but it was very bright, and ice was in all the ditches. A pull up to St D, after that I lost my way and had a particularly tough haul to the place . . . dinner and Melkisedeck's pipe.

Sun. Jan. 3. There came a note from L. Mrs Cortazzi is dead, she died in Paris. I went alone and walked round by the marshes. It snowed a little and was very cold. Thousands of turkies going in to be eaten . . . dined L. Nothing known but the fact. Poor afflicted Helena and Madeline! the poor old father! By very hard talking I kept myself alive – but later the miserable self-wrapped manner of L and his dead silence irritated me too much to bear well . . . I came away at 10. I really think it would be far better to avoid meeting so frequently. I was going to invite him to dine tomorrow his birthday but in some parenthesis he said he was going to shoot in Albania.

Jan. 4. Somehow I did nothing all this day. Had bookshelves put up . . . At 2 L called, but anything sadder and more unsatisfactory than his visit could not be. As for me I went out at 3 and saw the downfall of the Bastion and went up by the olives to the Ascension.

Jan. 5. Rose at 5.30. Greek till 8. Worked irregularly and suddenly came to awful grief $\overset{*}{1}\overset{*}{2}\overset{*}{3}$ [Each of these signs means an epileptic spasm numbered from zero each month]

Jan. 6. Greek Christmas day . . . Worked harder than usual.

Jan. 7. Very cold and cloudy all day. The coldest day I have known at Corfu. Wind very sharp. Painted at Lord C's Athos. Whiles badly, at other times better. By fits wrote Greek exercises and letter. Walked out to the one gun battery and back. Exceedingly cold, with a canopy of grey snowy cloud.

Jan. 8. Indian news. Havelock dead.

Jan. 9. Gage called and asked me to dine. I sent in the drawing of Athens to Mrs G. and worked really hard all day at the Clermont Athos. $\frac{*}{4}$

Jan. 10. Wet, rose late. Not well $\frac{*}{5}$. Wrote all day long. It rained and was otherwise odious, so I went out . . . Madeira very good.

Jan. 11. Frightful dyspepsia – no relief, sudden $\frac{*}{6}$. Then as usual deep sleep for ¼ hr. more epileptic then and later, though not so much as last year. [There follows a vague undetailed doodle of an antique Venus (?)] Dined alone wrote to Miss D for I see W Spencer is dead $\frac{*}{6}\frac{*}{7}$.

Jan. 12. Alack! alack! Rose al solito. At 6 came Papadop. all in tears – his only child being about to die. He was demonstrative but I allowed for grief and worked at my two hours solo. Found I had lost my little sketch book Mt Ida, Smyrna and many other sketches so I did no work but hunted for it in vain.

Jan. 13. Papadop's child is better, but he could not come for allegria.

Jan. 14. Lonely walk and 'a angry' saw L's dog and afterwards himself hardly spoke all the way to Condi Terrace, and this kind of thing irritates and annoys me so indeed that I quite dread the bore of so walking.

Jan. 15. Turville, most nice pleasant fellow.

Jan. 17. George's homily on life. Sixty is enough for a poor man.

It will be seen that the diary is not immediately oppressive, but his life looks like a poor student's life, his quarrel with Lushington, who in the diary is a difficult brute of a man, is obsessive, and he has made his painting into such hard work by pure conscientiousness that it is no relief to him. He should go and sit in a tavern, but on Corfu there were none, there were only wine-shops (to be found now, I think, only in the back lanes of Palermo) which he could not enter, as a member of the Master-race. So he went on, epileptic and lonely, recording snow and cold. '*Jan 20.* All things going wrong again. Clear lovely weather but very cold. L dined with me. While I was up to talking, but disagreeable – Drank too much $\frac{*}{11}\frac{*}{12}$.' On the 22nd he wandered around dreaming about Margaret Sandbach in Rome, 'that *was* a woman, spite of the foolish Dean-sisters'. On the 24th he drew in his diary the tiny, thrilling outline of a mountain. He saw Albanian Greeks 'plodding along to their adoptive olive-homes'. Next day 'going to the Princess's ball is out of the question, but I wish they would not ask me to dinner so often'. He notes but alas does not record 'George's discussion of a black slave who was brought to General Conyers', his old master.

'*Feb 2.* Mess dinner. Obliged to go out to pump ship in the wet, I cut away home.

Feb 3. L's millennial corpselike stiltiness. Good as I know L to be, he is most misabiliously unsatisfactory as a companion.

Feb 4. Unwell all night, diarrhoea all day, better at night.

Feb 5. Ill whether from internal cold and cold feet I cannot tell. Called L who got me a draught which did me good . . . dried off by the fire with rice and brandy and water.

Feb 17. Afraid of claret so drank 3 glasses of port whereby I suffer.

The scrupulousness with which Edward records every 'drank too much' and every dyspeptic twinge should not make one suppose he is a drunkard. He did come to a time late in life when he felt the need to cut down his own drinking and regarded other people's with a beady eye, but those days were far ahead. Part of the function of his diary was to compare one year with another for happiness and advancement in virtue and philosophy, but a more important part was to get rid of feelings that had no other expression, small irritations about cold and dirt, and rages. He is like a calm diplomat known for his even temper and amusing talk who rushes home and vents a diabolic malevolence on his diary that no one is meant to see. Sometimes in the diary Edward is simply muttering to himself. He records bits of gossip in broken Greek, and other people's secrets, usually by now public knowledge, in terms that are unintelligible to us. Once he has recourse to Arabic; probably he intends an obscenity he picked up from a servant, but he is unlikely to know quite what it means and his Arabic, like mine, is far from perfect, so one cannot be certain. He refers to the most exciting (to us) of his activities as if they were dull chores: his alphabets for children, for example, which he made for British children in Corfu in late February, while he was buying a tent and Lushington was teaching him to shoot a pistol because he was going to Palestine. He drew a parrot for the Governor's wife and recorded (3 March) a sweet and funny letter from little Hallam Tennyson to his Uncle Frank. 'We want to buy Mrs X's baby in Freshwater. We heard a gun shooting and we found a little Robin Redbreast dead. So we buried him in the garden and said God bless him, and Mama and Papa and everybody said, God bless him, for we ought to wish God to bless everything, and the angels. And they will come some day, and take away our souls to God.'

Then, in terror of the wind, he walked down through the silent Jewish quarter to the dark harbour. 'George and Spiro (his brother) rowed out, steamer to Bombay. Nearly fell into the water and so did Spiro, I not seeing the steps. So begins my Syrian tour.' He had intended to travel with Clowes, an old soldier friend who had served in the Crimea and

been a prisoner at Sebastopol, but in the end had only Giorgis for
company, and found him admirably suitable. The moment they are on
their way the diary takes on quite another colour. It was meant to be
written up, as he had been writing up Athos, for publication, just as his
sketches were meant to become the basis for finished water-colours and,
in spite of Holman Hunt, for oils. His comments in their raw state are
always interesting, though his adventures are ordinary enough on the
whole. It is still from letters that one can catch an atmosphere and a
vicarious pleasure more fully. All the same, it is only in the diary that he
says 'I am thankful as in 1848' about the scenery, and tells us of 'those
wonderful stuffed costume streets'. When the going is good or the
expedition too exciting, the diary is a blank, reserved for writing up later.
We know at least that they went by sea to Jaffa for Jerusalem ('8 tea, but
the odour was great. I do not know how the night is to be passed'). He
is more terse than Thackeray, though his tiny prose vignettes are sharper,
but his heart was set on a further goal, seldom visited, and recorded at
that time I think only by Roberts: he was going to Petra. He wrote that
up later, and Lushington published it after his death in April 1897 in
Macmillan's Magazine, as 'A Leaf from the Journals of a Landscape
Painter'.

The expedition was hazardous and it is only now that we see why Lear
let Lushington teach him pistol-shooting. Holman Hunt's adventures in
similar conditions were at least equally terrifying. Edward was to spend
a week at Petra and four days on the Dead Sea with an escort of fifteen
Arabs for £30 altogether, starting in the second week of April. On the
first night, 'Long after the tent was closed for the night, old Abu Daouk
returned from dining out, and an hour of discussion and noise of
quarrelling ensued, such as only angry Arabs can produce, and mostly
resembling the united gobbling of a thousand exasperated turkey-cocks.'
The following day one of the camels refuses to carry a cage of chickens
and 'the din of snarling, growling, screaming and guggling was considerable'. The whole of this description is worth consulting, as one of the
funniest bits of travel writing Lear ever produced. Whenever a cock
crows, the infuriated camel plunges and kicks: in the end she drags her
load at the end of a rope. After a few pages one of the camels is the big
white Hubblebubble, and two quarrelsome Arabs are Grumpy and the
Infant Samuel. From the literary point of view it is useful that Lear did
not know Arabic.

When they got to Petra, Giorgis said, 'Oh master, we have come into
a world where everything is made of chocolate, ham, curry powder and

salmon.' Edward was dazzled, both by the colours and the gleams, and sat down to draw. Alas, his pictures are fine but few, because they were very soon interrupted by demands for money that became more and more violent, as more than one tribe joined in. As the sun went down, the eastern cliff became one fiery red mass, with pink clouds resting on it. He saw the black figures squatting in a line just above the tents. A little after midnight Lear was roused. 'He be coming more and more of the Arab, Sir.' They were waiting for sunrise. Lear rose about four when there were about 100, demanding stores as well as money. Lear behaved as coolly as a Waterloo veteran, making a swift sketch of his own tent, and climbing a cliff to go on drawing, brushing the wild fig, thrusting aside the tamarisk, and startling the hoopoes, the rock doves and the partridges, until he heard a shot from the valley. The echoes circled like thunder among the precipices. They went on climbing and his Arabs shot a roe-deer and cooked and ate its liver. Lear then descended from a temple(?) he had reached, only to find there were now twice the number of Arabs around his tents, all quarrelling. He gave orders to strike tents and leave, Giorgis brought him coffee, bread and eggs, and Lear then calmly set off for a final sketch at the ancient theatre. Yells and roars pulled him back after a magical half-hour, and he saw Giorgis coming with a camel, and the bad-tempered camel refusing to be rushed by the Arabs, who seem to have been still arriving. There was a division of 'tax' in a cave by a local sheikh, and the uproar got worse. Lear's arms were held and he was robbed of everything down to hard-boiled eggs, except for his pistol and his watch. At the first shot, whoever fired it, Lear reckoned he would be dead. He therefore shouldered his way into the headquarters cave, manhandled the sheikh, and made him rescue the head of the escort, who was down. The man paid twenty dollars (on Lear's orders) and was released. Lear and his party escaped with their camels, leaving a diminishing trail of bribes. One admires the telling of this frightening tale almost more than the intrepidity. It is fascinating that having recorded it with panache, Lear then refrained from printing it.

He offered Lady Waldegrave a choice of subjects: Masada, Petra, Hebron or the Cedars of Lebanon. The *Masada* is a stunning image, which has recently been in the London market (Sotheby's, November 1991). The picture is as if Lear were very conscious of the history of that vast, dark ridge, as one must assume he was, since he had read every book he could lay hands on, including Josephus, before this journey, and referred Lady Waldegrave to his works. He knew, of course, that she was Jewish by blood; although she was nominally Christian, her favourite prayer, which her husband had carved on her memorial, did not contain the name of Christ or make any reference to Christianity. Edward considered a second visit the following year, though most dubiously, since a number of Americans had been robbed and murdered, and he knew well enough (though he did not say so to her) how lucky he was to have escaped with his life. His response was to demand a strong British military presence. The French and Austrians could not be touched, or so he felt. He particularly hated the quarrelling sects of Christians in Jerusalem. 'If I wished to prevent a Turk, Hebrew or Heathen from turning Christian, I would send him straight to Jerusalem! I vow I could have turned Jew myself, as one American has actually done!' He liked Lebanon and Damascus, but hated the villagers, the begging, the stoning, and therefore the Hellenistic baroque of Baalbek by association. He preferred Paestum and the Parthenon, as any ordinary scholar does. He really had extremely good taste. He got up at night to read Plato on the death of Socrates, he preferred Josephus in Greek to Whiston (sensibly), and was amused by the novelty of Lucian in Greek, though he hated Plutarch. His letters are like honeycombs, or rather they are like endless telephone conversations, and the best of them are his continual letters to Fortescue. 'I shall begin a letter and let it burn up gradivally, like the gunpowder which they throw on the fire.'

Edward just longed for Fortescue to come: 'I could put you up beautifully and feed you on ginger beer and claret and prawns and figs.' That summer (1858) he sent his friend a translation of 'Come unto these yellow sands,' from a version of *The Tempest* by one of the best poets of the Corfiot renaissance. He thought it pretty and amusing, a curiosity, and he liked 'Mpaou Vgaou' for Bow Wow, and the cock's crow, 'Koukouroukou'. Yet he is right about the translation and, more important, the possibility of wonderful poetry in demotic Greek. It is sad that he never knew that great poet Solomos, who did know some English families and even wrote poems to them. He had lived not far from Lear in a small house the painter must often have passed, but he died before Lear knew Greek. Now the days when Goethe was fascinated by Serbian poetry and translated it, and Byron attempted to do the same with Greek had passed: now modern Greek folk poetry was collected only by dry-as-dust scholars, and those were French or German: the English felt they had enough poetry of their own. There is a copy of that translation of *The Tempest* all the same, in the Readers' Club at Corfu. It has been annotated in pencil by an English hand. Could it have been Lear's? He drew the outside of the club in May 1857.

In June Lushington resigned and so did Sir James Reid, owing to the victorious influence of Bowen with whom none of our friends was now on speaking terms. Bowen is described by Lear in highly coloured language as being the creature of Greek intriguing influences, which does sound highly likely. The people of the Ionian Islands, on the other hand, not unreasonably aspired to join that Kingdom of the Greeks over which a King and glamorous Queen (Amalia) and a Greek parliament ruled, and under Gladstone that wish would be fulfilled within seven years, in 1864. Enthusiasm for this abdication by the British should not, on the other hand, blind one to the undoubtedly nasty smell which Bowen gives off. As a result, and since Holman Hunt was not coming, Edward Lear decided to leave with Lushington, and to spend his next winter in Rome.

In July he was tired of waiting: it was hot, he hated sailing, where one sat 'flapping and swinging'. He would go on learning Arabic and Greek in his Roman lodgings. In 1859 and 1860 he wanted to return to the Middle East and sort out his plans for an illustrated *Palestine*. Lushington had two nieces and a brother ill and fretted to get away. Giorgis had become a need, so Edward would meet him in Rome after the summer. Meanwhile, 'all the little time I have away from painting goes in Greek'. He was starting *Oedipus at Colonus*, thanking God he was uneducated and came to it fresh. Luckily for us, he would return to Corfu, because some of his finest, most searching and pleasure-giving island paintings were to come. They are scarcely brushed by the wing of sublimity. Mr McKay, the barrack schoolmaster, bought his piano, and he was off in August.

Edward's enthusiasm for Holman Hunt was undiminished, indeed he could hardly mention his painting without incandescence. 'He is undoubtedly *the* painter of these days.' Lear's topographical and island sketches do not reflect this surely mistaken view. The only analogy that I can offer is the enthusiasm of poets for Coleridge or for Leigh Hunt. It is no insult to their excellence as poets, greater than Holman Hunt's as a painter, to admit that their fans were mistaken. When one is lost in an art, anything that gives one hope, that cheers one along, is welcome. Things take time, and sometimes they take more than one lifetime to fall into place (in 1858, Cézanne was eighteen).

Wherever Lear went in England he was excited. His friends' marriages were shaking apart, Proby was dying, John Cross thrilled him by his tranquil, amiable household, he drew Langdale Pikes, Mr Hornby came in, 'how wonderful, the same as twenty-three years ago'. This was at Wansfell, just north-east of Ambleside, just north of Windermere, one of the few places in England you still had to get to by coach. Even in the Lakes, though, Edward suddenly found himself depressed, because he missed Corfu. His travels are not easy to follow, since he raced here and there as people could receive him. 'I must give up going to Ireland and stay a bit at the Adelphi', in Liverpool where his luggage had suddenly arrived: its timing depended on the vagaries of the Zante currant trade.

Knowsley buzzed with rumours: in this generation Lear's sympathies seem to have been deeper with the Hornbys. But the feudal generosity of the place, the slow, sweet servants refusing half a crown, 'there's no necessity for that, sir', and the prodigal grouse and champagne warmed him. Then it was Ashtead at the other end of England, the Bethells and a deluge of legal stories about deaf judges, a case of bestiality and Please, sir, it wasn't my pig. He adored Holman Hunt's paintings, *Behold, I Stand at the Door*, for example, and hated a sermon at Stoke Newington as he had a year before. In October Ann's life and state distressed him, and he was flung into an anguish of indecision.

> To go to Brighton? To see Helena C.? to take a place at the Isle of Wight? – and dismiss Giorgis? To start at once for Rome with unfinished work? to go to Madeira? To try to complete the five paintings here? to be involved in more debt? to attempt the Palestine small drawings? To write for Fraser? To set more songs? [This year he published five of the six he had ready of Tennyson's.] Story of Holman Hunt gluing the shoes, hammer, and tools of the idle workmen at the British Museum, when they had left the building, to the floor.

Lear's solution was to look ahead as little as possible: he did not like the idea of Rome, at least as it had been ten and twenty years ago. He called on Colonel Leake, stayed with Holman Hunt, walked 'by short cuts through a world of new streets and cabbage gardens' to Putney, to Mrs Cameron's. Then he dined at Simpson's in the Strand 'and oh! to see the little wheeling tables with assiduous carvers! Really, Daddy Hunt is a wonderful fellow . . . I fear he is legally in a mess, poor dear boy. He told me much and I read a long journal of this sad affair.' The mess was financial and sexual: Hunt had taken four years over his *Christ in the Temple* and would take another two, but 1860 would be his year of success, fashion and fortune.[3] In 1860–1 he was blackmailed, but the 5500 guineas he got for *Christ in the Temple* enabled him finally to say goodbye to his remarkable bohemian youth. In 1865 he married a Miss Waugh, and in 1875 he married her sister, though of his remarkable life those two were the least amazing episodes.

On 23 October, Edward read that Crete, Bosnia and Montenegro had all taken up arms against the Sultan. He celebrated by scribbling in his diary some splendid sketches of veiled women. He thought Seddon's *Jerusalem* a failure, to his own relief I think, and toyed again with a winter in the Isle of Wight. In November he heard that Gladstone was going to Corfu as 'Lord High Commissioner Extraordinary'. Edward packed for Rome, dined at Strawberry Hill with the Duc d'Aumale (who lived nearby), he began to cough and to freeze, and on 26 November he was in Paris. He lingered just a few days, but long enough to note that 'Nothing in city architecture was ever finer than Paris now.' They passed Elba at midnight, and he finally crawled into Rome in the first days of December, 'delighted to find I like it as I do'. He lived with English friends in the Piazza di Spagna until he should settle. Giorgis arrived too, 'Freddo son, Signor.'

Edward started 1858 with £213, some of it borrowed (Lushington £100) but he made £364 by selling pictures in August, mostly at £50 each, one to S. W. Clowes for £100. In 1859, by commissioned oils, he reckoned on about £600, and about £100 for ten-guinea water-colours. The corruption of taste that could pay thousands for Holman Hunt's religious painting and comparatively little to Edward Lear need not be discussed, but he was at least making a modest living and could travel. His 1859 oil of Petra is beautiful and strange, and his 1858 *Dar Mar Sabbas* is a thrilling, awe-inspiring study, done in sepia and water-colour washes outlined in pencil: it goes far beyond what appear to be its fragile means. It shows a monastery on the ravine of the Kedron, a place in the wilderness not far from the Dead Sea. His ability to grasp the solid structure of a landscape is well shown in his *Petra* sketches, and his calm and level eye, as undisturbed as any painter's in Europe 100 years before him, is well shown in *Jerusalem*.

CHAPTER TEN

THE DEATH
OF ANN

IN ROME Edward found himself distracted and freezing cold. Giorgis looked after him and fed him, but the chimney smoked – and 'the filthy people [his landlords] know and propose the remedy and will do nothing'. Prices had risen to £80 a year for rent, and he took a three-year lease, but he still had to go shopping for a portable lavatory, a bed, six chairs, a pair of bellows and a pepper-box. He called on Mrs Browning, 'saw her: nice little woman', and thought the Prince of Wales 'prepossessing . . . like his mother, God bless her'. He dined with Penry Williams once or twice at the Bell'Arte restaurant, 'that filthy place, how can he eat there every night?' The diary has become a deadly Victorian social record of visits by Lord Stratford, the Duke of St Albans, Odo Russell and so forth, almost as if he were in South Kensington. He is working at oils from old pictures, and he has nothing to tell us about how he arrived at this solemn and somehow loveless elegance. Through all this runs an undertone of personal pain, and below the anxieties the slow tolling of the death-bell.

John Proby and Lord Lyons (who had sent a doctor to Lear as a young man in Thebes) were dead, and others followed monotonously. It may be because, living alone, he cared more for his friends, but their deaths take up much of his attention as he gets older. His Canadian cousin Chester had died. Clowes has been with him and 'kept him above water', and it is only in a letter to Fortescue that he reveals that his first twelve days at Rome were 'the most weary and depressing I have passed for years'. Two or three times he came close to bolting to America. Then he took rooms in the Via Condotti and settled down to hope for Fortescue's company at Easter. His trouble was death, and weeping over it, but whose I am not sure, and perhaps it makes no difference whose.[1] Perhaps it was only his acute misery, which is obscure to us as it was to Giorgis. 'Whoever weeps except about his mother's death is a donkey,' said the Greek. As for Clowes, he was *hors de combat* with a broken collar-bone from falling off a horse.

Lear reported to Lady Waldegrave, when her pictures were finished, that 800 people had seen and admired them in his rooms. He had now seen his own paintings hung in eight different houses, so that his lightning visits in England took on a new complexion of reviewing his own work. But now war broke out between France and Austria. It did no good to the Italians, because France would not liberate north Italy as she had promised: at least this war was soon over. Its principal result was to add fuel to Garibaldi's all-Italian movement to fling out the foreigners and put an end to the idiotic Papal States, which of course in the end he achieved, and which Edward Lear lived to see. One may take Lear's final move to San Remo, which was just in Italy and not in France, as a bet, however timid, placed on the stability of a united Italy as opposed to French stability. For the present, he held on in Rome: if things got worse, all he could do would be to move to England and publish travel books there by subscription. He had never found any more modern or lucrative way of publishing anything he had so far produced. His comments on world events were becoming well informed at this time, so that he sounds like a serious, upper-class critic, but that does not make money. After the Indian Mutiny, in 1858 Lord Canning had more or less confiscated the whole of Oude, and in 1859 he got an Earldom, but Edward wrote sternly to Fortescue about ingratitude to Lord Canning in the difficulties of his career shown by Lord Derby's government. His views in fact were those of the army at staff level, where news came swiftly, predictions were dire, and a strong and wily sense of survival governed. In 1853, two days before Christmas, he drew Richard Burton in Egypt in full Arab disguise: we know nothing about the encounter, except that Burton was fresh from Mecca, but Lear would have had a respect for Burton's views, which, had they been adopted, might possibly have prevented the Indian Mutiny.

A letter from Lady Bethell on 6 February 'as lively (O woman!) as if she had never written *that* letter' suggests that she had been at her wits' end, which is all too likely for one in her position. This reveals an entanglement of misery we might have missed, but such letters, and diary remarks like 'Paroxysm' in Greek, and Lear's disgust at the crowds who come to see his pictures, do not really reveal him. One learns more from the way he judges people. It was very rare for Italians to go near him, but the Duke and Duchess of Bagnolo came.

> Duke stupid – the foolish longnosed man one has seen about Rome for twenty years past – quite absurd. She well dressed, intelligent. She said of Bassae, Jerusalem and Masada – it is like youth, age and death. The first is full of interest and life, the second of material greatness, the third so lifeless – which I thought not a bad compliment. But these visits bore me sadly. One from Penry Williams did not, and he liked the Bassae . . . Sunday. My own scirocco. Went to church though half inclined not so to do.

He told himself often that he felt 'less black misery than in earlier years'. Good weather so tempted him when it came that he dared not look out of the window until the chance of a client had passed for the day. Then he wandered out alone, 'semi-sad in the golden sunset'. At the end of March the Prince of Wales came to his studio at last and he melted with pleasure. 'Nobody could have nicer or better manners, nor be more generally intelligent and pleasing.' He stayed an hour and five minutes. Giorgis went on grumbling about Rome, its prices and chicaneries, its tourists whom he scornfully announced in Greek as 'Here come the Arabs', and even its bread rolls, which had four and not three divisions. 'When April came I grew a little soothed thereby, though Rome is a sad dreary prison to me nowadays.' He pined for his old expedition to the Abruzzi, more than ten years ago. Was he the prisoner of bad health (away from England) or of work and lack of money (so no expeditions)? One fears the latter. One day he felt ill, so he sat alone making a list of where he had spent every winter in his life, starting at his tenth, in Holloway: 11–13 Arundel, 14–15 Holloway, 16–18 Grays Inn Road, 19–21 Albany Street, 22–4 Southampton Row, 25 Marlborough Road, 26–33 Rome, and so on. Some of the early addresses are a surprise, but the biggest surprise is complete: all years until he was ten being a blank. His diary is a record of work and interruptions. A lady said *Jerusalem* reminded her of Kensington Gardens, and asked if it was governed by a mayor and municipality. And a young man inquired whether there were any trees in Greece, or had Lear put them in at Bassae for fun? Lear's interest became taken up with photography as a means of reproducing his black and white drawings. It was never satisfactory, but the solution always seemed close at hand, which indeed it was.

All that spring, rumours of war continued, and Edward went on toying with the idea of emigration to America. Soon after the end of his life that might have been the best thing for an artist to do, but it is not at all clear that had he gone in 1860 he would have survived, even if there had been no civil war. He was consoled by Miss Burney's memories, and by the occasional company of a new friend, the banker Edgar Drummond. He met Lord Leighton for the first time, the painter of whom Oscar Wilde said he applied moonlight like cosmetics, and thought him superficial or worse. Nearing the end of April, he at last hired a piano to cheer himself up, yet in May he was preparing to leave, because at the close of April war had been declared. So much for his three-year lease.

On 12 May he was forty-seven, but he did leave, watching the movement of troops again as he saw Giorgis away and crossed Europe. His reading as he left had been Sidney Smith and the *Oedipus at Colonus*: his Greek was not improving but at least was not sliding away. On the boat were 200 French soldiers heading for Genoa, and a Maharaja with hawks, quails and Arabs. In the train Lear 'made up a figure of cloaks and a hat and cigar to delude any newcomer. The Colonel was cross. He seemed to say that in the end everyone said that England would go against France.' They stopped for breakfast and dinner at Avignon and Lyons. Before midnight 'the punchy Colonel' (French) got out at Dijon, and the others slept as they could, until four or five in the morning, when 'we all woke and began to be merry', though Lear disliked the endless poplar trees, as he had done twenty years before in Lombardy. By half past six they were in Paris, 'Maharaja, hawks and all'. At Dieppe Lear sat happily through vespers in the Cathedral. 'No one shall make me think there is no real good piety in this people,' he noted defensively. The following day he got to the Husey Hunts at Lewes. 'Damp and cold and snuffly – Umph. All day long I wrote letters.' When they amounted to twenty-five, he went back to writing his Athos journal. In this mood, 'Church here is a scandal for deadness and ugliness, although the hills were lovely the East wind was diabolical and made me ill.' He was tired out, and small wonder. 'The domestic has destroyed my peace of mind by putting out *all* my things, even to fourteen pairs of scissors secreted in a bag.' He paid 5s. for a hat, 4s. 6d. for washing and postage, and 10s. for a carriage and the turnpikes, apparently to Ditchling and Keymer. On a lovely morning he got to Phipps Hornby's family, whom he remembered from twenty-five years before, and Compton Down from thirty years before with an Arundel friend, J. Sayres.

On 3 June he knew Frank Lushington had failed to get an Oxford chair he wanted, 'which annoys horribly; O dear I wish I were away from here'. Then in Greek, 'Certainly I should not go among them much more, these families that see nothing but themselves, as is natural.' On the 5th he went to the Tennysons: 'Day perfectly lovely.' He began at Ventnor, which he disliked as overcrowded (more than 130 years ago!), but he called on the Rev. Edward Peel at Bonchurch, with a note from Emily Tennyson. He was given lunch and walked part of the way to Shanklin; when he got there at three or four he turned inland, into the Downs, to Appledurcombe, then across farms, 'very often losing much time by being obliged to go round cornfields'. By about six he had got to Niton, 'some 26 or 28 miles I should say'. It sounds an idyllic but extremely roundabout route: the 'military road' along the coast had not yet been built. The following day, in the same lovely weather, he climbed Blackgang Chine (not yet a playground for plastic dinosaurs) to the hotel, and got to Freshwater by four. Alfred looked well but Emily haggard. He chatted with her and sang, and read 'Guinevere', 'which is the most astonishingly lovely of all the poems Alfred has written'.

The following morning began with a thick sea-fog and prayers before breakfast. Edward walked on the Downs with Alfred, who read out his 'Lay of Astolat' – 'most wonderfully beautiful and affecting, so that I cried like beans. The gulls on the cliffs laughed.' He found Emily friendly and angelic, but so ill she seemed doomed. He felt that she laboured for Alfred, but he seemed not to notice how hard. After dinner, he read 'The Old Woman', which Edward notes with more reserve as 'natural, and remarkably striking'. Breakfast next morning was 'not very pleasant, the dear little boys fidget me'. At eleven he walked out 'with Alfred and Evans' on the Downs. Alfred turned home but the other two pressed on to a view of the Needles, which Edward drew in his diary. They all lunched at three, but at dinner 'I think it a bad habit for children to come in then and feed, but I am very sorry I showed this to that wonderful boy Lionel . . . A kind of sensitive excitement here always is not good for such an ass as I am. Sang little.'

The following morning they went up Aston Down. 'Alfred doddled about a little, but has hay fever and a cold. I am less able than before to combine with him at times, he is so odd. Dinner, some singing, which owing to the bad piano is a misery to me.' On the 10th they all went to the ferry to see Alfred off to London. Edward recorded again, 'Emily is certainly one of the most utterly morally perfect women I have yet seen.' He was sure that he now liked Farringford better than any other place. All the same, even here in the springtime of affection he does not sound like at all an easy guest. On the 12th, with other friends, 'I do not like my idle life. Yet I dare not give room to anxiety as yet.' It took him twelve vehicles to get from Farringford to the Empsons at a vicarage near Romsey. Liking some friends' houses and hating others, he raced around England from Wookey Hole with Canon Charles Church of Wells to Appleby and the south bank of the Humber with John Cross, and back to 16 Upper Seymour Street, London.

His opinions about himself and about other painters seem to have set hard around this time. He wrote to Fortescue about the six paintings that were his year's work, two of them for Lady Waldegrave, how delighted he was that she was pleased: that made three successes at least. He totally disregarded his sketches, however exciting, and concentrated on the 'finish' of his 'finished' water-colours as of his oils. Some of the Upper Egyptian subjects in particular do convey an extraordinary calm, both of place and of spirit, as if they were by Corot. Nothing is more striking in them than their stillness. The rocks above the Dead Sea are dramatic by contrast, deep brown staring out into pale desert. The cliffs at Kasr es Saad, painted in oils in the 1870s, retain tranquillity even though sunset colours them. It appears that Edward Lear valued the dramatic qualities of his mountains and monasteries in the mountains, like Dar Mar Sabbas,[2] more highly for their excitement, and yet not at all until they were calmed and transformed into 'finish'. Yet the merest, lightest sketch of Lake Albano (12 October 1840), nothing but a cloudshadow, a cloudstain on water, dark grey on grey, is a perfect image:[3] every improvement would be a dis-improvement. In summer of 1859, 'I should gladly see Millais' worx, but do not greatly expect to like them. I am quite aware of the qualities of his mind, which I do not apprehend to be of a progressive nature, as are Holman Hunt's: but his power and technical go I have no doubt are wonderful.' His mistake surely hinges on the word 'progressive'.

He was working at three different journals, and trying out a woodcutter for illustrations: *Athos*, *Judaea*, and '*Albanian Zagorian*', none of which ever saw the light. He was placid and getting fat; the days when he would be shaped like an egg with a bald head and a huge beard were looming. On consideration he adored the Tennyson children and Alfred's new *Idylls*, and as for Emily in retrospect,

> I should think, computing moderately, that 15 angels, several hundreds of ordinary women, many philosophers, a heap of wise and kind mothers, 3 or 4 minor prophets, and a lot of doctors and schoolmistresses, might be boiled down, and yet their combined essence fall short of what Emily Tennyson really is . . . A twitching regret bothers me about having left the place.

He was on tenterhooks about events in Italy; he was experimenting with photographs and lithographs: 'I wish you were married, I wish I were an egg and going to be hatched.' Meanwhile, 'I am doing little, but dimly walking on along the dusty twilight lanes of incomprehensible life.' In July 'Guinevere' came out, 'prudes are shocked', and Lear had an argument with Bethell, now Sir Richard and Attorney General, who assured him Tennyson was 'a small poet', an opinion entrenched among clubmen who preferred Rogers and Sir Walter Scott, or the bright verses of Bulwer-Lytton.

Late in July Edward tried to heave himself out of debt by taking rooms at St Leonard's and painting. He permitted occasional callers, like Middleton who was Leake's nephew, and Anthony Chester's daughters, and on Sundays he dined with Sir John Potter's sisters or the Martineau family, where Holman Hunt was staying; otherwise he worked or read Greek. By September, *Athos* and *Corfu* for Potter were nearly done, and *Corfu* and the *Petra Theatre* for Mr Edwards were advancing, but two *Campagna Aqueducts* for Mr Heywood and a big *Petra* (eastern cliff) for Fairbairn had not got far. The *Judaea* journal was making progress, yet how to reproduce its illustrations was a problem that still defeated Lear. He 'bathed in the hocean but it was too rough' after a night of storm, '. . . were the beach sand it would be great fun'. He kept telling himself the quiet life did him good, but he did not believe it. 'Very sad exile life and lonely.' In August he went for a walk along the coast, 'with Carmel-like Beachy Head afar, and the sand-girt still sea-pools . . . Pevensey marsh with the "bullocks" dear Ann used to dread when I was five years old, and the old Castle, and lolling the dull road to Eastbourne. Burlington Hotel', where he read Tennyson to a Mr Kidd, a chance-met stranger, and had to borrow 6s. In this style he struggled into September. He felt the fine weather of August was a parenthesis, 'and one expects the Corfu (Albanian) mountains to come out at any moment'. Still, he was finishing paintings and tapping his patrons to pay for them. On 9 September he saw and drew the *Great Eastern*: Mr Brunel was ill in the Marine Hotel, so she tacked and came near enough for him to see the people and the paddle-wheels.

By October he would write 'last month was a sadly non-advancing one', yet once he got to London the autumn was not without its high spirits; even October had its moments.

Oct. 13. Of all the loveliest days of this wonderfully loveliest summer endless – perhaps this might be the softest and calmest and brightest . . . Overdrawn three dollars. Oct. 14. No words and no painting can give an idea of the perfect loveliness of this day and sea-view. Fell in with Martineau and Daddy on their way to me. Trivial talk on vain things, then

HH fell asleep in the moonlit calm open balcony. Walked to Hastings with them and back here by twelve. [Greek:] a great deal of wine.

His worry was Ann, in lodgings he disliked in Hornsey. Under Oct. 15 he drew a row of ruined columns from who knows where, imagined by the sea at St Leonard's or at Eastbourne. The 21st brought the Peace of Zurich, but it also brought the cold and the storms: Heywood sent him £52 10s. and he was off to London like a shot on 1 November. He wrote to Fortescue:

> *15, Stratford Place, Oxford St.*
>
> O Mimber for the County Louth
> Residing at Ardee!
> Whom I before I wander South,
> Partiklar wish to see; –
>
> I send you this. – That you may know
> I've left the Sussex shore,
> And coming here two days ago
> Do cough for evermore,
>
> Or gasping hard for breath do sit
> Upon a brutal chair,
> For to lie down in Asthma fit
> Is what I cannot bear . . .

This letter of eleven stanzas was no more than a frolic, a small cavorting around his friend. It expressed simply a desire to meet. He was going north on the 13th, and after that he would be back in London only to pack.

> No more my pen: no more my ink:
> No more my rhyme is clear.
> So I shall leave off here I think. –
> Yours ever,
>
>   Edward Lear.

In fact he soon felt better. He saw Colonel Leake, and Woolner, and heard how Mrs Leake (now ninety-two) was stopped by a highwayman while walking with her mother in Portman Square in about 1770. On the 13th Lear and Holman Hunt 'walked to Madox Brown. His piece of Work, a landscape in Essex and another painting were really true and fine: after all, *he* is the real first Pre-Raphaelite Brother', but he is never mentioned again. The fog returned, but Lear went north the same day and spent a week excitedly exploring the family of Mary Chaworth near

Newstead, because of their Byron connection: he also sold them seven drawings at twenty guineas each. The gift of his *Bassae* to the museum at Cambridge by subscription was mentioned in the course of a rapid and dizzying tour. Sam Clowes tried to back out, but when Edward looked surprised, he agreed to pay; letters came from Fortescue and R. M. Milnes subscribing; all the same, in the Clowes house 'the talk almost *wholly* gossip. A gloom insensibly pervades life here.' He had to stand a forty-two-minute sermon on the Woman of Babylon, and Lord Derby and (Dean) A. Stanley refused subscriptions. Lear thought Derby's letter very queer, and others of his friends extremely singular. But at last he saw the frame for his *Bassae* and the place in Cambridge where it would hang. He calls it the *Bassae Septuagint* or the *Subscription of the Seventy Elders*, or just the *Bassae* relief. His notes rise to screaming pitch about the cold, yet he did not leave England until 23 December: he got to Marseille on Christmas evening and was extremely sick on the boat on Boxing Day. 'The waves are really a wonder – deep blue black with silver crests – valleymaking, gulfing, – vast, forcible, opal-vitriol hued above, solemn inky below, gull-abounding, ever moving – terrible.' He got to Rome on the 28th, and rescued Giorgis who had got stuck at Naples without money, so that life resumed by 5 January 1860.

On the 6th he dined at the Angleterre, and Charles Newton showed him 'Photographs of Boudroom etc'. On the 7th he had to dine with Stansfield in a white tie, and draws a highly infuriated cartoon of himself wrestling with it. But that tie does not symbolize social jollity, since now that the war was over, there were only 200 or so English in winter residence, where once there had been 2000. This, of course, made Lear's life extremely difficult. He had his commissions to work at, but he found Rome more oppressive than St Leonard's that year; Giorgis was in a not unusual state of gloom too. All the same, he hired a carriage and saw the Campagna on his own; with Newton he got to the fifth milestone of the Appian Way. He was addicted to the melancholy beauty of those distances, the thistles and snakes, the snowy mountains, the striding aqueducts. He went to St Peter's, 'a place I can never like as I never did: – a vulgar, blaring, artificially devotional spot'. That was not the usual view then, nor is it now, even among the English; it is more usual among the Romans, but I must admit that I share it. The English church could not muster a congregation of above 150. He called on Storey the American sculptor, and thought him intelligent but violent, probably about the American Civil War. There were reports of disturbances bad enough to have his books taken down and his carpets beaten for packing.

'Worried and raved all day at these shit-begotten Roman filths, who make me pay 90 dollars a quarter and will do nothing for my comfort.' He began to take Giorgis with him when he went out into the country to sketch. On 29 January, 'the account of Pio Nono's rage and his speech this morning at the American College was wondrous. O dear Emily T.! and various people! – Now I live a living death here!' The following day at a reunion of artists organized by Charles Knight, Edward agreed with Penry Williams as to the likely course of events. The Carnival booths were all inscribed as 'Timber for the Barricades'. The following day a Mr More came [Greek:] 'and my goodness he was an idiot'.

In February Penry Williams came in and saw Clive's *Dead Sea*. He lost his temper and said it was 'not a picture'. (Cézanne was twenty at this time.) 'After all PW is very amiable and one must remember he is 59 (b. 1803 and came to Rome in 1826). We walked to S. John Lateran, for once it was fine and we saw the mountains. Nevertheless I deeply hate this place.' He saw Newton again too, and really liked him, although he foresaw his frustrations in the consular service. On the 6th Edward was deserted in the Campagna by a driver, whom he calls in Italian a fucking rabbit, but that night, having walked home, he received Cornhill with Tithonus in it, sent by Lushington. On Sunday the 12th he had almost decided to be away to England in April or May. 'Rockets as signals and soldiers as sentinels over them.' On the 13th he decided he would leave in May and take Giorgis with him. Then the following day, as he was going to bed, 'George said in Italian, "I never told you Sir, have I ever told you a fib in four years I've been with you? You never knew I was married? I've been married nine years, and I have three children, a boy of 18, a girl of 6, and a baby of three." There is no doubt these people are unfathomable. Niko, Elisabeta, and Haralampos, wife Tatiani.'

He looked for Tennyson in church the following Sunday, but he had not come. Giorgis was unhappy and Edward thought (as he did once or twice a year) of dismissing him. 'In England, if other changes [marriages of friends?] follow, a year or two in India or Armenia, or Australia. [Greek:] the best is not to be born, but since I am alone, the next best is to be always and always alone.' On Sunday the 26th 'they actually *did* send the public executioner out to Porta Pia in the carnival, and he narrowly escaped with his life. In other ways, they do all to compel the people to revolt.' March came, and the old thought, [Greek] 'O women past like all my other hopes'. His pictures made less progress than they had done; he met Browning, 'all fun – fun – foaming with spirit'. At home he read *Adam Bede*. 'There were demonstrations four abreast in the Corso for Garibaldi's birthday, and the cavalry charged, leaving ten or fifteen wounded.' One feels it hard to understand now why the Pope held on so long against the Italians, but even revolutions have to ripen, as fruit does. The Pope defended himself with a Bull of Excommunication, and at the end of March the streets of Rome were empty. Giorgis, at the age of thirty-eight, had finally learnt under Lear's tuition to read and to write. By mid-April Edward was cursing and packing furiously. Giorgis's daughter died, and Edward thought of taking him on a walking tour round the Cornice to the Riviera. At that moment, all the steamers were commandeered for the movement of troops. 'O God! can any lousy place of lice and shit be like unto this pigstye of impostors!' He might take Giorgis to Genoa and send him home by Marseille. He might write a journal with fifteen illustrations. Maybe central Italy would do? 'Let's go. We can't stay in this hole.' He hated the 'old priestlets'; when he did leave, on 10 May, he met fifty-six Papal *partaggiani* when he bought his ticket, and twenty-two of them were priests.

'May 12 (Genoa). Incredible amiability and good manners of the peasantry, one and all.' On the 13th he hired a boatman who said he was 'called really Francis, but no one uses my name. I am called Gallino (Chicken) and I reply to it'. They got to Porto Venere, and there Lear drew, retiring when it rained to a hole in the rocks. That was his birthday, and a happy one. The following day he 'did not like to tempt the silver wave, as the clouds were heavy'. So he sat on the beach drawing, with Giorgis for company, and then climbed a hill for a view of Spezzia, 'very beautiful, but it soon began to spit and piddle'. So it went on all day, and he found the cookery 'werry fishy' and the food vile. But Giorgis went tranquilly to sleep at eight, as the light faded, like the Albanian that he was, and Edward got up at four to draw mountains. They passed a marshy stream, then climbed up a long rise through a valley dense with olives and figs, to a fine view of Lerici, and down again to S. Erenzio. Shelley's and Byron's house looked gloomy enough, but the views were marvellous. 'Hence by the rocks and through a superb olive wood to Lerici', where they arrived at nine, drank some wine and ate breakfast. At four-thirty they bathed and then got to a marshy place: a strong peasant carried them over, but he nearly dropped Edward. 'When I waved my hat they all shouted with laughter. As pleasant a day as for years past.'

Everywhere he commented on beautiful faces and delightful manners. On 16 May he heard that Garibaldi had landed at Marsala, but from where they now were, the trouble coming at Rome was scarcely imaginable. Lear loved 'the soft-loud bells sounding out over the clear,

calm sea, the endless brightness of foliage, the brusque original independent fig, the dependent vine, the tremulous olive'. They had lunch at
Porto Fezzano sitting under chestnut trees, and fell asleep. There was
revolution in Naples, and they saw soldiers marching towards Bologna,
with the chaplain riding along beside the band. They left Spezzia through
chestnut trees, charmed by nightingales and by a single cuckoo, towards
Sestri and the most beautiful pine trees Lear had ever seen since Thebes.
The last note of this journey is about villas, 'better get rid of these and
put olives', then there are four days missing: he was not ill but just tired.
On the 26th they found a railway train that took them in four and a
quarter hours to Turin. Giorgis went off to Civita Vecchia by Livorno,
Edward past the splendour of the Alps. At four-thirty the following day
he reckoned Giorgis would have set out for Naples. He himself walked
to a fair at Susa, 'cuckoos, calves, cows and humans all gay'. But it was
time to go, and by the end of the month he was in Lewes. England had
responded to the war in Europe by setting up a rifle corps, which pleased
Edward when he saw it, after cricket on Friday.

On 7 June he walked with Clowes to the Zoo, where only the oldest
keepers remembered it as he did. 'The Balaeniceps was the most curious
beast there,' which from a cheerful sketch of it in his journal one may
well believe. He found the Nevill boy 'greatly improved (with rifle drill)'.
Alas, he felt that he himself utterly failed 'in the one trial most
important', and that Lushington too was 'as ever most remote and lifeless
as a friend'. Suddenly he had a flash of memory of his father 'and a gig,
a grey mare, Peggy, driving in by Theobalds Road, and shuddering about
a murder close by'. He met Lushington 'and a party of Prinseps –
shirked' at Waterloo, got some beer and biscuits at Lymington, and
crossed to Yarmouth in pouring rain. 'There was Mrs Cameron rushing
al solito.' The two of them took a fly to the Tennysons. At dinner
[Greek:] 'certain things I don't write down. The evening was pleasant
and quiet, and could have been very happy. At ten Mrs Cameron and
her train came, and odious incense palaver and fuss succeeded the quiet
home moments . . . We come no more To the golden shore Where we
danced in days of yore. Pouring rain.' The following morning he found
breakfast exceedingly uncomfortable, and when they went for a walk it
rained, so after lunch they tried again, but 'Alfred was most disagreeably
querulous and irritating and would return, chiefly because he saw people
approaching. But Frank would not go back, and led zigzagwise towards
the sea – Alfred snubby and cross always. After a time he wouldn't go
on, but led us back by muddy paths (over our shoes) a short cut home.'

Even so, he ran into the villagers streaming home from church. After dinner, 'Alfred on Norway catarax, and Cintra etc. – many times repeated – and on seasickness – [Greek:] I'm ashamed to say, but really – so I came to bed and believe that this is my last visit – nor can I wish it otherwise all things considered.' So the following day he walked to the Needles alone, and after lunch went to Mrs Cameron and sang, then went for another walk with Frank. When they came in they found she had sent a grand piano. 'Dinner more pleasant. Alfred's discourses on criticism – alas! At 9 or 10 Mrs Cameron, Miss Perry and Prinsep came, and I sang till 12.30. June 19. Off by 8.'

To Fortescue, the 'unchangeably good and gentle', he sent a letter in hexameters that summer. His mind must have hit on the idea because of Alfred Tennyson's controversy over translating with Matthew Arnold: Lear's hexameters are a pure skit, quite unlike Clough's 'Bothie'. As a device in English, the metre, which is always more or less ridiculous, probably owes something to Goethe, to whose personality it adds (in English) a pleasing touch of the bizarre. Monkton Milnes's translated epigram on a gondola must have been early in the field. But Lear speaks somewhere of the polyphloisboisterous sea, he has Homer in his sights, and this begins as a simple parody, like others of his poems.

> Washing my rose-coloured flesh, and brushing my beard with a hairbrush, –
> Breakfast of tea, bread and butter, at nine o'clock in the morning,
> Sending my carpetbag onward I reached the Twickenham Station . . .

He can do this effortlessly: it is a peculiarity of his ear that he can perform in hexameters as easily as Clough, and a sight better than Robert Bridges. It is not a great gift, but it is something, and all part of his unique and in a way alarming equipment as a poet. He took away a handkerchief and means to return it, that is all. He might come to Ireland, he would like to dine (always at the Blue Posts). If he had £200 a year he would roam the world and 'Marry a black girl at last preparing to walk into Paradise'. Here alone the metre has tripped him up. The whole letter is dated 9 July 1860, and the date is confirmed by Lear's horror at events in the Lebanon, which he expresses in prose to Mrs Tennyson on the 19th. It is queer that Lady Strachey should date it wrongly by a year, since it mentions her own birth as Constance Braham.

The letter to Mrs Tennyson describes a visit to the Archbishop of Canterbury, who was then at Addington Park, Croydon, his traditional residence. *The Victorian Archbishops of Canterbury*, a lecture by Dr Alan Stevenson[4] reveals him as J. B. Sumner, Archbishop 1848–62, 'Perhaps the obscurest of all the Victorian Archbishops' who left no papers and no letters, and was best known for his tact and prudence. He rose early and lit his own fire. Soapy Sam Wilberforce and his like did not flourish under Sumner, and his brother the Bishop of Winchester was the official translator of Milton's nearly atheist theological tract. He was not universally popular all the same. Phillpotts of Exeter, an immoderate Tractarian, quarelled with him, and R. S. Hawker, the poet and eccentric vicar of Morwenstow, maintained that Archbishop Sumner was such a toothless old mumbler that even his 'Let Us Pray' could not be made out.[5] Lear delighted in him. Edward is distinctly secretive about this unlikely conjunction, but for many years it was a regular visit, and appears to turn on his knowing a lady of the Archbishop's court called Mrs Greville, whom none of his everyday friends or family appear to have known.

> This good Archbishop is over 80 and as lively as at 50, walking in the park for hours – and never idle at all. There are many folk here – among others Mrs Moncrieff the Lord Advocate's lady, who is (my gracious!) so immensely large! How she was got into the narrow pew where we sit while the Archbishop "expounds scripture" I cannot think, and as I did not see her come out again, it is more than probable she slept there . . . Last night the Archbishop fell asleep during the singing of a song and drinking a very large full cup of tea. The cup of tea became more and more oblique; a tender young lady saw the impending calamity, but feared to interfere. Presently a faint squeal announced the accomplished evil – quietly and completely the whole contents of the teacup were in the Apron of the sleeping Primate – like a lake embosomed in black rocks. How to save dignity and yet prevent further ill? Gently they shook his Grace, and held his four-cornered garment till succour arrived. The kind old gentleman was amused as one who is never out of temper may be, – and we all laughed and rejoiced amain.

It is amazing how Edward fits into this most Victorian scene. He blends as it were with the old ladies and the knitting and the purple-vestmented domestics, but not without a touch of malicious glee.

He was searching for mature cedar trees for a painting nine feet long of the Cedars of Lebanon. Oddly he found very few in 1860: the Oatlands Park Hotel, Walton-on-Thames, Pepperharrow, and Paine's Hill. Lebanon itself was closed to him by the events of that year, when the Druzes set about massacring Christians and the Turks were unable or unwilling to interfere. Edward had planned to return there that very summer. Now, true to the PRB principles, he sought to amplify his sketches from English models. There was another search, even more frantic, for fig trees. At one time he was pursuing them as far away as Reading. The ones he finally settled on were in the old 'fig garden' supposed to have been planted by Thomas à Becket at the medieval Bishop's country house near Shoreham, where they still flourished at a vast size. Unfortunately 'development' has now taken place, with the consequent intrusion of the most horrible little dentists' villas, but one or two of the trees do still exist, though a modern Lear would find it even harder to track them down.

It was the London season, and Edward did some dining out: if the numbers were not too many, he records who sat where at each dinner. The Macaulays had him at the end of June with Venables, Thompson of Trinity, W. G. Clark, Lady Gray, the Stephens, Spedding and Frank Lushington; he enjoyed himself hugely at a party that would terrify most of us; 'Spedding ever very beautiful – real,' he noted. On another day at the Academy 'saw nothing I cared for', and 'the accounts of Sir Richard Bethell were disgraceful and terrible: his conduct to Mary frightful and were he within reach I would give him a severe shaking'. On the 14th of July he was at 'Pepperharrow Park, *most magnificent cedars*', then when he should have been elsewhere, he walked to Paine's Hill, 'great and fine cedars'. Meanwhile, to his great pleasure, Augustus Egg married. 'Miss North's tame salamander escaped and found its way to the maid's room.' In the last days of July he went to Nuneham, where Lady Waldegrave asked him to paint. He wrote her a nervous letter before doing so. It was a grand house from the last century in a park of that great, sleepy beauty that used to be so typical of England. The Harcourts were descended from the Archbishop of York, and later on they produced a politician and a peer, but the house, once it had central heating, consumed a ton of coal a day. The children would go down with the cart-horses to Culham station to collect it. Nuneham is still the same, from the outside at least, as when Edward Lear knew it, though it has changed hands; it is like an island, wonderfully cut off from Oxford. The first night Edward spent there, fourteen dined. The next time there was 'no party', which meant eight.

It was August and he was depressed. Seeing the calm beauty of what he painted at Nuneham,[6] it is hard to credit his depression. Even his pencil and water-colour sketch on his earlier visit is as lyrical as a Gainsborough, which it somewhat resembles. He worked on the terrace at dawn and at the Carfax, a monument in the park removed from the heart of Oxford to permit bigger and faster traffic at a time when seventeenth-century sculpture was out of fashion. It is at home now, in its Arcadian world.

But the loneliness of this life! After lunch gloom and cloud, and I as desolate almost as in Knowsley days. Walked to the Lock Bridge and meadows and half round the park – Knowsley often in my memory! [Greek:] Other days! Short walk with Fortescue. Superb Lady Selina! how grand and charming. Aug. 6th Very quiet evening making a Nalphabet for C. B. 7th Drew the outline of Oxford. Even now I do not know if the two pictures will ever be completed or thrown away. [Greek:] I am not happy, but when was I ever happy? . . . I am tired out, and how!

On the 9th the others left after lunch and he was overwhelmed by loneliness. The evening was purple and lovely but Edward was in despair. 'Chords long forgotten, and I thought long dead, have given out fresh sounds tonight when suddenly struck. [Greek:] Better take no notice of them.' On the following day, 'a glooglooogloomy feeling is over Nuneham if Lady Waldegrave is not there. When she is it don't matter how large or small the party is. Town by 12.' His most cheerful entry for August came at the end of the month, on an evening when he was slightly drunk, after working for the third day on his big *Masada*. 'Ah! very calm moonlight but dim and darkling! The *absolute quiet* of those stately moveless trees.'

In mid-September he was at Lewes, walking on the hills and coming home with the riflemen. He saw another fine park at Firle, a house which commanded a whole regiment of elm trees. 'A parky-fieldy, brown-cow-frequented, approach to an old house . . . The Gages appear to me homely and really good folks – with no "fashion".' They at least are still there, though the house is grander than Lear allows: the parky-fieldy, brown-cow-frequented approach deceived him, and it is odd that he does not notice the paintings. He walked out from Arundel by the mill and up the chalkpit to Burpham and Peppering a few days later, and there at least he was perfectly, almost magically contented. He went to the old yew trees at Kingly Vale near Chichester, which he loved and had drawn: but his picture now conveys little but inspissated gloom. His friend Sayers had taken him there from Midhurst in about 1832: 'something unearthly of feeling used to pervade this place', where now there were rifle-butts. Still, he drew a little. One day he had breakfast with C. M. Church, 'ever the same good Christ Church man, but years of *Theology* work their wills'. He went down to Dudbrook, a house of Lady Waldegrave's in Essex, where he sat up late with Fortescue and saw the Comte de Paris.

Then in the last week of September, Walton-on-Thames swallowed him up alive. Sometimes the boy failed to turn up and he had to carry his own enormous canvas. Sometimes the other hotel guests were boring, sometimes they had curiosity value. 'Robins singing in the cedar trees. Flies in this room. And hunt thereof.' Leafing through old letters, he pieced together the story of his brother Henry, who enlisted as a private and served seven or eight years in a foot regiment, but then deserted to join the cavalry. He was caught and sent to a 'condemned regiment', so he wrote to his father. The Duke of York agreed that changing positions was not desertion, so Mr and Mrs Lear went to Carisbrooke Castle and bought Henry out, and brought him home. 'What a bargain!! . . . I must have been 7 or 8.' It is likely enough that Henry had some connection with Edward's troubles. A further revelation soon followed, about another subject. 'Oct. 26. Colonel Hornby [Greek:] Lady Derby said If ever I become Countess of Derby, no Hornby shall ever enter the door of Knowsley! And she kept her word. No Hornby at Knowsley at Lady E's wedding.' The two families had been doubly or trebly linked by marriages in two generations; Lear preferred the Hornbys, and after the zoological Earl his Derby loyalty diminished, though he still felt himself a family retainer.

He corrected the proofs of more Tennyson songs and in November ('blue, blue firs and brown fern') he read *The Mill on the Floss*, which he thought unwholesome. He was deeply miserable. Rome was still danger-ous, even Penry Williams thought so. 'Shall I stop the large paintings, pay debts, and take out enough from "savings" for a year's Orientalism?' At the end of December the hotel boiler burst and his room was flooded. 'New rooms . . . weary work.' At the end of the year, he had £117 in Drummond's Bank, and £120 income from pictures, he gave £10 in charity and was paid £290 by three clients. A letter to Emily Tennyson (Jan. 14, 1861) reveals the vehemence of his sympathy with the winter condition of the city poor. He left his hotel with the cedars unfinished, and his future plans in the air. On 3 February 'Daddy Hunt came to breakfast, very pleasant morning and he kindly preached on all the pictures.' On the 7th he saw Alfred Tennyson listening to Tyndall at the Royal Society, and wrote to *The Times* about 'the American split'. His plans at this stage were, if he suddenly sold two big pictures, to go to Jerusalem, but otherwise to go to Greece in March: to see Elis, Crete, Epidaurus and the falls of the river Styx. But now Ann was ill: the creaking, murmuring note of his worry about her had gradually increased over a number of years. 'My plans are of course more than ever uncertain now.' He sold his *Civitella di Subiaco* for £150 to Sir Francis Goldsmid on 4 March, which he thought a good price; on the 7th he warned Fortescue of Ann's illness, and on the 11th she died.

Of all the pages of his daily journal, these are the most terrifying. Naturally he suffered worse than she did. He might of course have been absent, but as it was, because of the trouble in Rome, he happened to be there, and her death opened the floodgates of a grief that drove him almost crazy. *Essays and Reviews* had appeared, and Edward had been pleased with his water-colour of Cervara; he heard Lord Salisbury say, 'What is to become of us if you do away with miracles? And how rash of Jowett! He might have been a Bishop!' Edward saw John Gould (hardly altered – kindly and coarse), and Ann was 'very fading and poorly but in good spirits'. Then 'her pain dreadful but she never swerves in the least iota from cheerfulness. I could not stay, for exciting her is the worst thing at present. O! O! O! O! O! O!' She said, 'My precious, what a blessing you are here and not with the Arabs. Eye hath not seen. O my love, how disagreeable for you. How sorry I am. Bless you, my dear Edward, what a comfort you have been to me, *all* your life.' Two days later, she died quite peacefully, but Edward was heartbroken. When she was buried, and when he had paid five guineas to a West End doctor for two visits and an anaesthetist, he took refuge with the Tennysons. 'His conversation very nasty after dinner, how he's poor and ruined etc.' The following day: 'Alfred always [Greek:] drinks a lot, and now he talks about these nasty things, resolved to go home tomorrow.'

Almost insensibly the passionate grief disappeared, to surface again with no diminution of its force only on birthdays and anniversaries. Yet when he records 'Vastly, shockingly miserable and ill, body and mind', one knows what is the matter. They had talked about Ann having a rupture, so Edward thought he had one, but it was not that. 'May 3rd Zoo, boa eating dux and rabbits.' He dismantled his rooms, and arranged to meet Giorgis at the end of May, and drew Ann's grave at Highgate. He got his small cedars for the Clives into a mess and resolved to abandon them. 'Hurried to the train but lo! – just then off it fizzed.' He got to Italy, by train from Paris for the first time, in 1861, wafting through the Customs by waving a letter from Cavour. As for the unification of Italy, he recorded what Lord John Russell told him of a private interview of Pius IX with Odo Russell: '"If I could for one moment believe in the unity of Italy, I would place myself at its head. But I know it's not possible and you English know it too, and if it were possible you would prevent it, for you are well aware that you are inferior in every talent to Italians, and would suffer if Italy were a great nation to be your superior!" The old blashphemin pigg!'

CHAPTER ELEVEN

GREECE

JUNE the 1st found him in Turin, where six hotels were full but at last the Tre Corone took him in. The King was reviewing his troops, so Lear had stumbled from an English seaside place 'which curseth him who comes and him who goes', from the rough winds and seasickness of the Channel, into scenes of considerable animation. He teamed up with a travelling English merchant, wrote long notes on strangers and stressed to his diary how lonely he was. He trundled off to Genoa and Livorno (Leghorn), but Giorgis failed to appear. He gloomily noted 'old Albanian dog at the hotel' and at last Giorgis wrote to him in Florence. But his diary recorded only 'agreeable Singapore man and bride, saith tigers at Singapore eat one Chinaman a day'. Still, there were nightingales, he painted and drew on the bridges, and he began to settle. On the 12th he found he could get into the Villa S. Firenze by S. Miniato, high above the city: 'the *real* view of Turner; it is very glorious and I shall set to work at it thoroughly'. Florence was unspoiled and full of nightingales even in June. It seems to have remained so, according to the oldest aesthetes who were in their eighties in the 1950s, until the tram-lines confused the view with their overhead cables. What was left of the aesthetic aristocracy departed then like a migration of swallows. To Edward Lear it was all perfectly fresh, it was like what Walter Pater says in *Marius* of the greatest thrill of travellers, waking up in the early morning in a new town. '*How* can I *ever* have looked with delight at Gaspard Poussin or Salvator Rosa?'

Giorgis arrived after some drama of trains on the 20th, 'just as if he had not been away'. Edward planned to draw the Villa Petraia in earnest, then take six days over the three great churches, and after that to travel more widely in Italy or Switzerland. He was happy and therefore vague. Small notes are revealing about his life: one Sunday late in June he tried 'native beer'; at the Villa Niccolini the view was expansive but undrawable; Giorgis told him amusing stories about Corfu; at first he would eat two ices in the evening on the way home, then it was three, and finally (written shamefacedly in Italian) 'the usual four ices'. In July he was at Lucca where he found nothing to draw, 'the Carrara mountains are grand, but will not come in with the towers and trees'. This disorientation of distances from foregrounds was a problem to him life-long and he tried many solutions, the best probably in ten years' time in the Himalayas. His Florentine paintings are beautiful but seldom exciting, and yet the Tate Gallery has the most thrilling row of flame-like ancient cypresses painted at Villa S. Firenze on 8 June 1861. They were a mere water-colour study for the foreground of some vast canvas, in which the view beyond them is scarcely even adumbrated. They have almost the intensity of van Gogh: they combine the keenest natural observation with a sense of their quirky singularity of shape, as Judy Egerton points out.[1] His eyes were extremely open and sharp, he recognized his best subjects at once, and stalked them if they were saleable. Cattle with Thessalian wheeled carts scarcely merited a sketch, he did not stop for a long road lined with aspens festooned in vines: 'I should not like to live in Carrara, click click, tap tap, hammer hammer, chip chip.'

At last in mid-July, 'Made up my mind after some time on my way to draw, to go tonight by the Genoa steamer, irresolution which made Giorgis laugh, being so unusual ... The sense of loneliness was terrible.' From Turin, which he reached by rail, he set off in a one-horse car to explore the Val d'Aosta.

> There is a gloom about these Alpine valleys I can't abide. I doubt my staying anywhere long till I get to Lac Leman, unless indeed Courmayeur is more pleasant and lively ... Courmayeur. Mont Blanc has spread itself with a wonderful crescent of enormous dimensions. Very grand and vast, but destitute of all but immensity – graceless. A man goes about with a skyblue piano. No quiet in Switzerland and no approximation to harmony with the scenery in any way ... bus full of English. The clatter and bother of Swiss inns and travel is most odious to me ... Unhinged and altogether upset. I do not know what to do. I dislike and hate the Chamouni journey yet do not wish to give it up. Then I would fain have good drawings of Chillon, the Veeray view, but had rather be at work in Hastings.

He worries about Giorgis, whether to take him or leave him, then writes in Italian, 'Better I go to Corfu.' At once things settle. At Ferney near Geneva he draws a wonderfully beautiful, Claude-like landscape: the edge of the Jura, I suppose. He records a delicious fish lunch, though not as cheap as Turin. Then suddenly the railway tempted him and with very brief diary notes he rushed back to England, to St Leonard's, where he worked at his painting of the Villa Petraia. There on 1 September he passed 'Assuredly one of the purest, loveliest days it is possible to see on earth, not a breath of air, the sea a perfect mirror, hardly rippled.' But he was 'rayther in the morbids.' The root cause of his restless and desperate condition was the death of Ann.

Italy had been disturbed by Cavour's death and the various small upheavals that would lead to its freedom. English consciences were deeply disturbed by the crisis of the liberal *Essays and Reviews* and reactions to that: the crisis had been far worse and deeper than the fury over Tract 90 and Newman's break-away. The American news was terrible too, but Edward Lear's deepest anxiety was the longing to lay his head on 'an intelligent female's buzzim', as he wrote to Fortescue. His bed was like a petrified plum pie and the housemaid was a goose in crinolines. His consolations were simple dinners of sole and beneficial beer, walks at night beside the melancholy sea, and Palgrave's *Golden Treasury*, just out. But he hated the act of painting in oils, the tiny strokes, the dead stillness, the endless care over outlines, it was like grinding away his nose. Meanwhile Holman Hunt was painting in a field near Oxford, and five or six parties of fans would arrive there daily with baskets of lunch and autograph albums. Lear's *Cedars of Lebanon* were praised to the skies in a Liverpool newspaper. It should really have been his moment, but it was not.

He stayed with the Goldsmids and in London saw something of his intellectual friends, painters like Hunt, engineers and architects and Members of Parliament, and humdrum middle-class people for whom he felt affection. He knew that Woolner had moved in with Palgrave, and that 'a new spasmodic poet' called Swinburne was publishing, and he wrote long letters continually to Fortescue in Ireland. But by 12 October he had finished his *Petraia*, and by the 28th his complete *Nonsense* book, with forty-two woodcuts, was ready for negotiations with a publisher. 'Maclean also is to do a small work on the Ionian islands.' This stray remark is really epoch-making, because it is virtually our first news of what may well be Lear's masterpiece, his chromolithographs of the islands: we should follow its whole history, but first it is better to discuss the *Nonsense*, which he wrote to cheer himself up, and over which his publisher tricked him. The book was a huge success, it became the fashion, sold 4000 copies in six months, and had reached thirty-five editions by 1905: it is what made Lear famous; it led to his first American edition in 1863, and in a debased form it is still selling briskly. It contained 112 limericks, sixty-nine of them already published in the first and second editions in 1846 and 1855.[2]

In October 1860 he began work, and commissioned the first woodcuts (from his own subtler drawings) from the Dalziel brothers. Woodcutters were cheaper than lithographers, and he wanted to sell the volume outright to a publisher, rather than publish it for himself using McLean. To him in October 1861 he offered ten or twelve drawings of Corfu to lithograph; he was to pay Lear so much for the use of them, providing he gave up all his rights on the earlier nonsense publications. McLean wisely turned this scheme into Lear's *Ionian Islands*, the most desirable of all his books. So Lear went off to Routledge, who offered to buy 1000 copies of the *Nonsense*, but refused to buy the book as a package. Three shillings and sixpence a copy he felt might be the right price. Lear went at once to Dalziel as a printer and made a down payment for the first 1000 copies, and published them at Christmas 1861. By June 6000 were printed and 4000 sold, but Routledge had not paid Lear a penny for any of them, while Dalziel was understandably pressing to be paid. On 1 November 1862 Routledge did at last agree to buy the book outright, paying £125 in all. Edward was relieved to be free of the whole business and pleased with his winnings. Yet he must have been owed at the very least £500 or £1000, and the copyright of course was worth many thousands. The firm was Routledge and Warne, which is how this became a Warne's book a little later. There were nineteen editions within Edward Lear's lifetime with no profit to him.

There was little difference in his comic style, although a pleasing subtlety creeps into the cartoons, and maybe animals are more fearsome: the fish investigating the Old Person of Ems who fell into the Thames are hungry-looking, though they are not mentioned in the poem; the cow up a tree at Aosta has a formidable look; and the Old Man on whose nose most birds of the air could repose does express anxiety until they fly away, but then one fears he will feel lonely. Bulls and bears are naturally fierce, but so is the raven of Whitehaven dancing a quadrille, and the man who partners it will come to a bad end. There are other signs of scarcely suppressed aggression. The most fearsome drawing is of the Old Person of Bangor whose face was distorted with anger (he tore off his boots and subsisted on roots) and the most charming, which comes next to it, is the fat Old Man of the Coast, smoking contentedly on a post sticking out of the sea. The verses are levelly humorous on the whole, but the cartoons have an impish and independent life. The Old Lady sitting in a holly tree is particularly pleasing, so is the Young Lady of Lucca whose lovers completely forsook her (she ran up a tree and said fiddle de dee). There are more queer eating habits than ever, and some odd glimpses of fashion, such as the Old Person of Leeds, whose head was infested with beads, and escape is still a favourite theme. The small spotty dogs who were bought at Ryde with some clogs add wonderfully to the vacuous look of daftness on their owner's face. This book in short is worth the affection that has been felt for it. It is only a pity that it has overshadowed Lear's popular reputation as a painter.

In November 1861 Lear got back to Corfu, leaving a trail of long, gossipy letters from Trieste about his railway adventures. His adventures on board ship were not at all as cheerful: she was twenty hours late on what should have been a day's journey down the Adriatic, and at one moment they came near to turning back. Even the train journey by way of Vienna had been slow and hungry: in fact when the sun shines on him it is extraordinary how swiftly Lear becomes happy. He was happy in Corfu too, in spite of 'the balls and small, monotonous whist or tea-parties ... in this very very very small tittletattle place ... and a multitude of new and uninteresting acquaintance'. In fact he was so happy on the whole with Corfu that I shall reproduce a page or two of some selections from his letters made by Lawrence Durrell, since if you take them together and exclude diaries you get an incomparable impression of Edward Lear in an idyllic setting, even though he says 'the aspect spiritual of this little piggywiggy island is much as a very little village in Ireland would be, peopled by Orangemen and Papists ... with a resident crowded garrison'. The passages I quote began their public life as an appendix to *Prospero's Cell*, pencilled down in 1941, but when that book was published they were left out, until they were edited by Maria Aspioti and printed on their own in 1965.

Dec. 1st. The aspect meanwhile – (with which I have most to do – tho' unhappily no man be quite independent of the others,) is – so far as climate and country goes, lovelier than ever. Yet seeing it has never rained since April last, and that it is now daily perfectly clear and fine – the wise anticipate three months rain at once and continual.

17th. I wish I had more time for Greek: – if I had it my way, and were an axiom maker and Lawgiver, I would cause it to be understood that

Greek is (or a knowledge of it) the first of virtues: cleanliness the second, and Godliness – as held up by parsons generally – the third. O mi hi! – here is a noo table – sicks feet too – by 2 feet hate! I shall dine at one end of it – write at the other, and 'open out' in the middle.

Jan. 21st 1862. The woes of painters: just now I looked out of window at the time the 2nd were marching by – I having a full palate and brushes in my hand: whereat Col. Bruce saw me and saluted; and I not liking to make a formillier nod in presence of the hole harmy, I put up my hand to salute, – and thereby transferred all my colours into my hair and whiskers – which I must now wash in Turpentine or shave off.

Feb. 2nd. There is a man in a boat here under the window – who catches fish all and every day with a long five-pronged fork: a waistcoat and drawers being his dress. Why should I not do the same?

April 14th. Here's a bit of news to wind up with. After I had written the letter which encloses this, I heard a great noise, and saw four carts full of furniture, all being brought into this house – a proceeding which disturbed me with fears of being less quiet – seeing that a sixth added to the five families in this house, would not add to my peace. So I asked a servant going upstairs what the row was. 'It comes from Kozziris,' says the man. 'Mrs K is going to leave him and come and live here.' I said nothing, but I did not believe it: the Lord 4bid such a thing should happen. But when George came, says he, 'these things are to be sold by auction, for Sig. Kozziris is going to leave his "Posto" as keeper of the prison, and they are going to England, where they say Signora Kozziris is of a familia grande e ricca assai – and she will keep him.'

Easter Sunday, April 20th. I wish you were here for a day, at least today . . . I have been wondering if on the whole being influenced to an extreme by everything in natural or physical life, i.e. atmosphere, light, shadow, and all the varieties of day and night, – is a blessing or the contrary – and the end of my speculations has been that things must be as they may, and the best is to make the best of what happens. I should however have added 'quiet and repose' to my list of influences, for at this beautiful place there is just now perfect quiet, except only a dim hum of myriad ripples five hundred feet below me, all round the giant rocks which rise perpendicularly from the sea: – which sea, perfectly calm and blue, stretches right out westward unbrokenly to the sky, cloudless that, save a streak of lilac cloud on the horizon. On my left is the convent of Paleokastrizza, and happily as the monkery had functions at 2 a.m. they are all fast asleep now, and to my left is one of the many peacock-tail-hued bays here, reflecting the vast red cliffs and their crowning roofs of Lentish Prinari, myrtle and sage – far above them – higher and higher, the immense rock of S. Angelo rising into the air, on whose summit the old castle still is seen a ruin, just 1,400 ft above the water. It half seems to me that such life as this must be wholly another from the drumbeating bothery frivolity of the town of Corfu, and I seem to grow a year younger every hour. Not that it will last. Accursed picnic parties with miserable scores of asses male and female are coming tomorrow, and peace flies – as I shall too . . .

April 27. I wish I was married to a clever good nice fat little Greek girl – and had twenty-five olive trees, some goats and a house. But the above girl, happily for herself, likes somebody else.

May 7. A more gritty vexation is that I have done so little in Greek or in Greek topography this winter. Nevertheless I shall bring away the most part of this Island I fancy . . .

Lear's house that year was on what he called the Line Walk, where it now stands next to the National Bank of Greece. The prison governor's wife was Lady Emily Kozziris, daughter of the Earl of Clancarty. All these letters were to Fortescue: one may add to them from Lear's letters to Emily Tennyson, which in 1941 were unknown, though some are now published in the *Selected Letters* edited by Vivien Noakes. In December 1861 he wrote by an open window,

> with the clear mountains perfectly reflected in a mirrorlike sea dotted all over with sparkle sail-boats, and powdered, – far on each side of the two big men of war lying close to my door – with an infinity of white specks – (millions to wit) of what you might guess to be lotus flowers or sea mushrooms, but in reality they are seagulls, placidly waiting for their dinner from the big ships' kitchens. I do not remember ever to have seen such a month of purely beautiful weather at this season: day after day the same, – the same rose and crimson evenings, the same lilac and silver mornings.

Yet he says that when he arrived he was miserable, because all his friends had left the island, so he was on the point of journeying on to Athens, when he found his new house with a perfect north light, and lost himself in work. When the winter was over, he thought he might tackle Elis or an island, maybe Crete, or Epidaurus, before coming to London for the Exhibition, in the hopes that his *Corfu* and his *Lebanon* might draw in more commissions. In February he went through the works of Tennyson again, and selected 250 suitable lines to illustrate, without feeling he would ever live to finish them. His plans kept changing. Henry Grenfell MP commissioned 'my spirits falter in the mist', which in the end Edward painted as Beachy Head, looming white in terrific majesty, though his first thought was to do it at Freshwater or the Needles. To his diary in that same December, he remarked, 'I should not stay another year here. Certes. If I could only get Tin enough I would do all my destined topography, and then try to settle once and for all in England: near Highgate if I could. O my dear Anne.' He means the cemetery. When he worked at his big, slow painting of Florence he was 'looking back as far as six years old (the clown and circus at Highgate)'. His journals are never wholly idyllic: when he was perfectly happy he often wrote little or nothing in them.

About the most important events of 1861 he was most circumspect. They both happened far away in England: Lushington married, and he hoped that might let in a little light to Park Hall, which was already steeped in gloom, and Mr Harcourt died, about which he wrote a letter of careful tact and sympathy to Chichester Fortescue, though the big question that arose from the grave was obviously whether he would now or ever marry Lady Waldegrave. He did so of course, after a decent period of mourning and retirement on her part, and in so far as a fully mature marriage can be happy, theirs was so, although they were too late to have children. Lady Waldegrave now had almost everything that as a Jewish musician's daughter she can ever have wanted: a husband she had known many years, who loved her, who had some importance in politics, some experience of life, and excellent taste, the money and the substance as hostess she had attained as Mrs Harcourt, and the glamour and title of a Countess Waldegrave, to which she still clung. It was a remarkable career, which she finished off by marrying her niece Constance to a Mendip neighbour as Lady Strachey. This was the Constance who in 1907 scissored and published Lear's and Fortescue's (Lord Carlingford's) correspondence, with an introduction by Henry Strachey, a not unremarkable painter whom Edward had encouraged as a young man. A more varied second volume followed in 1911.

One must add that in 1862 Edward found that 'Craven's brother did wish to marry' Gussie Bethell, which put paid to his own intense but inchoate wishes in that direction. It was that October at Hackwood that he made a joke about a word in Virgil or Horace, *sequaces*, which he claimed to remember because of the ducks, or sea-quacks. The very same week 'CF very happy. Half think to go down to Dudbrook.' Then of another, much older lady: 'Col. Bolton's in 1834 was first time I ever saw her. Wordsworth was there and the old Earl and Countess of Lonsdale. She could consider no person to be human or Christian who was not Tory. In after days at Rome this disgusted me. Old Archbishop of York wanted her to marry G. V. Harcourt.' How long ago it seemed, now that he was fifty and had taken to musing, even in his diary. He remembered '*How* weary I used to be at Levens and Elford twenty-seven years ago' with Mrs Howard. On 5 November he noted where Noah got his honey, 'from the Ark-hives'. He 'sat a long time with dear little Gussie, who is absolutely good and sweet and beautiful', and then he was off again to Corfu. His pictures had not been well hung, though the advertisement (or was it the huge success?) of the limericks seems to have done some good, since thirty-three are listed as sold under 1862, though a gap follows, and one suspects they were not all sold in that one year. For example, he only began the first sketches of Beachy Head in October, when he stayed at Eastbourne in the Sussex hotel, yet it is listed under the same year. It is one of his masterpieces. We do know for certain that at the New Year of 1863, he had £1500 in the 3 per cent stocks.

It was essentially in the spring of 1863, at the last moment, that he made the coloured drawings for his *Ionian Islands*. Paxos, his first port of call, has perhaps altered less than the others, and as he first saw it, the island seemed enchanted. 'Moon like day. Murray sent man and boat pulled in to a little port, looked sparkly and bright and quiet in the moonlit silver and black shade.' He got to bed at 2.20 in the morning in a clean, small room, though he disliked the unstrapping and uncording he had to do on his own without Giorgis. He was up at seven choosing his view, 'grey limestone, endless filmy olives. Great colour and beauty of olive/sea vegetation, little of form. Difficulty of making Paxos picturesque.' In fact it was that failure that lay at the root of his success, apparent in each version. He drew a picture of perfect provincial peace and quiet, enlivened if at all only by a few normal-looking goats, but in doing so he expressed the true genius of the place, the mere olives, the mere rocks, the flat water, a very few houses. Of all Lear's lithographs, this and the *Zante* (Zakynthos) are the two I know best and love most. *Zante* is a grand, oriental sea-town where Solomos was born, whose poems Lear first bought in 1861. But *Paxos* is pure innocence. It is a triumph of restraint and of study, by one who studied the landscape like the subtlest of poems. Luckily a sketch for this beautiful picture was sold in Edinburgh last year, or rather the picture itself before Lear copied it on to the stone.

It is an arguable view that throughout these lithographs, or rather chromolithographs, on which Lear decided as a medium only at the last moment, and then with only the merest touches of colour, the prints, though they lack the dew-freshness and variety of the water-colours, gain more proportionately, are more perfect and more permanent, than what is lost from any other, earlier condition. There is more thought in their composition, they are in a true sense 'finished' as only the best of his 'finished' water-colours are. The image has stood still in his eye, or his soul has become a mere brooding over the landscape, or the spirit of place itself has totally possessed him. They are not 'poetic' in any sense in which his Italian paintings could be called so, or his *Beachy Head*, yet in another, quieter sense, they are most deeply poetic in their sober colours and their delicate lines. He had considered this series since 1857, and now he published the book himself like his first Roman book, with hardly any text, though what he does add is fascinating.

As late as August 1863, 'All yesterday I tried various materials, charcoal, lamp-black, pencil, chalk – by which to produce drawings fit for Photography – but all failed.' Harvard has a drawing of Palaeokastritsa that seems to be part of that doomed experiment. The idea then was to keep up his name as a topographic painter in readiness for the day when he would produce a smaller-sized *Topography of Greece*, 'to be one day printed with my Journals'. It was a dream of completeness, probably inspired by old Colonel Leake, whose very precise, topographic Greek journals were published late in his life. Lear's letter to Leake, probably his only one, is a moving account of the state of things in Corfu, and of how little the British had done for the island; it still lies unpublished in the record office at St Albans. Lear finished in October, and then settled down to write 600 letters inviting subscriptions. Financially he felt himself to be in a tight corner: hence the frenzy. The book was a success in the end, but it was also a worry: it appears that Edward never discovered a publisher ready to support him, and knew no other way of selling his lithographic prints but by private subscription. It makes an interesting footnote to the famous capitalist enterprise which was the motor of the Victorian age. His reason for publishing when he did was surely that the British colony of the Ionian Islands was due to come to an end, and as he preferred to act under British authorities, this was his last chance.

He was handed from official to official with letters of introduction; they made his work quicker and his arrangements simpler. He saw seals and caves and dim olive-veiled roads, 'endless pale blue grey rox, and asphodel, and long armed olives'. On St Maura (Levkas) there was a sea of olives spreading out 'really like a Claude or Turner morning view', but then some bits of rock in a foreground reminded him of 'my early Olevano studies, when I first began to paint'. He thought Kephalonia gloomy and severe with something very solemn in the vast ancient remains. Zante was elegant, it had infinite charm but no more: it was the great currant market and he felt its vines were 'one unbroken continuance of future currant-dumplings and plum-puddings'. At Ithaca he drew Vathy, and at Cerigo, the easternmost of the islands, Nerval's and Baudelaire's Cythera with the British gallows in its heart, he made friends with Bulwer and Massey. His book was out in November, holding its rugged mountains and its scarcely wrinkled seas in perfect balance. It was admirably undramatic. Subscribers included the Queen, the Prince of Wales, the Duc d'Aumale and three Barings, but not Alfred Tennyson.

There is no doubt that Edward enjoyed the travelling for that book. He was thrilled by new landscapes, vast glooms lit up by the flashing of a pigeon's wing, huge temples that an old man remembered high, before they thundered downhill to the sea years before, or were looted for later buildings; he notes tame deer and rat-catching 'the only pursuits of the lonely English) and a monastery with 'the old quince marmalade, raki and coffee', then a wonderful lunch, while Wednesday in Lent confined a priest to caviar and lemon, and cats sipped delicately at a trough. He saw Greek stones reused in many walls, and at Missolonghi 'the bare, mangy, fox-skin hills on each side – it is now my fate to walk between them'. August Egg died at Algiers, 'a dear good fellow, and one regrets he was connected with the narrow il-liberal Academy', but when Colonel Leake's widow died he uttered a single great cry of grief. He had loved the old lady even more than he admired her husband and his friend. He noted delicious, unexpected wine in a number of places, some of it twenty-three years old, some 'very dear, five pence a bottle, but six years old: a wonderful wine'.

He compared the attractions of England and those of his Greek paradise quite soberly one day in May.

> It seems to me that I have to choose between two extremes of affection
> for nature – towards outward nature that is – English or Southern – The
> former, oak, ash and beech, downs and cliffs, old associations, friends near
> at hand, and many comforts not to be got elsewhere. The latter olive –
> vine – flowers, the ancient life of Greece, warmth and light, better health,
> greater novelty, and less expense in life. On the other side are in England
> cold, damp and illness, constant hurry and bustle, cessation from all
> Topographic interest, extreme expenses: and at the south are . . .'

Here he breaks off. It is strange that he makes no mention of books or libraries, works of art or museums, doctors, since he had passed fifty, or any other of the habits and institutions on which we may pride ourselves. He appears to have despaired of marrying; perhaps now he just wanted to go on travelling for ever, to go on being as young as he could for ever. He had never settled down to an English career as an artist, and he did not propose to do so. There was not much to encourage him, and there is a great deal to be said for the choice he did make.

He went on meandering around his islands, though his notes became a little disjointed as he tired. 'George and I delighted in an old white tree trunk just like a recumbent camel . . . Mule kicks hole in basket and breaks bottles. Two little boys standing on donkeys' backs.' At Cerigo he drank excellent wine made locally from Smyrna grapes, 'resting below a pine tree and listening to the waves break – breaking on the sand. Very weary.' The next day, 'I sit on a wall and snort.' He complained of tooth-ache, fleas, the half-wildness of the people and a ferocious wind, the last of which at least is still to be found at Kythera. The Greeks, he says, are thieves who hate *nomous* and *dromous* (laws and roads). Even the landscape, the fifty or sixty ships rounding the most dangerous cape in Europe in a boiling sea, terrified him. All the same, 'larx sing'. He found four or five views, but nine bugs and fourteen fleas died in his bed in a night. 'Steamer may touch. Europa 11.40, blue heaving sea. 7.30 Zante, gayer and more beautiful than ever . . . My impressions as to what was good or vice versa as to Greek scenery were the same in 1848 as in 1863.' Yet he never drew it so well, he never fixed it so permanently as he did in his *Ionian Islands* of 1863. 'Unless I had payed this second visit I could not have been sure of this.' It took him most of June to recover. By the end of the year he had put another £500, making £2000 in all, into the 3 per cents.

Why was he doing rather well? It is partly the slow, inevitable spreading of reputation. It had been a good idea to open a room in his London lodgings as a private gallery, as he did in 15 Stratford Place in 1860, near his student rooms of ten years before. Then his commissions were solider now. In 1853 his *Quarries of Syracuse* had been sold for £250 at the Academy, in 1857 *Corfu* fetched £525 and that was what he asked from Lady Waldegrave for *Damascus* in 1858. The *Cedars* hung fire for some time, because he demanded £735, that is, 700 guineas: in 1864 Lady Ashburton wobbled over this high price, and finally secured it cheap by a well-timed offer when Edward was short of cash early in 1868. When she was dead it went at her sale for a mere £5 and disappeared, but that was when Lear's reputation had simply withered away, twenty or twenty-five years after his death. His setting so high a price on a picture had been an act of defiance that rose out of a disastrous dinner party with Millais. Edward was not avaricious, though every artist would like to think he is someone, not a nobody, and worth something.

The dinner went badly though the food was very good. What he could not stand was Millais' wife, her 'cold Scotch accent, her vulgar enquiries and half suppressed jealousy about Hunt (who is the Sun to a Candle compared with J. E. Millais), her catching at any Aristocratic names, her pity of batchelors . . . and her drawling stoniness disgusted me . . . He, at 30, is like a crafty aged French dancing master, and has neither depth nor softness in his character.' This estimate, not a usual judgment on a colleague for Lear to pass, has the ring of authenticity. At any rate, Millais had just sold his *Apple Blossoms* for 450 guineas and that is why Lear priced his *Cedars* at 700 of the same. Objectively he may have been right: right to try, right in his self-estimate, and right to reckon he might get away with it. Alas, that he did not. Lady Ashburton had married a Baring of sixty when she was thirty-four in 1858; she was a friend of Carlyle and of Tennyson. The painting had no people in it and no architecture: its religious associations were very remote. Still, that failure did not entail a general decline in his fortunes or a general slump in his prices, though it worried him, and his prices did decline.

It is difficult at times to prevent his journals from falling apart into a long history of indecisions. In January 1864 he heard that a Mr Wade-Brown was catching the boat for Marseille on the 4th: would he go too? Certainly not. Then he went, sleeping the night at the Grosvenor Hotel. His landlord and his landlord's wife grieved, 'it is a pain to go away'. This time he travelled by Ancona to Corfu, and by the 15th his routine was re-established 'as before the Fathers fell asleep'. Giorgis had lost an infant son from tetanus, but these family tragedies hardly cast a shadow on Edward's life. The Albanian hills on the opposite coast were deep white under snow, and he was still penning in the outlines of five water-colour drawings of the islands. Sir Henry Storks was at the Palace and Evelyn Baring, whom Lear had met in England as a nephew of T. G. Baring, was his staff officer. Evelyn had a distinguished career, which led to India under his uncle, then to Egypt on his own as an expert in financial stringency, and to the title of Lord Cromer, but at this time, and with Lear at least, he was the sweetest, kindest and funniest of young men, an ideal companion at dinner and a Godsend of efficiency. 'A certain placidity in this Corfu life is a charm – never before attained to except in the early Roman days.' Fifty copies of his island book arrived by post, and Storks, to whom the book was dedicated, did the decent thing, sending him £31 10s. for ten copies at three guineas each. There was a convention of not writing 'guineas' on a cheque: to the end of his life Harold Macmillan, for example, would subscribe to a club servants'

fund in guineas, which he would express as £3 15p. One is bemused into
such anecdotes by Lear's timeless tranquillity: 'the olives dropping as the
sun sank, with dark goats, with bright sheep thereamong'. The fear of
war over Schleswig falls like the smallest cloud-shadow in the distance,
and the genuine fear nearer Corfu hardly falls at all. In that winter
Edward perfected his art as self-caricaturist.

But the British were to leave Corfu, and their refusal to abandon the
guns which were the island's only defence, indeed their insistence on
blowing up the batteries where these guns had been placed, was causing
the bitterest resentment. Edward feared the expense of London and
hated the idea of Athens, but he knew he must go, never perhaps to
return. Colonel Wright, whom he met at the Palace, had contrived to
visit Palmyra with his wife, by the influence of Lady Ellenborough, for
only £15. 'Conceive what a bore it must have been to have gone with the
Wrights.' The note of tartness is unusual, and now every hill and village
haunted him with memories and filled him with sadness. 'Three or four
sails only slowly skimming by – and one heard the songs of the boatmen.
The transparent green and purple brown below the near water edge ...
Try not to regret this place.' If the first consul appointed were one of his
friends from the island tour, then he was all but tempted to linger on
when Corfu became Greek. Or he might pack up everything for England
and make off to Palestine. In March he had eyes only for 'bright grey
and pale yellow lichened trunks shining out from the dark glens of
foliage, here and there broken by bits of bright green with long streaks
of shadow. And the silver edged – as it were – ever moving sheep.' Are
these visions special to a short-sighted man, or are they dream-like? At
any rate they are a match in words to what he did in water-colour, and
they seem to me to rank among the highest attainments of the Victorians.
Edward had come home at last, and he had done it only by knowing that
he had to go away. 'Go off as soon as I can' ... 'I shall now go' ... 'Did
nothing and went no-whither' ... 'Unpacked and painted' ... 'The
green and gold, and the shadows, the light-catching myriad-arm
branches of the olives! Returning saw a drunken sailor sleeping by the
roadside and wished I could do something for him, but did not know
how' ... 'Rumours of panic and civil war to come.' The English were
justly terrified of what the Greeks were saying.

On 2 April it was still 'O asphodels O olives O shadows'. On the 3rd
the sea and wind were violent. He had seen the great battery blown up.
On the 4th 'Politi thinks all the Jews will go sooner or later.' At five that
evening he left by steamer with Evelyn Baring, paying Giorgis £9 10s. in

wages and school fees to the end of May and a 10s. tip. On the ship he
set down his musings.

> She sits upon her Bulbul
> Through the long long hours of night
> And the dark horizon gleams
> O'er the Yashmak's fitful light,
> The lone Yaourt sails slowly down
> The deep and craggy dell –
> And from his lofty nest, loud screams
> The white plumed Asphodel.

In a day they were round Kythera, and in two days Edward saw
Sounion for the first time since 1849, and that evening they docked at
Piraeus. 'Here were rockets and patriotism but no bother for us.' The
following morning he saw the WONDERFUL newly excavated theatre
of Dionysos, the Theseum and the Acropolis. One of the few columns
of Hadrian's temple of Zeus had fallen since he saw it last. He called on
the old historian Finlay who had fought in Byron's war and known him
well: Finlay was rewarded with a Greek property, but it was too close to
Athens, and a later government confiscated it for the King's palace. He
called on that ancient, hawk-like figure, Sir Richard Church, a still more
distinguished remnant from the War of Independence. He found the old
servant who had taken him round the Morea with Lushington and up to
Tempe in 1849 and happily parted with a dollar.

Maybe the dollar that he gave Andrea brought him luck, because he
was off to Crete, which was still under the Turks, and there he wrote the
best journal of his life, and still in that mood heightened by parting that
had inspired him at Corfu, he painted some sketches which are incomparable. Luckily, most of them are now in the Gennadion library at
Athens. Some of his last Corfu paintings are to be found in Philip
Sherrard's brilliant and indispensable *Edward Lear, the Corfu Years* (1988)
with a far more generous selection from diaries as well as letters than
Durrell's pamphlet. Those painted at the last moment are not more
impressive than for example the cover picture (1862) or what he put into
his island book, at which I do not cease to wonder; it was not only a
sense of parting and sunset that sharpened his eye, it was also novelty.
The light is new and different every day, so the influence of novelty is
not always easy to spot. He spent the last three weeks of April and the
whole of May in Crete, constantly travelling with Giorgis, and there can
be no doubt about the freshness with which he saw it.

CHAPTER TWELVE

CRETE

CRETE in our lifetimes has notoriously been to the rest of Greece what Greece has been to the rest of Europe; it has been wild, undeveloped, unspoilt, quite lost in itself, and in a new sense what Pericles said of Athens, the Hellas of Hellas. It was already about to play that role when Edward Lear knew it. Pashley (1837) had made it famous, by doing what Leake did for the mainland, but of all the Turkish provinces Lear visited it was peculiar. The Byzantine aristocracy, as far as it survived at all, had taken refuge there, and Crete had fallen to the Turks only when their energies were flagging at the end of the seventeenth century, so that Cretan refugees, who mostly went to the Ionian Islands, could still be distinguished in Zante and Corfu, and they carried with them their ballads and songs and their long verse romance, the *Erotokritos*, which in Crete itself every shepherd still knew by heart in the 1940s, and some in the 1970s, and from which essentially the 'first' national poet of Greece, Count Solomos of Zante, learned his business.

Crete was more or less unexcavated until Sir Arthur Evans dug at Knossos in 1900, though its innumerable ancient sites were charted by Pashley. Under the Turks it produced by slave labour olive oil, cane sugar and marmalade, that is, oranges preserved in sugar, and it was the principal supplier of sugar to Europe until the rise of slave labour in the Caribbean: so there were numbers of black slaves from upper Egypt in Lear's day, as well as the cheerful, toadlike Turks, the Albanian soldiery who were mercenaries, and the independent-minded Greeks. At the eastern tip, Crete once boasted a banana plantation. One of Lear's most startling drawings to a modern traveller is of the monastery of Arkadi, looking demure and pretty and quite lost in the wilderness under Mount

Ida: then one realizes this is Arkadi before the explosion; just after Lear's time it came under siege, and the Abbot blew up himself and most of his monastery and all his monks, rather than fall into Turkish hands. It was brave of Lear to adventure through such a province.

He intended to publish this journal and illustrate it himself, but he never did so: the publishers thought there was no market, and lithography was coming to an end long before colour photography had been born. The journal was published at last with his sketches in brilliant colour and his old edited diaries intact, by Rowena Fowler in 1984. Of all his travel books it comes closest to what he would have liked. Lear had written up or rewritten and formalized his original diaries in August 1867 at T. G. Baring's (Lord Northbrook's) house in Hampshire, and finished it at Christmas. He thought at first of two volumes, one with Crete and the other with the Corniche of the Riviera which he had visited in November 1864: it is hard to realize how unspoilt that still was. He dropped it, though, and an Egyptian journal followed at once; then in 1868 Corsica distracted him, and that alone saw the light in his lifetime. Spratt's survey was published only in 1865, a year after Lear's Cretan walk. In 1866 there was an uprising in Crete, which was put down with terrible savagery; that is when Arkadi was ruined, and in a way it marked the end of an era, because the Cretan struggle could end only in freedom, as it did a generation later. The situation in 1864 is neatly enough pointed out when a huge crowd of pilgrims invades Lear's Austrian Lloyd steamer at Syra: 'Great row in separating men from women: one man and wife dismissed: Eimai eleftheros – Hellenas (I am a free man – a Greek).'

They had a rough crossing and Crete was blotted out by heavy rain, but at five they got into Chania. 'The 160 or 200 women and children all vomiting and wet through were a sight to see.' They would be deck passengers. Edward thought the port spectacular and drew it exquisitely. A black man was recommended to get him and Giorgis and their eleven objects of baggage on shore, which he did efficiently enough, but then came the hotel, 'a most filthy and wretched hole'. It was called the Constantinople but has now luckily perished, though I recollect some most vigorous fleas in Chania 100 years later. The harbour all the same must have been a dream of beauty: he saw that the next day, but at the time he was relieved to be out of it and to leave the hotel and see his letters of introduction do their work. An Italian who was Dutch consul took him in for the night and fed him; he met a Frenchman who remembered Pashley, and was assured he could safely go wherever he liked, all over the island. Giorgis did not fare so well, but he does not seem to have complained. His eruptions of indignation when they occurred were more temperamental and never expected. After a day or two Lear would generally confess he had been in the wrong about whatever had been the apparent cause, and his worst threat was to pay George off and pay his fare home.

Everything struck him as picturesque, the port, the bazaars, the black men and women, the great galley arches of the Venetian sheds, all the Cretans and the mountains, and 'the queer village of the blacks, with houses in a cluster', outside the city walls. He could scarcely pass a peasant without popping in the epithet 'picturesque', and he saw the plain and hills as like Sparta, which from him was high praise. All the same, he was so discouraged by wind and a slamming window, and by a dog that gave him fleas and a sleepless night, that he half felt like going back to Athens; luckily Giorgis, who had slept worse, laughed at him. The White Mountains gleamed, he thought of Olympus and Palermo: when he went out drawing on his own, 'two Turkish soldiers, one black, came and said "bono" and offered me a cigar'. Tobacco was by now one of the few remaining exports. He hated the stony roads, 'as bad as Cerigo', but the views were growing on him. He played and sang at the English consul's house and wrote out some of his Tennyson songs, then on 15 April he and Giorgis set out for the hills, beginning by exploring Akrotiri and the area near Suda Bay. By that day he was already drawing wonderfully, and catching exactly the spirit of the landscape around Chania. 'The Suda Bay view is very Sicilian in its variety of isolate form, but bluer – grayer – *Claudier*; though it is not unlike the colour around Hybla Megaris (the shore near Taormina).' He was getting it more and more precisely right, even in words.

He called on the Pasha, and walked as far as Mournies, which means the mulberries, a lovely village some distance away. He saw ravens and hooded crows, bee-eaters, orioles and hoopoes. He was reminded of olive trees around Tivoli, 'so strange and dreamlike in life', but the trees were less good, and they crossed deep dells full of lemon trees. They were assigned a guard by the Pasha, whom Lear was not so rash as to refuse, since a refusal might carry a suggestion he was an anti-Turkish agent, and he must simply put up with the disastrous impression his Turkish soldier would make on Christian Greeks. But at last, on the 21st, in cloudy weather and with stomach-ache, and with Zeriff their guard on a horse, they began their serious journey. By nine in the morning it rained. All Edward says is 'the same thyme, cistus, lavender and thorny euphorbus abound . . . Oleanders, and the black arum, and squills'. At least the smell must have given them pleasure. They got to Ayia Triada in three hours, and the Abbot offered them a breakfast of coffee and sweets, then eggs, olives, caviar 'and *astonishing* wine'. The sun came out, and one feels they are really started, but bad weather drives them back to the same monastery. Next morning's breakfast was bean soup, olives and 'snails'. The Abbot asks with concern whether the English eat these, and is a little comforted when Edward assures him how fond they are of sea-snails, which is the Greek for winkles.

They woke with yellow-green sunlight on the vines and figs, and the mountains of Sphakia very clear. All the same, Lear did not feel the scene merited drawing, and as he turned back to the consul's house that was the end of their first journey. The following day they got lost among olive trees and lemon trees near Perivolia, but nightingales were singing and the colours were amazing: the gardens in particular thrilled him with lemon, orange and plane trees, vines and pomegranates, vast aloes, myrtles, sheets of cistus. It was, after all, April. 'Olives very large. Three lepers. Asphodels.' There were, it turns out, whole villages of lepers around Chania. Next they tried Platania, the loveliest of villages once, but vine disease in 1862 had ruined the vines and so the plane trees after which the village was named had been cut down. The lanes were refreshing and nightingale-haunted, Zeriff's horse was carrying Edward's bed as well as Giorgis's, and saddle-bags of drawing things and spare clothes, but the disappointment was great. By now Edward was certain his whole Cretan expedition was to be ill-starred. His mood swung about: they had lunch in grass and buttercups under two or three huge planes, enchanted by the tremendous noise of nightingales. Giorgis said it must have more brains than other birds, because it never sang quite the same twice. Zeriff smoked his hubble-bubble, streams trickled, the air was fine. They got to Gonia, a monastery where 'the wine as usual is absolutely astonishing and not unlike a light port', but which harboured fleas. It is apparent from the relatively trivial subjects Edward drew that when he complained of 'nothing drawable' he had a point. Incredible as it is to us, the loveliest of places was unexciting to him unless it had a particular drama or association. Even at 'Pashley's fountain' there was only one plane tree left. They had soon explored much of north-western Crete, but Zeriff was uneasy there, and the landscape perhaps is less rewarding than the eastern direction, which they had proved only to Ayia Triade and Mournies. They could not explore the White Mountains, or, I suppose, the gorge of the Samaria, which really is exciting, because of the Turkish fear of the Greek mountaineers of Sphakia.

Then at Kissamos of all dull places, or near it, in the simplest of lilac and brown drawings, though it is made with astonishing, swift skill, we strike gold. It is the rapidest of washes, as if sea-waves had washed the sand; the colours are both threatening and lyrical, and it was all over in ten minutes as it came on to rain: 2 p.m. on the 29th. The picture belonged to George Seferis once. It rained on and off all that Easter weekend and mist drifted around the mountain-tops, clearing just enough to show what you were missing. Things went little better at first in the direction of Rethymnon. From Aptera they reached Karydi, by way of the Moslem village of Armeni where Edward was taken to see great plane trees and water-springs in a garden, and no one would accept money for food, drink or favours. Crete he thought had few paintable scenes, full as it was of loveliness. Yet on the morning of 5 May he painted the lake at Kourna, which lies under cliffs, as well as anything he ever drew, and the following day Rethymnon from below Episkopi just as wonderfully. Three weeks later he was drawing Psiloriti like a man inspired. It all makes one wonder whether his gloomy mood about Crete did not overshadow his mind and words, while leaving his hand and eye perfectly untrammelled. Indeed, it must be so. He admits to a charm rare in the world, and thinks the lake 'very fine and Cumberlandish' (but it is better than that and he draws it better). Giorgis goes off to find wild grapes. He protests about sleeping in a hovel: 'We've slept with pigs once in the twenty-four hours and isn't that enough?' He has just observed a man taking lice out of his head and killing them with the edge of the coffee-pot. 'I wish I had made a drawing of Ida between the large oaks.' The oaks were full of blackbirds.

He hated Episkopi, where he stayed with a deaf doctor and his rough but decent brother-in-law. There were numerous Turks in the village but these were Greeks. Lear thought 'the doctor, poor fellow, has much of the gentleman in him'. He wanted Giorgis and Zeriff to sit down with Edward, but they would not. 'Why not? They're free men just as we are.' Edward drew Rethymnon several times like an angel, all the same, and the bay of Armyro. The fact that he was deadly bored there does not affect him: indeed it is just a funny story, written down to entertain himself and then us. He and Giorgis went to the beach and the gardens, they sat under a huge mulberry tree and counted their blessings. Strangers, to whom they must have been objects of curiosity, would say,

'Liking the shade? Good.' No dog barked (except at other dogs) or threatened to bite either, whereas in Moslem villages they fought in packs. The garden people seemed happy and sang; the marrows flourished. A little boy ran up and gave Edward a big bunch of lettuces, which Giorgis washed in the sea, and disappeared again. In the early morning of 9 May, after two days, they got up early and left. Lear had hated his foolish provincial hosts, above all for their eating habits. He found nothing to do at Rethymnon, and 'the lepers at both gates are horrible here'. So they went to Heraklion by ship.

They set out at three and got to bed in Heraklion at eleven. 'O bugs! I caught 34! Read newspapers . . . Ruined cathedral, ruined but splendid walls . . . Town mealy-ruiny, earthquaky, odious . . . a nastier and less interesting Turkish town I was never in.' His guide to the mountains was to be Captain Korakas (Crow), called the Garibaldi of Crete but 'now in Turkish pay, only not paid'. A photograph of him survives in a black turban and breeches, with a huge rifle and his belt stuffed with pistols and other weapons: his moustache alone speaks loudly of heroic ferocity: he was a true Cretan, and the same face, a little older, stares out of the centre of the 'Cretan Pantheon 1889': he died fighting. The Captain is to meet him at Ambelouzo and conduct him further: his plan is to go to Sphakia, approaching from the south. This must mean the upper, not the coastal Sphakia, the heart of the White Mountains, that is, and of resistance to the Turks. It was not possible to approach coastal Sphakia from the south except from the sea. Korakas will guide him to Askyphou, where he will seek help from a certain Vandinos. This would be an exciting scheme even today; in Edward Lear's time it was hair-raising. Yet it seems to be his own idea; at any rate he does not dither and he does not protest. It is not clear whether Giorgis knows what he is in for. It is the first time since they acquired him that they have got free of Zeriff; who is carrying the baggage?

They passed through Knossos and saw only heaps of Roman brick, though there were plenty of nightingales and Edward drew a lovely view at 7 a.m. Giorgis gathered watercress and near Fortetsa they came on the 'tomb of Caiaphas' and some Byzantine walls. 'I don't doubt it was the acropolis of Knossos once on a time.' Their guide was slow and wooden-headed so they paid him and sent him home. 'Black man comes, and little boy, and peasants, and I draw them. They are all good tempered and laugh; small boy almost cries at drawing of a donkey, and is impelled to give me two lemons. I gave him a pencil. Peasants like Life Guardsmen. 1 p.m.' So on they went, drawing here and there and having tiny adventures all day. At last they hired a mule and its man, and a guide of a kind, and got to Arkhanes where floors were earthen and Edward and Giorgis ate snails for the first time in their lives. They enjoyed them, luckily. The wine was good too, and dinner ceremonious with many toasts and compliments, but Edward's camp-bed caused amazement. Giorgis slept in his bed on a dresser, the host and the mule-leader in a big square bed at the far end of the room, and the lady upstairs among her silk-worms. In the middle of all this was a huge jug of the most beautiful rosebuds. Next day they were allowed to pay only for coffee (because it had to be sent out for from the village café). Before half past six Mount Ida, or Psiloriti, came into sight behind Iuktas. 'Stop and draw till seven, a grand mountain scene. Birds calling, mists floating.'

The series of wash drawings that began here was magnificent. Was it the birthplace of Zeus or the antiquity of the Cretans that inspired Lear? Scarcely, but no doubt these things were present in the awe-inspiring penumbra of the great mountain, as with appropriate differences the idea of a savage absolute of liberty must have been present in his dark, dramatic Masada and in his terrifying ridge of Souli. All the same, Psiloriti is a more human mountain, though it is equally august, and the same may be said of his paintings of it. He was hard to please still: 'scenery unwieldy,' he noted, 'with huge lines of green hill, and above, the Ida range.' The simple charm of his rustic outdoor life preoccupied him like the fussiest of foregrounds, the delightful, wavy shade of the mountain planes and the warble-twitter of birds cheered him. At twenty to five and definitely unwell, he got to the house of Bernardakis, where he took water and quinine and coffee. 'I and George both think it better I should give up farther journeys in Crete.' The heat was increasing (now that it had stopped raining), he found little of the 'picturesque' he sought, and the dirt and bad food depressed him. Bernardakis, 'a small old deaf Cerigotto', gave him stocks, roses, wine and uneatable biscuit knobs, which sound like Cretan rusks, but the fleas bit him and the evening and the conversation bored him. Supper was good soup, a tough fowl, some tough artichokes and an omelette. 'I have never known any travelling so hard as this in Crete.' The muleteer was sent to another house because Bernardakis had a daughter; he sulked and went, and even Lear was surprised. There was no po, which always vexed him, and the stinks were sublime and various, and the fleas devoured him, and the old man coughed. Lear and Giorgis were up by half past four.

He judged the form of the hill at Ayios Myron to be good, and his medicine was effective. He drew at Venerato, a scene of some grandeur, though wide and shadeless hills had hidden the big mountain. What he loved and resented was the green, undrawable valleys. The formula of their pleasures was always the same and he endlessly repeated it. He loved the climb, for example, up through leafy valleys towards Ay. Thomas, and drew there with what had become his usual small bunch of Cretans lounging about to create a foreground, the distant mountains vague and the paradise of trees like the fleece on a particularly woolly sheep, which accounts for the numerous nightingales. He knew the wild cypress well enough to draw it with affection now, in light or shadow. Undoubtedly he felt it was what he had mastered in the gardens of the Villa Petraia in Florence, where he drew it more than once. But there really is something special about Cretan cypresses: indeed, in his day there were remnants of cypress forest in Crete, though he never realized that. The ones he drew on the afternoon of 15 May on a knoll to his right are beautifully lifelike. Meanwhile he kept brooding over the past, even in this edited form of the diary. The day before it was the house at Peppering when he was about twelve, today the cawing of the rooks brought back 1823, when he first heard the rooks of Sussex: it also brought back the same tags of Shelley as these moods always did, 'days that are no more' and 'O world, O life, O time, On whose last steps . . .' which he had set to music himself. With the memory of Peppering yesterday he had thought of Tennyson's 'Break, break, break'. These rags and tatters are as near as one can get to the core of his feelings. 'The longer one looks at this place, the lovelier it seems . . . a kind of sadness – tears, idle tears – comes over me, so much here reminds me of England, and of other days.'

In this remote place he stayed in the spotless room of a lay-reader, in a village full of ruins and of trees where his hostess was a lady in a muslin dress like Lady Canning's, and the conversation was about birds and about politics. He was told the nightingales bred and never left, and the swallows left only in October. But why had the English destroyed the fortifications of the Ionian islands? He lied to them, saying he knew nothing about such matters. He felt he was in paradise, but they had cherries at dinner and Giorgis got the squitters that night. At five in the morning Edward was out drawing the village in its rocky setting; he makes it formidable and wonderfully mysterious. 'The great rox,' he said, 'are magnificently picturesque.' He appears to mean dramatic and Calabrian, and a certain touch of the mountains does link his lovely picture to early work, but this is far more skilful, more various, more fully realized in space, and the last of the mist on the further mountains is thrilling. 'Oddly enough, George remembers some similar rox and ivy in some of Penry Williams's paintings'. If Mr Williams was here, said Giorgis, he'd have a lot to do.

By seven that morning they had come to where they saw the plain of Messara to the east and big mountains to the west: they were well to the south of Iuktas and heading for the southern tip of Crete, circling slowly round the south of Psiloritis. The day was already hot but the air was fine. There was no shade, and after three hours of trudging Edward already looked forward to getting back to Chania in ten days' time. There was no further mention of Sphakia.

> George, after long discourse on Ceylon and elephants, has gone to sleep, as Konstandis has done a good while since. The Suliot snores, which for once I allow, as he had no sleep last night. He is disgusted that the Ay. Thomas host put water in our wine; not so I, as I wanted to drink a great deal, being thirsty. The she-mule, an amazing beast for leaping over walls with a backful of luggage, flaps her tail and is woodenly tranquil. The wine was certainly utterly diluted: we drank it out of the foot of the candlestick, which like my tin cup is broken.

They were on higher ground, musing away noon after an early lunch in the cooler air. The grey clouds seemed to Edward very English, but people were busy gathering mulberry leaves to feed their silk-worms. They were three or four hours from Ay. Deka (the Ten Saints), and now Konstandis woke up and wanted to start. Lear said it was too early, and this was so pleasant a place, why hurry to leave it? So the mule-man lay down again, and went straight back to sleep, and Lear went on musing. Suddenly he remembers Harding, who drew a Swiss scene from a sketch by Hullmandel in Volume 4 (1832) of the *Works of Byron*, and in fact four in all of the pictures engraved. 'Ah J. D. Harding! I could have liked once more to have seen you! Wide apart as we were in all thought, yet you had some astonishingly original and true perceptions: and moreover I owed you for some benefits. I write this because I am recollecting some of JDH's illustrations of Lord Byron.' He thought also of Gale and Fowler: R. L. Gale was Fowler's brother-in-law and went with him to Italy in 1834–5; Daniel Fowler was two years older than Lear; Harding, whose pupil Fowler was, must have been twelve years older than that, an insurmountable barrier in one's early twenties. But Harding had been a pupil of Prout and had written a tourist guide to Italy, and Lear gave Fowler some sketches signed *By Lear after Harding*.[1] Fowler was a Canadian and his life has recently been written as *The Painter of Amherst*

Island, but what Lear remembers is Gale and Fowler together when he first knew them, probably in Hullmandel's studio; they had come back from Italy two years before Lear had gone there. They are his main connection with Harding. 'I am feeling that I have received – not much personally – but much through Gale and Fowler; advantages of which I acknowledge the value far more now than then, and which I regret I never showed a wish to repay.'

'Anything more hideous than the long wrinkled hills with scraps of purple above them, clouded and gray, can't be. Ugh! winding ever over dry weary hills.' They were near Gortyn and they could see the island of Paximadi (the Rusk) peering out of the mist off the southern shore of Crete. Lear's disgust at descending, and at Cretan travels in general, was extreme, and became a joke between him and Giorgis. 'Descent by an ugly pathed narrow gorge of frightful hill.' These are among the most beautiful spots on earth, but one must add in his defence that he was walking, not driving, and that he was tired and not too well. 'A pile of sliding stones and earth on each side and no outlet of picturesque or grand whatever and all covered in gray cloud: a bad Westmoreland pass.' He might be describing Wookey Hole on a rainy day in January. When he comes out on to the plain, he finds that so commonplace and dull 'as is the sky, that draw it I can *knot*'. They got to their horrible village, and a beastly hole full of silk-worms with dry stale bread to eat and nothing to drink, where Pashley had stayed in 1834. 'Lots of old columns, friezes etc etc about.' I am certain he was not exaggerating, since I recollect something similar (bar the silk-worms) more than 100 years later. Only those who have walked all day, to dine on raw lettuce, Cretan rusks and a glass of water will sympathize with poor Lear. He did see some signs of beauty in unevennesses of the ground, the grouping of olive trees and the masses of ruination. 'The supper was uncouth and nasty to the last degree. O that supper! which even George could hardly bear.' It consisted of snails, cheese pies, and boiled chicken. When Giorgis went in to make the bed, the old man whose house it was gave Lear a tap, and said, 'When will our unfortunate country be set free? You know, you know very well – but when?' 'Maybe one day,' answered Edward. It seems that 1866 was already brewing.

It was a relief to be up at half past three. By a quarter to five they were walking west towards Mitropolis and Ambelouzo. At the ancient theatre he drew the plain, as elegantly as ever, and with more features than the Roman Campagna, but the sketch is slight enough. Still, it is moving, like any simple sign of human habitation, and it is unmistakably Lear's.

He rather liked that view, and he was sorry for the old man, to whom he gave money: one of his sons had gone into exile because of a murder, and the other was deaf and dumb. He did not remember Pashley, only his Greek guide who was dead now. It rained heavily. Edward wrote, 'Desolate yet beautiful spot!' At Ambelouzo Captain Korakas had not yet arrived, but on they wandered as far as Pobia, and Lear did begin to grasp the princely position of Gortyn and the extent of its remains. Pobia is as far south as they ever got, due east of Paximadi: it used to be studied twenty years ago as the very type and exemplar of an isolated Greek village, and a book was written about it: it did not seem attractive. It is not far from where a colony of hippies lived in the late 1960s, lying about naked on the rocks, plundering the fields and slaughtering farm animals: they provoked the Cretans to an extreme of indignation and xenophobia.

At the topmost house of Pobia they were met by Mrs Korakas, and then the Captain, a 'big, hearty man'. The view of Psiloriti was a fine one, but persistent rain wiped it away, and the sketch Lear made that evening conveys more a thrilling village, to connoisseurs of villages, than an astounding view. The upper room of the house was hung with carpets and with arms, and there they ate 'the supper of a king'. Korakas discussed the villages on the way to Sphakia, and seemed to assure Lear he could go where he chose, but Lear's Greek was still imperfect, and his Cretan dialect unhoned, so he could hardly understand the Captain; at any rate he could form no clear idea about places and persons: no doubt the Captain was circumspect. At night fleas tormented Edward, and the Captain alarmed him by climbing peacefully into bed with the muleteer. The following morning Korakas took Lear to a high place where he saw and drew the perfect Psiloriti, high and faint in the clouds beyond the Chinese rocks. Then the Captain ground beans for coffee, as any Greek countryman would do before 1939: but to Lear the wait for bread to be baked and coffee ground and roasted and then brewed was intolerable. 'He has suddenly begun to comb his head close by me.' At last the agony was over, and Lear gave pencils to the children, and at seven headed downhill to the plain: Korakas went with him to the end of the town. Edward drew 'Claudelike olive scenes', and it was here that he passed armed men riding.

As they moved back towards the monastery of Arkadi near the north coast, which is close up under Psiloriti and due west of it, they saw more and more of the mountain, and it excited him more. The rain poured down, the mule misbehaved and the muleman stole artichokes which in furious rectitude Edward threw away; they got wet through and met a savage dog: but he was determined to reach Apodoulou. Whenever he tried to draw the mountain it withdrew, or rain fell, or he had to press on. They ate lunch in a storm of wind and packed to go on, but it was Lear's musing time. 'Why do Dr and Mrs Dunn, the Danses, and other early fooly people come before me now? Meanwhile clouds hide all mountains, and Ida might be Penmaenmawr for aught I see.' The Dunns and Danses are lost beyond conjecture, and as for Penmaenmawr, it is a little mountain lake near Dolgelly, the native place of rains and mists, underneath Cader Idris. We did not know Edward had ever been there.

He had complained of descent, now he complained of climbing. At the top of the hill 'the snowy line of Ida' revealed itself. It seems probable that this constant peering and study and these many glimpses of a landscape are what led to his swift mastery when he came to draw. What he most wanted, I suppose, was the right dramatic or picturesque subject for a large oil painting which would sell for a lot of money. He found that in Ida, though the painting he made, based on his sketches of 24 and 25 May, owes almost more to his thirst for formal perfection than it does to his study of what he saw. The foreground is rocks, to the left a handy olive frames a third of the picture with a more or less faceless group of Greeks engaged in what looks like a Platonic dialogue. The middle ground is trees, rising to the right almost to complete the frame. Beyond the snowy beautiful mountain is very faintly inscribed on the distant air. The effect is somehow a cross between Lear's *Bassae* and his later and far more exciting *Kinchinjunga*.

They found Apodoulou somewhat overrun by drunken Moslems – those of this part of Crete all drank – but among them Edward picked out the Greek nephew of his old friend Robert Hay. Robert had bought a slave girl of the Psaraki family of this village in Egypt, brought her to Crete and married her, though she was now in Scotland and he was dead. She and her brother had been taken as slaves after the Cretan rising of 1821, when gruesome things were done, but in the end her brother contrived to buy himself out of slavery. The family, one of whom became the village priest, lived long enough to entertain Arthur Evans, in whose day their ruinous house was exactly as it had been in 1864. Lear noticed 'chairs, a bed and good English bolts, locks, etc etc etc, but every part decayed and in the hands of savages. Rabbits, a goat, swallows etc, rush and flit about the rooms.' The rabbits were still there to greet Evans.

Next morning Psiloriti displeased him, being now too near and
dome-like. It might have been better, he felt, from the road that led
roughly south-east to the great monastery of Preveli. It is a pity he never
saw that, but he was sure Psiloriti would be clouded. He did not go
anywhere near Sphakia either, which lay to the west, near where the
Samaria gorge splits the White Mountains for twenty or thirty miles. 'As
things are, Chania is my aim.' He does not seem ever to have looked for
the guide to Sphakia who was recommended in Heraklion. By a quarter
past seven the muleteer had whacked the mule, which had leapt,
scattering luggage. 'Ida far more drawable now, but of course has become
clouded.' It was still only the 19th. He was still learning about Crete, in
his engaging way. 'Good Ay. Myron wine costs 200 to 250 piastres-the
barrel, which is 100 or 150 *okhades*.' The myrtles were huge but Psiloriti
behaved like a girl, veiling herself this way and that in clouds, being
unwilling to have comparisons made of her. 'Going through great olive
groves, all property of the Monastery of Asomatos, at which George says
he is sure they will say they are poor and have only two eggs. George
bursts out, resolving to buy a fish at Chania, and to roast it himself
without oil.'

When they got there it was only by showing the Pasha's letter that
they could get anything at all to eat. They got a small plate of stewed
pigeon, one of eggs and some nasty pasta between them. Even the wine
was not good, and as for the coffee, it was undrinkable. If you feel that
these are harsh judgments, remember that several miles of walking
sharpen the hunger and thirst cumulatively, and that by now (apart from
their amazing reluctance to eat snails) they did know what was what.
There is no doubt a touch of anticlerical feeling in what Giorgis says
about the monks, and of course in what Lear says. Giorgis said to pay
them nothing, but Lear did pay them a little, and off they marched
towards Arkadi, which the hopeful Abbot had said was near when they
first arrived. And so in mist and rain and without an afternoon sleep they
did in the end get to that beautiful, Venetian-looking monument of
architecture, sitting above the deepening ravine that leads northward to
the coast. The Abbot 'is a very jolly man and hearty, and gave us all
sweets, water, coffee and *raki* in no time. Also I am well washed and
comparatively comfortable.' They were comatose until supper, for the
poverty of which the Abbot apologized, but it was 'stewed pigeons, three
sorts of salad, a dish of honey, cherries, beans, cheese, etc etc and with
very good wine, though a little to sweet'.

The following morning they crossed the ravine and made for Amnates, where they could see Rethymnon in the distance. Edward drew Arkadi looking most elegant, and behind it the hills rising up towards the distant white pyramid of the mountain. His diary begins to resemble the prose style of Belloc. 'At a wineshop outside we get some wine. There are the noisiest hens here I have ever heard.' They set up their encampment for lunch, under a mulberry tree again, at the gardens near Rethymnon, unloading the mule and jumping him over the garden wall. Here the dress of Crete began to alter: it had been mostly dark blue with tan boots and scarlet accessories; now it was 'the semi-Bulgarian drab black jacket', but Edward liked his lunch. 'We also had perfectly good wine. The lunches of Cretan travel are therefore ever to be celebrated ... George and Konstandis are fast asleep (why the muleteer takes off only one boot remains a mystery).' They passed Rethymnon at five that evening and came soon after to a village called Atsipopoulo, which was on their road for the next day. They slept, in so far as they slept, in the house of the village mayor. We learn from this grim experience only because the mayor was so pompous: 'Lords from Paris and all the world' frequented his house, he said. Edward thought, 'He is like a gigantic Lord Somers.' He liked Somers, so this is hard to construe: perhaps he referred to the dizzy grandeur of Eastnor Castle.

They walked hard all morning and six hours later settled themselves, exhausted, under a vast olive, beside a loud waterfall. George found some watercress and earlier Edward had bathed in the sea. 'The beauty of vast flox of goats on the sand; the blue bay of Armyro beyond and the snow range above.' That evening they stopped at a khan, a travellers' rest providing nothing but water and shelter. They had walked for ten solid hours. It was near a river, the third that day, and Edward noted, 'From the river a lovely scene is beheld, and I half think the river scenes of Crete are its best claim to beauty for paintings.' Maybe Lear's *Rivers of Crete* would have been as attractive as Turner's *Rivers of France*: but the moment passed. As he went to sleep in the khan, his last recorded thought was, 'Even yet, I hate the thought of giving up Sphakia, for Askyphou is only four hours off!' The following day they were at Halepa near Chania.

On the 24th he made a lovely drawing of desolate Suda Bay and then set out for Phre. 'I drew three times, each time delighting more in the beautiful scene, the great charm of which is the dark, full green of the olive, and the lilac hills and the broad pure snow above.' He thought Apokorona combined all the great and lovely elements characteristic of Crete, though the sketch he made there at eight in the morning does not go far to expound his meaning. It is subtle and disturbed, rising to huge mountains, that is all. In his prose, the same words figure as always: green bright quiet, the birdsong, rivery rills, bright snow: perhaps they are enough. His emphasis is heavily on green and greenness and 'green and good'. He goes on to marvel at the universal suavity of the people. It is all as if his baggage is packed and he is reaching a summary, while his sketches on the road to Phre at eleven-thirty in the morning and Mount Ida from Phre at six in the evening do not summarize but they reach a climax. The first of these is near Stylos, where the headquarters for the 1889 rising was, and is used to illustrate that in the account by Venizelos published in 1971. Lear's peacefulness with two donkeys and their foal and distant women with baskets could hardly be in heavier contrast with the heroics of that time. But there is indeed a terrifying quality in the life and nature of the Cretans underlying their remarkable suavity: it crops out at times. I do not know what except steepness, strength, purity corresponds to it in the landscape, but whatever it may be comes close to eluding Edward Lear.

'Never till now have I had much respect for Ida. A dreamlike vast pile of pale pink and lilac, with endless gradations and widths of distance, and the long curve of sand from Rethymnon hills to Armyro. So I drew till long after sunset.' The following morning he was out and drawing before sunrise, at half past four, an utterly different picture, the first all purple delicacy and vigorous trees, the second with browns and brown-blacks reluctantly giving way to a kind of purplish-grey. The mountain is lucid, distant and untouchable: it somehow recalls Towne's analytic style in the English Lake District. The two drawings are a remarkable pair, and no other artist in Europe could have done them. He drew many times on this second day, but he was still obstinately sure that the White Mountains could not permit picturesqueness. He walked a long way that day and at night slept deeply. He woke in the consul's house and at once made 'designs' from yesterday's sketches; he had already begun the process that would lead to 'finished' pictures. In the next few days he relaxed. 'Walked in the garden and gave the monkey some onions.' Then, 'the sea air was delicious, but I have never seen any sunset here warmer in colour than those of Hastings: a sort of pearly mist involves all the isle. But the Sphakian mountains, though now almost snowless, are very grand ... Sang sixteen Tennyson songs.'

The steamer came in at two in the morning: it was the *Persia* again: she sailed at half past six. It was the last day of May, and as it dawned he made a last, most elegant sketch of the harbour. It is curious how often he drew cartoons, very funny and among his best, of the long-horned Cretan goat, the *kri-kri*: yet he had never seen one unless in a zoo. They survive (if at all now) only around the Samaria gorge in the White Mountains.

CHAPTER THIRTEEN
SUCCESS

WHEN EDWARD LEAR came back to England he was at the peak of his powers as a painter, at a point which Turner had reached at Hastings twenty years before, when he could go further only by dissolving colour and light and almost form itself in paintings of such modernity that they make Whistler look old-fashioned and rival Monet in his garden. Turner of course was a conscious and deeply intellectual artist; it is probable that Lear's progress in his art was blocked, for one reason or another. Yet in the course of 1864 he finished Sir W. James's *Campagna*, Bruce's *Cephalonia*, Jameson's *Florence* and Fairbain's *Iannina*, and 220 drawings: in another year he had 200 of Crete, and 270 of southern France, and not only his industry but his intellectual freedom was great: he had read and marked Renan and threatened to become a unitarian. He read widely and worked hard: he could 'lithograph all day and live upon cold mutton'. He was anti-imperialist and anti-war: the Maori war in New Zealand in 1863 horrified him, the American civil war deeply depressed him. All the same, the Greek anti-British feeling and rhetoric over the end of Corfu infuriated him. He was a sharp, discerning judge of persons, whatever side they were on in religion or in politics, and humour flowed from him that must have arisen from some deep well of sweetness, some irrepressible longing to play. He was endearing in his letters as perhaps he was in his art: but in his art also perfectly serious until the image was, as it were, wrapped for presentation, and at that stage somehow he often shared in the failure of all the Victorians, in the falsity of their whiskers.

In Crete, as we have seen, he had constantly been vexed by the lack of a chamber-pot, which it was Giorgis's job to find him in each place.

Once he seized on a tin wash-basin, once he was forced outside a monastery in the dark and found himself locked out for the night, until he woke a priest (at ten at Arkadi); but Giorgis never complained of his tasks. They were on the way home and in a hotel at Piraeus, when vengeance struck: 'found my room intolerable from stinks of three months unlooked at chamber-pot'. Edward showed Giorgis round the Theseion and the Acropolis and fled for London, tormented by mosquitoes, to arrive still seasick at Victoria station. Ten days afterwards he was soothed by spending two or three evenings with Alfred Tennyson in London, hearing his poems and finding him most amiable, cheerful and pleasant. He enjoyed the dinner at Woolner's too, queer as it may seem to the reader. They had 'rustical Soles, good lamb and peas, pudding and cheese, sherry, surprising Burgundy, and olives'. Edward thought Woolner had great originality, but did not like Palgrave, 'of all men the most frightfully antipatico to me, his voice and gross vanity'. Edward's social life was too hectic in London, he did not mind that or the work, but eating and sleeping were the horrors for him. In September he went back again to see Bowman's Lodge. He had known for a year that it was to be pulled down, and had alarmed an old lady who showed him round by knowing every cupboard and every corner; he had pacified her with half a crown. At that time he claimed he had come across it more or less by chance, on one of his regular visits to Ann's grave in Highgate Cemetery. Now he drew it with impassioned accuracy, noting 'Houses here', and 'Mother's window cut in half'. On the side of the road where it was you could see only the new shops in front of it, but from the other side you saw the top part of it divided into three dwellings.

In October he was vainly attempting to get a map of the Riviera: the fact that he could not is some indication of how wild it was beyond Cannes and Nice. Suddenly the old Lord Newcastle, who had been Fortescue's rival for Lady Waldegrave's hand, had died. Fortescue had married her quietly, in spite of some opposition in his own family: he had proposed by letter, not daring to do it face to face, and called for his answer. She wanted him, and this match had been Mr Harcourt's dying wish and advice to Fortescue: he became the happiest of men, as he deserved. In mid-October, Edward had been to see the Tennysons and would have had a pleasant evening 'had not Mrs Cameron come in'. He thought Emily was sadder than before and dreading the day when the boys must be sent away to school. Alfred was more expansive and effusive than usual. Then news came of a proposal to cut a railway close to his house, which deeply disturbed him. He and Edward walked to the Needles. 'He doesn't seem to enjoy scenery now [to him of course it was not fresh] and ever talks about the accursed railway. At dinner he was "far from over wise" . . . AT's ravings about England going downhill – "Best thing God can do is to squash the planet flat."' The following day the Tennysons told him all about their interview with the Queen, how she had curtseyed low to Alfred and shaken hands with Emily and the boys, and how Emily had said, 'You know, Ma'am, we are all Danes.' 'Lunch. AT's manner is assuredly odious at times.' They walked together all the same, to near Alum Bay 'which they are just spoiling', and called in at the shepherd's cottage, and later Lear gave his 'outspoken opinion about his morbid absurdity and unphilosophical bother', which Alfred apparently accepted. The following morning he was in a captious mood all the same. 'I believe no other woman in all this world could live with him for a month. It always wrings me to leave Farringford, yet I doubt – as once before – whether I can go again.'

At the turn of the year 1864–5, Lear had £2100 in the 3 per cents. In ten years' time, 1874–5, when he had built his house, he would have £1950 in Consols and £1650 in 3 per cents. This coming decade, therefore, from the ages of fifty-two to sixty-two, was one of substantial progress and success. It is important to bear this in mind as he shivers with worry and wails at his numerous misadventures. It is also true that his diaries are full of untapped self-caricatures and sketches, outlines of mountains, plans of paintings, ornaments for his garden, and at the moment when a 'Spiritual Medium Bazaar' opens in London in 1875, the beginning of a brilliant series of cartoons, alas unfinished, of 'spiritual objects', for example a Spiritual Snail whose head is that of an impudently cheerful flea, rear body and tail a cat's, and shell snail-like. He had explored the comic possibilities of snails in letters spiralling in the shape of snail-shells to Evelyn Baring in Corfu, but the theme was not exhausted.

In the New Year of 1865 Edward arrived in Nice where he found some old friends and swiftly made new ones. As for his work, he worried about it constantly. 'Suddenly resolved to see if I could do four £5 drawings in a day or even three. I began small drawings of Nice, Villefranche etc and by four had nearly penned out all.' The following day he had a cheque from Thomas Hankey and 'at three came Lady Duncan and bought a five pounder. Worked at a Tyrant'. These 'tyrants' were copies he made of pictures he had already painted. He worked on a number at a time, putting in all the outlines, then all of a certain colour, in a series of processes which were in a way mechanical. He appears to have invented this system about 1862, when in sixty days he produced sixty 'finished' pictures in water-colour for ten or twelve guineas each. The reason for his adopting this course of action was his despair of oil painting, but in fact it was a commercial success. The method was taken from that of aquatinting lithographs, though it is not quite the same. Vivien Noakes is severe about the result. 'They are worked according to a formula, and reveal a lack of the imaginative searching which must exist in every satisfying work of art.'[1] I am doubtful of this, since the imaginative element can work in an instinctive, instantaneous flash or very laboriously, and the despised mechanical element is only an efficient method (before colour photography) of copying his own work. The best of these 'Tyrants' are, as she goes on to say, indistinguishable from his finished water-colours. That 'the worst are very bad' is something I have never observed among the many hundred Lears I have seen, but the bad ones may well lurk among the thousands Vivien Noakes has seen. She maintains that 'their production and exhibition did lasting damage to Lear's reputation'. I am not at all so sure of that. Lear felt that all studio work was a pain and a bore, and there one must sympathize.

Essentially his life in Europe depended on Giorgis. In Nice he worried over him and thought of letting him go. '*Per me*, I would go to Rio or Ceylon or Spain for two or three years – and so change the grooves of life.' But that was after a row over the Russian church; the following day they were back to normal, and 'Vell, if this ain't vorking for nothing, vot is?' He got into a fever because Gussie Bethell arrived. Then the Tsarina of Russia wanted to visit him. 'It would be better to sell no more drawings here than to involve oneself in endless risk of loss of time and temper by contact with Royalty.' Russians at that time treated the Riviera as an extension of the Crimea, but they were never good payers. In mid-February Giorgis got into one of his fits of rage. Once before he had said life would be stupid if we didn't have an outburst now and then, but Edward worried about them. There were tears and he thought again of letting Giorgis go. I do not think Giorgis liked France, and by what transpired later I suspect he was drinking secretly. Anyway, it all passed over. By the end of February, 'Blue olives, blue sea and blue Estrelles. This day was perfect in loveliness, sea a sheet of emerald green, real ultramarine like a Maccaw's tail feathers.' Giorgis finally agreed he should leave because of his family. Edward explored Cannes, where he found 'a sailoryacketty kind of life' he did not enjoy. He heard from Evelyn Baring who was in Malta and did not like that. Edward finished colouring his drawings, and had Giorgis photographed, and packed for London. He went for walks among olive trees and talked olives and olive trees with the peasants, but he was in London by Easter, halfway through April.

'20th. Farquhar very kind, but suggests asking a thousand people to come and see my drawings. At times I think I will break up all and go and live at Jamaica ... Mr Price Edwards looks for a large Jerusalem that I was to sign for him as a testimonial on leaving the Customs at Liverpool ... 24th. Order 1000 circulars, come and see my drawings.' He encountered Sir Arthur Buller next day. 'But what sort of place is Nice? Is there plenty of immoral society, which I like? Nothing like a fat arsed woman!' – a modest and decent Legislator, Edward noted. Among much gossip, he notes that Catherine North is now Mrs Symonds. He dined out a great deal, once with sixteen people at Digby Wyatt's. Wyatt was now an established architect to whom Edward had written in 1863 (14 November), the two Wyatts being brothers both by blood and profession. Lear met them at Rome in the 1840s.

> O Digby my dear
> It is perfectly clear
> That my mind will be horribly vext,
> If you happen to write,
> By ill luck, to invite
> Me to dinner on Saturday next.
>
> For this I should sigh at
> That Mrs T. Wyatt
> Already has booked me, O dear!
> So I could not send answer
> To you – 'I'm your man Sir!' –
> Your loving fat friend
> Edward Lear

In 1865 Lear's father's old banker, Prescott of Roehampton died by suicide that May; in Leatherhead Mr Street had lost his money and seemed to have a mania about some mining shares; Lady Ashburton regretted her means would not permit her to acquire the *Cedars*; young Percy Coombe confessed to 'having lived extravagantly', but with no details, and Lear rightly suspected worse. On the credit side of life there was Miss Jekyll, 'the mysterious, finely clad', and a sort of young fan or apprentice, Underhill, whom Lear helped 'to learn lithography at Day's'. When his exhibition opened people came in numbers and he made £75 the first day. Lord Spencer then bought another six, 'yet this English life is sad'. He went to a dinner for fourteen in one house, ten in another, then fourteen again, eight (Sir E. and Lady Strachey) and eighteen, all in ten days, as well as large evening parties like the Speaker's. When he fled to the country it was not only to see Church at Wells, but to dine at Whitsun with Fortescue and Lady Waldegrave at their nice new house at Chewton, where he was one of twelve. This was a bright, quiet June weekend, and Lear did not go to church, though others did. 'Later there was no end of a row about the Fetishmonger church. Gen. Malcolm left in a rage, Lady W. nearly did but CF prevented. Mrs Malcolm approved.' It seems to have been a High Church service, but Fortescue regarded all country church-going as a matter of propriety.

Lear travelled back to London for the rest of the season, reflecting ruefully on 'such £4 costly visits'. The pace of London life, since he was now so fashionable, was hectic. He was thrilled to meet his old friend and recently his hero A. P. Stanley, Dean of Westminster. He got invited to lunch, but the Stanleys forgot and went out. He saw the Symonds and Miss Gush and her aunt and went to a toyshop for the Church children. The Prince of Wales came in and wanted ten Palestine drawings, while a peer in attendance picked up and blew 'some queer india-rubber whistles' which were meant for the little Churches. At York House he was one of twenty-four to dinner, and somewhere else where he met Richard Curzon, one of sixteen. He began to note down the jokes after these dinner-parties: he claimed to hate them, yet he seems to have been the easiest of men to please. On 14 June, to his relief, he dined alone and the Prince sent £99 15s. by Lord Knollys. In the midst of all this, almost incredibly, Lear worked, and Holman Hunt sent him a letter that Miss Waugh had refused him. The long saga of that painter's liaison with first the one and then the other Miss Waugh was, I think, what cemented their friendship. Lear loved intimacies and was starry-eyed about the loves and sufferings of all his friends. He was not so enamoured as before of Holman Hunt's paintings: he felt that his friend was a failure when he painted on a big scale (as he often was himself, and by now maybe knew it or suspected it). On 21 June he went to see F. Church's 'most magnificent paintings, Aurora Borealis and Cotopaxi'. Lear loved this American painter for his boldness, for his topographic explanations, and for the *Heart of the Andes*, an eagle among amazing peaks, which he knew by 1880, I suppose from an engraving.[2] He loved the 'National Graphic' side of him: a painter who was an explorer, almost a reporter.

Richard Bethell, Lord Westbury, was in trouble at the end of the month, indeed, Lear often suggests worse scandals about him than burst at the time. His fall from grandeur as Lord Chancellor seems to have been the turning-point that led to a remarkable and rumbustuous decline. Gussie's feelings about this are nowhere recorded. On 25 June when Lear dined there she was ill; on 3 July his fate was in the balance, a vote of censure was passed, and on the 14th he had resigned. Edward is apparently more interested in an old friend called Ellis Ashton who was seventy-six: 'I am deluged with stout and porter, all the enthusiasm of 1831.' But he dined at Hackwood in a party of eight on 8 July and on the Sunday morning, the 9th, he had a conversation with Lord Westbury: how his friend the Countess would meet him in Turin to buy an estate, and about the Gonzaga title of Duke he could then assume, and how Hackwood was all to please Gussie dear child, who had sacrificed herself for her mother. 'I now see truly that all that is said of him is only too lenient.' Dinner was odious.

The summer drained slowly away. He was thanked by Tennyson for a drawing of Cogoletto (for 'The Daisy'), but Alfred was in a queer mood, and dressed in grey. 'Would he were as his poems. Said he'd write another Farmer. I said he could publish a Farmercopia. This disgusted him.' Cholera in Dalmatia and Greece put an end to some Greek plans he had never mentioned before. De Vere had been shot and nearly killed by a soldier, and Decie told Lear that some such event had always been expected, he was so abusive and so much hated. This was a brother of Tennyson's old friend from Cambridge, the poet. Edward saw a lady dressed in the new fashion, with a train streaming behind her and hair to match: there is a sketch of her in his journal. In his serious painting which was the Liverpool oil *Jerusalem*, he got stuck, but he found Holman Hunt's advice useful. Half-way through October he was still quite undecided where to go, or when, or whether to send for Giorgis. Lord John Russell suggested Cabinet office for Fortescue as Colonial Secretary; if he got it, he promised to buy one of Lear's major paintings.

In November 1865 Fortescue was made Secretary for Ireland: Edward's reaction is enchanting.

I threw the paper up in the air and jumped aloft myself – ending by taking a small fried whiting out of the plate before me and waving it round my foolish head triumphantly till the tail came off and the body and head flew bounce over to the other side of the table d'hôte room. Then only did I perceive that I was not alone, but that a party was at breakfast in a recess. Happily for me they were not English, and when I made an apology saying I had suddenly seen good news of a friend of mine, these amiable Italians

said Bravissimo Signore! ci rallegriamo anche noi! se avessimo anche noi
piccoli peschi li batteremo di qua e la per la camera in simpatia con voi!

By 1866, there was another election, and Fortescue's fate was in the
balance again, 'nor does the Irish cloudy sky appear to get brighter'.
Edward had 'no more energy than a shrimp who has swallowed a Norfolk
dumpling'. Early in November he was in Venice, in a city suddenly of
heavenly silence. There he waited for Giorgis. There also he ran into
Val Prinsep and saw his latest painting: 'design good, colour bad,
execution worse. But I am no judge.' At last he met Giorgis, whose boat
had broken down at Syracuse, in Malta, where he would settle for the
winter. But from this time on Giorgis had begun to yearn for the Piraeus,
which he thought a great advance on Corfu.

Lear's life in Malta was dull and melancholy enough, but his sketches
were elegant, of course: only less inspiring than those of Crete or Athos.
The exceptions are his paintings of Gozo, where the cliffs are a cross
between wonderland and Beachy Head: there is one Mrs Roundell used
to own called *Cere*, which is as astonishing as it is beautiful, the image of
a genuine natural wonder, like something from the Western Isles of
Scotland. A Maltese collector who lives in western Gloucestershire,
almost in the Severn Valley, has got many of them together again, and
they are well liked. But the Maltese must be already well supplied with
the excellent drawings made by the British Navy, of architecture as well
as shipping. Drawing was at that time taught to young naval officers,
who would draw the entire coast where their ships patrolled, with every
gun and gun emplacement, in case of need. Many a country house has or
once had boxes of those sketch-books, like extra-illustrated Admiralty
Pilots to the Mediterranean. The skill was just like what Paul and
Thomas Sandby learned in the Army school of drawing in the Tower, in
the 1740s. Valetta harbour was a favourite subject, and for the connois-
seur there were British and French ships bombarding places like Petro-
paulski in the Crimea in the 1850s, drawn, if you were lucky, by the
Admiral-in-command from his poop, marking the splashes of the cannon
shots from the shore. All this sort of thing Lear ignores: it is as if he
never encountered it, and perhaps he never did; the officers thought
themselves amateurs and were too shy.

He missed Evelyn Baring, who had gone off to observe the Americans
at their civil war, but he did make a new friend called Strahan. His life
was like the old Corfu life, only without Lushington, in a garrison town
with access to the Palace, and expeditions to Gozo and all over the

island. But he lamented the lack of trees, and he complained as usual about the weather. When the Scirocco blew, 'He only said, my life is ugly, my life's a bore he said.' This variation on 'The Lady of Shalott' is the first musical hint of 'Uncle Arly', the last poem he ever wrote. We do not know when he started it, but he was now entering the phase of his lyric poems, which are as spellbinding and as unlikely, as original – however much they are parodies – as anything else he produced. Half-way through February he was already planning to be off. He intended Palestine but could not decide whether to take Giorgis. Then he considered going north in a Dalmatian steamer, which could drop Giorgis at Corfu. In April he worried about war between Austria and Prussia, which might shut the Adriatic altogether. He took a McIver steamer to Trieste, but even when it stopped at Syracuse he did not know what to do next: stop at Messina, go to Naples or Marseille or where. He went to Corfu. The esplanade, the old parade ground, was green with grass grazed by flocks of sheep. The streets had new Greek names. He went by a deep green road to the Ghetto, now Ayia Sophia Street, succumbing almost step by step to 'the sunlit, dozy lotus life'. It was like the resumption of an old affair. Little by little he gave in to the colours, the mountains, the sheer beauty of Corfu, which after his long endurance of Malta he found overwhelming.

> The still calm, a twitter only of birds; the thick carpet of grass and flowers; the great olives all around: their shadows throwing a short-lived darkness on the rocks and herbs below. Far down, the world of olives with outstretched arms and motionless foliage, and *how* green the light between the olive branches. The too great abundance of wild onion is the only drawback.

Corfu between 1864 and 1914, between the British Army and the motor-car, must have been a kind of heaven.

In the last week of April and 1 May he wound his happy way up the Albanian, Montenegran and Dalmatian coast, with the 'creax thumps and Turx' of a small steamer, hoping to be home by 1 June. On 10 May he heard of Garibaldi's 20,000 men and made a panic rush for Ancona or Fiume, and was in Trieste by the 15th. He arrived home in deeper gloom than ever. 'The marriage fantasy will not let me be ... To encourage it is to follow a thread leading to doubt and perhaps more positive misery. Meanwhile the ignoble toil of these worrying drawings.' He settled for mild habitual misery, telling himself verses from his adolescence.

Like a sudden spark
Struck vainly in the night
And *Back returns the dark*
With no more hope of light.

Life dropped back into its grooves. He thought of moving his gallery to Mackay's, he met Jowett 'who is like a cherub', the Austrians collapsed, there was a riot in Hyde Park, railings down, police and Life Guards out. He dined with twenty-eight at Strawberry Hill and heard the Government had yielded. On 1 August, 'Warne's don't want no more nonsense, nor do Routledge.' He had been suffering his spasms or epileptic attacks, and one day in mid-August he suddenly noted,

> Before I rose reflected on days long gone when I was but eight if so many years old. And this demon oppressed me then 'I not knowing' its wrong and misery. *Every* morning in the little study when learning my lessons: all day long: always in the evening, and at night. Nor could I have been more than six I think – for I remember whole years before I went to school at eleven. The strong will of Sister Harriet put a short pause to the misery. But very short. How well I remember that evening! Thus a sorrow so inborn and ingrained so to speak, was evidently part of what I had been born to suffer, and could not have been so far avoided willed I never so much so to do. And this is at times a great consolation to me.

For reasons I have already explained, I think this is frontal lobe epilepsy, and not some sexual peccadillo, although some kind of sexual consequence would of course explain the degree of shame. It is interesting to hear that he did go to school, about a year before going to Sussex. On the 23rd Gussie wrote, 'Emma's wishes and thoughts are not difficult to divine, but again I say it would not do. The perpetual misery of all the belongings!' and on the 27th another letter from her upset his quiet. He did not talk or write about it.

Meanwhile, a man from Warne's told him they did, after all, want some more Nonsense. I am not quite clear what is meant, since after the third edition of the limericks in 1861, the major poems and songs seem to be datable by their working manuscripts to the 1870s. So far, there have been only the faintest preliminary mutterings. Perhaps the *Nonsense Songs, Stories, Botany and Alphabets* of 1871 are involved, but they were not recited as early as this, and the best of them not written. Normally he would speak of showing or giving any poem or song, soon after it was written, and would note that he recited it to friends. However this may be, the situation with Gussie was resolved. 'The gulf is not to be passed

'... and yet it seems hard too, and were I ten years younger I would act differently.'

Edward was taking Portuguese lessons, presumably in preparation for Buenos Aires or Portugal. By the end of November Giorgis was at Marseille, and in 1868 Edward went first to Cannes, and after that as if the idea had fallen like a spark out of heaven, to Corsica. He had been deeply restless ever since Ann died, and now there could be no sensible resolution of his disquiet until he bought or built himself a house he could call home. That would have to be somewhere in the south. Apparently it could not be in Greece, I suppose because of the probability of political disturbance and of foreign wars there. Eighteen sixty-six had seen the Cretan rebellion and the heroic defence of Arkadi with terrible loss of life of monks, priests, men, women and children. The place was not completely destroyed only for the typical Balkan reason that a large part of the gunpowder meant to kill them all was too damp to explode: but many whom Edward and Giorgis had known were dead, from the Abbot downwards.

By the end of 1866 Edward had determined on a journey to Jerusalem and up the Nile. In terms of painting, the Nile was one of the great successes of his life, though he did not much enjoy it. He had a cousin from Canada with him, who whistled away the days and scorned the antiquities of Abu Simbel. Edward was also much affronted by some of the first package tours in history, Americans travelling in groups of a dozen or more. His finances were not easy, Fortescue lent him £100, and he had commissions. Monkton Milnes had ordered a Nazareth, so that in December his intention was to draw only high up the Nile (except Denderah), or else make straight for Jerusalem, and draw everything as far as Tyre and Sidon and even Palmyra. By March 1867 he had done the first half of this journey and was back in Cairo. His water-colour of Abou Seir (4 February, 1 p.m.) is one of his triumphs, because it precisely and most beautifully conveys a landscape one has never seen and could not have imagined. This lovely drawing of slack water near the Second Cataract is in the Leger Gallery's *British Landscape Painting* (1992), their centenary catalogue, and could be seen early in 1993. Lear had not been to Egypt for thirteen years and it fascinated him now more than ever: upper Egypt was of course new to him; he loved it but could scarcely tolerate the Americans. 'One lot of sixteen, with whom was an acquaintance of my own, came up by steamer, but outvoted my friend who desired to see the temple of Abydos, because it was Sunday, and it was wrong to break the Sabbath and inspect a heathen church. Whereupon the parson who was one of the party preached three times that day.' At Aswan, the same party spent a Sunday evening watching the dances of quite naked women.

It was while he was in Cairo that Edward heard of the death of Holman Hunt's wife, the first Miss Waugh whom he had married in 1865. He appears to have been a good deal nicer than most people to their son Cyril. He did go to Palestine, with all the usual apparatus of a dragoman, tents, a fish-faced boy 'like a turbot', and of course Giorgis, but the expedition was abortive. As he came home at last from it he and Giorgis gloomily picked out the landmarks of Crete and the places they had known there. Edward's feelings about such matters seldom burst out except in rage, which he thought was part of his illness, and what Giorgis felt is usually as obscure, but they sorrowed together over Crete. The slave route of the Nile, and the part the Moslems played in that, had created a fearful scandal in England, which Edward would not have missed. It appears in his letters and journals only in his extreme indignation about the dancing of the naked women, for which they were heavily paid. It was clear enough in Crete that he did not in the least like the Turks, and automatically took the Greek side, though without militance: he did not think much of the Arabs either, but he was not given to generalities about peoples, except when harried by some minor official. When he found the Cretans taking his flea-powder as snuff he recorded the incident without comment. He did of course think that people from strange places were extremely funny, that is the foundation of his limericks.

In Cannes he saw something of Symonds but he himself was really at a loss, and frantic with indecision, longing for Palestine again, thinking of Corfu because of the beating of the sea, lavishing equal attention on caterpillars and landscapes. He saw boats leave for Corsica, and in the second week of April he had made his preparations, which were intellectually thorough, reading Valéry's guides, buying photographs, and getting a letter of introduction from Prosper Mérimée.

> I can't decide in my mind if it is wiser to wait death in one spot, making the spot as pleasant as may be, and varying its monotony by such pleasant gleams of older life as can be obtained, or – to hurry on through constantly new and burningly bright scenes, and then dying all improviso as may happen. Considering all I have passed through from six years to fifteen is it not wonderful I am alive?

That was 19 March, the day he went to the boat office. But earlier there is an important item of Symonds information, on 24 January he waited three-quarters of an hour for Symonds, 'and drew the Owl and Pussy for his children – with what effect, we shall see'.

This certainly looks as if the poem already existed. He seems to have written it for little Janet, and therefore its first manuscript would be the one he gave her on 18 December 1867. This manuscript was reproduced in the small book *Queery Leary Nonsense* (1911), but after that it got lost. Another manuscript with some differences of wording was given to the Clive children at Perrystone near Hereford in 1868, but by the time their house was burnt down (in our lifetimes) it had luckily been sold to Harvard, and so had an 1870 manuscript. The secret of this plaintive lyric is that it is genuinely a lyric, a song: Lear wrote music for it too which has not survived, and in November 1869, staying with the Lushingtons at Park Hall, he wrote to James Fields of Boston, his new American editor (Hazard of Philadelphia had brought out his limericks in 1863, but Field ran a magazine, *Our Young People*), about dates and details, saying 'that dear old gentleman's grandchildren have been screaming about the songs I sang'. Since songs are in the plural, there is no saying what his repertory may by then have been: we do know of a nonsense story, 'History of the Seven Families', written for the Fitzwilliam children in 1865: it was published with a whole miscellany of dated and undated items at Christmas 1870 (dated 1871), some of which must have been in his head and in his repertory before he put that book together.[3]

In the manuscript illustration, the cat and the owl are the same height, with oddly similar features. But the owl and the cat and the pig all have multiple origins in children's rhymes which are like folk poetry: it was Lear who composed this plot and brought them together. The cat and fiddle is an old inn sign: fiddles were made of cat-gut and the howling of cats occasioned much comedy, some of it nasty. So in a drawing Lear made for Symonds' children, probably the one he made first, the cat plays his fiddle, then the cow jumps over the moon, then the little dog, a distinctly pig-like little dog, laughs to see such sport. This nonsense verse must be among the best known of all, and it was printed in 1765.[4] It was quoted in verse in the sixteenth century, and casually by Byron. Whether the cow's supralunary leap suggested the voyage I doubt, and how the owl, famous for silence and for hoots, got to meet the cat, who knows? They are creatures of the night. Edward was simply making up a rhyme with traditional characters for Janet. As they sail away, the cat and owl can be seen in the drawing, just as the cat was with his fiddle in Hey diddle diddle: only now it is a guitar which the owl twangs to his beloved.

The owl looked up to the stars above
And sang to a small guitar,
O lovely Pussy, O Pussy my love,
What a beautiful Pussy you are . . .

They sailed away to the land of the Bong-tree, where they found a pig, who sold them the ring in the end of his nose, and they were married next day by the turkey who lives on the hill. They dined on mince and slices of quince (does he mean that solid, delicious substance he elsewhere calls quince marmalade, which looks like jelly-cubes and is still served sliced in Athens?) which they ate with a runcible spoon. Originally it was a muncible spoon. Turkeys would be seen coming into town before Christmas in Cannes as in Corfu. But why is the spoon in the poem? Because in Hey diddle diddle the fork ran away with the spoon? There is plenty of precedent in nursery rhymes and in the strange poetry of mummers' plays for the bad behaviour of kitchen utensils, and that is the source of other poems by Lear. At present all we need to establish is that his first nonsense song appears to be a sweet romance with a sadness and strangeness that arise only from its impossibility.

There is another memorial to Lear's friendship with the Symonds family which is a lesser production as poetry, but important for the light it throws on his life. One must remember that Mrs Symonds was his old friend Miss North, whom he had known when she was a girl, and the poet and historian's sister Mary was the second wife of the third baronet, Sir E. Strachey, both of whom Lear knew in London. The Lord Strachie who later married Constance Braham, Lady Waldegrave's niece, was a cousin. The poem (9 December 1867) is a dialogue in couplets in which John and Edward exchange growls about their lives and Catherine adjudicates. They hate their exile and the foul winter weather. Chimneys smoke, the firewood is wet, poor Giorgis now speaks Albanian, Greek, English, Italian and Arabic, but not French, swells in carriages threaten to run Edward down, their servants despise him, John complains of noise, Edward of invading German tourists, John of mosquitoes and Edward of flies. Catherine says they are both bores, but Edward is old enough to have more sense. John must nurse the baby for seven hours, and Edward must go back to buttonless cuffs and endless mutton,

To make large drawings nobody will buy –
To paint oil pictures which will never dry –
To write new books which nobody will read –

... Till springtime brings the birds and leaves and flowers,
And time restores a world of happy hours ...

The solution does not enter very deeply into their ills, and perhaps that is just as well. It is something that Lear's self-portrait as well as his portrait of Symonds amused them all.

The book on Corsica is the most efficiently written, and it is still an excellent guide to that island, in which the worst change has been deforestation. But it was the last travel book Lear was ever to publish, and the reason surely was the nightmare that he suffered getting his sketches into a condition where they could be reproduced. Those that he turned into finished drawings and paintings are thrilling: Corsica has the dramatic quality he had learnt how to transmit in southern Italy, and his passionate love of forest trees was an asset to him. His *Forest of Bavella*[5] is among the most thrilling of all his sketches. He drew it on 29 April, with pencil, sepia and water-colour washes. At the time, he thought it 'one of the most beautiful sights that nature can produce' and with the varied light on the high peaks and the closer darkness one can all but smell the spring air. This is, as Vivien Noakes observes, one of those rare water-colours where he creates 'an atmosphere of mist and water-laden sunlight'; it could not have been attained by any other means, and it could certainly not have been reproduced before colour photography. In this book he abandoned lithography, and the wood engraving is certainly effective, but it is not entirely satisfactory. He was a perfectionist, caught in the long crisis of technique.

The book, dedicated to Frank Lushington, was published in 1870 by R. J. Bush of Charing Cross, with the translation rights hopefully reserved. He admitted he had gone to Corsica only because Palestine was impossible, but claimed he always travelled alone by preference, with his india-rubber bath and his camp-bed. It is a curious thought, but at least he admitted to the presence of Giorgis Kokalis, a Suliot. For the engravings, with some exceptions 'drawn on wood by me from my own sketches', he had to thank a handful of wood engravers working in Paris, who did him proud. He fully expounded his forebodings about the journey, the work abandoned at Cannes, the bad crossing, the broken promise that this or that journey should be his last. He remembered Oenone: 'And from that time to this I am alone, And I shall be alone until I die.' He made frantic notes about banditti, vendettas, moufflons, cream cheese and copper money, then suddenly he was in Ajaccio with its bathing-machines or Ebenezers, its chapels and flat caps and the rural stillness of its streets.

He liked the *Helix tristis*, a melancholy snail, he liked a herd of black sheep and their tarry shepherd. But it rained and blew a hurricane, he would not ride and could not walk, he took rambling excursions in a two-horse car with 'my man Giorgio'. He already worried about the time when Corsica would be as covered in villas as Menton or Cannes, Torquay or Norwood. This was to become a theme of the rest of his life: he was fifty-five and beginning to be old. Tourism had begun to startle and irritate him, villas had begun to cover the ground where once he could expect to feel free and alone. His first explosion about it had been in a letter describing the Isle of Wight two or three years before, but now he noticed it was a universal plague. It is a curious thought that the villas of Torquay before 1870 (I do not know those of Norwood very well) and of Menton and Cannes of the same date have for us a certain charm: they are even nostalgic with their large gardens and their quiet roads. At least in his time the maquis was intact. That word was imported into Europe from Corsica in the 1939 war, but in the last century both the word and the thing were idyllic: the myrtle, heath, arbutus, broom, lentisk, crimson cyclamen, hellebore and the nameless shrubs.

He saw black goats and sheep and pigs and drank coffee out of glasses. There was a certain sense of the operatic about things: twenty conscripts feasting with a wine barrel, the feuds between tower and tower, the 4000 cork trees. He met a boy who knew his Buffon, at least the pictures, which Edward used to copy out at home. 'The lovely morning light falling on the dark red and silvery gray cork stems and the changefully clouded mountains are full of beauty . . . How like this is to the old days of Roman campagna life.' He saw bee-eaters on the telegraph wires, and great timber carts and teams of a dozen mules dragging a 100-foot tree. His illustration of Bavella looks like something devised by Magnasco. He loved the golden haze, the streaming torrents, the cuckoo echoing from the crags and the thousand blackbirds. Even the wine at Tallano was sensational. A little boy told him the names of his goats: Blacknose, Silverspot, Greynose, Cippo. 'Perhaps if you stand still she may let you scratch the end of her nose.' The groves of fruit trees resounded with hundreds of nightingales, except when they were interrupted by what appeared to be general target practice.

It will be seen that this was a highly enjoyable outing, and why should it not be? It was intelligently chosen, the range was not beyond him, and he had mastered the reference books, including those that spoke of the arrival of refugees from southern Greece. The name Bonaparte could easily have a Greek origin, and the feuding lords of towers do sound like the families of the Mani. But Edward had no trouble; nothing went wrong for him. He does tell some splendid anecdotes about feuding: the lady called Colomba who disliked the building of a threatening tower at Fozzano and stopped it by picking off the masons one by one, while a child in her arms established her innocence, and her party were just playing cards with their guns beside them, deserves to be remembered. It is a pity Lear never heard a Corsican *vocero*, the lament for murdered men that was sung by women swearing vengeance, just as it was in the Mani. He came across a pleasant lunatic who believed he had eaten two policemen and nearly starved himself to death in his misery. He then decided they had both died of hunger, and began to eat happily. The only sad thing in this book is unkindness to animals: horses driven over a precipice and thousands of blackbirds slaughtered and exported every year.

Even the process of commissioning the wood engravings was enjoyable in a way, since although it was a worry and not simple, it meant living in Paris. Lear hated the fuss and fidget of country houses, he did not mind being alone in a great city. He left cards on a few old acquaintances, but he did not at all care if they were not returned. Paris was rather new to him, he liked its physical splendour and its military bands. Still, by 28 September 1868 he was peering around England looking for ten acres to build a house. He had vaguely thought of one near Tennyson in the Isle of Wight; now Surrey was likelier. Really it was a kind of mass instinct: all the other birds were settled or settling, and he began to be anxious there might be no room for him to make his nest. He heard that Frank Lushington had lost his two boys 'and what is more has been living with Venables the mighty'. Tennyson was off to Paris 'for a run: how queer is the smallness and egotism of such a man. It is so melancholy at Faringford now that Horatio and his children are there (as if E. were *not*!). Why did FL's boy die? Teeth. I nearly died of teeth. I was given over and lay for dead for a long time. He is leaving Moxon's for Strahan's.'

On 15 December Macmillan refused Corsica totally. Giorgis was ill, but then recovered. It is evident during the illness that Edward had come to be very fond of him and to rely on him. At last Bush took on the book 'if cheaply got up'. Lear spent Christmas at Lewes but when he got to Folkestone he could not resolve to leave England. Finally, on the last day of the year 1868, he left at eleven and got to Paris in the evening. He had £3000 in the 3 per cents, he was selling pictures, slowly but surely, though £100 was usually his top price (to Sir F. Goldsmid). He went to Cannes again to find Giorgis. The chief things he now felt were his hatred of church, his admiring veneration for Darwin, and his passion for broccoli, to which he made continual reference. He is not a person of reliably sound views, of course: but an obnoxious teller of obscene stories called Abraham Hayward is called 'as Dizzy used to say' (long before Tennyson said it) a Louse upon the Locks of Literature. Lear was so shaken by a ride one day that he thought the country round Rendcombe, not far from North Cerney and Cirencester, terribly ugly: an opinion he admittedly withdrew later. But the process of getting old was for him like that of getting a little drunk; he was becoming crosser, more quickly cross and less restrained about it.

CHAPTER FOURTEEN

THE HOUSE AT
SAN REMO

IT IS HARD as one slogs through the diaries of a dead age to prevent
a sense of routine and quotidian repetition from overwhelming the spirit,
but the truth is that in spite of all ups and downs Edward Lear's spirit
was unquenchable, and his zest for life, in his barest water-colour
sketches, his most expansive finished paintings, his most casual passing
jokes and cartoons and self-caricatures, was more alive than most
people's; the diaries taken alone are the feeblest guide to that, and even
the letters somehow cumulatively bury him under a sand-dune of
preoccupations. On 24 January he 'offered to take charge of Dick the
Doll, which little Mary Liddell was delighted at, and gave me many
parting dicta thereanent. So I carried the big doll to the Hotel des
Princes, wrapped in two handkerchiefs and the Saturday Review.' Sunday
came and Giorgis came in as usual for a small glass of wine and a cigar.
That led him to talk of his house at Kastrades in Corfu, his sons, his
mother and his wife. On the 29th little Mary Liddell came and took back
her doll, which Giorgis assured her he had taken out for a walk every
morning. Mérimée sent some specimen woodcuts done in Paris, and on
1 February 1869 Edward finally decided to use French engravers.
Meanwhile Giorgis expressed a wish to see Nazareth 'and that lake
where the Lord fished'. Lear noted that for himself he supposed 'this
snaily hermit life' was not right, but it was not unpleasant. He had put
together his Corsican exhibition: Mérimée secretly did not think much

of anything he saw by Lear but outwardly they were most polite, and inwardly Edward cannot but have been proud.

There is a Harvard sketch of Ponte del Vecchio, for example, the usual sepia and water-colour, done at two-thirty on 1 June the previous year, which for swiftness and spectacular effect with the minimum of means is as brilliant as any sketch of mountain scenery: the mountains billow away like clouds, yet they are precise, they are just visible in the mist, and the thunderstorm is still palpable. In fact thunder pealed as Lear began to draw, and he had to abandon work and run for shelter: luckily for us, the storm was over at six in the evening. 'The mountains all at once became ... perfectly clear ... the great snowy summit of Monte Rotondo, if that be it ... the line of crags and dark pine woods all along the centre of the gorge, the immense granite precipices hanging just above the rapid stream, its profound shadow and narrow depths here and there lighted up with gleams and flashes of brightness' inspired him both in words and in colour. This picture never gave birth to an oil, although he painted at least three oils of Bavella:[1] it is not always easy to see what the criterion was for selecting certain scenes for immortality in oil. Mrs Lees-Milne has a small oil painting of great intensity, pleasingly dark in tone, taken from Delphi looking down the gorge towards the sea: Lear painted that from the sketch once and never again, it has no ruins (they were still underneath the modern village, which was moved a quarter of a mile in the 1890s to make excavation possible) and no stray gods or hamadryads (though in 1849 their addition had been normal practice), but this picture has an extraordinary intensity of beauty, like a Samuel Palmer. Lear was distracted from one exciting line of progress by another, as he was from one place by another. The Ponte del Vecchio drawing survives as plate 38 in *Journal of a Landscape Painter in Corsica*, but the sketch shows a fleeting effect of light and storm which wood engraving cannot convey.

It may well be that Lear was frightened for a time at least of embarking on oil paintings of great size and ambition. They were every artist's ideal because of their comparative permanence and the amount you could charge for them, and they hang now in places like Lancaster House. The Victorians filled the walls of their new enormous buildings with them, at Eastnor Castle, for example, and at Rendcombe; but I imagine that those vast rooms must have begun to go out of fashion as central heating became a serious demand. That existed in the 1860s or 1870s, but it was not in demand, indeed it was so inefficient that it was scarcely noticed, though in our day people do live in smaller, warmer spaces, and the pictures they buy are consequently smaller. Lear could still aspire to sell enormous paintings to someone like Lord Aberdare, Henry Bruce, and he did go on executing them, but I think only by commission. He had reduced his prices for those in stock late in 1866, though artist friends advised against it: the *Cedars of Lebanon* to £525, cutting 200 guineas; *Masada* to £315, with the same cut; and *Beirut* to £210 from £315. His banker, Drummond, had bought *Beirut*, Lady Lyttleton *Masada* and Lady Ashburton the Cedars.

Edward's explorations showed unusual stamina. He found a Watteau in a house at Grasse, he climbed up to Croix de Garde for some heath, he was working extremely hard at old paintings such as Zagori and a gate scene in Crete, he was endlessly interrupted, then 'a sudden bad fit came on (it has been threatening some days) of frightful violence, which gave a sort of cataleptic pause of an hour'. It was the fourth in three weeks: under these conditions his sheer persistence seems to an outsider morally heroic, though it may be that resistance to his disease is at the bottom of many of his remarkable qualities. 'Lady Grey bought the Zagori I had put up ten minutes before for ten pounds.' When he took a day off it was to sketch, and to walk in 'the filmy woods'. But he reckoned two more years in the Riviera would be enough. There was still snow on the hills at the Saut de Loup on 1 June, a little to his indignation. Holman Hunt wrote to him that Beaumont and Martineau were dead. 'As for me,' he recorded, 'I half think of getting to Mentone drawing early next week, and then going to England at once, and getting out the Corsican book with twenty water-colours of my own drawing, and as many vignettes by Dalziel. But one changes so often it is hardly worth while to record decisions which never hatch.' Miss Campbell, his fellow Corsican expert, arrived to warn him 800 Germans were expected in Ajaccio, 'and so, exit Corsica'.

He really wanted to settle down, and the process had begun. He heard from a Mrs Close of land to sell near her house at three francs a metre – 15,000 francs, £600 for a 5000-metre plot, with another bit the same size available. Edward thought more trouble was taken over these winter homes than they were worth. All the same, within a week he was inquiring at Nice about houses (from Taylor, the agent) and had half a mind to take one. M. Arimandy would sell a small plot for £1000; Edward felt he should postpone. 'I hear the roaring of the sea, but there is no wind and it is pleasant.' He could not look on Cannes as a nice place to live in, but he could not at the moment think of anywhere better. Meanwhile, he was buying blocks and preparing vignettes and giving three groans for Corsica, which ended on his happy visit to Paris, where he dined at once with his old Athenian friend Lord Lyons the Ambassador, and dithered over how many vignettes or whatever to commission from whom. 'The music of the band is wonderfully fine, and the contentment of such crowds most surprising . . . Overpayed Pibaroud for so much work which pleased the old cove. What stinx in that house! . . . England and the journey there is a dread and a horror.' Pibaroud had produced an electrotype for him, but it does not recur, so it was not satisfactory. The rest of the work was, however, so as soon as he got to London and had seen Fortescue, who never altered, Fanny Coombe, who had gone blind, and Martineau's widow, he went to Bush to arrange publication and had the first thirty-four subscriptions within a week. Half-way through August he had 333.

In one of those stray insights into his early life that come and go without warning or explanation, he suddenly says on the 22nd, 'My Uncle Tom Lear bought no end of Turners and other painters, among the rest that early Millais, the dinner scene with Isabella and the brothers, to me the best of all Millais ever did.' He then draws the painting very well, but this important uncle goes as swiftly as he came. His name arises in the description of a lunch with Woolner. One does not even know whether Tom Lear was a real or a notional uncle. He is never mentioned in connection with Edward's early life, so he may well be notional. August trailed on, Edward was chased by a bullock, the subscriptions reached 446, he longed to get away, he dined with the Wyatts where Decimus Burton talked too much, and in September he was showing interest in Frank Lushington's news of building plots at Bournemouth, where a Mrs Sutton had bought 160 acres at £20 an acre (£3200). 'As for Mrs Lushington, no words can depict her miserable, most miserable and desolate look. It cannot be right for the living to live with the dead.' It seems that the tragedy of the Lushington boys' deaths is what so firmly cemented Lear's late friendship with Frank Lushington. Of all intimacies to which he could be admitted, that of grief was to him the deepest. Before the end of his life, having so wide an acquaintance and so good a memory, he was grieving over the recently dead at a rate of more than one every week. Even this autumn he was writing after names in his diary, 'But ah! how soon to die!' Still, his list reached 500 and he was writing out one of his stories for a child: he dined that night with the Grenfells at Taplow, with Russell of *The Times*.

On 25 September he went to Haslemere where Alfred's pony carriage took him up the wonderfully beautiful hill to what he justifiably calls the

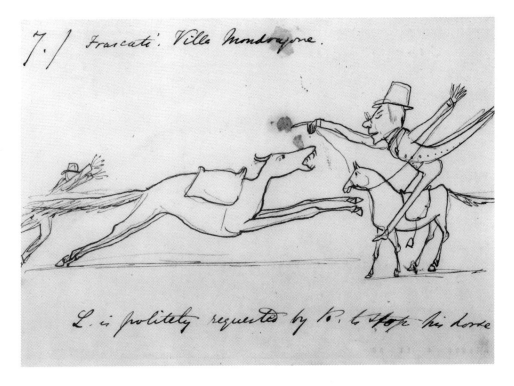

7. / Frascati: Villa Mondragone.

L. is politely requested by K. to stop his horse

8. / M. Porzio.

K. enquires amiably of L. if his stirrups are
sufficiently short.

Self-caricatures of Lear's adventures with a horse. Charles Knight taught him
to ride in Italy.

The Monastery of St Paul,
Mount Athos (watercolour).

Luxor, from the Royal Collection (finished watercolour).

Evelyn Baring, Earl of Cromer (oil by John Singer Sargent).

Lord Northbrook (pencil sketch by Frederick Sargent).

Zante (Zakynthos), finished watercolour.

The Monastery of Stravroniketes, Mount Athos, 1861 (oil).

Montenegro with Albania in the distance 1870–2 (watercolour).

Rocks at Jubaipur (oil).

Mount Kanchenjunga in the Himalayas (oil).

The Road at Giza, 1873 (oil).

Monastery of Arkhadi, Crete (finished watercolour). Sketch 1864, finished 1876.

Note to T. G. Baring, Lord Northbrook, Viceroy of India.

Indian sketch of elephants, 1873–4.

The Cedars of
Lebanon, 1858
(sketch for oil
painting).

Lear in 1862.

Lear pursued by Foss
(letter to Hallam
Tennyson, 1885).

Palazzo Tennyson. He liked it and found it comfortable, even apart from its amazing views. Only Alfred and Emily were there, but at dinner, after what Edward felt was too much to drink, conversation went badly about Horatio and his children: 'the breach with Park Hall seems always wider, nor do they take much interest in Frank and his'. Edward breakfasted with Emily, which was a pleasure to him, and looked through drawings with Alfred, who was easier than in the past; then they took a cheerful walk and looked at a bit of ground at £700, 'but it by no means follows I could live happily even if I built a house there'. On the Monday, Alfred chose two pencil drawings, then he wanted to change to coloured ones, then large ones, 'then he worried about how much he might adorn the outside gallery[?] for £10 – how he should cut out such expense . . .' Lear was offended; it was as if he were selling rugs door to door. He had spotted it was really Emily who was buying his drawings, and he lost his temper. 'We all exploded', but Emily insisted on giving him a £10 cheque for *The Moon Broadens*, and Alfred put him on the track to Black Down House. At dinner there was no sign of temper at all, Lear apologized and Alfred said he 'cared for nothing of all that, but that you said Everybody thinks you are a worrier'.

It was Lear's turn to worry, because the following day he found a place at Bournemouth for £1650; 'hard even to think of deciding on such a big leap in the dark'. By October his list was up to 547, and he met H. J. Lee, a man 'learned about bombyxes' who promised to send a memoir on the subject, and did so. The bombyx is indeed an amazing creature, a caterpillar by Linnaean convention, though in Greek a cocoon or a silk-moth, or a wasp-like bee, or bee-coloured wasp, black in colour with a wicked sting: Pliny said it was Assyrian, whereas, according to Nicander, the bembyx, which may or may not be the same beast, lived up mountains. They could even be the same as a *bombylios*, the most enormous of all bumble-bees known to Aristotle. They clearly merited a monograph: the Greek name *bombyx* just means a buzzer, so the field is wide open, but Lee's memoir seems to be unknown to Davies and Kathirithamby (*Greek Insects*, 1986). Can it have been privately printed? Some years before, Lear had been asked to give up his Associateship of the Linnaean Society unless he would go on sending them scientific information, and he had not used the letters ALS since the 1830s, but he was genuinely interested in queer creatures, and still noting them in his journals: *Bombyx processionaria*, for example, on 15 March 1868 and on the 31st, just before Corsica, and whether cows eat salmon (the same day). Now his list was up to 830; he called in London on Thomas

Hanbury of La Mortola, the great gardener and introducer of oriental plants to Europe, and in a flurry of farewell notes fled to Cannes, and called at once there on Taylor about buying land. He could have bought some with a house for £1200 plus £1000, but 'I would not have it as a gift, beautiful as the views are – to be in the middle of a clique of swells.' On the train he had chosen to sit with smoking Arabs whom at least he could make laugh, rather than with Monaco drawlers, and he thought the Princess Royal and Princess Alice of Hesse-Darmstadt, whom he met there, might in a lower rank have been called flippant and common, which he rather liked: but he was pleased when they left. What he loved was Giorgis's cooking. At Christmas, he sang Tennyson, and gave away his *Corsica* book. He was genuinely an eccentric, and isolated in the world: but he was energetic, and he still had £3000 in the 3 per cents.

At the beginning of 1870 he was worn out, with work and indifferent health: this is the condition he is never willing to diagnose in himself. He wrote to Field in Boston that he intended his *Corsica* as a flagship or pioneer for *Crete*, *Egypt*, *Palestine* 'and other journals I have kept and illustrated', and for magazine publication in *Our Young Folks* he offered his 1865 story for the Fitzwilliam children, 'Lake Pipplepopple'. 'The Owl and the Pussy Cat' appeared in February 1870, 'The Duck and the Kangaroo' in March, and 'The Daddy Long-legs and the Fly' in April.[2] He had left some 240 paintings in London for McLean to try to sell while he was away: this was not an unsuccessful venture, it swelled his income a little, and if I make Lear appear rapacious about money, the reader should remember that he gave a Corsica drawing intended for his own book to Thomasina Campbell for the frontispiece of hers, which came out in 1868, and when he found himself unable to get to Nazareth he not only returned to Lord Houghton his advance on commissioning a picture, but threw in as interest a lovely old drawing of (or rather from) the ruins of Phyle. This was one of those Athenian frontier forts where the *ephebes*, the young men of Athens, had to do their year's military service in the fifth century BC. It is a beautiful spot, guarding the mountain track to Thebes: the ruins are undisturbed to this day, because it is not on a road. Lear spent much of this winter working at two large Corsican pictures for the Academy, which in its wisdom hung only one, *Valdoniello*, and his wonderful Egyptian subject, *Kasr es Saad*.[3]

In late January in snowy weather he was out searching for a spot to settle, and half inclined to take one, then 'looked over Nonsense for Learical Lyrics but finally fell asleep', and that night he slept well, a rare event. All the same, he was deeply depressed, and without that indefinite

hope which buoys up young people. The story for the Fitzwilliam
children, of which the manuscript is now in the British Library, might
have been designed for falling asleep over: the families are all illustrated,
and they were parrots, storks, geese, some sleepy-looking owls, guinea-
pigs, half-asleep cats, and fishes. Their children all set off to explore, but
they ate one another, the geese were tormented by a flea who is the
origin of Mr Floppy Fly, the guinea-pigs battered their heads on a
lettuce and the owls flew down a well, the cats died of exhaustion chasing
a Clangle-Wangle, and the fish followed an insect into deep mud. The
things they were chasing danced a hornpipe and the parents jumped into
pickle jars and pickled themselves in brandy, vinegar and pepper. This
charming tale is possibly too horrific (or maybe nothing is too horrific)
for the tiniest children.

The story of the four children is less tragic: it was written for Gussie
Bethell's nephews and nieces in 1867. The tale is longer and more moral,
being a long exploration. It is interesting from the point of view of the
lyric which followed about the Owl and Pussycat that they sailed in a
blue boat with pea-green spots, with a cat to steer it and a Quangle-
Wangle as cook. This creature is almost never quite visible, being hidden
by the cat or the sail (as he is later by his hat), though there are flies
which buzz happily and he looks like some minute flea-like insect. His
foot gets so badly hurt he has to sit with his head in his slipper for a
week. It will be seen that this kind of story is not far from what fathers
make up to this day, and there are a few scattered hints that Lewis
Carroll, a friend of the Tennysons as Edward was, read and remembered
his works.

The botany and the cookery that went into the same book are too
slight to provoke comment. Bluebottles, parrots and pigs figure in the
botany but storks have had their last outing and may rest. The lyrics are
another matter. 'And who was so happy, O who As the duck and the
kangaroo?' The idea and the illustrations are charming and original:
Gould had gone to Australia and excited Edward about kangaroos as a
very young man, and he had seen them, I suppose, in the Zoo which he
still visited. The Daddy Long-legs and the Fly are more serious and
imaginative. The Long-legs is a cousin of the Quangle-Wangle, the
theme of all these stories and poems is exploration, but this one when
spoken in the right tone is masterly: by the right tone I mean the fly's part
in that of the traditional village natural, of whom Baldric was an example
in the television series *Blackadder*: I have heard him perform this poem
brilliantly on the radio. The fly is so shy of court and so admires Long-

legs for his singing, they are so philosophic over their illsuited legs and so happy at the solution of a boat. Off they go to the Great Gromboolian Plain, and there they play for evermore at battlecock and shuttledore.

The Gromboolian Plain introduces the Jumblies, who went to sea in a sieve: that is what witches were said to do, and James I believed he had seen them at it. The trick survived proverbially, I suppose in the mummers' plays. But the lyric rhythms of these lyrics are those of Thomas Moore, not of the *Irish Melodies*, of course, but of that ridiculous sequence, *Poems Relating to America*, and within that the ballad about 'The Lake of the Dismal Swamp'. Moore is a poet probably as under-estimated today as he was overestimated in Edward's youth, and we know that he and Fortescue would laugh for hours over the absurdities of poets. They doubled up with mirth over the story of Tagliacozzo, a village in Calabria where Edward had been, though his footnote on the subject is in Latin. The joke itself is unfunny, but the story of their enjoyment of it as young men is, as Lear tells it, amusing and even charming. 'The Dismal Swamp' is an open invitation to parody, and I have no doubt that it was one of Lear's party-pieces. It leads to 'The Dong with the Luminous Nose'. Other poems in Moore's sequence are distinctly Learian, such as 'When I have seen thy snow-white wing/ From the blue wave at evening spring', which is addressed to Flying Fish. It would not take much adjustment to turn into a nonsense poem. The whole sequence has interested me for years because it is a travel poem, a journey of exploration in verse, but it does contain fearful piffle, and 'The Dismal Swamp', about a Canadian Indian love legend, is among the worst. Original as Lear's verse was, and in its disarming way beautiful, it derives from his own interest in natural history, from traditional verses such as he often copied out for children like 'Hey Diddle Diddle', from mummers' plays obscurely remembered or half-remembered, and from parody of poets like Moore. The Swamp suggests the great Gromboolian Plain and the hills of the Chankly shore, or at least America does, and more closely inspires the Dong with the Luminous Nose: the nose being a cousin of Edward's own nose, often drawn as enormous.

> They made her a grave, too cold and damp
> 　For a soul so warm and true;
> And she's gone to the Lake of the Dismal Swamp
> Where all night long, by a fire-fly lamp,
> 　She paddles her white canoe.

> And her fire-fly lamp I soon shall see
> And her paddle I soon shall hear;
> Long and loving our life shall be
> And I'll hide the maid in a cypress tree . . .

The entire poem deserves to be looked at for its curious degree of absurdity. But Lear's parody cannot avoid taking off on its own, as the 'Owl and Pussycat' poem did, into one of those lists of provisions that delighted Lear, a cranberry tart, and a hive of silvery bees. The provisions are mummers' material. The trouble about them is that mumming was an annual ceremony in villages, but the text was never written down because the actors were often illiterate, so although some features are strangely invariable, the words get peculiarly mangled, and the result in performance was something as comic as Shakespeare's Pyramus and Thisbe in *A Midsummer Night's Dream*. Indeed, Robert Armin's book about fools, village naturals under the protection of someone, tells us a good deal about the world of mummers.[4] It is from them that Edward took the character of the fool which he wore himself in his last lyrics. The touches of sadness are also traditional. The disturbance of things like frying-pans with a life of their own is a persistent convention and theme of the mummers. Like the nutcrackers and the sugar tongs, they faded away – and they never came back!

That 'never' is the key to 'Calico Pie' and its music. Nothing ever comes back to Edward, and the song is pure, scarcely disguised grief for an earthly paradise lost; the fact that it is toys or mythical creatures that disappear in most of the stanzas does not disguise the fact that he begins with birds not unlike swallows, and ends with his beloved insects, crickets and grasshoppers.

> Calico Drum,
> The grasshoppers come,
> The Butterfly, Beetle and Bee,
> Over the ground,
> Around and around,
> With a hop and a bound!
> But they never came back!
> They never came back!
> They never came back!
> They never came back to me!

Is it a cry of regret for the lost lyric moment, or lost childhood, as so much poetry is? Possibly, but it is wonderfully decorated with creatures, real or unreal. Only the fish, being by nature dull so far as he knows, are given toy characteristics. But what is extraordinary in all these verses is their lyric progress, the noise they make. Lear was a master of the way alliteration and internal rhyme work in verse: few poets have shown such rhythmic and verbal mastery, though I do not think he first learned it and then applied it to nonsense. He learned those skills where they most purely survive in English, from traditional children's nonsense poetry, of which he had a huge repertory. Even the Herculean labours of the Opies do not enable one to trace all the variations he adopts in traditional poems, and there is no book from which he can have learnt them all.

'The Spikky Sparrows' is metrically simple apart from its rebarbative but painfully accurate refrain. 'The Table and the Chair' is simpler still, and charming in a slight way: the introduction of duck beetle and mouse at the end is a little strained, but it rounds off the volume. 'The Broom, the Shovel, the Poker and the Tongs' is the most mummer-like: 'Ding-a-dong! Ding-a-dong! If you're pleased with my song, I will feed you with cold apple tart!' It is a short song, and undeveloped, but the characters and their violence ('I'll certainly hit you a bang!') would be a marvellous invention if they did not already figure in children's rhymes and in mummers' plays: between these sources it is hard to establish the priority, since a scrap of mumming might well survive in the nursery, but the mummers might easily have incorporated some tatters of children's rhymes in their act.[5] To Lear the entire tradition was indistinguishable from scraps and cobwebs and tunes at the back of his mind. Yet if there ever was a 'working-class culture' in England, Edward Lear drew on it: how, we do not know.

In the early spring of 1870 he was grieving over Crete. 'Lonely and painful echoes alone are their long passed songs, of a tune long past. My eyes are full of tears, my heart of grief.' He must mean those traditional Cretan songs that we know now, that he heard there but never wrote down, among the numerous 'complimentary toasts' that he does record, like the song *Tha katebo*, 'I will go down, I will take my gun and will go down the mountain.' They are powerful songs, but they would be hard to record, and of course dangerous: yet it is plain that he heard Cretan folksongs and that they lingered in his mind (*Diary*, 17 March 1870). Better perhaps, he wrote the next day, to pass the rest of the years in seeing new places and in living how one can – and not in endeavouring to make good pictures. He goes to San Remo and explores there. Immediately the name of Congreve crops up in a land deal: the priest would sell land and Congreve a bit more. Congreve became a friend of a kind, or at least a close expatriate neighbour, whose sons Edward befriended. There was an explosion of surprising violence, as there so often is among tightly linked expatriate communities. Congreve himself was a pupil and disciple of the great Arnold of Rugby, his brother was a Comtian positivist, his own marriage was not happy, or at least not faithful, and his attempts to earn a living or carve a career were more or less pitiful, but this long saga occupied much of the rest of Edward's life. Now Edward walked up hill to S. Romolo above Congreve's house and the place where his own would one day stand. 'Congreve's brother taught two of the Lushingtons, (V. and G., not the Park Hall ones), they are very Rugbeian altogether.'

In April he was sketching a house and paying Congreve for land and the right to put in an approach, a matter over which Tennyson had trouble in Surrey. The architect was Gastaldi. On the 8th, 'up by lemon and olive groves to S. Bartolomeo': it was bound to do. Edward hated what he called the cliquishness of Cannes, and found 'the miniature style of the landscape unacceptable after the larger forms – though they are not so delicate or refined or pretty – of San Remo and its neighbourhood'. Just before Easter, a vendetta in Ajaccio left ten dead, which must have confirmed his choice of the mainland, and three days after Easter Sunday he signed an estimate for £1200. On the following Sunday he went to church and heard a sermon, 'Balaam's ass and other follies'. That came out in a savage letter to Woolner about what he thought of Holman Hunt's new and disgusting fundamentalism: he never in his innocence grasped what an ass Holman Hunt was, or to what degree he was on the make.

> I had spoken about the increase of rationalistic or antimiraculous thought, and hoped his future pictures would point or express such progress. Whereas I find I never made a greater mistake; and on the contrary, he is becoming a literalist about all biblical lore, and has a holy horror of Darwin, Deutsch, and I suppose Jowett and A. P. Stanley, though he don't name them. You may imagine that I shall nevermore touch on this subject: – meantime, if he should paint Balaam's Ass or Gideon's Fleece it would not surprise me.

His two new subjects were *The Triumph of Death*, and *The Triumph of the Innocents*, but Lear was bound to keep them secret. In the same letter, Lear's house is due to be ready in November.

> As I have sold no drawings this winter and have no commissions ahead, I shall endeavour to live upon little Figs in the summertime, and upon

Worms in the winter. I shall have 28 olive trees and a small bed of onions: and a stone terrace with a grey parrot and two hedgehogs to walk up and down on it by day and by night. Anyhow I shall have a good painting room with an absolute North light, and no chance of its being spoiled.

People had called at his studio that last winter, including the Westminsters and the Rothschilds, but no one had bought. Who can say why? He cannot have been out of fashion or they would not have come, but it may be they thought he was old-fashioned. Certainly some of his best drawings of Corsica might as easily have been painted in the late eighteenth century, which was not such a compliment in 1870 as it would be today. According to Lear, all the English commissioned busts from the mediocre and dying Academician Munro (whom Lear helped to look after) and they spent the rest of their money buying drawings by one another from church bazaars. 'As for Munro, when I tell you that he has just gone off to Nice to make a bust of the Grand Duchess of Russia, you may suppose he is not so very bad as I certainly thought him last year.'

In the summer he went to Certosa del Pesio, a former Carthusian monastery in the hills not far from Turin, sold by the French in 1801 and now a hotel for the discerning Piedmontese. He took refuge there to wait for his new house at San Remo to be ready, while Giorgis went off for his annual holiday in Corfu: Giorgis always looked more and more cheerful as that day approached. Lear now had the scheme of having photographs taken of all his pictures: he would have been first in the field had he done so, but nothing came of it. Lord Derby commissioned a new picture, as his grandfather had bought *Olivano* and his father *Windsor*; Lear was pleased with the sense of continuity. All the same, as one generation followed another at Knowsley one senses a certain cooling: it is evident in the more formal, artificial style of Lear's letters. However that may be, the *Olivano* was his second picture in oils ever sold, the first being *Civitella di Subiaco* for Lord Charles Percy. Now he would do a big water-colour of Corfu for £100: his aim at the time was to become an Associate of the Old Watercolour Society, a dignity that he never achieved, though prolonged study of its history does not reveal any possible reason why not. It was apparently a disadvantage to live abroad? He had hoped to be commissioned to paint Knowsley, he says, to paint it again, but that project also failed.

It is curious, considering his usual nervousness about European conflicts, that the Franco-Prussian War, when it broke out, meant little to him, only 'a bore. But if France wants to devour others, I can't but recollect that Prussia did devour some of Denmark and other places: so I don't see one is worse than tother'. Later of course the war impinged on him, but he does not appear to have foreseen that. He was out of touch with messes and staffs and governments. 'I live the queerest solitary life here . . . I hate life unless I WORK always . . . The scenery is of the most remarkably English character as to greenness – but of course the Halps is bigger: I never saw such magnificent trees, such immense slopes of meadows, and such big hills combined together; the Certosa Monastery itself however is a beast to look at.' He was planning work for next year's exhibitions, and the coming *Nonsense*: but Bush was only the agent for his Corsica book, there were still 300 copies unsold at 30s. each, and although Edward owed nothing, the £130 now due to him from Bush did not cover the costs of engravings that Lear had met, so *Corsica* was still a net loss.

His house was Villa Emily, named, he said, after a New Zealand niece, although one wonders whether Emily Tennyson might not have been lurking at the back of his mind. It was quite a long, white place on a hillside with guest rooms, study or library, a studio and an exhibition room. The fashion was, he discovered, to let small villas: poor Congreve, whose wife was now dying of cancer, had built four that summer and let them all, for £72, £120 (two) and £200, and Edward was aching to do the same. Congreve had also made a little by taking in pupils. Moving into the Villa Emily was no joke, but at last he got his furniture from England and he and Giorgis worked like demons at unpacking and setting things up. He cannot conceal his pleasure. He had sent Bush £60 in advance for the new *Nonsense Book*, no longer called *Queery Leary Lyrics* as had been planned, but something less embarrassing. It was amazing all the same what a persistent genius Lear showed all his life for not making any money at all out of things. That summer the Tennysons' neighbour Sir John Simeon died and Evelyn Baring's son was drowned in a Bay of Biscay disaster: only tragedy relieved the appalling hopelessness of his life.

That and of course his work, which continued as tranquilly as if it were being produced by someone else. The first painting to be finished in Villa Emily was of Montenegro: a painting of a striking beauty now in the market. 'The difficulty of "finishing" in water-colour on a large scale is more and greater than I looked for.' A few days later, 'It is more effective, the detail is worked out, but it is coarser, the colour is gone.' He wrote to Lady Wyatt about it: 'The Montenegro is a cold and gloomy scene – *as it is intended to be, for it is so in reality*: and I have done one bit of rock so well that you sprain your ankles directly you look at it. In the foreground I have taken a great deal of pains with a large figure of a Montenegrine, and he was really like life.' He heard a trumpeting and found this figure had picked up his handkerchief from the table and blown his big nose. 'I had instantly to sponge out the whole man, for I thought, if he can take up a handkerchief, he may take up spoons or money ... O dear! I wish I had done this dreadful drawing and that I had sold it.' All the same, the picture is a fine one.

Frank Lushington wrote him 'the kindest letter any friend ever wrote to a friend; how much more of a friend he has been to me than even he himself knows'. In early winter when workmen were kept away by the cold he mooned about his house and gardens. Hanbury was now his neighbour and Edward wanted to buy him out, since his land near San Remo was unused, and Edward wanted both a larger garden and a barricade against the world. Daniel Hanbury wrote that his brother the merchant was still in China, and he had no power over the land in his brother's absence. At least Edward's friend Morier liked his lyrics, Charles Kingsley raved about them, Field had taken 500 copies, Bush wanted another volume with limericks next year, and on Christmas Day he discovered the *Spectator* of 17 December, which contained a generous review of the new *Nonsense*. It was time someone praised him: he had just reduced two £200 paintings for sale in London to £50 each; it was nearly a year since he had earned anything at all. He even thought of selling his house and just wandering about until he died: once again he thought of the unexplored vastness of America.

As time went by he became too close to the Congreves for comfort, but what tied him down in San Remo was the pleasure of gardening, which he now discovered, and conveyed in voluptuous caricatures. His sister sent seeds from New Zealand, Dr Bell sent them from Selborne, he bought plants from a dealer near the Archway and collected them from India, so that in the end he was really too entangled, too enthralled, as all gardeners become, with what would happen next, ever to want to go away. He drew parrots and caterpillars and snails of a superhuman size as his companions and friends, as he had once drawn pelicans and wild geese. If he was not a happy man he gave an amazing imitation of one. He gave money to the local charities, did the local expeditions and enjoyed the local festivities: he was always busy, particularly in the garden. It should really have been a formula for a happy old age.

In 1872 appeared *More Nonsense*, held over by Bush's advice because it contained more limericks. We know that one of the lyrics from the 1876 collection was written earlier: when he stayed at Certosa di Pesio in 1870, the little girl who became Mrs Winthrop Chandler (*Roman Spring*, 1934) observed his glowing and bubbling and twinkling and announced she would like him for an uncle. He was delighted, and sang to her his 'Owl and the Pussy Cat'. 'He took me for walks in chestnut forests; we kicked the chestnut burrs before us, yonghy bonghy bos as we called them.' She was given an alphabet too, one letter a day, which has vanished now, but luckily it was printed, and its C for Cat,[6] with its tiger stripes and its truncated tail, is the predecessor of Lear's innumerable drawings of his cat Foss, who arrived only in 1872, and cannot possibly be the origin of this Bengal tigerish creature. But on 11 December 1871, we know from Lear's diary that he was hard at work on the manuscript of 'The Yonghy-Bonghy-Bo'. The character of fool in it follows the direct coincidence with a scrap of mummers' play text, and now that we know where he got his fat-face or potato-headed fool from, we are justified in reading the same character into all the many times he has drawn the same figure since childhood. The traditional words differ slightly from version to version: this is the Fool's entry.

> Father died the other night (My father died a month ago)
> And left me all his riches;
> A feather bed, a wooden leg
> And a pair of leather breeches,
> A coffeepot without a spout (He left me a teapot without a spout)
> A jug (cup) without a handle,
> A guinea pig without a wig, (A tobacco pipe without a lid)
> And half a farthing candle.

Other variants are a stewed stool foot, an old top hat, and his gun and volunteering cap, long sword and leather breeches. In Ireland it was 'My Aunt' who died, and what she left was a pair of calico breeches.[7]

The poem is the story of a sad wooing. As a performance it was greatly prized by Lear's friends, but as an old man he could break down singing it. It is called 'The Courtship of the Yonghy-Bonghy-Bo', and the original drawing at Harvard is certainly subtler and unimaginably better and more delicate than the rather awful woodcut which now precedes it. The queer thing about it is that people forget the story and remember only the list of all the worldly goods (In the middle of the woods) Of the Yonghy-Bonghy-Bo: precisely the traditional material with its unaccountable attraction. The worldly goods of the Yonghy-

Bongy-Bo were an old and well-loved list, since they occur in a play set in 1658, Cowley's *Cutter* (a name like Slasher) *of Coleman Street*, with no indication that they are a quotation or an allusion. The audience must have recognized the list at once. Its comic force is that it describes the room of one of the ruined villains, Cutter (Act 1, scene 6). 'Half a chair, A chamber-pot without an ear' etc. But the whole poem is lovely, and its touches of modernity are almost too painful. The turtle is his own, naturally, but I am not sure where the hens came from.

We can see now that writing lyrics had become second nature to Lear. The only question that remains about them is why they arose when they did, so late in his life. The fact that they were not obviously seriously meant was essential to them. They were for performance; they were an opportunity for Lear to pretend he did not mean them, did not mind, while in fact he minded extremely, he meant every word. This is a trick picked up from the singers and chanters in drawing-rooms in an earlier age, who might or might not mean what they sang. It is not a young man's trick. There is a stray note of thanks from Lear to Evelyn Baring in 1864 or so for the loan of his two-volume Moore, and it may be that was the moment. I do not think his dismal swamp joke arose from solitary giggling, but Lear and Baring were tremendous gigglers together, and touches even of quite serious Moore are to be found in unexpected places: in this poem, for instance, in which the sea of exciting exploration has suddenly widened into the estranging ocean of the Atlantic, the Bo is on his turtle:

> Through the silent-roaring ocean
> Did the Turtle swiftly go;
> Holding fast upon his shell
> Rode the Yonghy-Bonghy-Bo.

Why silent-roaring? Is that not an unusual and slightly unLearlike epithet? He was not underwater, the turtle is illustrated carrying him on the surface. I suspect an influence of one of the most beautiful of the Irish songs of Moore, one which Lear is bound to have known: 'Silent O Moyle be the roar of thy waters . . .'

It is a relief to know that with all the local intrigues that soon began to beset him, with the oddities of his diet and the rather large amount he began to drink, leading to a struggle which he triumphantly won with no dramatics and without anyone but Giorgis noticing, he went on composing his handful of lyrics until his dying day, and they got better and better. I do not think that his painting went on improving: it stayed more or less the same from now on (he was sixty in 1872) until his sight began to fail. Even at that time, it is possible that the dramatic black to which he reduced his works in his wildness and perhaps his misery, even in this final metamorphosis when it was without colour, without almost any quality but a terrifying inner strength, his last style may have more to do with his determination to find a way of reproducing his lifework in books than with his failing eyesight. His heart was failing too, as it had been since 1870, and he had been told he had exactly the same heart condition as his father had, so one day he would suddenly drop dead.

Still, there was life in him that year: more than there is in much younger men.

CHAPTER FIFTEEN

TO SEA IN A SIEVE

'OUTLOOK SOUTH – but who knows if one will live to look out at it?' That is what worried him at the New Year of 1871. The Sandbach children also annoyed him a little. 'Do you know, I really don't see how they *could* have gone to sea in a sieve . . . So the family not only lost their two horses, but their sugar-tongs and nutcrackers?' They were no worse than some of the adult clients who came to look at his paintings: but the lack of sales had begun to be serious, since now he had only £1000 left in the 3 per cents. 'I always get everything darker than I set out to do, owing to the haste necessary to complete what I begin: nor do I, as I ought, make a small coloured design first.' It is not a noticeable fault in most of his work, but it does indicate an indiscipline, a boredom when things took too long, that was possibly his deepest trouble: that and his lack of confidence. Sir W. Denison died that January: 'O the Woolwich and Chiselhurst and Shooters Hill walks!' By February he began to be hooked by his garden. 'Bernadino diggeth the terrace.' He went to a merchant and bought ten trees and some pampas grass. He was 'vexed, hurt and grieved by a song on the assassination of the new king of Spain', but by the 13th he had his ten orange trees planted: bulbs came from Selborne and cuttings from Congreve. Edward planted seeds and wrote out their names on wooden labels. He loved looking out always through the same screen of olive branches to the sea in the distance. 'It is difficult to fancy nicer loveliness and quiet than *might* be got at here.'

He transplanted vines, his cistern was dug, the *pergolata* (pergola) went up like scaffolding to make a vine-covered walk. One can scarcely wait for these things to come to be, because one has seen his heavenly garden sketches, which are mostly of terraces, at Harvard. It is the luxuriance that excites him, the entangled profusion of his pergola walk. The closets were damp and full of mould and beetles by spring 1871, but he was offered two mimosa trees. His pictures were selling at that season quicker than they were being painted, but it was local troubles that got to him. He had lent three garden keys to English people, who calmly robbed his garden of flowers, never sent the keys back, and left the gate open as well. He was worried about Hubert Congreve, the elder of the two brothers and now his pupil. He told the boy's father he should be at school, because he was too forward, which went down very badly. The relationship was a complex one: on Lear's side he became more and more deeply devoted to Hubert as time went on – besotted even, in a ridiculous and paternal way, and desperate to protect the boy from his troubles over his own father. Hubert liked the attention, but he is self-conscious and never a good witness either to what Lear was thinking or to the impression he made on others. His posthumous memoir of Lear appears to me unreliable, if only because he was an ordinary young man with the average number of things he wanted to hide, but Edward Lear was not at all ordinary.

When an east wind blew 'he only said, my life is dreary . . . Looked over and made notes on the whole Tennyson book of 1852 [he means the sixth edition of the 1842 poems]. I am really such a fool as to think of beginning a hundred of those subjects all at once.' He made a sketch of an eagle, and noted it was exactly a year since he decided to buy the ground. He worked at his Tennyson pictures, but suddenly a consignment of peach trees arrived. He now could not show or sell his pictures because of the war. Meanwhile 'the boys are all beating Judas's bones'. He planted marigold seeds his sister Ellen had sent. There was a fearful row with the gardener that April over the number of days he took off for the feasts: Edward could hardly grasp this endearing Italian habit, even at Easter, but the gardener won in the end. Edward was often lost in dreams. Now it was 'Charley Hullmandel's evenings when Stanfield made the scene of Charley's manufactured boats[?] and when after supper about 1 am JM Turner actually sang a song. For the world goes roundy abound abound a boundy, the world goes roundy bound abound.' Giorgis fed him with blackbirds and bacon on toast, or quails and stuffed artichokes: 'What celestially good food.' Still, 'We come no more To that golden shore Where we dreamed in days of old. O Knowsley! O Bovisand! O Woolwich!' Those are all Hornby habitats. He made designs for a Riviera book he knew he would never finish. When people left he was upset, as he had been in Rome as a young man when Digby Wyatt and others had ridiculed him. He had only two small oils in the Academy.

On 15 May, Congreve startled him by making some assertions about men's sexual treatment of women, 'known he said to all doctors but not to the many, which had led more or less to the women's rights movement (which he opposed)'. There can be no doubt what Congreve was talking about, and it is rather sweet of Edward to have been startled: but he was not experienced as a sexual partner. He was happy tying up his passion-flowers. Another day a fit came on him and left him senseless for two or three hours. It was so violent it could have happened anywhere and would have been irresistible, but fortunately he was able to lie down in time. The training of peas surprised and delighted him: 'Selborne' was in bloom, and the sweet peas almost. *Malpe trifida* came out, and all through the siege of Paris his garden comforted him. 'Garden is quietening. Fleas is not.' On 19 June came another enigmatic reference to his childhood: Fred Harding (a cousin in America) died. 'It is just fifty years since he did the greatest evil done to me in life – excepting that done by C: – which must last now to the end – spite of all reason and effort.' The second of these sounds like what he believed was the original cause of his epilepsy, but bad as it no doubt was, he is not likely to be right about cause and effect.

At the end of June he gave dinner to the Congreves. 'No better boys have I seen than these.' All day long the sky was intensely blue, and it was time for a holiday for Giorgis and therefore for himself also. He thought he might travel to Genoa, maybe even as far as Rome, but what he called his semi-rupture worried him, so that staying alone and travelling alone were equally disagreeable thoughts. Days wore themselves away to useless fritters. He designed pictures for the following year, the Congreves left, a weasel or a polecat got the Congreve chickens: at last he was off to Genoa by the train; he had never found the Corniche scenery so beautiful before. He loved the unexpected views as the track ran behind towns, and the water reflections in the Nile-like sea. San Remo was exquisite in its colour and calm. 'Old bridge, mulberries, aloes, reeds, figs and crash of zigzag cicadas, aloe hedge. Medlars. Tamarisks. Griale is passed but I was fast asleep. Immensely lovely bit past Finale. All these places quite different from 1864, more full of brightness.' I have travelled that route, lovely with vast mountain-slopes full of carnations, in a tiny modern train like a very clean tram, but it was more populous and combed and civilized than it had been a hundred years before. Certainly no one left in a trap for Spezzia at 3 a.m., as Giorgis did.

Edward got to Rome, but it was too hot to breathe, and he felt he was walking on graves. He thought about Mondragone 'where poor Charles Knight tried to teach me to ride'. He crossed Italy in stifling heat; at Falconara 'ever so many little boys come down astripping and pull huge cattle into the sea'. Rimini impressed him, and at Bologna he took paper and chalk to the Accademia gallery, but then he did not like the pictures. There is no sense in criticizing any of this: he just did not know what to do with himself. In August he got to Padua, 'no mistake about summer in this country'. At Conegliano he thought the trees might be Catalpas. He turns out to have been in a fastidious, almost snorting mood because he was stalking picture subjects. What occupied him most was the Ravenna forest for the Old Watercolour Society: or maybe Sermoneta or Gaza or Athos? In the morning he was dazed by the dreadful boom of bells – the Bellzebub quarter – all these places felt somehow the same. A stray acquaintance called Sumner told him plenty of gossip which his thirsty pages lapped, how A. P. Stanley had been offered Dublin, how the Queen had boxed someone's ears for making sheep's eyes at Prince Albert. Then Edward went down to Genoa. He read over the ninety pages of his *Riviera* and knew it was not good for much. Then Milan, Turin, and at last his old Certosa, which would have truly been a paradise had it not been for the fleas.

On the 27th he was home at San Remo, lingering around the Villa Congreve, melancholy enough and accompanied by Stripes the cat. The mosquitoes were unbearable, but he was able to work, if only at a drawing for his next children's book. H. Farquhar offered to pay him to take his two sons up the Nile and as far as Palestine, but he would not go; he said he could not. He outlined Athos and two Egyptian subjects on canvas. He was planting Tocsonia too, which a thunderstorm bent down at once, but he tied it up again. Frank Lushington was coming out at last, and it was half-way through September, so Edward sent for Giorgis by telegram, and rushed off to meet his friend at Avignon. Giorgis, who hated the sea with passion, arrived on 5 October, having lost his luggage overboard in a bad storm off Elba. Then there was a fuss over some lost spoons, 'which I found where I had put them' at 3 a.m. a fortnight later. In October he planned a barrage of flower-pots round the cistern, he planted onions, he gave away half a dozen plants, he bought a barrel of Marsala and filled seventy-two bottles. In November he reread the Antiquary.

Giorgis had adopted the olives, and rather to Lear's annoyance spent entire days at his olive harvest, though the result sold for almost nothing. Meanwhile, the gardener spent his time building himself a hut, and the Lord of the Manor, Edward, assailed the Cavaliere Hanbury with 'a drawing of the bits of ground I want'. He poked in his cellar and found a lot of wood which he recovered, 'because if Congreve has started fires, why shouldn't I?' He made a design for the line 'They sate them down upon the yellow sand'. Hanbury offered two little bits of ground 'if I give up a bit to square it. So matters are likely to hang fire.' In those same November days, Lear was much disturbed by a rumour the size of a man's hand, that Congreve had got a servant pregnant and sent her away. Giorgis knew all about it already, and he and Lear agreed in disapproving. It emerged in time that Congreve had been the rival of A. H. Clough for Arnold of Rugby's strongest affections. He had taught under the great man, and had just been appointed as Second Master or Deputy Head at Marlborough when his wife became ill: he left England at once, but she soon died and so did his eldest son. He married again, and this second wife had died too. His sad story filled Edward with sad sympathy, but I cannot help feeling it was more in the forefront of his mind that green cabbage caterpillars were attacking his stocks. He dined with Congreve and showed his new *Nonsense* book, 'but there was crackling of thorns under the fire'. San Remo got a new station: 'I went out and it had ceased raining, and lo! a railway whistle! and there sure enough on the beach by the new Station was the Macchina and three Carri of legno and two of engineers who went off puff puff to Spedaletto!!'

In December, he planted twenty pepper trees, and the gardener put in eighty or 100 rosemary roots. But there was more Congreve scandal. Little by little, with confrontations and heartsearchings, it came out that Congreve had been sleeping with this girl during his wife's illness, his wife knew it; when he sent the girl away he went on seeing her, he re-imported her under another name; eventually Lear spoke out against this, and so things rested at Christmas. The good news was that Hanbury agreed to the new boundaries. 'Moonlight spiffin as Hubert would say. Bernardino marks the new boundary with sticks . . . Bernardino prepares the wall' while Edward and Giorgis fill the waste places with beans. Congreve now confessed that the girl was quite untrue to him anyway. 'Verily women are queer critters.' There was a great deal of popping along to talk to the Rev. Mr Green, who was apparently still proposing to marry them out of hand. This shocked Lear, chiefly because of the children. One cannot deny that at this stage of his life he does seem guardedly happy, pleased with his house. He had nearly £1000 wrapped up in oil paintings, and still £1000 in the 3 per cents; in the course of the following year his savings began to climb again, to £1950 in the 3 per cents, because by then he had completed the last payments for his house. His worry about Congreve was like a hobby compared to his passionate feelings about his own family in the past.

Letters were now a more important lifeline to him than ever, but they are no longer a young man's letters as he explores the world, prim to his sister and gleeful and funny to his closest male friends. He has a past in common now with nearly all his correspondents: only occasionally with a new friend like Evelyn Baring or a newly discovered old one like Marianne North, the botanical painter and sister of Mrs Symonds, there are unexpected outbursts of joy and hilarity. But with staple friends like Emily Tennyson the tone is on the whole sober: he lapsed from jokes into caricatures to Alfred only when cajoling him into granting an autograph, which he knew Alfred hated doing, for a friend. Emily had written to tell him Hallam was to go to Trinity, Cambridge after Marlborough, and his younger brother Lionel from Eton to University College, Oxford, where Alfred and Emily knew and admired the Master. The Oxford plan did not last long, as the Master was swiftly promoted to a Deanery. But some letters, from this period if from no other, have perished, and the news about the boys is recorded only in Edward's diary. Of course correspondences were punctuated by fits of silence. When he wrote to congratulate Emily on Lionel's engagement early in 1876, appending a brilliant self-caricature, 'I find an old Envelope, intended to be filled up to you thousands of years ago (but I cannot write by Lamplight in these latter days, and the whole daylight is crowded with work) . . .'

Only the large archive of his letters to Fortescue, and often now to Lady Waldegrave, whom he treats like the Queen but at the same time with confident familiarity, is more or less complete, in its censored or scissored version between covers, and in the magic haystack of the Somerset Record Office at Taunton. It was to Fortescue he confided in January 1870 that his new book was to be *Learical Lyrics and Puffles of Prose*, and with him and his wife that he discussed politics in a remarkably sensible manner. And then also

> O pumpkins! O periwinkles!
> O pobblesquattles! how him rain!

It was to her he wrote from Certosa di Pesio that the private patronage on which he had been relying and which after all he had so carefully cultivated all his life was bound in the nature of things to come to an end, so now he must concentrate on public London exhibitions. Hence presumably his sudden enthusiasm for the Old Watercolour Society, which as he foresaw rejected him: and hence his starting to send pictures to the Academy after a sulk of some years. The work he was doing was careful and lively, and from a formal point of view better than ever. His Italian *Alpine Col di Tenda*, which he apparently gave to Hubert Congreve, is a flowing and majestic composition in sepia wash. He told Lady Waldegrave he reckoned the odds would be Tenda one whether he could get his shoe on after the climb, which thought kept him on Tenda-hooks. The view of the pass reflects the grand solution he had found for subjects of that kind in his huge Montenegro drawing, in which a solemn and thrilling landscape opens out between great wings of rock: but this is a mere sketch; the small township of Tenda huddles together in the middle ground, with rock less well defined beyond it. It is important that the Montenegro drawing is 'from sketches', not 'from a sketch'.

Lear's financial worries in 1871 had at some stage been bad enough to produce the offer of a loan from Fortescue, but he had turned that down: the sale for £100 of a Corsican forest to Goldsmid (whom it turns out he first knew through Henry Bruce and his wife, Arabella Beadon) and the commission of two more at £25 each relieved that crisis. Since Giorgis found he could do all the indoor work and preferred to do so, and the gardener dug, drew water and cleaned boots for 10s. a week, Lear's small economy could trundle along. He could still stay with the grandest Anglo-Italian families, where he had usually known the wife for years: the Duchess of Sermoneta at Frascati being Charles Knight's sister, and the Princess Teano being Ada Wilbraham, cousin to Lord Derby. He was on close enough terms with grand visitors like Archbishop Tait of Canterbury to know that he was henpecked by the female members of his family, who had frightened him away from the Riviera. Still, the truth of Lear's life was loneliness. His sixtieth birthday was due, and he had difficulty going up and down stairs. 'I think of marrying some domestic hen-bird and then of building a nest in one of my own olive trees, where I should only descend at remote intervals during the rest of my life.'

He corresponded with Mrs Parkyns, once Emma Bethell, now the wife of an Abyssinian explorer; she was the mother of eight daughters and expecting a baby, but feared a boy would spoil the set. This engaging lady was told in December 1871 that Edward had just written 'Mr and Mrs Discobolos', and she already knew all about the Jumblies. Indeed, she had two prose stories of Lear's called 'The Scroobious Pip' and 'Polly Pussybite', which might easily have perished altogether: he feared they could have been too long to copy out. The Bethell story of 'The Four Children' had been short enough to copy and send to him, otherwise we would have lost that too. And how many others? 'Polly Pussybite' was done in 1866: the drawings for it were traced for publication, lost and found again in 1872, and published only in *Teapots and Quails* (1953). It was Emma Parkyns who produced the 'Four Children' story of Violet, Slingsby, Guy and Lionel, Gussie Bethell's nephews and nieces. Emma Parkyns had, I think, wanted Edward Lear for a brother-in-law, but her opinion had perhaps wavered, and now that matter seemed to be over. Gussie had added a note to Emma's letter, and Lear's reply, although benign, was not conciliatory. Gussie said the clergy were his *bêtes noires*, he said he thought she would marry one, and explained how he had called someone's Reverend brother-in-law a miserable cretin of a ritualist.

He was pleased with the success of his *Nonsense* in 1872, and wanted to produce 'The Yonghy-Bonghy-Bo' at once, on its own if necessary. Little Henry Strachey, who would grow up to be a painter, recited it, and it made a furore in Lear's expanding and contracting world of Riviera expatriates. 'It is queer (and you would say so if you saw me) that I am the man as is making some three or four thousand people laugh in England all at one time – to say the least, for I hear *2000* of the new *Nonsense* are sold.' He longed to say a word of comfort to Congreve, but dared not do so 'for fear of agitating him'. Congreve said, 'I am ill, Lear, very ill,' which Lear felt he could see. He was reading Miss Edgeworth's letters, which he found 'curiously interesting but too breathless'; that is how to think of Lear: new seeds arrived from Jane Husey Hunt, his heart palpitations were bad, his sister Ann would have been eighty-two. Giorgis gave him a new dish, *spanakopita* with guinea-fowl and his own roast potatoes. There was a railway accident near Nice that left sixty dead, and the following day Edward had a fit so violent he thought that he was dying too. Congreve assured him, 'Lear, I am not going to marry her.'

New people of some importance in what followed begin to appear in his diaries and his letters during the early 1870s. Kay Shuttleworth was his neighbour and owned an obstreperous yapping poodle: he had thought she might be Lady Shuttleworth, but for certain she was half-sister to Marianne North and Mrs Symonds: Old North the MP had been the second husband of a lady from Lancashire who left a rough and gloomy ancient house which the Symonds sisters well remembered. Kay never grew in the least degree close to Lear, and there was trouble of her making to come. Then there was Tozer, an excellent travel writer from Exeter College, Oxford, who descended on San Remo and bought four Lears, which Edward delivered with a fifth in exchange for his *Highlands of Turkey*, a work unrivalled for nearly 100 years afterwards. Tozer's Lears were left to the Ashmolean Museum, Oxford: they were exceptionally well chosen, so that of all small English collections of which one is tempted to say the same, this is outstanding, where Lear is to be seen at his best on a small scale.

In February the east wind set in. Edward was reading Turner's life, probably with some alarm. 'It don't really matter what Shakespeare or Turner were (though it would be pleasant to know), seeing they have left proofs of almightiness.' Tacsonia 'Volk', Snailcreeper, yellow hibiscus and wallflower appeared, but the castor oil plants all looked miserable. Narcissus and crocus were already beautiful. Congreve was confiding, Emily Tennyson was like 10,000 angels boiled down, Lady Charles Percy talked of old times: she was Edward's first friend or patron in Rome. At the end of February came news that would change his life: T. G. Baring was going out to India as Governor-General. Lear's first reaction was 'I shall never probably see him again.' He was sowing lupins, sweet peas and sunflowers. It was a leap year, so he drew himself as a fat and bearded goose in flight, Congreve threw out Mr Green and was sad. Lear rearranged his studio for oil painting in the summer with long natural light, 'putting away Montenegro for ever'. He seems to have developed a vengeful feeling against it, as he often did when anything took a long time. Has it a certain sadness, like a Biblical painting, or one of the gloomier historical ones? The people in it, of whom there are an unusual number, and without whom its foreground would be bare rock, are very much a crowd scene, though he has tried hard with two of the faces, but the stillness of the light and the landscape is both mysterious and (as I have said) majestic. It is by no means a picture in the usual modern taste.

'A tooth, false or real I know not, broke off and swallowed was.' On 9 March Baring, who was now Lord Northbrook, asked Lear to come to Cannes, 'and then go with him to India and stay a year. To give up once more the chance to see Agra, Delhi, Darjeeling? I can't decide at once.' On the 10th he replied, thanking but declining. Was it because he feared the journey and the disturbance, or was it some fine feeling about the imperial lavishness of the present? He negotiated over more land, argued over mandarin orange trees, inspected thirty cypresses, and in pursuit of the exhausting question whether cows eat salmon dined with Lady Charles Percy, where Miss Dempster said she knew the very cows, which were sold from her father's estate. On the 23rd Lord Northbrook renewed his offer to pay Lear's expenses right through India. He wanted to walk from Nice to Menton, but the weather was bad. (The habit of such long walks was becoming 'old-fashioned at that time.) They did at least dine together. 'Too much champagne perhaps; long sitting and smoking and stories.' The following night they dined alone and then Edward saw his old friend off to Cannes: 'affectionate and upright. Whether I go to India or not I thank him all the same.' On Maundy Thursday *Clyanthus puniceus* bloomed from his niece's seed: 'a magnificent flower like a lobster's claw, four bushes of 'em.' He was re-reading *Persuasion* and on Easter Day his geraniums came out. Everything smelled of stocks at dusk that April, and the garden took most of his time.

Then it occurred to him, why not buy land and build another house on that while he went to India? The new ground was not so cosy or so picturesque as what he had, but it was less vulnerable to disturbance and had more 'capabilities', and it could be had for £920. He would have to borrow, or could he sell the Villa Emily for £3000? He thought he would buy the 11,000 metres anyway, and sent for house plans from England. He dithered about the ground but settled on buying it. He asked Drummond's to sell his last £1000 of 3 per cents. The following day, 20 April, Lord Northbrook bought the Montenegro for £100. Edward's mind was 'all at sea and cloudy' about whether to choose India or not, whether to build or not, whether to publish his Egyptian and Riviera journals or not, whether to get to work the following day on the Tennysonian paintings or not. The last at least he did. 'The crag that fronts the even,' he wrote, and then 'Moonlight on still water'. The new bit of ground was uphill, but somehow not exposed, and Mr Bonatti agreed to £800 and to give up his request for an access road through it to a quarry: the Bonatti family wanted Edward to go to Genoa to sign.

The first house-cat, Potta, had wandered away and got lost or died on 30 October. On 30 April, 'The (second) new cat a kitten of two weeks old came today, an object I am glad of for two reasons, mice and distraction for Giorgis. Rats are playing the deuce in the garden – biting tacsonias in half where they want to make a passage etc.' Walking over the new ground, Lear spotted 'an odd sandpapery ouzelly sort of bird in that stream'. In his own garden the delights were endless: a blue Selborne delphinium was the new attraction, not to mention the nightingales. 'The cat truly exemplary, begins to be quite tractable and amusing.' His tacsonias and passion-flowers do extraordinarily well. 'The cat Potiphar is an eminent person in this establishment ... Potiphar sits on one knee quietly enough.' Then, 'I suppose I shall buy the land ... Half wish I had not bought the land.' On 17 May he refers to the *Telegraph* as the *Daily Jabberwok*. This is the year (1872) in which *Alice Through the Looking Glass*, with the 'Jabberwocky' in Chapter 1, was published (the official biography says 1871); it sold 8000 copies at once, and by March someone at Cambridge had put the 'Jabberwocky' into Latin: Lewis Carroll cannot have got its joke name from Lear's private diaries, even though Lear influenced him so that he even wrote a limerick. Can Lear have got it from Lewis Carroll? Only from gossip, I think, and from jokes circulating at the time, otherwise calling the *Telegraph* the *Jabberwok* is obscure. The jaal-goat of Mount Sinai is in the old Oxford dictionary, but the jabberwok is not.

Edward went to Genoa in the end, missing 'Giorgio my servant and friend, and Potiphar my model cat'. The cat followed him about and loved him: 'Potiphar the unrivalled and excellent disports around the room.' Lear was in love with it in return: 'P. rushed out and sat in an olive tree.' Gastaldi agreed on the site of the new house, but Edward was more intent on burying his old slippers in the garden. He got to Marseille reading Tennant on Ceylon, and found it was only seventeen hours now to Paris: within a week he was in England, amazed at the novelty and beauty of the Thames embankment. Yet 1872 is the publication date of Doré's London with all its terrific horrors and its grime.

Lear found G. S. Venables greatly aged but greatly softened and improved. His picture at the Academy was not as badly hung as he had imagined, and he sold two to the Drummonds for £107. He felt at this stage that he would not go to India unless he could go 'on my own hook to Ceylon', which he had always longed to see and where I assume he thought his visit might be expensive. 'The feeling of dependence and control which this offer must needs tie me to for many months would I believe at some moment or other prove insupportable, though I am well aware how much good the regime would do me, could I go well through with it.' His objections and conditions in fact were to do with his own neurotic condition, but Lear knew himself. He thought the Albert Memorial fine work, but scattered and somehow unsatisfactory. He drew a little, he considered Autotype, and half-way through the month he thought he was going to India after all.

Lear hung about England for a long time, feeling more and more disposed to his Indian adventure. He worked hard at a painting for Tozer based on a sketch of Frank Lushington's, and he visited assiduously. He sang 'The Yonghy-Bonghy-Bo' to the more than eighty-year-old Mr and Mrs Bell at Selborne, where he found the villagers would use nine sixpences to make a ring to cure fits, and keep a knife clean to cure the wound it made. 'Prayers early and late, one bottle of port, all solicitude.' He went to the Drummonds at Cadland, and to Stratton, the Baring house. 'Clear and lovely lawn, flowers, long deep shadows of the trees: gardens and avenues of Stratton, which place has for me more of a home feeling than any other.' He drew it to illustrate Tennyson's 'Daisy', and it did indeed look like the old English thatched half-timbered farmlike house *par excellence*. After dinner Lord Radstock played the organ, though what that was like who knows? Back in London Lear paid Autotype for two facsimiles, which he did not like. He went for a long walk round Chislehurst looking for land to buy near Lushington, heard from Williams of Smith and Elder (once Hullmandel's), that the Cornhill were unlikely to take on his journals, went nearly out of his mind with excitement at the National Gallery Turners, and bought three sets of teeth for nine guineas. Bernard Husey Hunt had advised him early in August to go to India, to retain the new land and garden, but not to build on it yet, and to pay Lord Northbrook back in paintings. This simple and sensible solution worked on him. It had really been worth coming to England for it.

He saw Chantry's picture of A. H. Hallam at Wickham Court, and Mrs Howard at Ashtead, and late in August, so deep in the long vacation that the grass must have grown up unscythed and untrampled between the cobble-stones of the High Street, he stayed with the Tozers at their elegant new house, 5 Park Villas. Oxford was all very well in August, he thought, being neither the first nor the last to think so, but not in November. 'The longer one lives to contemplate Turner', which he did in the remarkable water-colours in the Ashmolean that Ruskin had acquired, 'the more wondrous is the gigantic wonder.' That collection includes the most accurate of fish, the heron's head, and a landscape dissolving into mere light. It still looks every bit as spectacular as he thought it. At Mount Lebanon (1835), at Jericho, the Convent of S. Antonio, at Boscastle (1824) and Margate, the old genius had crossed Lear's tracks, and nearly everywhere was supreme, though I do own to not much liking the Ashmolean Turner of the White Cliffs. But even his simple drawing of cows is brilliant beyond emulation.

By this time Lear was becoming tired out and unwell, and while on a walk with his friend Evans at Duffield, he fell climbing a gate and broke his glasses. He refers later to this as an injury to his eye, but he must in the course of his life have fallen some hundred times, and it may be that his eyes deteriorated gradually and the headaches arose from that. He makes wry observations on persons and places that seem worth recording, only there are too many of them. I like 'a natural, visible vein of swelldom' in Lord and Lady Bagot, and 'rough, kindly and good but hardly agreeable' of Lord Lyttelton. At Rendcombe he noticed 'a curious selfcontainedness, the surrounding landscape seems made to fit it', which it does. He loved Lord Bathurst's park and admitted that it gave him 'a quite *new* idea *of an avenue.*' Somewhere here he saw 'the nasty little fellow Hayward' again. He drove about 'parks and shady places' and collected the names of passion-flowers. 'Emily Strangford has built a new place at Naples, but will go to Madrid if she don't go to Calcutta, which I hope she won't.' At the end of September he rushed to the Highgate Nursery and then made for San Remo, where Bernardino was at the station to meet him and the flowers in his garden had grown preposterously. Then he was off to India.

He went to Corfu to fetch Giorgis who looked pleased to see him. 'Met King and Queen of Greece on oss back. My, how I slept.' On the 7th the two travellers boarded the *Ungaria*, 'huge boat of odious arrangement: half lower deck full of cattle, other half straw'. The boat was also crowded with humans, and Lear could get only a four-berth cabin below, not something one would recommend to a man of sixty. 'The real first deck is actually impossible, owing to the nuisance of Levantines: woman vomiteth all about and another hideously fat suckles her child in full society, churning her immense "bossum" in the most flagrantly nasty way. Cerigo and now Crete fading away as daylight goes.' After a day or two 'some of the filthiest second class now came out in silks and blue glory. Those brutal Arabs. A few mosquitoes.' Edward does not sound in the frame of mind that would augur well for his journey. If he felt like this in the Mediterranean, how was he going to like India? Part of his trouble was surely cold horror at that daunting question. Alexandria at least was now a huge and prosperous city. 'Got two seats in a carriage easier than I expected. Cairo by one PM. About to mount donkeys, but the brutal boys so bullied me I had to cut off and walk, whereat those fiends followed and molested us nearly to Boulak.'

Garden City (Heliopolis) was new to him and so was the Nile Bridge, but he was disgusted with Egypt, the two pyramids barely showed above the trees so he gave them up, he hated the sense of a filthier Riviera. 'Doubt if I shall get beyond Suez or Ceylon.' It was the following day that he realized Northbrook, who had asked for this Egyptian picture, had meant the viewing-point to be farther on than the bridge.

The following day the bridge was open for ships. Edward waited three-quarters of an hour, while nothing happened, but then,

> Nothing in life is so amazingly astonishing as this new road or avenue, literally all through the Pyramids. I could really hardly believe my own senses, remembering the place in 1867. There is a house built for the Prince of Wales. Not one of these wonders can be really seen or thought of, owing to the monstrous devil-nuisance of the loathsome aborigines. Worked an hour and three quarters. Frogs, beetles, and many rats were my friends.

The following day he was at the island causeway: 'Great lines and circles of palms and egrets, and were one sure of quiet there is much of poetry in the scene, but it wants thought and arrangement, and as it was impossible to avoid these Egyptian pests, so it was hard work to draw.' Attempts at lunch were equally fraught. 'I drew again at the head of a great acacia avenue, but flies made the work impossible.' Inside the hotel, thinking to eat at the *table d'hôte*, he was 'upset by the noise of some Levantines'. Next day he got to Suez, and one feels that never can a drawing expedition have been so ghastly. And yet it produced two really remarkable pictures in a new, monumental style. One feels at once the sweep and shadowy grandeur of the avenue, and the sheer fineness of the pyramids, something that does depend on precise distance and viewpoint. They 'coalesce in light', as Christopher Fry says somewhere. They are really two of Lear's most successful pictures.[1]

But it is important not to lose the momentum of this generally hellish journey. They got to Suez at seven in the evening, with a chance-met friend, and 'a cluster of horrid Arabs clawed us up. My companion thinks there will be no chance of a place to Ceylon: if so I will return to San Remo.' That was not a serious threat: he penned out his new drawings and he slept well, and next day he watched a steamer come through the canal,

> and rose mountains as the sun set, every line brightly cut out to Jebel Suthr(?) of 1849 memories ... Steamer 600 tons. I have had two bottles of Médoc and one of Beaujolais – as Hugh Nevill writes – RUIN. Going

up to look at the moon. 18th Messagerie boats equally good and large and one goes on the twentieth ... Can't decide. Lose three in a hundred changing money here. Bots. 4 Beaujolais, 5 Médoc.

On the 19th he changed money at Lloyd's agent for a half of one per cent, and then bought two tickets for the Tigre. 'Doctor's stories of the boundless vice of Egypt. Tribesmen's evening entertainment. The Prussian consul told him at the opening of the canal the most popular entertainment was a giant negro buggering seven boys in a row for two hours.' (This is in Greek.) On the 20th the boat had still not arrived, but on the 21st he sent his luggage to the Agency, and had his smaller things put on the Mahon barge at six in the morning. 'On French agent's advice we go on donkeys.' He then ordered their things off the barge and on to a small boat. Customs men came, and Edward felt he might miss the steamer. There was no wind.

'My rage was extreme, and as at Thessaly, I suddenly resolved on an opposite course – being nearly mad with worry, noise, delay and uncertainty – so off went all the things to the Station, before 8 a.m., and the *Indian bubble is burst*.' Breakfast and wine were fetched and Edward and Giorgis set off back to Alexandria. 'My head was *very* bad, and at times I really *do* think my reason is shaken. Giorgis shocked.' Next day, 'The frightful row and murderous savage beastliness of these savages of Alexandria! Had it not been for a soldier's whip we could never have got through.' Giorgis took a ship for Corfu, Edward was to meet him at Brindisi, and perhaps see Otranto. 'As at Jerusalem in '67 and Larissa in '49, this abrupt change is afflicting and savours of insanity. In vain, in vain, I look back for a reason for the determination of heart and mind in those days of Suez. Nothing but that miserable blow [falling off the gate] seems to me to account for it.' On the 23rd, 'grief prevaileth, at times to excess ... The end of the monologue is don't go, make the best of San Remo and perhaps go next year.'

Before I leave the reader to make what he wishes of this heart-rending story, there are some details one can clear up. The first is Edward's almost unnatural hatred and fear of Arabs and lower-class Levantines. Observe that the Egyptian soldier used a whip to control them, and it was quite common in the last generation to beat them with one's stick: I remember a very old Englishman living in Cairo who was still doing so long after Nasser. This dark streak of savagery in Egyptian life was really there, and Lear's racist remarks, which are quite uncharacteristic of him, were provoked by a ghastly experience. What he says about sex is as true as it is nasty; Durrell's *Alexandria Quartet* contains plenty of that kind of thing. Egypt in the early 1870s was a horrible place, with actively malevolent mobs. The attempt to put down slavery dates from Gordon, who was still to come. Edward Lear had been mishandled by a mob, and had behaved perfectly at Petra: can that have left a mark on him, or was it his childhood fear of black men? Hardly so, since the complex if it was one left him perfectly free and happy when he got to India. He just felt he had gone mad with heat and worry, and that was all that worried him. It appears to me that he was so near a breakdown of fear and rage and horror, that what he did was the most sensible thing. It is a pity he did not travel out with Lord Northbrook. Later, he said, 'I think the sense of compulsion, the want of total independence, was the biggest ingredient of the breakdown of India.'

He heard torrents had cut the railway to San Remo, and there was talk of brigands, but he got home, and so did Giorgis: the railway was now the only safe road, unsafe as it was. One of the Corniche bridges had been carried away, and passengers got out and walked; there were numerous landslides, because San Remo had suffered twenty-one days of continual violent rain. It was November, and too late to visit Otranto that year. The cat which Giorgis had taken to Corfu had got lost there; Bernardino's child had scratched the names off all the careful plant labels, 'so Botany is confounded'. But on 4 November Potta's twin brother arrived, sent by Madam Poplawska with half his tail missing. Because he was a twin he was called *Aderphos* in Greek, or Foss for short: we have no photograph of him, he jumped out of Lear's arms just as one was about to be taken, late in both their lives, so we depend on numerous extremely funny and affectionate cartoons. Edward adored Foss and it was mutual, but the Foss we know belongs more to the world of nonsense stories and songs than he does to the real world.

The idiot Vicar preached on whether Nathaniel was Bartholomew or vice versa: Edward still often attended these punishing sessions. Giorgis cheerfully settled down to pick olives, Foss sat with the dignity of cats on a chair on his own. Edward wrote calmly enough to his friends about why he did not 'purSuez Eastern journey further', making it sound the most reasonable of decisions. All that winter he read what were then the nine volumes of Horace Walpole's *Letters*, which he enjoyed, and in the spring the eight volumes of Moore's *Memoirs* edited in the mid-1850s. In summer he devoted himself to making Ipomaea, passion-flowers and Cape Jessamine rush all over his pergola. 'Vines is vines it is true, and very beautiful – but they give so much bother of sulphur putting these days that I eschew them.'[2] When visitors observing a beech tree in his painting asked whether that was a palm tree, he put on his soberest expression and assured them it was a Peruvian broccoli. Perhaps he was thinking of his friend Marianne North, who had explored an entire, remote forest of Peruvian pines or monkey-puzzles.

He made his mind up that July to sail for India from Genoa on 24 October: ships were crowded at that time of year, and this time there was to be no nonsense about his berth. Foss was 'very reputable and follows Giorgis like a dog'. He was banished for scratching 'but has insinuated himself back by the fireside'. Edward negotiated with Hanbury about ground again, but found him cryptic and cautious: he showed pictures of La Mortola, the large hillside garden estate of the Hanburys, 'to win him', wondering whether he might pay £1000. Journeys had cost £838 the previous year, including London as well as Suez, and not going to India had cost £1000 in lost commissions, but money was easier now, he had over £1200, and thought of buying land again. Then on the whole he thought he might prefer spending his money in seeing the world. The quarry was to be exploited anyway, and so the ground there was not sold. Congreve also saw salvation in acquiring unspoilable sites at this time.

When April came, he planted two Japanese medlars at three francs each and twenty more cypresses at fifty cents each. He wrote to Fortescue asking him to make Congreve Vice-Consul, another road to salvation. The town annoyed Edward now with its carts of stones, but he was ill and hard at work making copies of 120 pictures, for a return of £1000. That had taken seventy-two days, and left him free at Easter to return to his Tennysonian pictures. He had pondered so long over the poetry that humour and parody were bound to break in, though his respect was real, his admiration for the poems profound; needless to say, the parodies were never published by him. They are repeated here because they show with what closeness he could follow the sound of poetry while parodying its sense.

Like the Wag who jumps at evening
All along the sanded floor.

To watch the tipsy cripples on the beach
With topsy-turvy signs of screamy play.

And the crag that fronts the evening
All along the shadowing shore.
– *Eleanore*

To watch the crisping ripples on the beach
And tender curving lines of creamy spray.
– *The Lotos-Eaters*

Tom-Moorey Pathos: – all
      things bare
Delirious Bulldogs – echoing, calls
My daughter, – green as summer
  grass: –
The long supine Plebeian ass,
The nasty crockery boring falls: –

– These two are both from
To E. L.

Tomohrit . . .
The vast Akrokeraunian walls.

Spoonmeat at Bill Porters in the
  Hall,
With green pomegranates and no end
  of Bass.

Moonlight on still waters between
  walls
Of gleaming granite in a shadowy
  Pass.
– *The Lotos-Eaters*

This joke would not have pleased the Laureate, but there is no evidence that he ever heard it: unkinder and less skilful parodies of him existed. We have this in two slightly different versions, one in a letter to Mrs Ward in July 1873 when she was newly married, and one to Fortescue in September, in which the reading is 'To catch the whistling cripples . . .' and tott'ring falls gives way to boring falls, and a shower of Bass to what I have written. It is not a matter of great moment, and I have amalgamated the two. But five oils represent a vast and brave investment of time. *The Morn Broadens* was already sold to Fortescue; it was his old *Civitella di Subiaco*. Lear also tackled *Bavella* and *Beachy Head* in oil for this series, and when he died the Tennysons acquired his unfinished Enoch Arden painting of *Someone Pacing There Alone.*[3]

In 1873 he spoke of a new will, since he reckoned he would now leave £1500 in pictures, leaving his house not to his family in New Zealand, who had done very well like many others there, but to a godson. The Villa Emily was changing, of course: Kay Shuttleworth's property below it was let to Germans for six years (Lear did not like Germans), and now he never saw Congreve.

Edward liked Miss Edgeworth's *Absentees*, he loved his fire-flies and the chirp of his sparrows, he was banking his money, he was writing his parodies down, 'the nasty crockery always falls', and on 27 July he suddenly composed 'The Akond of Swat'. He must have been reading about the Afghan border, where those titles were commonplace. 'I must go away in September for some weeks, but where or what, who knows but the Akond of Swat?' He had fixed Hanbury's wall for him and Hanbury offered him a room at La Mortola whenever he wanted one, so that was going well. His pictures inched their way to improvement. He threw away letters, musing always about the past. He remembered his sister Jane's epileptic attacks when he was a child and had not known what they were. He thought how lucky he had been, nearly always to feel the onset of his own and preserve his privacy. He reckoned Aunt Kitty had to do that for Jane. (That is another character we have never heard of before.) 'Fleas is few, flies is fewer, gnats not come yet, and altogether life might be very pleasant if accompanied by a female.' That summer Lord Westbury died leaving £300,000 and no executors. 'Foss ye cat catcheth grasshoppers.' *Ipomoea learii* bloomed.

Giorgis went off to Brindisi instead of Marseille. 'Not a very great matter would make me give up India for the last time.' The railway was broken and the rivers flooding. Lear finished a pelican picture, and mosquitoes arrived in swarms half-way through September. His notes about luggage and Customs create a certain tension: he is clearly prepared to find some obstacle insuperable. He was in an anguish about Giorgis leaving first, and in deep anxiety about leaving Foss behind: but Hubert Congreve was to be his bailiff. Even when he had set out for Genoa, when the passengers had to walk here and there, and Edward missed a train at Rapallo, he seriously considered walking back to San Remo to see that Foss was all right. He did get back in the end by train, and 'Poor Foss would persist in following me right down the steps and into the road.' Edward took him back to Bernardino. His old friend the painter Marstrand died in Copenhagen, two years after his first stroke. 'He was the F. L. of those days, and I cannot dare to think of them.' At last, on 24 October at four in the afternoon, he boarded the *India*, but a last-minute delay of twenty-four hours made him so furious that he had all his luggage taken off; he was on the point of not going at all. When he was at last on board again, he thought of doing quarantine at Leghorn and sending for Giorgis in Naples. He decided after two days to go on: 'great sea, steadied by sails, bright green and blue water'. He slept all night, Giorgis met him, and he sat up in the moonlight as they passed Stromboli 'with good old Giorgis, glad of my thickest cloak'. They really were on their way to India.

Before they had left the Mediterranean, Edward composed another lyric. It may depend on the fact that *Gee* in Sanremo dialect meant spinach. He began south of Crete on 29 October, and finished in bad weather, below decks, on the 30th.

> The Attalik Ghazee
> Had a wife whose name was Gee
> And a lady proud was she,

> While residing by the sea.
> Said the Attalik Ghazee
> Who resided by the sea,
> 'My own beloved Gee
> I am suffering from a flea
> Who has settled on my knee.'
> Said the Begum Lady Gee
> (Who resided by the sea),
> 'Why! What is that to me!
> Do you think I'll catch a flea
> That has settled on your knee?'

All the morning when he began this small poem he was watching Crete with Giorgis, who had called him at five to see it. The journey to Bombay was tiresome at times but it took less than a month and we owe it some sharp observation of shipboard conversations. 'You wear spegtacles alway?' Yes. 'They vill all grack in one: one pair is no use.' But I have many. 'How many?' Twenty or twenty-four. 'It is no good, they vill all grack. You should have got of silver.' But I have several of silver. 'Dat is no use, they vill rust. You must got gold.' But I have some of gold. 'That is more worse; gold is always stealing.' When they got further on their journey, there was a gentleman who complained of a rat ah ah ah rattle. He gave Edward his views over coffee one evening. 'It is my own idea – idea ah ah my own idea, that if the wind had been ah ah right ah favourable for four days, we should have arrived in Bom ah Bombay, the coffee is not hot, in Bombay arrived in Sugar! my own idea.' Taking on coal every two or three days, they puffed their way south, and at last, on 22 November, their twenty-eighth day, they docked at Bombay.

CHAPTER SIXTEEN

INDIA

EDWARD had finished another bit of comic verse on the boat, full of strange bits of Indian, or Anglo-Indian, which he was learning. The Akond of Swat really existed, but the Attalik Ghazee was invented, an Attalik being a Persian administrative district: the third effort was still more fantastical, 'The Cummerbund', published in the *Times of India* while he was out there.

> She sat upon her Dobie,
>   To watch the Evening star,
> And all the Punkahs as they passed
>   Cried, My, how fair you are!
> Around her bower with quivering leaves
>   The tall Kamsamahs grew,
> And Kitmutgars in wild festoons
>   Hung down from Tchokis blue . . .

Nothing much happens until she is eaten by a Cummerbund, who is a first cousin of the Jabberwocky. It is a pleasant bit of verse with an entertaining, exotic landscape beyond the reach of Tennyson, but it is neither here nor there: a pass-time, that is all.

Pause for a moment to watch the two highly eccentric elderly gentlemen descending from the steamer. Giorgis was five years younger than Lear, born in 1817, so he was fifty-five, but while he was in India he would begin to break up. He somehow got it into his head that in India they might both get rich. It was to him a land showered with diamonds: at least it appeared so later, and in retrospect he felt that in India Lear had failed him. It is hard to know what he meant by that, but certainly the grandeur of Lord Northbrook will have impressed him. Northbrook at the time was fighting a severe famine, working extremely hard at it and winning golden opinions; less than twenty years had passed since the Mutiny. There was a streak of melancholy in that great man, as there is in many Barings; one should think of him on his last night in England, dining quietly in London with Fortescue, Drummond (not the banker) and another Christ Church friend from some thirty or more years before. His younger and brilliantly efficient assistant was Evelyn Baring. Naturally there was a stiff protocol which Edward sometimes found vexing though very often it was cut for him. What Giorgis wanted most was to see an elephant: Edward is said to have got to ride on one in some official procession, but I do not think he did.

At a lower level, the India of 1873–4 was not such fun: Edward was soon warned by Dr Sydney Coombe of Dinapore, late of Arundel, that Giorgis ought not to travel with him, since the English (and Indians) would assume he belonged to an inferior race, because they never encountered servants, except for the multitude of native servants, and to travel with a Greek servant was asking for trouble. Edward records this conversation, but told his friend that he proposed to do precisely nothing about this idiotic rule. All the same, it must have added to the strain they were both under in India. Edward was careful and even spiky or crabby in his initial approach to the sub-continent: he could still be as enthusiastic as a boy, over the baby elephants at Dinapore, for example, but his deeper mood was more sombre, his appreciation as a painter was slower. When it was all over and he left for home, he decided he would come back again, because his work was unfinished. How could it be, in a year? Even Canada, even Australia, could not offer such wonders to the eye as India could in 1873–4.

The Indian journey was written up for publication, and it was given to Lord Northbrook with all its extremely rich illustrations; he had it bound by Bayntun of Bath in two vast and heavy folio volumes, which are now at Harvard; they must constitute one of the greatest treasures that survive from the British period in India. The diary itself also survives and was edited by R. Murphy in 1953, in a volume now hard to find. It really deserves to be done again with the kind of pictures used for Lear's *Crete* and *Corfu*. The sketches and finished pictures are amazing, so that a lifetime later one still says, 'So that is what it was like.' Lear's numerous plant studies are beautiful enough, and when Northbrook was later promoted to an Earldom from his Viscountcy, Edward gave him a detailed and expert opinion as to which kind of palm trees he should use for supporters. He brought home a lot of seeds too. Among his paintings, although the set pieces are astonishing, and the Kinchinjunga above all,[1] in its very different, unexpected way, the crowded shore at Benares, and the blue and tawny Mahee, which is a view of mountains over swampy lakes[2] on the Malabar coast, certainly impress: yet it is the swift sketches at Harvard that have such immediacy.

I would have said 'with the single exception of Kinchinjunga', where the first sight of the mountain peering out of the sky over the dark forest background is unforgettable, and impressed me more than any other thing in the Academy Lear exhibition ten years ago; yet there are two drawings of the same subject done on 18 January 1874, at 8.30–9.30 a.m. and 2.30–3 p.m., which are so wonderfully lively and stinging that I do not think even the substantial solemnity or sublimity of the oil painting is better. It is most carefully considered, every move in it creeps forward like a game of chess played very slowly. It is as breathtaking as it is exciting. The Harvard sketches[3] look like the work of some marvellous painter one had never heard of, probably French, somewhere between 1780 and 1830. At Kanchenjunga, as it is now called, the artist and his proper subject came face to face. He was in his early sixties. The Taj Mahal probably excited him more, but that does not submit to sketches and his is mostly a study of cypress trees. His forest at Roorkee with strange monuments in the distance is marvellously eerie,[4] and his *Poinciana regia*, his lotus, the forest in his Poona river view are all very satisfying: one would happily have paid the 5s. any of them must have cost in the 1930s: but the palms and banana trees(?) at Calicut on the Malibar coast that he drew on 21 and 22 October cannot ever in history have been so exquisitely recorded.[5] They are a masterpiece of botanical drawing. His Hanwell is a slighter but similar sketch. The trees he had drawn at Barrackpoor a month or two after he arrived in India are amateurish by comparison, and yet when they are adapted for a Tennysonian illustration later on, they are a thrilling design. It took him months to get his eyes used to Indian trees, yet in the end they were his great victory. In the oil painting of Kinchinjunga, done a year later when he was far away, he reverted to his old bad habit of great banks of trees, exotic certainly, but whiskery. The mere sketches of vegetation in 1874 which I so admired owe something perhaps to Edward's concentration on his Mediterranean garden; it was a skill that from then on he never lost.[6]

Kinchinjunga is a tall Himalayan peak, seen from Darjeeling: perhaps there can be no much more spectacular view on earth. Lear made three pictures of it, one for Lord Northbrook and one for Lady Ashburton, both now privately owned by Americans, and one for Lord Aberdare, which belongs to the Cynon Valley Borough Council, to whom Aberdare left it. He gave Edward a free choice as to what he painted, but this is in all India the supreme, purely topographic view. There is one point in the Hindu Kush mountains in Afghanistan, above a mile or more of waterfalls towards the Pakistan border, where the Himalayas are suddenly visible with their eternal snow; certainly no sight I have ever seen is more startling or more august. Until he saw this great mountain, in January 1874, Lear was worried about the perfect subject: he thought of Benares, but it was too fussy and his eyes were not good enough for all that detail: anyway, although it gave him several pictures it is really too conventionally exotic, and I doubt if Lady Aberdare wanted burning ghats in her dining-room. He cavilled at Kinchinjunga too, when he saw it.

'Kinchinjunga is not, so it seems to me, a sympathetic mountain; it is so far off, so very godlike and stupendous, and all that great world of dark opal valleys, full of misty, hardly to be imagined forms, besides the all but impossibility of expressing the whole as a scene, make up a rather distracting and repelling whole.' But that surely was just painter's nerves, which did not alter his power of sketching. The mountain revealed itself in amazing and snowy splendour every morning at dawn, and was blotted out as the day went on, so he began to stalk it. 'Kinchinjunga at sunrise is a glory not to be forgotten; Kinchinjunga PM is apt to become a wonderful hash of Turneresque colour and mist and space, but with little claim to forming a picture of grand effect.' He liked what vegetation there was. 'The foregrounds of ferns are truly bunderful – only there are no apes and no parrots and no nothing alive, which vexes me,' he wrote to Lady Waldegrave. He bought a lot of photographs as usual, and in San Remo he settled down to paint in December 1875: he finished the Ashburton and the Aberdare pictures by May 1877. Vivien Noakes in her RA Catalogue calls this scene 'a supreme example of the sublime in its traditional (eighteenth-century) sense . . . Lear's concern . . . was to evoke the contrary feelings of attraction and repulsion', and that is no doubt true if one has his sensibility, though in some cases, including my own, horror is swallowed up in wonder. It was adapted later on to be one of the great unfinished Tennysonian series, where it illustrated 'All things fair' in 'To E. L. ', the place of honour maybe.[7]

Bombay excited him of course, because it was India. The only drawing I have seen from there must be done later as it is shadowy and romantic and has waving palms in it, but at the time of his arrival he writes, 'Flowers, trees, rupees, hotel. O new palms!! O flowers O creatures O beasts.' Telegrams flash, he is to make for Lucknow, and in two days he has taken to the railway. He sees green cockatoos, buffaloes, lotos growing, and egrets: there are 'beautiful scenes, even at shadowless noon ... Superb hills. Queer shaped hills. Very curious forms of hill. Mangoes.' Even at a wayside station, 'What flowers!' He is like a man new created, or like a child home for the holidays. 'Pale, far hills, light green trees, very like Crete to my surprise. Jubbulpoor. Kellner's hotel. Bed (hard).' He notices sparrows indoors, squirrels, a bluejay, and to Giorgis's great wonder they see their first elephant. On 2 December Edward saw Lord Northbrook in camp, and agreed to spend Christmas in Calcutta. At the same time he met young Doctor Coombe: 'Mem. No more private houses for either self or servant.'

'Valley of rocks, huge granite boulders with actual live dusky elephant at one spot, like a live boulder.' He saw the falls of the Nerbudda, which he thought were like the First Cataract of the Nile. He was not being dismissive; the resemblance interested him; he drew the marble cliffs of that river with most skilful precision.[8] At Lucknow he saw a great procession, but Giorgis could not go and so Edward missed his first elephant ride. It was a long, slow, military affair with troops and over sixty elephants. There were eleven or twenty Durbar elephants which cavorted and trumpeted; they had belonged to the royal family of Oude. Lear several times drew caricatures of himself in a pith helmet being run away with by an elephant, but I cannot find that he ever did get to ride one. He drew a wonderful scene of elephants washing in a river in a forest, yet that was only like a snapshot, a swift memoir of a day. Sometimes he despaired to a nearly comic degree: at Lucknow, for instance, when he felt ill and miserable and his luggage had got lost, and he meditated return to Bombay and Genoa, but that was before Evelyn Baring took him in hand. Still, at Benares he felt it was all a mistake, as he listened to the fife-like squeals of the kites, and then the song-like crying of jackals, Away, away! All through December he considered deserting, whenever something went wrong. He was comforted really by flowers like *Poinciana regia*, and birds such as a small green bee-eater that were new to him.

For the Governor-General, Calcutta meant hard work, and Lear seems to have disliked the place. At Benares his aim had been to outdo Daniell, whose paintings of it he had thought dreary, but at Calcutta at the New Year it was just 'O the misty sultry blueness and orangeness of

Calcutta mornings'. His stool broke, a red ape invaded but was repelled, and Giorgis spotted a crocodile on their way north. On 13 January 1874 they saw the Himalayas for the first time. 'The mountain views are incredible yet I fancy at moments not so lovely as some I have seen in Greece, barring the incredible vegetation here.' The evidence that belies this statement is his paintings. Even the little Buddhist shrine that he moves about in the foreground of his oils was really there, and it excited him. 'Near sunset at the little Buddhist shrine with Kinchinjunga clear and rosy heighted beyond.'

At the same time he was disturbed that all his letters to scientific people were useless, because every one of them was dead and gone. Occasionally he quarrelled with Giorgis, who had fits of bad temper. When offered melons he said, 'No vorrei mangiar cipolli!' and Edward considered sending him home. After every quarrel they would be contrite: there was no single severest attack, but travelling around India in heat in monsoons and in very variable comfort was a test, so that in the end they were both becoming rather ill. India could be lethal to the English: Tennyson's son Lionel died on the way home, and many gravestones in England commemorate English names of the Indian dead. At the crumbling antique fort at Chunor, Edward discovered a battalion of invalid soldiers, one of native infantry, one company only of the 107th, and some political prisoners. At Gwalior he met Colonel and Mrs Willoughby-Osborne who had spent nine years in Bhopal. He suffered a sleepless night there from crickets and Islamic drums, but then he wrote, 'Giorgis's perfect patience is a blessing, for at times, what with my bad eye and other bothers, I seem nearly to lose my head.' His days had gone like this: Agra the 18th, Jubbalpore 8, Lucknow 10, Cawnpore 5, Dinapore 5, Calcutta 30, Road to Calcutta 10, Chumar 4, Arrah 1, Allahabad 1, Agra 10. He begins from Agra because he had seen it from the sea and longed to land, as well as for the fame of its monuments.

It is a curious truth that Edward Lear was more greatly excited by the very idea of Agra than he had been by anything in Crete, except maybe Sphakia. The reason is that in the seventies of that century, prehistoric, Bronze Age Crete was totally unexcavated, and where there were ruins and an ancient name then the surface was Roman or late Roman or Byzantine. There was a wall like the ones Edward saw in Crete at the site of Olympia, when that still lay untroubled, ten feet under the mud, and when the excavators arrived they simply brushed it away, cleared it and removed it, before their serious investigations ever began. Crete was a blank, but India was known to be ancient: even Anglican bishops knew of the amazing antiquity of its languages, and the earliest Buddhist ruins of the north and the Moghul ruins of the Taj Mahal period and earlier were photographed and widely known. There was even excavation of a kind, an interest rather than a skill picked up in the English countryside by squires' sons from the tumps and bumps and tumuli and heavings of the ground which were the enigmatic witnesses to history. Officers in India were by no means uninterested in such matters, and there were learned societies where opinions could be aired. Agra was famous as a Moghul capital. Even in the despised Calcutta, Edward studied the ruins, as well as drawing the immense banyan tree and the bamboos in the Botanic Gardens, which were more to his taste. On 2 January he had bought forty-two photographs.

The worst news of him in 1875 is things like 'Luggage to Poona a strain . . . On the whole unwell, rhubarb and tea . . . Mrs Peate tortures us with piano . . . G. was sulky so I sent him home, but couldn't find the bridge and was a monster unto myself so came home myself . . . How utterly hateful are these doorless rooms . . .' But he wrote out 'The Cummerbund', which was an enormous success, and met a little girl who had learnt 'The Owl and the Pussycat' by heart at school. On another front, he was amazed by Gover's *Folklore of South India*, and most excited by some of its songs. What utterly dumbfounded him was the rain, which descended in torrents in September: it equally dumbfounded Giorgis. Still, in all practical matters Evelyn Baring was helpful and his arm long, although there was not much anyone could do when Giorgis had a bad attack of enteric: he and Edward sometimes seem to be staggering round India like a pair of cripples supporting one another. It is amazing that there were enough clear days to get so much work done.

At Delhi Edward was drawing well. 'The quiet of all the place, dreamy and silent flocks of apes, flash of green parrots, sparkling of brass.' On 15 March he had 'far better health than I have known for years', but on the 21st 'think of leaving India as soon as I can . . . can't walk, or cross by boat or elephant'. Then suddenly the morning views captivated him: they recalled Italy and the pictures of Claude. The three small domes of a tomb on the other hand recalled three poached eggs. He took the Ganges canal from Roorkee to Hurdwar, where he had become enough of an old Indian hand to argue the merits of travel by jampan or by tonga: 'jampan more like dhooly but more room'. At Simla, 'Doubtless this is one of the world's loveliest landscapes . . . Himalayas mighty uninteresting.' He was determined not to be over-impressed, to be connoisseurish about places, and he was tired and I think frightened.

When he was gently burgled one day he wondered if he should leave
India at once. Then he started philosophically to compose limericks.
They begin from real life.

> There lived a small puppy at Narkunda
> Who sought the best tree to bark under,
> Which he found and said Now
> I can call out Bow wow!
> Underneath the best cedar in Narkunda.

> There was a small child at Narkunda
> Who said Do you hear? That is thunder.
> But they said, It's the Bonzes
> Amaking responses
> In a temple eight miles from Narkunda.

> There was an old man of Narkunda
> Whose voice was like peals of loud thunder,
> It shivered the hills
> Into colocynth pills
> And destroyed half the trees in Narkunda.

While the rain fell they were imprisoned: Edward could not just pack
up and leave. But the vast treasury of what he had seen grew and grew.
'I can't remember any storm so magnificent. Some parts of that vast
snowline are of the finest I ever saw . . . crimson rhododendrons bewilder
by their beauty . . . great numbers of trees covered with white roses . . .
Grove full of boas like creepers . . . Rain, moths, beetles. Tales of
scorpious snakes.' When the rains were over he decided that 'As at
Calcutta, champagne has kept me alive.' Then a curious bit of gossip
which perhaps well reflects conversation in the rainy season in a hill
station. 'Le Mesurier as a boy knew Sir W. Napier's family in Guernsey:
Nora had dormice but their tails fell off along of drinking milk.' He
hated the shaking of the railways; it demoralized him that August, but
he could still record 'the strontian brilliance of young green rice'. (This
Greek-sounding word is the name of a parish in Argyll where the
mineral, well known to colourists in the nineteenth century, was first
discovered in a lead mine in the late eighteenth.)

Half-way through August the railway deposited him at the gardener's
Mecca of Bangalore, where the Lal Bagh was the Kew Gardens of India.
He 'never saw a more beautiful place'. Later in history Bangalore was a
vast royal engineers' camp: but those who were there remember the
same creepers that delighted Edward still running riot everywhere. Late

in August Giorgis had a sulky fit at Madras, and climbed up on to the roof on his own. It sounds better than the one in May when he 'sat with his back to me and grunted amain'. They were both tired out and neither of them was well. Edward longed for Egypt. 'O beautifully endlessly endowed Nile! O weary and stupid India!' When Giorgis had an outburst of rage and criticism, he gloomily wrote, 'If I have been as he says a bad master to him we ought to part; if not still we ought to . . . Rest of this Indian affair best given up.' But suddenly Giorgis was cheerful again, it was 'ultramuggily hot', but a stray major gave the old Greek a box of a hundred cigars. On 10 September Edward was not sleeping. 'As well Giorgis is with me.'

At Srirangam he was thrilled by the temples and the sculptures. 'In all India I have seen nothing as impressive'; here he found a Sanskrit scholar like an aged human moth hovering among his manuscripts of 'old Hindu literature, some filthy enough'. At the next place he was bored by a museum of 'harnesses and gold cloth'. He comforted himself with a 'deep blue or sulphur coloured' pea or vetch which grew luxuriously all over the ruined fort. As he got further south, so they sound more and more lost. At Ooty in October, 'went out with Giorgis, moony-moony, and down to the bazaars'. This meant they arrived at Lord Hobart's when that nobleman and his household were half-way through lunch. Edward and Giorgis withdrew, of course, and went home, only to find an invitation to that lunch waiting for them. At last they came to Calicut. 'Roads of such redundant beauty one can hardly dream.'

He admired Giorgis beyond measure for his quiet patience. The nearest he came to a complaint about the climate or the seasons was to ask, 'Please, Sir, how many monsoons are there in India?' Edward noted his own feelings with almost equal stoicism. 'The naked women are mostly old and horridly disgusting, and I am disappointed in seeing so few young ones.' In Malabar, he dreamed of transforming what he saw to beautiful, Indian versions of Claude landscapes. It is interesting how often he mentions that wonderful painter, more I think than in any other place, and certainly far more often than he had done for years. 'Palms . . . Devon-red soil and wonderful figs in foreground, with pure pale-blue heights beyond; but the pictures must be long-shaped.' It is as well to leave him wandering down the west coast of India at the end of October, too dazed to know quite what he wanted next, in order to interject a long, continuous passage of his landscape prose written up in a more formal style. This was picked out by Murphy[9] and in its way is equally revealing.

So very remarkable an Oriental view I have never seen or even imagined; for although the infinite lines of the low hills and higher mountains are all quite à la Claude Lorrain distance, yet the texture of coconuttery is something quite unlike what can be seen, except in this and other extended coast scenery; myriads of small white flashes, and as many myriads of deep, shady dots, caused by the light and shade of the great, innumerable palm fronds. The rivers in this view are wonderfully beautiful while the sun is low; and all the colour-changes of grey and misty lilac and palest opal shade (not opal though, for that is clear, whereas here all is misty and damp) makes a world of divinely exquisite beauty. The hills too are elegant in form, and in truth, the whole scene is a perfectly magnificent specimen of eastern landscape, most difficult to reproduce on paper, but wonderful to contemplate. A wood of palmyra palms, their crisp, hard fans rattling in any breeze, and their ringed broad columnar trunks rising from an undergrowth of young coco-trees. Beyond the village, all is green until it gradually becomes sandy to the seashore, where the ancient pagoda stands in complete loneliness above the fretting waves.

The fall-out of Indian sketches pasted into stray albums as well as the folios presented in the end to Lord Northbrook is particularly abundant. The trees, for example, are some fourteen inches by eight: *Rhododendron arboreum*, banana, banyan and mango, Arenga Sacch., tree fern, Talipat palm, Palmyra, Areka and Jambool palm, the bread fruit tree, the deodar (the cedar of the North Indian mountains), mimosa (not in blossom), and a sketchy bamboo. The landscape sketches clearly include the sketches for Kinchinjunga. There are seventeen of these, showing variations only of trees and light. All this prodigality is to be found at Harvard in a folio album that contains cuttings from the *Spectator*, all kinds of landscape sketches from Egypt, Albania, Malta, Sicily, Athens (drawn from where the Athenian district called Metz is now, taken in 1848), Corsica and the Riviera. There is even a drawing on tracing paper of an arch in the Roman Campagna. Some few sketches have gone: at one blank a note says 'Bought by Lord George Quin 1880'. But the principal repository of Indian material is Lord Northbrook's albums.

These are really very like a photograph album, in which small drawings, about six inches by three, have been pasted. They are done in pen and wash, and give much the same impression as early photographs give. Perhaps this is a case of art imitating machinery. I saw only what is evidently the second volume, headed 'Vol II Central India 1875'. It begins at Oonkar Mandhatta on 11 November: at that date in 1874

Edward was still at sea, so that Volume 1 must contain nearly a year of his record. This second volume is impressively sober and thorough; in the first month among the birds and camps and palaces come the camels of Numbhera and the elephants of Chittore. Some drawings are in full colour, some in light washes, some in pencil. A view near the palace at Odeypore is particularly lovely, in brown wash on blue paper. An album of drawings later Edward seems to be at Jodhpore, which looks hot and formidable in pen and wash. Then he takes the road to Ajmere. His drawing of lake and hills in the first days of December is superb: he really loves this scene, and draws it again and again. Here the album ends, with three or four empty leaves.

The reason for this is not easy to discover unless it is simply a job unfinished: in the album there are a few added topographic comments, but no more. Certainly on 9 November 1875 Edward and Giorgis landed in Ceylon. The likeliest solution is that the dates of the album are confused. Some encounters with disagreeable people have been left out. Those of the diaries are a continuous series and so they are much likelier to be right. Unfortunately this problem had not occurred to me when I had the album in front of me at Harvard. It is after all the kind of mistake Edward did make, when noting dates many years after the event, and Jodhpore is not in the south but the north of India. When they land in Ceylon, Edward and Giorgis had just suffered the pains of purgatory from illness, from filthy food, Customs officers, and so on. Northbrook was expected on the 15th, but meanwhile, 'Torrents, holes numerous'. Edward and Giorgis walked to Wakwalla: it made them feel a bit more human to have done so, and they were pleased with the daturas in the forest and the hermit crabs on the beach. But by the 20th they were seriously unwell. 'Mist of all kinds, gloom and damp and in the evening torrents.' On 2 December Giorgis had abdominal pains and a bad attack of dysentery. On the 4th the doctor was not pleased, and when he was a little better the next day, told him to go to Colombo. Game to the last, Edward noted the fine vegetation. On the 9th Giorgis really did seem better, so on the 12th Edward took him away by boat. At Calicut one doctor told them it was the most fatal of places for fever, but another recommended strong soups, puddings and port. The Arcot boat took them to Cochin, a filthy den, Edward said, where the mutton was raw and yet smoked, the potatoes arrived cold and hard an hour late, and the rice pudding was wicked. The only explanation available was 'Him cook, he drinksy drunksy'.

Still, Edward was not so easily beaten. Giorgis was better, and Edward found a Christian boy called Samuel in the synagogue to be servant to both of them for a few days. At last, on the 29th, a boat called *Assyria* took them away, bumpily and broken-screwed, and on that they passed the New Year of 1876. They passed Goa and arrived at Bombay. There Giorgis got two letters. The Greek consul at Alexandria wrote that his brother Iannis, who was the nearest thing in that family to a success in the world, had died. He learned further that his wife Tatiani's illness was owing to her own bad behaviour, that his eldest son Nikos had gone to the bad, and that the other two, Lambis and Dimitris, had also gone wrong. One wonders who wrote this letter. Naturally, Giorgis needed to get home as soon as possible, and in fact he arrived in Corfu at last exactly six weeks too late to see his wife alive. The letters had reached him on the 7th of January; on the 9th, Edward told Evelyn Baring what had happened, or as much as he needed to know, drew some money, got 120 photographs which cost £24, and bought two tickets to Brindisi.

So Ceylon, which had been his dream and ambition, had turned out a nothing, because of season and because these two elderly gentlemen were not in good health when they got there. It is at least true that the virulent fevers of those places can vanish as swiftly as they invade; nothing else can explain their survival. But there is little doubt that by lingering in the swamps and then trying Ceylon in the rain, they were taking risks. As for the service they got in India, Edward felt in retrospect that it had been atrocious, and that the class of civilian managers was to blame. Lord Northbrook was kindliness itself, but India was a phenomenally backward place under the British. The simple natives hope he will impale his solar topee on a tree. In spite of what British officers constantly assured him, Edward found that Indian servants treated Giorgis badly, as a member of an inferior caste. Financially, Edward had done well, since his expenses seem to be under £1000, and his commissions worth well over that sum. He had the material for a large number of 'finished' drawings, and one subject at least for three oil paintings on a large scale, which turned out over the next two or three years to be as good as, or arguably better than, anything he had ever painted.

His sprained back (from getting into a boat in Travancore) was rested and a bit better. Perpetual surf beat on the pallid line of sands, and far beyond them you could see the mountains, 6000 feet high. 'The menagerie here a goat, two cats, three apes and a parrot. Giorgis always better.' He had already soldered up a parcel of 560 drawings, four books of journals, and nine sketch-books, in June 1874, and on the boat home he sorted out his 1500 drawings and chose fifty for an Indian journal. In four weeks that passed quickly he was at Ancona at five in the morning and at Genoa in a day. 'Put more detail in your Riviera views, there is extreme delicacy in all, but you never put enough. The great broad greys this afternoon are lovely. Once more to olives and lemons here after that great and extraordinary India ... Garden beautiful, with Oranges! Foss somehow seems to know me dreaming ... Scores of villas. Crowds of Germans.' The villa had been burgled, though he lost little, but he picked his oranges and gave them away at once to some elderly friends, and he unpacked his pictures from Poona. He heard from Dimitris in Corfu that his mother had died on 12 December, so he cabled at once that Giorgis should bring Dimitris with him to San Remo.

It is hard to see what else he would have done. He was a creature of strong natural impulses and very warm-hearted. Also, he did not want to lose Giorgis or to throw him out of work or to tear him in half. There was now no real home left for Giorgis in Corfu: the family might help the other two boys, but Dimitris, the eldest one, was in trouble and now without a mother. Of course Edward thought the household in San Remo could carry him. The decision was somewhat fatal in its final consequences, but Lear could hardly have foreseen those. It is a saga that unfolds from this moment, and Edward's life becomes lethally entangled with the family history of the Kokalis from now on. Still, he did not know that; he was re-establishing his relations with the Lushingtons and the Fortescues, to both of whose families he really remained an outsider, however cherished. Intimacy had been one of his overpowering longings ever since childhood: with Giorgis and his delinquent sons he achieved more of it than he could stomach.

It is worth appending to this chapter, since it has discussed Lear's journeys in India, a stern report he wrote to Chichester Fortescue on Indian hotels. He liked the system of dawks or bungalows, resthouses provided by the government where you furnished your own bedroom and bathroom and ordered your food and drink (they ran to English beer and sometimes wine), and were otherwise left alone. 'Their paramount good quality is you *lose no time* while in them, nor, as I don't want the services of the people, do I lose my temper either.' For the traveller with Giorgis or his equivalent, or the modern independent traveller who carries what he needs, these places are ideal. In the morning Edward would be up by five, and the pair of them would be off by six in the morning, and in the evening dinner took about half an hour. All this was ideal for Edward, it was the hotels he hated.

The second mode of travel, Hotel halts, is in 19 cases out of 20 odious and irritating, indeed I can only name three or four good Hotels as yet visited, out of dozens. Mostly the Landlords are people occupied about other matters, and leaving the visitors to the care of their own servants – most people bring three or four or more. The hours for meals are at stated and often inconvenient times, and quite unsuited to my hardworking life: and the time lost by the table d'hôtes and dawdling is a frightful drawback. The rooms are neglected and dirty in many cases, and the food ostentatiously varied in name and appearance, but pitifully monotonous as to its bad qualities. Your tea is brought to you cold slop ready mixed in a cup; – and with all these and many more inconveniences you have to pay double the sum which in a dawk bungalow would have secured you very tolerable comfort and independence. I have known instances of carelessness and impertinence on the part of Innkeepers that would be incredible in England. One, when I begged for a chamber utensil – (I grieve to say they call it Piss-pot throughout the land; – Pisspot dumpy? you hear constantly at your door in a hotel – meaning, Do you want it emptied?) coolly stared at me, and said, walking away, It is plain you have not been long in this country! – another, when I wanted to start and pay his bill, said Can't mind you Sir, till I've looked after the osses.

He was lucky things were no worse. He is simply drawing Fortescue's attention to the usefulness of the strange novelty of dawks, by contrasting it with the glum provincial hotels, and (as he goes on to say) the inconvenience of staying in other people's houses. He would have found the hotels quite as bad a few years before in Canada, had he travelled there with Charles Dickens, who writes about them in his *American Notes*, but gives an explanation which must surely have applied equally to India. Having described their ghastliness, Dickens points out that the reason for it is that the military officers, who were numerous, dined in messes and did not patronize the civilian hotels. The same cause in India must surely have produced the same effect. The languid management of these places, as perhaps of much else in Indian life, sounds like something deeply rooted, but its roots are shallow enough, and have to do with the imperial attitudes of the colonial lower middle class a generation before Kipling.

Lord Mayo, an Irish peer given to the utterance of fine phrases which contradicted one another, and policies peppered with ifs and buts, had died by assassination while dutifully visiting a penal colony in 1872, so that when Northbrook arrived, he found the sub-continent in a restless and resentful condition. He had been privately educated and went late to Oxford where he got a Second: as Viceroy when his time came he deserved the highest honours, most of all because for the first time in history he remedied a Bengal famine, which we are told was the worst famine to hit India in 100 years. In 1872 he was forty-six: his experience had been in a long list of brief private secretaryships, and in the House of Commons since 1857 when he was thirty-one; he had served at the India Office under Sir Charles Wood and had navigated the bill to abolish army commissions by purchase, under Lord Cardwell in 1868: that success was what brought him to notice. It is of course true that he was an aristocrat and a rich man: his father was a baronet who lived at Stratton in Hampshire, his great-grandfather had directed the court of the East India Company in his day, his wife was a daughter of Sir George Grey, a notable Whig influence on him.

He behaved as one might expect one of Plato's guardians to behave if he had been educated at Christ Church. While the famine raged, he hardly left Calcutta for eighteen months, which is why Edward saw so little of him. He calmed India all the same, abolished income tax, rejected an upsetting municipalities bill in Bengal, and cut public works, producing a surplus of a million in spite of spending 6.3 million on the famine. He imposed price regulations and forbade the export of rice, in spite of howls of protest from the merchants. When Gladstone fell in 1874, and Salisbury came in, trouble was bound to follow, but in one way and another Northbrook resisted him. Policy in Afghanistan was bound to become more aggressive, but by coolly referring its details to experts who could be relied on to thwart it, Northbrook postponed the worst for two years, when the agents Salisbury wanted in Herat and Kandahar were appointed by Lord Lytton. Northbrook further defended India against Salisbury's wish to promote Lancashire cotton at her expense: but this was already the age of telegrams, whose speed utterly altered international affairs and long-range governments: the telephone would be the coup de grâce. The same is true in Church affairs as in diplomacy: the cases of India and Australia illuminate each other, government in both became immediate and from London. Northbrook waited for the Prince of Wales's visit to pass off in the winter of 1875–6, and resigned in April.

One other highly characteristic action that Northbrook carried out in 1875 serves to light up the sort of country India was. He had trouble from Baroda, where an attempt had been made to poison a British agent called Colonel (later Sir Robert) Phayre: Northbrook removed the Gaekwar, using an independent commission of inquiry to do so, and then restored native government. The tiger's claws were drawn in fact.

It can scarcely have been obvious at the time, but the foundations of a modern society were being slowly laid. Lear probably felt it had gone far enough: he was a liberal, but less Whiggish than Lord Northbrook: for instance, he was offended by criticism of the House of Lords, which all parties then assumed to involve the monarchy itself, from Americans, who were of course quite free with their views; it positively horrified him when coloured with atheism, and adopted by English intellectuals. No doubt it would be fair to say he had seen enough change for one lifetime.

The Viceroy kindly gave him an elephant-shaped paperweight for the New Year, of which we do not hear again, beyond a note: 'how like his kindliness'. Edward had been making lists again, and wrote to Fortescue from a pit of exhaustion or depression in March 1875: 'It is very provoking not to have seen twenty-five or twenty-six things I particularly desired to visit, yet even had I been well I could not have done all those before April, and so if they are to be done at all with a view to a perfect collection of Indian scenery, I should have to go out again, say at the end of 1876, but of that matter there is plenty of time to think.' He did realize that he could not possibly survive in India without having the Viceroy to ease his passage.

I did *not* enjoy Ceylon: the climate is damp which I *hate*: it is always more or less wet, and though the vegetation is lovely, yet it is not more so than that of Malabar, where the general scenery is finer. Ceylon makes people who arrive there from England scream: but then I did not come from England, and so was not astonished at all, nor did I find any interest in the place, as compared with India.

What he liked was Hyderabad, the subject of one of his finest Indian paintings, and Nizam, but the rains kept him from Anagoonda, 'the finest of all Hindu ruins'. He did see a number of temples in the region of Madras, but both in the south and in the north he missed a great deal that now grieved him not to have seen. These places 'were alas! left unvisited, and go to form a great heap of repentance'. He found the Nilgherry hills 'like a bad, sham Cumberland, and I loathe the fogs and cold', though he admitted they were very grand around the edges. Something analogous might almost be said of the Cotswolds, but there he never seems to have discovered the edges. He sent Lord Carlingford, as he now was, a list of thirty-six Indian subjects, including three *Kinchinjungas*, three *Himalayas*, and one *Elephants*, of which eight were commissioned.[10]

In 1876 or so he jots down a list of forty-one Indian subjects in the flyleaf of a copy of *Sense and Sensibility*, Bentley's 1870 edition but signed and dated by Edward as owner at San Remo 1876, and then by F. Lushington, Templehurst 1888. In this new version of the list the last five are new to it, two of Gwalior for J. A. Edwards, Kandy and Benares for T. Hanbury, and a third version of Jubbulpore rocks; but since some of the names in the list of March 1875 disappear, it will be best to show them side by side, since they show Edward Lear in the careful process of marketing his art.

1875

1. Marble rocks. Nerbudda Jubbulpore.
2. Ditto. Different view. Finished.
3. Benares. Lord Aberdare.
4. Benares. Bernard Husey-Hunt, Esq.
5. Benares. Finished.
6. Village scenery, Calcutta.
7. Kinchinjunga. Bernard Husey-Hunt, Esq.
8. Kinchinjunga.
9. Kinchinjunga. Lord Carllingford (sic).
10. Descent from Darjeeling Plains.
11. Taj. Agra.
12. Fort. Agra.
13. Gwalior.
14. Brindaband.
15. Togluckabad – Delhi.
16. Bamboos and Himalaya.
17. Hurdwar. (Perhaps for Col. Greathead RE).
18. Himalaya, Simla.
19. Himalaya, Simla, from Sir C. Napier's house. Lady Aberdare.
20. Himalaya, near Narkunda.
21. Matheran (cum scantily cloathed women).
22. Wai.
23. Poonah.
24. Hyderabad (Deccan).
25. Mahabalipur Temple.
26. Trichinopoly.
27. Elephants.
28. Tanjore Pagoda.
29. View near Conoor, Nilgherries.
30. Road scene, Malabar.
31. Sunset, Malabar coast.
32. River scene, Ceylon.

33. River scene, Ceylon.
34. Kandy. S. W. Clowes Esq. MP.
35. The Temple of the Tooth, Kandy. S. W. Clowes Esq. MP.
36. Road Scene near Galle, Ceylon.
   (This last is upright and would not pair.)

1876 or later

1. Jubbulpore rocks.
2. Jubbulpore rocks.
3. Benares. B. H. Hunt.
4. Benares. Lord Aberdare.
5. Benares.
6. Calcutta village.
7. Kinchinjunga. B. H. Hunt.
8. Kinchinjunga.
9. Kinchinjunga.
10. Pugdundies (?).
11. Taj Agra
12. Fort Agra
13. Gwalior
14. Brindaband
15. Delhi
16. Bamboo
17. Hurdwar
18. Simla. Lady Aberdare
19. Simla
20. Nurkunda . . . (?)
21. Matheran
22. Wai
23. Poonah
24. Hyderabad
25. Mahabalipur
26. Trichinopoly
27. Tanjore
28. Elephants
29. Conoor
30. Malabarland
31. Calicut beach
32. Kandy. S. W. Clowes
33. Ceylon ruin. S. W. Clowes
34. Ceylon ruin
35. Kandy Temple
36. Road in Ceylon

37. Gwalior ⎫
38. Gwalior ⎬ J. A. Edwards

39. Kandy ⎫
40. Benares ⎬ T. Hanbury

41. Jubbulpore Rocks

Through Lear's confusions over numbering, it will be seen that only Carlingford and Colonel Greathead have dropped out, and Edwards and Thomas Hanbury, who had a special interest as a gardener and introducer of new plants, as well as a druggist, have been added. *Trichinopoly from the Sea* and the *Marble Rocks, Jubbulpore*, were later owned by Lord Northbrook.

CHAPTER SEVENTEEN
THE FALL OF A HOUSE OF CARDS

LEAR had written to Fortescue from Italy about Colonel Pattle, a brother or cousin of Lady Somers and Mrs Cameron the photographer, who was called in India Joot Singh, the king of the liars. There was a story of a man seen floating across the Atlantic in a hen-coop who refused help except for a box of matches, as his had got wet; hearing this told at dinner, the Colonel had burst out, 'It is no fib but the truth: I was the man.' When they said peas would not grow somewhere, he assured the table he had grown such giant peas there that a herd of Government elephants was lost for three weeks, hidden among his peas. Lord Carlingford said General Vernon was a worse liar, but Lear replied, 'I have heard of that Vernon fibber: Lady Hatherton told me he declared he had seen two cherubim on Mount Ararat, and that he fired at them: one flew away with a buzzing sound and an inestimable perfume, the other was wounded in the wing. The sportsman took him home and kept him alive for six weeks on milk and eggs, but just as he was getting strong, the cat ate him.' Edward was recovering his spirits; in April 1875 he wrote to the widowed Lady Wyatt a letter of thirty-two puns on the word mint, asking how to make dried mint.[1]

He saw Congreve two or three times a day and had a long talk with him about his eight or nine years of marriage. He showed the boys his collection of Indian photographs: a great wonder in the Europe of 1875. Foss kept escaping; as soon as he was brought into the house he would whizz into the cellar, and so away by a broken window. But in a matter of days it was 'dinner, Foss assisting', and Giorgis would come in for his Sunday cigar. Edward sold a few cheap pictures and saw a lot of the grand old ladies who frequented the Riviera. 'Walk with Lady Hatherton, as delightful as ever, though she was so in 1834 in Dublin.' He settled to make 'thirty-six pictures of the £30 size'; he had fourteen already. It was Easter and the gardener announced his intention on Friday of going home until Tuesday; Edward gave him an old suit. Nothing could be lovelier than Bordighera, the sea and sky, 'and Corsica clear as light on the horizon'. The diary really sounds more like retirement than ever, almost like a convalescence. *Poinsiana regia* began to grow.

'Muddled and doddled in the garden. Giorgis says the Buffalo wants to sleep in the Kitchen. That won't do.' The Buffalo was the gardener. Then on a day when he had ochre-washed all thirty-six of his drawings, he heard the Lushingtons' little girl had died. But life at the villa simply continued: Foss nearly caught a wild duck in the yard, which flew out to sea: it turned out to be one of Congreve's. Birkett Foster came, 'beautiful artist'. Edward's sixty-third birthday passed and then Hubert Congreve's seventeenth: Edward gave him Loudon's botany, H. and F. Lushington's small book of poems, a saxifrage and an opera glass. He explained to the father all this was for *his* kindness, 'not but what Hubert deserves it'. Arnold the young brother was delighted too. 'Two phier phlies eggspatiated up and down the walks, keeping to regular path like respectable Christians.' Giorgis remarked one day, 'Il mare e come il Nilo.' Edward had begun to feel his Indian pictures were all understated, but when he counted up the value of his hanging pictures it amounted to £1240, so he cheered up.

At the end of May his thoughts had turned to London, where lodgings were now £8 a week, and he heard there was a Spiritual(ists') Bazaar which tickled his fancy. He ordered rooms and tickets, went to the port with Congreve, ate four ices, numbered over the names of his plants: carnations, Guernsey lilies, hollyhocks, datura, geranium, passion-flower and solanum, which last, if I may intrude, I regard as the most deadly weed and puller down of walls, but Edward Lear liked it. He liked anything that climbed or rambled or dangled: he liked to see a robust habit of growth. The photographs of his garden show a mature young jungle. He set out for England at eleven on the 11th of June and got there on the 14th with a Lyons merchant and his daughter, '*how* they did eat cakes all day'. He dined with Lushington and the Venables, and installed himself in 8 Duchess Street. 'The number of moths here is

frightful. Study large but mothy. Walked to the Zoo and dined there.'
He sent out his 370 invitations to his new rooms at once, took a small
back room in addition for another £80, and held his breath. He dashed
round first to see the Watercolour Exhibition, 'interested me much
particularly as to the various modes of execution – so much more liquid
than my own. Glennie's distances beautiful, but foregrounds wanting in
much.' It is well-nigh incredible, but he still lacked confidence. As to his
own work, he spoke of 'a small but laborious Simla sketch of rhododen-
dra', which I recollect as cool and casual-looking, and by September the
20th 'the two Simla drawings seem to me about the last water-colours I
have ever done, barring the Montenegro'.

Sales were swift and must have cheered him. On one day before the
end of June he sold £306 10s.' worth of drawings. Yet he was still
overmodest. 'I wish I could do trees as V. Cole and some others. If I
could surely one would produce far more interesting work.' He was
crazy about the paintings of Marianne North: partly because he loved
her, no doubt, and had known her family so long, partly because she was
dauntless in going to remote places and bringing back a strong
impression of how they looked, but partly, I suppose, for the robust,
rather primitive enthusiasm of her botany. Her *Memoirs of a Happy Life*
would make anyone like her; she incarnates the toughness, the spirit of
Victorian women pioneers, but her paintings are so startling as to make
one blink. She paid for her own gallery at Kew, which opened in 1882,
and in 1875 she had just come back from America and had her eye on
India, where she arrived in 1877. She used to squeeze the pigment
straight from its tube on to the canvas. Her birds and her butterflies
were as vivid as her vegetation, and the distant mountains are a deeper
lilac colour than Lear's. Edward still sternly thought, at a dinner for
sixteen with R. Ansdell R A and Sir T. Shuttleworth, how odious the
conversation of the Academicians was. He met Miss North at a dinner
for ten, more of his own sort, but missed Holman Hunt who was
supposed to be there.

Signs appear that he was getting tired of his gruelling programme. He
had to give up a journey to the Lushingtons because of the shaking it
would entail on the railways. 'Besides, Edmund would be there which
learned as he is would be depressive.' On 14 August, 'only four sold,
seven unsold to get rid of, a terrible task; the longer I work on them the
less well they turn out, I am only saved by running downstairs to play
the piano'. He overhauled his will again, he had shingles, sometimes he
drank too much, a habit that had crept up on him in India. Now Giorgis

would soon be coming back to San Remo, leaving Dimitris and Nikos with his wife's aunt. On 9 September, when that should have happened, Edward was cramming work into every day: on the 14th he finished Simla, 'only one more to complete', and at last did so, having 'dined unrepentantly at Simpson's' where hearing a name he knew mentioned behind him he broke in with 'I knew his wife's sister', but it was a confusion. He sank back into San Remo with relief. The Congreve boys were cheerful and Indian ipomoea was all over the railings, flowering splendidly.

Giorgis had brought Charalampos (Lambis), 'a sharp-looking little chap'. But Congreve was 'weary, dreary, sad', and Edward now learned that his ex-mistress Ellen was working actually in Italy. Thomas Hanbury called, and he seemed sad too. The house 'goes on abuilding of itself', and yet half-way through October 'He only said my life is dreary'. Two days later he laid down 126 squares for the oil painting of Kinchinjunga. The doctor definitely diagnosed his shingles, the masons working at some walls he designed, like a fascist war memorial just coming into bud, annoyed him. 'Soup and tongue and spinach and a bottle of Graves, and rightly or wrongly I feel better than ordinary ... The Ex-King of Spain walks to and fro ... Lunch one thrush, one glass of marsala ... When all these people come to be paid What a horrible bore it will be Said the Quangle Wangle Wee.' He threw out his gardener for cutting at a tree, and one called the Stammerer applied for the job. The one he took was Giuseppe Ferreri, and Edward set him to plant iris and ipomoea: it was mid-November. As they got to know each other better, he discovered this man had been in the Crimean War, at Tchernaya and Malakoff. Miss Shuttleworth came to see the garden in December, and now Edward was writing out poems for Bush for a book of comic lyrics: on the 5th, 'Lady Jingly Jones'. Three days later a Miss Poynter called – 'alack! a really ladylike and accomplished woman – but – Too late, oh far too late, Mr Yonghy Bonghy Bo.' If there had been any doubt that Edward wrote his songs about himself, let this resolve it. The news of the rest of the year was that Congreve would marry his mistress as soon as Hubert was twenty-one, in three years' time, Holman Hunt had married another Miss Waugh, and Foss, 'who goes to sleep in remote places', had to be hunted and brought back to the kitchen. Edward had £1950 in Consols, £1650 in 3 per cents, and about £664 here and there. I think it was his record.

It is hard not to make the whole of 1876 into a garden record. Only two of the Bangalore ipomoeas survived, he bought bamboo, white

Banksian rose, Kennedyias, bougainvillea and wisteria, but as he harvested his last mandarins in Easter week, he found rats had eaten three dozen, sitting on top of the pilasters to eat the nearest. He clearly admired these rats. Giorgis was in a temper about Dimitris, as much about 'Is he learning Italian?' as about 'What is his religion?' and Edward thought of buying them all a small house in Corfu. In August he sent off the Dong, the Pobble, and Yonghy-Bonghy-Bo's pictures to Bush in London. He had already penned out all but one of the twenty-two books of his 'Indian scraps'. Thomas Hanbury came to see him, and he went to la Mortola on 17 August. 'It is hardly possible to imagine anything lovelier and more Italianly romantic than Mortola now is – gardens, palace, all so improved. Thomas Hanbury one likes more as one knows him longer.' On the 20th, 'Shall give Lambi £5 a year from Sep. 1st.' J. F. Lewis the painter died, and Lear wrote a letter of almost extravagant warmth to his widow.

The Bangalore mauve ipomoea came out in September and old Terrick Hamilton died at ninety-five, 'kind to me since 1840'. Lear's diary reminiscences of old people wandered wildly: he suddenly noted more than usual of one of those songs that had haunted him, and gave it a context: 'dear Lady Hornby, to whom one used to sing:

> On through the storm
> And the summer warm!
> And on through the winter cold,
> But we come no more
> To that golden shore,
> Where we dreamed in days of old.'

Was the music to which he sang this innocent old ballad that of the piano? Probably so, in the 1830s. He acquired a new semi-grand piano in the autumn of 1876, and a cask of marsala. He had a day out with Giorgis, who turned out to be on terms with all Irishwomen, he dined on thrushes and sardines, and gave Hubert and Arnold Congreve their first landscape lessons. Hubert drew beautifully and he took him on a drawing expedition to Bordighera.

This, therefore, is the moment to discuss Hubert's essay, published by way of preface to Lady Strachey's *Later Letters of Edward Lear* in 1911, when Hubert was an engineer of fifty-three. He had been ten or eleven when he met Edward Lear in 1869; he remembered a tall, heavily-built gentleman with a large curly beard, in unusually loose-fitting clothes and enormous round spectacles. At first he was disconcerted by some preposterous joke but he was won over at once by the twinkle, the kindness, and 'a wonderful charm of manner and voice. He became very intimate with us' as a next-door neighbour, and often sang in 'what must once have been a fine tenor voice'. His favourite comic song was 'The Cork Leg'. Giorgis carefully gave the boys the plainest of English food whenever they came to dinner, but Hubert assumed that was because he was not a very accomplished cook. The key to the queer food he often did serve to Edward alone is probably cheapness: spinach in season, certain fish, calves' heads and so on. Hubert was first taught drawing by Lear in 1871, and in 1911 he was sure that he was meant to become an apprentice painter. That is a fantasy, whether Edward's or Hubert's: it never occurs in the diaries; there is a moment when something must be done with Hubert and art does seem possible, but Edward is perfectly clear-headed about the decision not to pursue art.

Hubert describes the sketching expeditions (which he misdates):

> Lear plodding slowly along, old George following behind, laden with lunch and drawing materials. When we came to a good subject, Lear would sit down, and taking his block from George, would lift his spectacles, and gaze for several minutes at the scene through a monocular glass that he always carried; then laying down the glass and adjusting his spectacles, he would put on paper the view before us, mountain range, villages and foreground, with a rapidity and accuracy that inspired me with awe-struck admiration.

The drawings were always done in pencil, then inked with sepia and brush washed with colour on winter evenings. It is always the freshness and light power of touch that amaze one in these field drawings. When Lear died, he left 10,000 of them. Hubert quotes a letter from Lear about how his time was spent in 1883, when he was over seventy, but that is about an old man's routine, and even the account of the sketching expedition makes the old pair sound older than perhaps they would have appeared in 1876. What Hubert does remember is Edward's passionate interest in acclimatizing Indian flowers: in 1882 he had coaxed four of his beloved Indian ipomoeas to flower at his second house, the Villa Tennyson.

Giorgis was beginning to be ill more often: a lady bought him a glass of vermouth which seemed to do him good, so Edward dashed off and bought him three bottles of it. Then Lambis needed medicine, so Edward dosed him with castor oil. The boy fell from his chair in a faint, and Giorgis was very frightened. But life went on, of course: the Vicar

preached on Christmas Eve on the Pope as Anti-Christ, and Edward
gave his tacsonia blooms to Miss Murray. After Christmas Giorgis was
better, and Lady Ashburton paid a bill for £740, and Lambis got over his
toothache, even Foss was better. Congreve, however, decided Arnold
was going to die, and told Lear he was selling the Villa delle Palme, but
he wanted to leave Hubert to become a landscape painter while he
himself made off to Tasmania with the mistress. Then it turned out he
was going to stay in Europe with her really. On New Year's Eve Hubert
came in for some caterpillars Lear had found for him, and talked about
wanting to be an artist.

Eighteen seventy-seven began with the garden in bloom: mandarins
ripe on the trees, narcissus, cassia, maurandia, hexacentri, buddleia just
coming out, roses, lithospermum, nasturtium and saxifrage. Lear told
himself his motto should be, 'Have ten years' work mapped out before
you if you want to be happy'. He had few commissions left to do, but
about £1100 worth of 'possible paintings', and by this time of his life he
was continually making pictures from earlier notes and sketches, deliberately choosing to work on several different regions at the same time.
At one stage they might include Athos, which gets more and more
beautiful in the later water-colours, Argos, Ravenna and Gwalior: the
diversity was a device against boredom. Early in 1877 he hung sixty-
three saleable paintings. Congreve gave up the idea of Australia, and
Edward, who felt protective, wondered when Hubert should be told
what was going on; 'See how far he goes in drawing first.' Giorgis
announced that Dimitris was going to be a shoemaker, because Nikos
ran the risk of call-up in September, when names were chosen at random.
By the end of January the garden was sprouting daturas, narcissi and
china roses.

It now appeared the mistress's family might arrive: Lear wrote to
Congreve who replied, 'I will think of it', and then next day all but
authorized Lear to tell Hubert. Edward did tell him in the end in
February; the boy 'wept as if his heart would break', and said, 'I am sure
it was her fault . . . How can a fellow bear the stigma of a woman who
has caused the ruin of a whole family?' He ended up kissing Lear and
assuring him he was not to blame. It is clear that Victorian blame-
placing instincts were thriving, and no doubt we would have acted
differently, or given Hubert different advice. My only reason for telling
the story in this detail is to make it plain that Lear's obsession with
Hubert, if that is what it should be called, was protective and paternal. It
was also unrealistic: in a day or two Hubert was quite composed and had

recovered his savoir-faire. Meanwhile, Congreve was attacked by other people for irreligion, and even Edward wished he had not given up all church-going. When Walter heard that Edward had broken the news to his son he was much affected, took both Lear's hands in his and thanked him. Finally Hubert remembered having seen this lady when she was a servant flitting about in a nightdress in the small hours. 'I am confirmed,' he said to Lear, 'in my conviction that she was not a good woman.' Lear saw Congreve daily at this time and was still delivering caterpillars to the boys.

Giorgis was not well, and he had to go home for a while, which gave rise to the question should Edward go with him, and if so should he perhaps take Hubert? The sea was rough, but with some dithering he decided to stay in Italy and let Giorgis go, saying goodbye at Brindisi with kisses. It was early March, and as he travelled north he could see Vesuvius and thought of Proby. As for Hubert, 'he will not be a painter I see'. Edward was not at all well on this winter rush up and down Italy; he had what sounds like flu. But in Rome an old waiter greeted him as 'Mr Edward Sir' and old Dr Danbery said, 'Have you done any more painting, Mr Lear?' And what fellow artist was it who asked, 'What's that tree Lear?' 'It's an olive, have you never seen one?' 'No and I don't want to, if they look like that.' Surely not old Penry Williams? More probably someone in England, doubtless an Academician. Hubert remembers this journey with Edward, Giorgis and Lambis, in very different terms. First of all he was surprised to be made treasurer, and trusted with a huge bundle of notes. Then in Bologna on the way, he says, 'Lear threw off the melancholy which had hung heavily on him throughout the journey' and showed 'almost boyish delight in the sights and the museums'. There is no mention of his health and no comprehension of the responsibility he felt. He did feel Edward's depression in the cold and snow of Brindisi.

At Naples he says Edward revived.

> I found him again outside the station, surrounded by a crowd of outporters all struggling to get hold of his bag, Lear hitting out right and left and shouting Via, via, pellandroni, the scamps all enjoying the (to them) good fun. The scene was so irresistibly funny that I was helpless with laughter, and before I could intervene my old friend had tumbled into the wrong bus, out of which nothing would move him . . .

Lear, he says, showed eager interest in Hubert's unrestrained delight at the sights of Naples: he does not see that this was a kind artifice and no more, nor does he hear as we can do the note of irremediable sadness mingled with Edward's affection in the diaries. He records only that 'the week we spent in Rome was one of the fullest and happiest we ever spent together'. It was five days of consummate acting. He heard Lear singing Tennyson songs with deep feeling to an old lady who had tears in her eyes, but when Edward suddenly left the room he did not see why. Hubert was very young for his age.

On the day he got home, 'Misery even more terrible . . . Thank God prayer has done some good. I have to pack a lot of things and go. It is the best plan I fancy . . . No one understands about Giorgis . . . Congreve's moroseness is awful to bear.' Even Foss made him unhappy because of Giorgis, but at least Giorgis was safe in Corfu by then, and a little better. On 24 March he remembered his first 'morbid fit' ever, which we discussed in Chapter 1. At this time Lear came very close to what one would call a breakdown. 'This kind of life simply stupefies me and the cruel loneliness of every day drives me wild.' Mr Waterhouse came and drew but Lear could not speak, so he fled. Giorgis sent messages to Foss: tell him when I come I will bring him a *triglio fritto*. It had been the most unhappy March since 1861. In April Frank Lushington wrote a reasoning letter about not giving up San Remo, 'and I suppose I shan't'. At least Giorgis was getting better, but even the garden was small relief. 'Like Mithridates one is getting used to poison by using it.' He came after Easter to rely on Hubert, who was level-tempered: 'H. came, so my day became bright,' or else it rained, 'Walked sloppily on the terrace and discoursed with Foss, who however was far from polite.' He found 'Sir J. and Kay Shuttleworth much aged and altered'. The diary becomes unbearable and even a little perverse. 'Invited to La Mortola but it cannot be.' At the end of April he decided to go to England in June. 'The break-up here will be dreadful but it must be done.'

While Edward was still uncertain whether to go to Corfu or to England or neither, Giorgis said he would come back in October. He must have known a lot about Edward, yet I do not believe he knew what despair his absence had caused: no one seems to have guessed. Before he left Edward dined with the Congreves, he recorded 'great fun and comfort' all the way to Menton in the train; Hubert and Arnold saw him off, 'Bitter and dreadful agony when I saw them no more.' In four days he was in London and had to buy an umbrella. He had arrived in Marseille at nine at night and in Paris at five in the morning. He crossed the Channel not that day but the next and then went on to London after the third night, but if he had been young he could have got to London on the second day from San Remo. The service had very greatly improved. Edward dived into a whirl of society and of painting and selling. He gave drinks to Hallam and Lionel Tennyson in the Criterion, and raced down to Aldworth in June, where he found the 'view greatly betreed and very fine, the house more habitable. Emily younger, handsomer, diviner than ever. Poet more genial, though of course he had his growl about the public after dinner.' Alfred read him *The Village Wife*, Cobb and his enemy, and Sir Richard Grenville. 'Begged Alfred to write a Moslem sonnet to counteract the Russian sympathy of his Montenegro sonnet,' which Emily agreed repelled her too.

On 9 June he got home to London to find an invitation from Lord Northbrook to meet the Prince of Wales. 'I shan't go.' On the 10th he went, though to be honest he was more interested to meet a sister of the Miss Hurt with whom he had crossed to Dublin forty-two years before. He wondered whether to bring back Giorgis with two sons instead of one. He heard that Hubert was to be an engineer. Hubert says his desertion of art caused a rift between them so that Lear avoided him for a long time; we have seen how untrue that is; Hubert cannot have had an inkling of what the old painter was really feeling in 1877. In August he was preoccupied with a journey to Corfu, and with how to look after the Kokalis children if their father died. At Stratton he wrote, 'It is too late now to seem as if one of a family, and I always try to avoid feeling so anyway. Yet in no case is this more difficult than with the Northbrooks, where all is so natural and good.' A friend wrote, 'Come to see me in Baltimore,' and he thought maybe one day he would. Then suddenly early in September he heard Giorgis was unlikely to recover, so he rushed to Corfu.

At Paris he thought of getting his old servant a house or sending him on a voyage. He had made a settlement on him in his own will. He saw the Congreves, 'ate too many phiggs, drank too much wine'. At Brindisi he trembled but he knew he was doing right. Then on the 15th 'that wonderful lilac coast, and in a boat Giorgis, Lambis and Dimitris'. That day he drew a lot; Giorgis was weak but furious with his sons because Lambis had set the plates on the wrong side at table, Nikos muttered, and Dimitris would not eat grapes. Still, the sight of old Giorgis with his family melted Edward. Giorgis told Edward the only alternatives he had were to stay in Corfu now, with all three of his sons around him, and to look after them there, or to return to San Remo and bring all three sons with him. Edward was impressed by this argument, but he did not know what to say to it, and so he said nothing, and the decision was put off. He knew all the same that something like that would happen in the end. 'He allows he *must* do one of two things . . . I know not what to advise.'

As he went walking with Giorgis in great heat, Edward was taken short in the road and went behind a church to do what he must. Giorgis said, in Italian, 'I need to show you something.' He was trembling like a leaf in the wind, and said, 'That iron cross marks where my Tatiana lies.' Lear said, 'You will see her again later,' and Giorgis answered, 'I know very well this is only bones, but her heart and spirit are not lost: we shall meet in Paradise. If she is not in Paradise, who can go there?' Lear asked if he wanted a stone put up. 'No,' he said, 'this iron is enough memorial.' It was this conversation that made Lear so happy about his visit to Corfu, I think, although he did not fail to notice his own loneliness as the boat left the island. 'The sun is bright, and the loveliness of Corfu greater than ever. So I set to work to draw . . .' On the 21st Edward was back at Brindisi, but resolved to go to Corfu again if Giorgis got any worse. On 27 September, Hubert left for England, amidst much melodrama, but finally he was gone, leaving his cousin and his younger brother. 'Jack and Arny are less than nil!' We have one painting of what must be Hubert, among trees on the green slope above their house, holding a straw hat. He looks an ordinary young man, which is what he was. But now that he was alone in London, Edward became more solicitous than ever.

He gave the boy letters to Frank Lushington, and to a Colonel of Engineers, and wrote to warn Emily Tennyson he had asked Hallam to ask Alfred if he might bring Hubert down to Aldworth.

I have never asked anything of this sort before, but I am so anxious that this lad should know someone whom he might not only like but respect, that I have allowed myself for once to rush in where angels fear to tread, in hopes my request may lead to some good for a youth to whom I am much attached, and whom I respect also, – for he has no vice of any sort, and indeed I cannot fancy anyone of twenty years old being sent out on a London life with less anxiety as to his conduct in it. One of my great desires, (I write this in confidence), is that he may have other society than that at his Uncle Richard Congreve, where Lewes, Bridges, F. Harrison and other men of talent abound: for though Hubert is not at all a lad to be easily influenced by theories, yet the kindness of relatives united with literary society may have an ill effect by degrees. At present I know the young man remembers all his Mother and second Mother taught him, and he is wholly not only without any tendency to materialistic doctrines, – but on the contrary goes regularly to church. But he never speaks on the subject, because his own Father's opinions are like his Uncle's, and as a good son he thinks his silence is due in this case.

Edward felt passionate sympathy for children left without their mothers (as he had virtually been), for the Kokalis family, and the young Congreves more than for most, because they were close to him. He bought Hubert all his Nonsense books, and gave him sketches. The new volume of Nonsense in 1877 was *Laughable Lyrics*, published for the author by Bush as usual, but this was the last volume Lear got round to issuing in his lifetime, surely because the endless hopeless gloom of dragging around publishers bored him to distraction. This book actually contains a Lear alphabet illustrated by someone else, though the drawings Lear had intended to be used are at Harvard. He thought of entitling the new collection *Learical Lyrics and Puffles of Prose*, or possibly *Sage and Onions and other Poems*: if this means a weeping sage, then the pun *Learical Lyrics* is comparatively acceptable.

'The Dong with a Luminous Nose' begins the book. The nose as illustrated is like a perforated warming device, or like that motor tyre of coloured bulbs which Scriabin brought home from Cambridge on which he proposed to show which colours denoted which musical phrases by changing colours as he played. There it still is indeed, in his rooms in Moscow, looking neglected. The Dong is jollier altogether and goes back to Edward's consciousness of his own large nose as a boy: but it also goes back to Tom Moore's dismal swamp poetry.[2] It is typical of Lear that being the last poem he wrote for this book it was placed first, in the position of honour. He had a right to be pleased with it: the Great Gromboolian Plain is a fine invention, and the lost Jumbly girl who deserted him with all her tribe is a pathetic device of some charm. The Dong in the distance becomes an eerie vision or a ghost, maybe just a firefly. Lear knew the Greek word for a firefly, which is arse-fire, and it is possible that word enters into his idea.

'The Two Old Bachelors' are parodies of Lear Furiosus. They have nothing much to eat except a tiny slice of lemon and a teaspoonful of honey, when one catches a muffin and the other catches a mouse. They go hunting an old Sage up a mountain to chop up for sage and onion stuffing, but he repels them vigorously,

And when they reached their House they found (besides their want
  of Stuffin')
The Mouse had fled; – and previously had eaten up the Muffin.

It is a desultory tale, in which the couplets are always a delight, and the only forceful character is the Sage, who is illustrated. When the book was called *Sage and Onions* this must have stood first. After it come the Pelican Chorus with its music, and the Yonghy-Bonghy-Bo with his music. The pelicans have a pleasing, crazy quality in their chorus, though the main part of the stanzas is very close to ordinary, adult poetry. 'We live on the Nile. The Nile we love. By night we sleep on the cliffs above. By day we fish, and at eve we stand On long bare islands of yellow sand . . .' These birds, and the storks and cranes that go with them, had been an obsessive theme of Lear's as an artist, as a scientist and as a traveller all his life,[3] so it is almost inevitable that they should appear in the sad, comic lyrics. They really are sad, none of them ends happily, even this one, in which the King of the Cranes took the Pelicans' daughter away, having won her 'With a Crocodile's egg and a large fish-tart', merges into the world of the Dong; the Pelicans never expected to see their daughter again, they just sat on the rocks and watched the moon, and thought of her on the Great Gromboolian Plain.

The Yonghy-Bonghy-Bo is sadder still and his sadness is of a traditional kind. He is a romantic, rejected lover, a knight errant of unhappiness like Mr Poker and Mr Tongs whose world is like that of nursery rhymes, where kitchen life is anarchic.

> The cock flew over the table,
> The pot began to play with the ladle . . .
> The sow came in a saddle,
> The little pig rocked the cradle,
> The dish jumped on the table
> To see the pot swallow the ladle.
> The spit that stood behind the door
> Threw the puddingstick on the floor.
> Od's bobs says gridiron can't we agree . . .

It is the world that featured on the stage in 'The King of the Cannibal Isles', about 1830: where the owl says 'Wishy washy weedle, fiddle faddle feedle', and the cannibal language sounds exactly like Lear's: 'Poonoo whishky-wang, flibydee flobydee boskybang.' As Shaw said, this kind of joke of Lear's is very old. A was an Apple pie under Charles II, A was an Archer and shot at a frog under Queen Anne. 'Buzz quoth the bluefly, Hum quoth the bee' is in Ben Jonson. As for Moore and his plaintive easily parodied verses, there are lines in him that Lear could have written.

O had we some bright little isle of our own,
In a blue summer ocean, far off and alone.
... let us roam no more
Upon that wild and lonely shore ...
... Tomorrow I sail for the Cinnamon groves.

'The Pobble Who Has No Toes' is one of Lear's masterpieces. An interesting and slightly deviant manuscript of it exists in the National Library of Scotland, and the printed version is in some ways inferior. 'Before he went he *swaddled* his nose' is surely better than *wrapped*, and '*mice* and buttercups fried with fish' is surely better than *eggs*. Sadder still, in the printed version the whole final motif of the Pobble spotting King Jampoodle's daughter 'a-eating of crumbs and cream', and her demanding his wooden toes, which unscrewed, and their perfectly happy marriage, has got completely lost. The manuscript has ten verses instead of six, which the book has.

It is dated 24 May 1873 when Lear was at San Remo and extremely happy in his lovely garden, but the poem must be written earlier. It is with one exception the only happy ending he ever did write to anything. Had he lost it or did he revise it deliberately towards sadness? It ends as we have it in the book with an ironic clang. It must I think be deliberate revision, since he surely cannot even after India had intervened have completely forgotten about his last verses? 'Mr and Mrs Discobbolos' part one ended happily, when the couple fled from the worries of life, but in the second part, which was written later and published only in 1888, Mr Discobbolos blows up the entire family in despair: they are sitting on a wall and like Humpty Dumpty, whom Lear had drawn as a nursery rhyme and Carroll also had adapted, he ensured they could not be fitted together again. Last of all come 'The Quangle Wangle's Hat', which does end happily in pure fantasy with all the creatures dancing and playing, but there is scarcely any plot at all, so it is in a class of its own, then 'The Cummerbund' and 'The Akond of Swat'. 'And at night by the light of the Mulberry moon, They danced to the Flute of the Blue Baboon ...' Still, even this happiness is not a final statement, because the process of composition as he grew older was more or less regular: a book was just a collection, and he might be writing something else before it was printed. I have decided not to give the last seven stanzas of the Edinburgh 1873 manuscript here, because although that version is charming and explains some peculiarities of Lear's private mythology, yet the sad and masterly ending in the printed book does have an authority in its sadness and irony, and in the tragic figure of Aunt Jabiska. The Oxford edition of Edward Lear's comic writings which will supply this lack has been long awaited.

In October 1877, Lear got himself a Maltese servant called Philipo Bohaja; Mrs G. Howard died and left him £100; the Earl of Derby wrote him a letter about the horns of deer; politics were disturbing, Edward hated Gladstone and Christian quarrels; Lord Northbrook insinuated gloom about Batoum. It is in Turkey in the Mediterranean, and the Russians wanted it. Still, at Christmas Hubert came home and he and Lear went for a walk together. Lady Somers 'postponed for the twentieth time – O, Pattle!' His last thought on New Year's Eve was 'dear good Janet Shuttleworth!' Yet within a year he was to suffer a stroke of fate worse than any other since his remote childhood. It crept up on him with a certain calm inevitability. He was now financially a substantial man: in October 1877 he intended to leave £1500 to Emily Gillies, £600 to Giorgis, a hundred or two to godsons (Coombe, Nevill and Lushington) and the Congreve boys (£200 to Hubert, £75 to Arnold), £50 to Lizzie Senior, £2825 in all. In January he seems to have owned £1950 in consols and £3500 in the 3 per cents. He picked 450 mandarins, which gave him far more pleasure than the money and were more carefully counted and accounted for. When the year ended he had just the same consols and £100 more in 3 per cents.

Frank Lushington asked Hubert to the Tennysons to hear Ioachim play and Lionel asked him to a ball. Old Dr Bell's edition of White's *Selborne* arrived. Edward was working hard at orange-farming, and linking his garden to a new road of Congreve's with a new terrace, and working hardest of all at Northbrook's *Kinchinjunga*. He had finally penned out no fewer than 2300 Indian sketches and now had seven bound notebooks to tackle. He records a 'frosty conversation with Walter Congreve's brother Pope Richard'. In February 'old Mr Hanbury came over with no coat on his 84th birthday with two sons for a lark'. Edward heard conflicting stories about Giorgis in Corfu, so that by May he had almost decided to go again to visit the invalid. 'Then came Thomas Hanbury, joined by Mrs K. Shuttleworth. By and by I found they had business and fled.' Maybe he would take Giorgis away somewhere on a voyage, but if so, where?

It was the second day of May, and this enigmatic reference is all we know about a negotiation between Hanbury and Shuttleworth which must surely have ended in the sale of the ground they owned, and the trees on it, to build a new hotel directly between Lear and the sea. They were walking the ground together, and Lear's sense that they had private business must have been aroused by some shyness on their part about how or maybe whether to tell him. Edward in those few days was thinking only of Giorgis: he felt the illness dated from India, and for this as well as other reasons he felt responsible. Then Frank Lushington came for a visit; the garden was more beautiful than ever: even 'dear old Pentaphylla' was 'not dead after all. Would it might be an omen . . . Wonderfully happy days'. When Lushington was gone, Edward's only company and only 'tie to comfort' was old Foss. 'Came back and supped on bread and butter pudding. Amen.' Evenings were quiet and golden in his library and he was turning back to his Tennyson subjects when in mid-June he was disturbed by a flurry of telegrams.

There was cholera at Marseille, and Giorgis was arriving at Naples in two days' time. Then he had got there and was leaving for Marseille, so he must be met at Genoa before he got there. Edward had already considered going to Monte Generoso for the summer. He heard from Corfu that Giorgis had taken a Count's house at £50 a year. Then it turned out he could not land at Naples being too ill, but he had landed at Foggia and got on a train for Bologna. Edward had got to Genoa: 'Poor old Foss came out to see me off, keeping close to me and butting me with his head.' Now the Count in Corfu was protesting because Giorgis had backed out of the arrangement 'as Master may disapprove'. At last on a Sunday at the very end of June, Giorgis got to Genoa: Edward took him to the Upper Acquasole Gardens to see a tiger, and the very next day straight to Generoso to a Swiss hotel where the Stracheys, the Lushingtons, the Symonds and the Fentons used to stay. It was half a convalescent home or clinic, invented by a Dr Pasta. Edward went the second day they were there to 'the spot where I made a sketch in 1837'. Giorgis was not as tired as he feared, but he fainted one day as he got off a mule, and asked as he came round, 'Have I had a drink?' The doctor in Corfu had mentioned 'some alcoholic abuse' in his diagnosis, but the old man had denied it indignantly.

Edward was painting all the time. He drew Monte Rosa, and he had already applied his 'fifth process' to thirty Tennysonian images: blue Latin and ochre. Now he experimented on ten of them with indigo. Giorgis spoke of working at Patras or the Piraeus with his three boys, and Edward thought that might well be the best solution for them. He was on the twelfth or rubbing-out process. Finally he decided he had taken the first ten of them as far as he could without going back to San Remo to consult his original sketches. Giorgis was better 'but he is 72'.

He was not as old as that really, but he did look more than his age. On 3
August Edward coloured sixteen birds for little Charles Pirouet: they
were a colour chart and a joke at the same time. Edward was a pioneer
of educational toys. He and Giorgis took a steamer on the Italian lakes,
and by 25 August they were home, where Foss greeted them and the
Maltese servant departed. Edward would not colour his Generoso sketch,
he thought, but just wash it in blue. It was decided Lambis should be
sent for, and Giorgis should go and fetch him. Edward fell easily back
into his routine, in which Leslie Stephen's book on Dr Johnson merited
a long, approving sentence, and snails for dinner at S. Romola an
exclamation mark. He thought Gussie was happy, more so than if she
had been married to him. Walter Congreve was moving to Alassio, a
small town down the coast a little, with Arny and the mistress, and his
villa turned out to be let to Bridges the atheist. 'Beginning of an end.'

October the 24th. 'All the trees or nearly all below my ground are cut
down – and I heard today that the hotel is to be the very largest in San
Remo. It is possible that it will hide all my sea-view. But I do not allow
myself to think of this ugly affair.' Of course he thought of it, and as
matters got worse he spoke and wrote about it too. On 1 November,
'Went up to the land above me to see what was to let and sell, but I
doubt my ever building again.' On the 8th, 'Returned by horrible
Hanbury road too shaking to look'. On the 20th Walter Congreve at last
married his mistress, and Arny migrated to Alassio with all his canaries.
In December, 'Foss in his basket: how it would have been if Gussie
hadn't married Parker.' In January 1879 Edward was satiric and somewhat savagely so. 'Went down the garden and so was horribly out of
humour with the Great Bee Stanbury and Jenny Shuttlecock Hotel.' The
shoe that hurts him announces Uncle Arley.

> O dear how disgusting is life!
> To improve it O what shall we do?
> Most disgusting is hustle and strife,
> And of all things an ill-fitting shoe – shoe!
> O bother an illfitting shoe!

'The annoyance about the firing and blasting of roots in the ground
below mine, and the noise of the cartmen all day make my life miserable.'

'At times went down the garden but the noise and shocking ram made
me return ... Giorgis, his care of old Foss is very funny and good.' He
sent to London for books, Vathek and Fanny Kemble and Trollope's life
of Thackeray, and ten children's books. He rushed up and down looking

at bits of ground. 'Hardly any places have been so mercilessly mangled as these of S. Remo ... The growth of the great Bee Stanley Hotel is a misery say what one may.' In March 1879 he got 605 oranges from his trees but expressed no pleasure in them. The Rev. Mr Fenton called on him to investigate his fury about the new hotel, which had now reached a point where people took sides. He gave Lear the impression that he felt his complaints were real and not fantasies. In fact Edward was quite practical. He had worked out that three nice plots were too far, but a certain Gandolfi had land which was unspoilable, even though it was a little noisier: he could get it for £2000 which would leave him an income of £48 a year. The Margherita grounds were pretty 'but all those villas are so hedged in and surrounded'. The truth is that Edward knew exactly what he wanted, and it was a great deal. That same force, that hunger for building-plots and seaside hotels that hemmed him in now, was a wave on which he had ridden like a surfer in his day.

In April an old friend called Grace Hitchcock sent him a photo of her cat Jobiska, and he thought of visiting her in southern France, but it was dangerous weather, the railway was broken again and wreckage was washed up on the shore: the Tozers came to see him and encountered thunder, lightning, hail and rainbows, on Easter Sunday 1879. Edward, or rather Lambis, was now breeding rabbits in the cellar, and Mrs Augustus Egg called; Edward noted that Mrs Frith had got very fat. The hotel grew nastier every day, and Edward became frantic about how to raise the money to buy ground and build a new house. That summer Lady Waldegrave had died. Frank Lushington was a support, as Husey-Hunt used to be, but his visits could not last for ever. The hotel went on growing while Lambis, who was twenty-one now and therefore earned more money, constructed a Palace of the Rabbits out of hutches in the cellar. The garden had lost its old charm of distances and the sea, but it still had an interest. He went to the Pasta hotel, where he read *Can You Forgive Her?* and wrote out his 1848 and 1849 journals, and wondered about £500 worth of ground, or 10,000 metres for £900. He spent time at Varese while Giorgis went home. His struggles and despair, which he tries to suppress from his journals, were terrible, but the outcome was bound to be an uprooting of himself. The Villa Emily must abandon ship. He was a painter, after all, and the building was not just an aesthetic insult, it ruined the light.

He planned to borrow the money 'from seven or eight people' and pay them back from the sale of the Villa Emily, without realizing how hard that would be to sell now, how little he would get for it in the shadow of the monster hotel. He thought of Derby, Northbrook, Somers, Lady C. Percy, G. Clive, J. Cross, and Evans (who had come and stayed recently). Lushington had no money and he does not mention Fortescue who perhaps had as little now that he was a widower. The new house would cost £3000 (with £2000 for land) and he must hope to sell Villa Emily for the same amount. This was the course he adopted. But there was more bad news: Lambis had debts in the town and was in trouble over women, so he would have to be sent away. He had been going daily to the café to drink and then to a brothel. Frantic negotiations took place, but old Giorgis and Foss were imperturbable. Derby disapproved of lending money, he might only buy something. Somers said he had no money, and indeed it is likely enough that he spent his annual income and more; only Northbrook agreed to lend. Meanwhile, Edward worked out that Giorgis and his sons had cost him £75 that year and £28 more for debts: he was hearing Dimitris his prayers (by heart, in Greek). Before Christmas, Cross offered to lend £100 and Derby to buy pictures for £500: he bought £270 worth but offered to buy more. He wrote at the end of the year offering the other £230 of his £500 share for nineteen pictures, no less. All of these people were seriously rich men. But Lear at the end of 1879 had £1950 in consols, £3600 in 3 per cents and £1590 in various banks. It appears therefore that he could have moved, and built, even without borrowing. Still, he was sixty-seven, facing old age when he might be unable to earn, and the money he had now might never be replaced. The Nonsense and the travel books had not been great money-makers, and his paintings were not earning a lot that year.

CHAPTER EIGHTEEN

THE VILLA TENNYSON

AS LATE as November 1879, Edward still believed or half-believed he might retreat to New Zealand. He even issued a manifesto to the public about how he, an artist, was being ill-treated. All the time this was going on, while he pondered feverishly on building sites, read Macaulay, and wrote desperate letters, and while Mrs Brocklebank assured him that Jenny the Gerwoman was sorry to have grieved him and knew of no hotel ... all this time Edward was working at his paintings. The day after Christmas he wrote, 'Last night a runaway horse with half a broken carriage, tonight two bicycles near demolished me.' His eyesight was becoming less reliable than it had been. But 1879 as it withered away had produced from him of all unlikely things a creed, 'one all can unite in, or most. I believe in God the Father Almighty Maker of Heaven and Earth. And in Jesus Christ our Lord, who was crucified under Pontius Pilate. I believe in the forgiveness of sins, and in the Life Everlasting. Amen.' Its interest is personal, no doubt, but it has an attraction beyond its date, as *In Memoriam* has.

He worked as hard as ever in 1880, so that by July he had finished eighteen of the pictures Lord Derby had ordered from his list. He told Emily Tennyson on 16 February 1880 that he had in the end borrowed money from Northbrook, Somers, Aberdare and Carlingford, also 'Clowes, Cross and others', the money to be repaid when he sold the Villa Emily. As soon as the year began he started to pay for the new ground, between the old lower and the new upper Berigo roads, not far from the Villa Emily. Only the road and the railway lay between this new land and the sea, so unless the fishes began to build, or Noah's Ark anchored offshore, he would be safe. He listed the value of his stocks for Frank Lushington, gave Giorgis handsome presents for the twenty-fourth anniversary of entering his service almost as if they were an old married couple, and comforted his friend Lord Carlingford, who said, 'I can get on so well with you but hardly anybody else,' and fled into the garden. Fortescue (Carlingford) poured out old stories about his wife's life: how when George Harcourt went to Elba he so bored Napoleon that Napoleon got rid of him by pissing against the wall, how the eighth Earl Waldegrave tried to prove his nephew the seventh was illegitimate, how the seventh never forgave him, and tried on his deathbed to get Lady Waldegrave to promise to leave no money and no property to any Waldegrave, how this Earl in a drunken frolic was accused of beating a policeman or a watchman and was given six months in the King's Bench prison, and she drove straight there and stayed with him; how it was she at that time who carried out the Strawberry Hill sale, in about 1843. When Lear wrote to Emily Tennyson about his friend's loss he wept all over the paper.

Whenever Edward got into a rage it lasted longer now than it used to do, and he wept more as he wrote letters. He had a furious rage with Giorgis over an old woman delivering charcoal by the wrong gate, and as usual thought of packing him and Dimitri off to Athens. In April he went to England: the journey was a brief agony, then he was plunged into London political gossip, trailing now and then on his slow, painful feet as far as the Zoo, and curing himself of diarrhoea with whisky and water. His headquarters were in the Lushington house in Norfolk Square, in order that he should hold an exhibition in it, without the expense of his usual lodgings. He did see his old friends, but he was hell-bent on selling paintings, and sent out some 685 invitations. Lord Leighton bought some, 'pleasant and friendly as ever', Edward met Shelley's sisters, both nearly ninety, and his own sister Ellen, a most distressing piece of wreckage alas. He met Gladstone too, and saw a good deal of Lord Northbrook. He also saw Lionel and Eleanor Tennyson; Lionel had wanted to be Northbrook's secretary; they worried him over Alfred, who early in June 1880 had 'taken a shine of going to Canada'. It is a pity he never went: he would have been excited by Niagara, and might have been photographed as an Indian Chief. Lear's publisher Bush went bankrupt owing him £33, but Lear went on pootering about London (only at a higher social level) and sighing for what might have been if Gussie had married him. For some reason two young Anglo-Indian girls floated into his mind, one a Miss Sinclair: he had taught them drawing in 1830, at Madam Zieltskye's in Tavistock Square. 'I well remember Madam Z's vast turban, and my poor sister Cordelia's injunctions before I went into the drawing room.' He noted that 'Mrs Malcolm, last of the Archbishop of York's many (Harcourt) children, is greatly aged.' He met a man in the Stereoscopic Shop, who remembered him from Hullmandel's in his parrot-drawing days. On 1 July he dined with Hubert at the Zoo, his mind on the past even then.

> I had just finished my exam at King's College and he carried me off to dine with him at the Zoological Gardens. You are just beginning the battle of life, he said, and we will spend the evening where I began it. It was a beautiful evening in July and we dined in the open and sat under the trees till the gardens closed, he telling me all the story of his boyhood and early struggles, and of his meeting with Lord Derby in those gardens, and the outcome of that meeting – the now famous book, The Knowsley Menagerie ... Lear when at his best was the most inspiring and delightful of companions. He was then absolutely natural, and we were like youths together ...

The emphasis on the Knowsley book is a pardonable mistake, so is the idea that it was famous, but the phrases at the end of Hubert's piece, 'not a great painter ... a great personality' are less forgivable. I am uncertain whether Hubert was a booby, or only grew up into a booby later. Yet Edward lavished affection on him, so that it might almost seem that Hubert was part of his break-up, but it was not so: the intensity of his involvement with the boy was a result not a cause of Edward's inner disturbance, as is his over-reaction to the building of the hotel, and only one among a number of results; all that Edward ever showed to Hubert was a purely comic kind of avuncular intimacy. There is a letter at Harvard with a whole long poem to Hubert, full of jokes based on how he is never going to be an artist (15 March 1878). 'We have got two blackbirds as sing surprising, and as Foss went out and looked up at the cage for two hours every morning, we hoped he would learn to sing too.' That was the level of their usual communication.

What kept Edward sane was mostly his art, and the late studies of Monte Rosa and Monte Generoso show how accomplished he had become. It also appears true to me, though it is more difficult to demonstrate, that the finished water-colours done later are better than those done earlier. The improvements are not just abolishing an ilex and substituting a *Pinus maritima*, they are abstract, to do with the balance of colours and the geometry (to use the term loosely) of his compositions. The Knowsley treatments of Suli and Montenegro are, as he said to Derby in 1881, of a formidable gloom, but the *Syracuse Quarries* done then and the *Parnassus* are admirably full of light. Whether the gloom in his mind affected his work, I greatly doubt: his work had a life and logic of its own, particularly in subjects like Masada and the Heights of Suli. He wrote in October 1880:

> It is plain that owing to my very defective sight which cannot work without a distinct outline, I have to make that outline so dark that it interferes with the light and clearness of the drawing, all through its future progress. It seems nearly impossible that I shall *gradually* achieve colour and form together. Just now it is on the cards whether I give up this Cataract Alfred Tennyson finished drawing. A pretty 'kettle of Fish!' as the pious Baboo wrote.

In July 1880 he produced the twenty coloured birds for Evelyn Baring's little boy that were reproduced forty or so years later: they are of named colours, one being a runcible bird (a kind of marmalade colour?). On 15 August he was luxuriating in the Boydell prints of Shakespeare he remembered from boyhood. They are works of the eighteenth century, by artists like Wright of Derby. He went to Aldworth too, where he discovered that Emily and Alfred now so hated Gladstone, that Hallam was not allowed to stand for Parliament on his side. A young group was playing tennis at Aldworth, and there was a seance after dinner (16 August) but things improved later. Edward never ceased to be interested in techniques: he tried drawing on cards with a Stylograph at this time. But before September he was in Italy with Giorgis and all three of his sons, doubtful of happiness but looking forward to a visit from Gussie. Giorgis said £40 would set up two of the sons in Brindisi. Lear's headquarters were now at Varese, but his new house was growing; he had referred to it as Villa Oduardo but now it became Villa Tennysonia, and a little later the Villa Tennyson.

Suddenly Nikos was chosen for the Army. Everybody wept and the going and coming speeded up, Giorgis said he should go to the Army unless he could be bought a café at Brindisi. Edward calculated he would have to spend £7 a week on Giorgis and sons, but no café was forthcoming: Nikos then escaped from the Army and arrived in Brindisi anyway. At this appropriate moment, £5 arrived at Dr Pasta's hotel from Boston, for part two of the Discobbolos family, in which they are blown to smithereens. At this stage Nikos began to demand money from Giorgis, and Edward sent him a little at a time, and went on doing so. He was turning the Villa Tennyson garden into a garden. He was reading Hans Andersen, whom he thought 'a real poet, but *too* melancholy'. Lear uses the word poet loosely: he thought Arnold's *Light of Asia*, which Lord Carlingford sent him, the most wonderful poetry, and liked to tell the story of how Dean Stanley had been called the Professor of Ecclesiastical Poetry by Mrs Grote, and how the Dean had called Lear the Prof. of Poetic Topography. There is some substance to Stanley's compliment, but Lear liked the *Light of Asia* for its vision of Buddhist purity.

On 26 October, ten days after the technical note about his eyesight and his painting, 'dim belief I shall not be able to paint anymore – sale of both villas and all drawings, with a retreat to Otranto or Bova or whatnot . . . Nikos needs forty-five or fifty pounds for a trattoria . . . Shuttleworth devilry prevents me seeing much of heaven or earth . . . sell all new property . . . go away hence until eucalyptus are grown . . . one can only go on'. Giorgis told him his Marsala was too powerful; it was in fact heavily spiked with spirits and Giorgis discovered that it ignited when placed near a stove. He cut Marsala and tried to cut wine, but found it an unprofitable manoeuvre. In February 1881 his gardener died, apparently of blood-poisoning, a man whom even old Giorgis called a kind of angel. The new gardener knew more about the names of flowers, but it was not the same. The consolation of this period is the re-incandescence of Edward's old friendship with his widowed friend Lord Carlingford. At first it was just a few sweet, saddish jokes, the attempt to bring this severe Anglo-Irishman out of himself, and back into politics, but they both had a second flowering at more or less the same time, and it shows.

Carlingford re-entered politics after two years of mourning, as Lord Privy Seal. The jokes about this private marine animal flower in a profusion of caricature in Lear's letters. The fishy joke was recorded in London by Sir Mountstuart Grant Duff GCST in 1878: someone had said Mereweather was as fat as a porpoise, and Julian Goldsmid had replied, 'Fit company, my Lord, for the Great Seal.' Carlingford followed the Duke of Argyll, who resigned, into Cabinet office in April 1881: Northbrook was one of his colleagues. Lear wrote him some letters of sinewy political analysis and he replied in kind, but the basis of their friendship was a deep warmth: it had been to Carlingford that Lear had meant to leave his diaries. It is hard for anyone now living to penetrate this aristocratic old politician, whose diary was so sparkling and yet who

seems carved out of granite: he was a romantic, who went on worshipping
Lady Waldegrave for many years when she was unattainable, so that 'and
Mr Fortescue' at the end of every social list printed became a public
joke: he went on through marriage until her dying day. I know of no
other friends of his but Henry Grenfell, a Christ Church man, MP and
Governor of the Bank of England from April 1881, who Lady Strachey
says was his best friend, Lord Northbrook and Edward Lear. His sister
may furnish a clue, since she married that wild man the orientalist and
Catholic convert David Urquhart, and their son Francis Fortescue
Urquhart was the Balliol don, Sligger Urquhart. He owned a fine
collection of Lears too, and by my calculation through Lord Carlingford
as his uncle he was a second cousin of Lytton Strachey.

Lear wrote to his friend that April 1881, at the beginning (as usual) of
his lifework:

'I have really begun five out of the three hundred Tennyson illustrations,
but as yet with little success ... When the three hundred drawings are
done, I shall sell them for £18,000: with which I shall buy a chocolate-
covered carriage speckled with gold, and driven by a coachman in green
vestments and silver spectacles, wherein, sitting on a lofty cushion
composed of muffins and volumes of the Apocrypha, I shall disport myself
all about the London parks, to the general satisfaction of all pious people,
and the particular joy of Chichester Lord Carlingford and his affectionate
friend Edward Lear. The new Villa Tennyson is nearly done, and the
flower supporting arches are all removed hence and put up there. Eight
men is a digging and a manuring all day – and costs sixteen shillings a
week. In the house here, abomination of desolation begins to show, for 56
immense cases already hold all books and drawings.

At this stage, we must face another problem: that of a poem which
Lear appears to have written twice, at intervals of years, having it would
seem forgotten it in the meantime. The upheaval of India and then this
upheaval intervene. The reason for discussing it here, and neither earlier
nor later, is that Lear scribbled some notes about a property in Volumes
1 and 4 of a copy of Addison's *Spectator*, of which Volume 2 is dated,
Edward Lear San Remo 1877, and page 25 of Volume 1 is dated 2 July
1886, 'numerous gatherings in all volumes' remain unopened, but the
endpapers of Volumes 1 and 4 contain working copies of 'Incidents in
the Life of My Uncle Arly,' and a sequel to 'The Owl and the Pussycat'.
When did Edward Lear write this poem? Frances Partridge gave the
manuscript to the London Library sale two or three years ago, and the
auctioneers thought *c.* 1886 might be the date: his diary leaves no doubt

that the poem was finished in February 1886, from something 'begun years ago for Lady Emma Baring', who was Lord Northbrook's daughter. But the Royal Academy Lear exhibition showed a different working copy of 'Uncle Arly' which is at Yale, on the front endpapers of the *Letters of Horace Walpole*, Volumes 8 and 9 (1866 edition), which has 'Edward Lear 1872' on the title-page: the RA Catalogue dates this copy to April 1873, when Edward was in bed with bronchitis (in fact it was early May).[1] This is a time when he is highly likely to have been writing a poem for Lady Emma Baring, whom he expected to see soon in India. But when poets scribble verses in the blank leaves of stray books, there is really no final way of dating them. When the poem was at last finished to his satisfaction, in March 1886 he made about a dozen fair copies which he sent to friends: Harvard has one made on the 7th for Wilkie Collins.

It had been clear for some years that 'Uncle Arly' was in his head: I have transcribed hints of it where they occur in his diary, but no doubt I have missed some. It was to him the echo of a song, a theme sad from its conception, but stated in the end with perfect clarity. It remains curious that the *Spectator* version has a lot of variants that were discarded, and one stanza that suggests the reading of Addison even more strongly than it does Horace Walpole.

> When in early life he wandered
> Here and there, he madly squandered
>   All his property away,
> So that when he came of age
> He was in a frightful rage,
> When they brought him lots of bills
>   And had nothing left to pay
> So that when they brought a kettle
> Full of ugly bills to settle,
>   But his bills he could not pay . . .
>
> From the fields and from the hills
> Every day they brought him bills,
>   When at first he came of age
> So he thought he'd go away.
> When he'd walked about for years
> And had shed a lot of tears,
> Then he said, my island home
> Is a long way from here.
>   clear
>   no longer roam.

This does not sound anything like the final version, but it does sound like the early conception of the character. To make the mystery darker, this scribble has a perfect version of stanza one, but the Walpole's *Letters* version has a perfect last stanza. No conclusion will be reached before they are both carefully compared, if then. Meanwhile, I cannot help wondering whether Lear did not roll these poems around in his mind for years, picking and rejecting among what he remembered of them. And yet these working manuscripts look exactly like the record of composition on paper, to which writing down was an essential. I will leave any discussion of the entire, very beautiful poem to 1886.

The unfinished draft of a sequel to 'The Owl and the Pussycat' was printed from the same flypapers of the *Spectator* by Angus Davidson in his *Edward Lear*.[2] It is largely in couplets, and deals with the children of 'The Owl and Pussycat', who live at Sila, a forest in eastern Calabria, where their mother whose tail was striped and five feet long died by falling from a tree, and their father grieved nearly to death, 'with the feathers of his tail he wiped his weeping eyes'.

> From Reggian Cosenza many owls about us flit
> And bring us worldly news for which we do not care a bit.

It is obscure what happens to these creatures, but they are sad because never more can they see the far Gromboolian Plains. The father goes on grieving in Lear-like strains, but their money is spent and the owls are annoyed because they take no interest in the politics of the day. It is a feeble, expiring chant that never came to anything, and Lear did not intend that it should, because he declared with some emphasis that Uncle Arly was the last poem he would ever write.

The year 1881 began with Dimitris creeping in to repeat the Lord's Prayer, and his father for half an hour a little later. As it went on into sloppy, droppy, weather, Edward was troubled by his bowels, and he let out more than was prudent of his venom against Miss Shuttleworth to the Vicar. She now maintained Hanbury had said he would tell Lear their intentions at the first opportunity, and she had assumed he had done so. 'I half wish I'd gone to New Zealand at once, or shall I go now and live in Toronto?' On 6 May, 'He only said my life is queery, it's very queer he said. He said it queerer gets and queerer. I would I were in bed.' He went as far as Brindisi to try to settle Nikos and Lambis, but at Bari he found that *trattorie* were being set up by the score and failing every week. On his return he had a row with Giorgis who shouted that his sons would not be waiters. In June Edward's *Philae* sold at Christie's for £63, Foss vanished up a chimney but came down again, and on the 7th Edward slept his first night in the Villa Tennyson. In July he was at Mendroso on what had become his annual painting holiday, with Giorgis and Dimitris, but Nikos was in Milan. At the end of that month A. P. Stanley died, whom Edward had loved and admired since Alderley days in the early 1830s. Dimitris began to struggle with Italian. The other two were still writing begging for money.

In August the Pasta hotel sheltered Edward; the calm beauty of it 'brought back infinite days and years of outdoor delight'. Yet on bad days he suffered temper, pain, indignation, shame. Nikos was declining jobs, Lambis thought he was really ill, and they drained money steadily away. At the end of September what was left of the Villa Emily garden was ruined by high winds that tore down the eucalyptus trees and the pillars on the terrace. Next day, 1 October, the Villa Tennyson garden was awash and torrents poured into the cellar. Nikos was spitting blood when his father went and fetched him home. Edward suddenly recorded about his own youth that 'No doubt remains that he (my father) was imprisoned for fraud and debt, and two brothers for desertion and forgery.'

There were calm evenings, of course, but 23 October, 'He only said, my life is dreary! There seems no hope, he said. He said I am aweary! aweary!' He tried to arrange an apprenticeship for Nikos at the Hôtel du Midi, paying them forty francs a month, then found another that would offer him keep now, and pay him when he was worth it. In December Edward was drawing Campagna buffaloes, Giorgis was discovered to be sweeping out the Villa Emily on his own, by his own wish; then Giorgis went wild and got very drunk, and the entire family erupted with one another. This would have been farcical if it were not tragic, and if Lear were not so tragic a figure attempting to pacify and control them all, and if we did not have to read about it through his anguished eyes. At the end of this year he had £1950 in consols and £600 in 3 per cents, with £154 in other banks.

After a week or two of 1882 the storms had settled, but it was now known that Giorgis drank, not only because of his wild behaviour at the New Year, but because he had been seen doing so in cafés by the hotel manager. The money Edward hoped to get for the Villa Emily was now down to £3000 and in fact it would be less. He drew Foss and the first beans came up in the new garden, Dean Church of Paul's bought some pictures; he was a brother of the Charles Church of Wells who ran a theological college there, and was Edward's old friend and travelling companion. Lord Somers spent even more. In May Edward had a letter from Gussie on his seventieth birthday. 'Who knows if . . .' he wrote. Lambis was sacked, no one knew why, so Giorgis went and brought him home, and Dimitris controlled the pair of them. In June Edward was wondering if Giorgis was often or always tight. Nikos said the old man wanted to go, and Edward, having spent £921 on them over nine years, began to wonder if twenty-seven years in service was not enough. Giorgis began to rave about India: who would have gone there for £3 a month? He wrote to Lushington, because he was a judge and used to tip Giorgis. One day the old man disappeared for ten hours, came in, said 'Goodnight', and went to bed. He raved with fury, 'No present from India, not even a photo! I'll go to Genoa and get justice! I know the world, I've been round it . . . I will go to England and get justice! . . . Money? I have millions, I have a palace in Athens . . . I'll go to England and get quite pissed!'

The next heard of him was a telegram sent at six in the morning from Toulon: 'Please send 200 francs Poste Restante Marseille for me to go to England'. Edward sent at once to the Greek consul there, saw to Nikos's and Dimitris's lessons, and went on painting. Meanwhile Giorgis telegraphed Lushington, still from Toulon, for money. Edward sent telegrams to Giorgis, to Lushington and to the consul. The telephone existed, and he had used it, but not from San Remo. Edward wrote: 'I have a conviction that he will not live.' The three younger Kokalis sat on the kitchen doorstep together, as they had done as children in Corfu. Nikos was sent, and after a few days Giorgis arrived at San Remo, so weak he could hardly walk. He had lived on a hill above Toulon for two days without food and scarcely conscious. He was in deep grief, and when the consul read him Lushington's letter, he wept. On the train he was as weak as a child. 'Monte Generoso as soon as possible is best.' It was the last day of June, and Edward began to celebrate by diving into the sensations of landscape and his garden and the crash and fizzle of the waves. Throughout this crisis he had been perfectly level-headed. He found out from Dr Pasta that the alcoholic problem was deep-rooted. At the hotel Nikos, who had gone ahead with his father, wanted to bring Edward his boots, but Giorgis said it was his job and he did it. Edward was working at 'All the land was dark' for an Autotype. A letter from Corfu warned them that a year in prison or three in the Army awaited both Nikos and Lambis. Edward thought of packing them all off to Cyprus.

Giorgis turned out to be deep in debt in many directions: yet he had never had a debt. Now he felt so ashamed he wanted to go home to Corfu. Edward was too grieved to go out. 'I fear, I fear, I fear I must send him in late September.' He loved Giorgis, he could not stand the thought that never again would he come in and say, 'Padrone, dove andiamo?' Giorgis insisted on Corfu because he could not face San Remo, because it was the scene of his disgrace. No one seems to have sought to persuade him that what had happened to him was a kind of breakdown, or that it had been overdue. There was a robbery and break-in at the Villa Emily, so the police arrested the gardener and the two Kokalis brothers. At last, by the end of September, 'Giorgis immensely better and cheery. Garden now in extreme beauty, Ipomeas especially. Rev. Carus Selwyn sent £52.' The hotel manager, Bertolini, wanted a second waiter as well as Nikos, but Lambis knew no French 'and must shave whiskers'. Edward was now teaching French to Nikos and English to Lambis and Dimitris. 'In a week their expenses 45 to my 55 francs.' Giorgis and Lambis quarrelled about the events of 1878. 'Gave Lambi a franc to have his curled moustache shaved.' In the middle of a tangle of these and worse upheavals, Giorgis suddenly bought a lot of guinea-pigs, 'poor dear old Giorgis'. Edward took on Nikos, who was out of work, for forty francs a month.

The quarrels went on into December: yet Edward says 'days happier than I could ever expect so late in life', and Giorgis and his sons write 'Forno Albanese' ('Albanian Cooking') over the oven in the back kitchen. The quarrels are intense, though. Giorgis buys some appalling oil paintings. He goes for walks and when a stick is suggested he says, 'You wish me take speckles too?' He says, 'My sons respect me less than they do Foss.' He calls Dimitris a vagabond, he says Nikos ruined him. Lambis calms him down. 'All this and much more occurred.' One day Edward and Giorgis go together to the cemetery where the gardener's grave is. Edward went there alone on Christmas Day, when he had settled his Albanians to their dinner and seen to the presents for Giorgis. His own present to the old man was a large tobacco jar in the shape of an Indian elephant. Sometimes he felt very ill and giddy, and for fear he might die wrote a paper one day to see that Giorgis got £25 and Dimitris £10 if he suddenly died. Giorgis was not well pleased by this arrangement; he felt he should have money of his own, at his age.

Eighteen eighty-three began calmly with 'a blessed monotony of life – old Giorgis very cheery and calm'. F. W. Gibbs assured Edward that Dean Wellesly had told him it was not the Prince Consort who forbade the Athanasian Creed, with its hellfire and damnation, to be recited in his Chapel at Windsor, but George III, 'because I won't allow my subjects to be damned in my own chapel'. The Rev. E. Carus Selwyn, Lear's favourite late-won friend and patron from Cambridge, and Plumptre, the Dean of Wells, and his wife, F. D. Maurice's sister, came to see him in these halcyon days. But Lambis was next in trouble and Nikos was coughing again. Lambis was ill and crying and the doctor inspected them both. Lambis's employers said some wine was stolen. Giorgis had back pains, but he recovered and showed considerable amusement at the news of a railway in Malta. Nikos was spitting blood and needed a fire in his room. By April Edward thought that Giorgis was back to his normal self, yet he worried when the old man went into San Remo for a haircut. Sometimes he envied him for being so lively and so content. Then Lambis disappeared and ten bottles were missing. He had been to the villa, but Giorgis had refused to see him, and Nikos and Dimitris refused to let him in. There was a women's quarrel, and it seemed Lambis had slept with one. His employers the Watsons threatened deportation but Nikos bribed him with 150 francs to go to Genoa; Giorgis saw him off at the station.

'April the thirteenth: Fried oranges again.' Lambis demanded money from Ancona; it was sent, but a girl said he was now at Pisa. He had also pawned the Watsons' cook's watch, and Mrs Watson alleged he had a wife and two children in Pisa, a Greek girl he had married in Brindisi. Giorgis was pleased at this, because it would mean he was a grandfather. The old man was not at all well that spring, he took to his bed with a cough, so Edward sent him up to Mendrisio as soon as he could. After an appalling fuss, with consular intervention and heaven knows what else, Lambis, after lurking long in Brindisi, was packed off by sailing boat to Athens, and Dimitris sold his rabbits for four francs. In July Oenothera was 'in full splendour, and the illustrious Cobaea, astonishing flower'. Edward took the family saga quite tranquilly now, and toddled off to the mountains to find Giorgis. But Giorgis was not recovering: he was getting weaker; on 1 August, Nikos knew he would die; Dr Pasta said he would not recover, though he might linger on for a year. At this moment, Lambis reappeared at Brindisi; Edward telegraphed the consul, disclaiming all responsibility. Giorgis said he had three or four days to live. The English doctor arrived with egg in brandy, beef tea and mustard plaster, but on 8 August, at five in the evening, Giorgis died. Edward wrote, 'O dear Giorgis, you are gone, but O be as good a guide and angel to me as for so many years.'

He was deeply shocked. He quoted *In Memoriam*, and went wandering around Italy with Dimitris, with lessons every day. He sent £10 to the importunate Lambis from Bologna. For months he thought about Giorgis though the loss was too painful to be very much talked about. He sent Lambis a trunk of clothes but Lambis wrote from Naples that clothes were no good, he was in a hostel for the destitute. Edward was conscious of death and of little else. He cut a Mrs Dawson because she mentioned Hanbury and La Mortola, in a hotel at Perugia. It had a window towards Assisi. He compared Lake Trasimene to a Claude: and at the tiny railway station of Terentola, which is not far away, he took the train home. The first sign of life in Edward was at the very end of October, when he read about the Troodos Mountains in Cyprus. He became crazy about them for his future summer retreat, because he would not be going back to Dr Pasta's hotel. He did pay for an eloquent gravestone. A doctor wrote from Naples, 'Lambis very ill – I dare say.' On Christmas Eve Edward wrote a letter and tore it up again, but the next day he did send twenty-five francs. Alfred Tennyson's peerage could not stir him up to go back to his Tennysonian pictures. 'There is no outlet of hope for that set of 200 abortions.'

The old Greek had served him as valet, cook, servant and companion for nearly thirty years. Before that he seems to have married and had those of his children who survived in a brief interval after another eight years as servant to a General Conyers, probably in Corfu. He was an admirable servant, with an extraordinary patience and sweetness, and he obviously loved Edward and depended on him, until he began to break down after India and the death of his wife, and the realization that he could not provide for his sons. It is hard to describe how wild Souli was: it was an isolated mountain village from which his parents had come straight to Corfu as refugees very shortly before he was born. The morality of Souli became unstable when the tight community of the place was disbanded, but it still prevailed in Corfu. The impersonal burdens of the new Greek state, like military service and taxes, were beyond Souliot comprehension, and the boys had run wilder than their father ever did, in his absence. They now felt a feudal dependence on Edward, which he was reluctant to acknowledge except in the rather English terms of a social contract: they must behave themselves and be honest and clean, then he would do what he could.

There was among the other inhibitions of life in a Greek mountain village a subtle and complex system of sexual morality which appears to have prevailed in Corfu, as it still does in the remoter parts of Greece, which was relaxed in Italy. In a village like Souli, you would get a knife in you if you touched someone's daughter or sister, and probably in Corfu much the same: but Brindisi was the ferry port and the border port: once a Greek set foot there, he was loose from that commandment, and that is why the three sons of Giorgis behaved less well than their father. As a consequence, they picked up syphilis. Giorgis in his extreme of anguish and bewilderment wanted to flee to Lushington, he had been impressed by him and knew him since Corfu as the judge, and it is clear that he really felt he had been wronged, he had been meanly treated: because whether or not Edward loved him, some provision had to be made now for his children. Edward on his side was in a fearful state of worry about money, things could not have happened at a worse time. It is evident from the gestures he had made that he did feel paternally about Giorgis, but he did not know what he could do for the best: this was a double tragedy with two Lears in it. Edward's troubles now appeared to be catastrophic and irremediable by the end of 1883.

Yet he went on painting, and went on to some degree supporting the sons of old Giorgis. He began 1884 working at paintings of Bassae and Corfu, and a lovely and fresh Ventimiglia. He feared that Nikos was terribly ill. His father had died of congestion of the lungs and Nikos's lungs were clearly weak and diseased. Edward also felt guilty about Lambis, who for the time being had disappeared. His frenzy about reproduction of his own work, his Tennysonian images in particular, was because at this stage of the century, from the money that artists made, at least half came from the right to produce prints from their originals, and he cannot not have known what large sums were involved. It was in 1883 that Thomas Holloway bought a Turner, a Gainsborough and a Constable at Christie's for £3675, £2835 and £1249 10s., to decorate his new college at Egham; they were all in oils. He was a former grocer, rich on patent medicines, who paid high prices: the most was for an idiotic work of Landseer showing polar bears and wreckage (6500 guineas), and nearly as much for some absurd naked ladies. But Frith's *Railway Station* had sold for £4500 in 1860, and then for £16,300 with the right to make engravings, and Holloway was lucky to get it for a mere £2000 in the 1880s. It was fame or popularity, created by the Academy exhibitions and by newspapers, that generated this added value of the right to engrave. Boydell's Shakespeare prints had been made on the same principle a generation before, though with less success.

At this moment Cameron Grant recommended woodcuts, someone else said to try Hogg: in the middle of this confusion, when his books needed a publisher, when he felt guilt and shame, when Dr Hassall gave

Nikos's left lung a very bad report and Edward was further thrown by a tax demand, the Villa Emily sold at last for 40,000 francs. Even then, Edward was not quite sure whether to pay off Lord Northbrook, his chief remaining creditor, in full at once, which would leave only £100 in the 3 per cents. There was a hope that a botanist called Kettlewell might buy his lovely *Ravenna Forest*, a long picture. Nikos was settled in a hotel job with 900 francs a month. Edward was working at Asphodels for his *Argos* foreground, then at Gwalior and two Ravennas. He settled to a new trial for Autotypes, and in April recorded that it 'may or may not yet require no end of patience and energy'. He was re-reading Stanley's *Dark Continent*, and a book on North Indian zoology. Mrs Leake had left him her husband the topographer's watch.

All through April he was ill, but he kept at his painting. He found out Dimitris was secretly sending money to Lambis, and of course repaid him. He took Dimitris on a journey to Vicenza, since he begged to be taken, if necessary just for his keep, to learn French. At Milan Edward saw Dean Church: he had visited a region of mulberry trees, Recoaro with its green hills and mountain tops, and S. Donnino which was ugly but full of nightingales. In June he tried a rail journey with Nikos and Dimitris, 'only Foss objected strongly'; Nikos was installed at Salsomaggiore, and Dimitris came home to San Remo, but lifting a lot of mounted sketches forced Edward to lie down and rest. In July they were off to Recoaro; Edward felt Nikos was better but Dimitris felt he was worse. He was often sick, but Dimitris had his French lessons, and Edward's first five caterpillars of new Tennysonian sketches emerged from the state of chrysalis.

His diary was blotched with tears over Giorgis, and on walks he had to be helped along. In August he learned that Lord Northbrook and his daughter Emma were sent out to Cairo. 'It is getting dark, and the evening bugles of the Alpine soldiers are a pleasure.' He went crazy about Palladian rotondas and theatres and about Vicenza. At Milan he saw the Natural History Museum and the Zoo. By the time he got back to San Remo he had done a number of fine drawings, but he had been suspicious, furious, sad and worried about money, and Lambis had sent a crazy telegram. Dimitris now claimed to have sent another 200 francs; he seemed to have been lying about money: finally he cried and confessed, and Edward arranged to keep Lambis supplied. Then a debt of fourteen francs to a coachman emerged, and Edward said, 'I am so angry I can neither write nor speak.' At the end of September he drew the oleander in the garden.

'I can't help feeling all two hundred Tennysons must be completed in black and white – may even go to the expense of photography.' He was still evidently imagining a book published at his own expense, beautifully illustrated. There were such wonderful books in those years, but it does sound like a dream. Nikos was a little better, but Edward and Dimitris did not speak for a time. Had the boy stolen a seal? No, because luckily it turned up in Lear's pocket. Then ninety francs disappeared and he remembered 110 that had gone that summer. Should he send them away and give Nikos a pension? The 200 turned out to be money paid to doctors to cure him of pox. At this point Edward paid Dimitris off with fifty francs for a month and twenty-five for bills, but Nikos could not do all the work, try as he would, so in November Lear hired a new servant called Luigi, and Dimitris withdrew, first of all to a kind of peasants' tavern nearby. Nikos improved a little but he sat sadly by the fire in the kitchen. 'I must die in Italy,' he said. Dimitris demanded money from Corfu where he was in quarantine: he needed eighty-three francs to get out. The cook was found to be watering the wine; both Nikos and Luigi accused him. Only Lambis seemed a bit more cheerful with his money; Nikos was sinking. A new cook called Cesare came at the end of 1884.

Edward now had £1950 in consols still, £2000 in 3 per cents, and he had made a new will. He attacked his chrysalis Tennysons again, in June 1885, in sets of ten; he had done forty-two, all mounted: by the end of July he had done eighty-two and by the end of September 130. In the course of that entire year his invested money did not alter; only his current account at Drummond's rose a little. He was working in black and white with an amazing concentration and vehemence that shows as great power: in a very few cases, perhaps two among the whole series at Harvard, say, one can see that his eyes are failing or else his mind is not well, but the evenness of his temper at work and usually in life in these last years is startling. He noted in January that his bodily health was good, but his mind was not well, yet he went on doing what had to be done. He was delighted with a chromolithograph from E. Martineau: he wrote the sweetest letter to Hallam Tennyson's wife. On 12 February he heard Gordon was killed, Russia was threatening Herat, Dimitris was demanding 'the money you owe me' and Lord Rosebery followed Carlingford as Lord Privy Seal. Carlingford's private secretary had got a year in prison for fraud and forgery a little earlier.

On the 20th Edward found Nikos crying with pain from siphylis, which the doctor easily treated. He caught it from his first woman, in Brindisi, and his father had known about it. It turned out that old

Giorgis more or less starved Lambis, Dimitris never ate at home, and used the money for a woman who then got Lambis into trouble, who then had two other women in San Remo. The story is sordid and entangled and unhappy as Nikos told it, and the whole family seem in the end to have had clap. 'In the next world,' said Nikos, 'I will see my mother and no one else, I do not want to meet the rest of my family.' The most or the only unexpected thing about all this is that Edward muses in his diary that he can hardly blame them as they were not educated like him, 'Considering I myself in 1833 had some sort of siphylitic disease'. No doubt that was in the days of Husey-Hunt and his friend Harry Greening 'who was in those times the life of all our parties, albeit through him partly I got into bad ways' (diary, August 1881). It does serve to establish once and for all Edward's relative normality. On the last day of February, Nikos said, 'Master, you have always been so good to me,' and never spoke again. He was unconscious, and breathed with difficulty for three days, and on 4 March he died. He was thirty-four. On the 16th Edward's blind and last surviving sister Ellen died at the age of eighty-four; her wealth reverted to her husband's family. The last surviving member of that generation of Lears apart from Edward was now an old man of eighty-two in Texas for whom Ellen had just built a house.

> I lose not only an admirable servant, but a companion whose great intelligence and whose perfect disposition could hardly be surpassed, nor could his faithful affection to myself, nor his admirable help to his parents. The conduct of his brother Dimitri troubled him terribly, but with a true Suliot courage he hardly ever gave way to sorrow . . . Almost to the last he would go on keeping the accounts, and often read a good deal of Greek and French . . . he hardly ever uttered a word of complaint.

The letter was to Carlingford. He was working then at Nuneham elm trees from sketches made in the last few days of July 1860. The Oxford Professor of Poetry had been to see him, Tozer had sent him Bent's *Cyclades*, and people kept suggesting he should write an autobiography.

> And this is certain; if so be
> You could just now my garden see,
> The aspic of my flowers so bright
> Would make you shudder with delight.
>
> And if you vaz to see my roziz
> As is a boon to all men's noziz,

> You'd fall upon your back and scream,
> O Lawk! O crikey! it's a dream!

On the evidence of this sad but controlled and amusing, affectionate letter, it cannot be said that Edward was a crushed or a defeated man. Life had done its worst, or nearly so, and he might in the end blow out like a candleflame, because he was weak and not well. But in the less than three years he had to live, he was still making new friends and loving old ones, and still producing work of the highest quality of anyone in his generation of painters, and in these late 1880s poetry which no one but Tennyson (until Hardy) could rival for its lively and startling originality. In June 1884, while Carlingford was in attendance at Balmoral, Lear had sent him a version of the first stanza of 'Uncle Arly', 'just to let you know how your aged friend goes on'.

> O my aged Uncle Arly!
> Sitting on a heap of Barley
> Through the silent hours of night!
> On his nose there sate a cricket;
> In his hat a railway ticket –
> – But his shoes were far too tight!
> Too! too!
>   far too tight!

The version on the *Spectator* fly-pages has him 'Silent through the weary night', and abolishes the repeats after the first 'tight'. The conception, though perhaps not the whole poem, was set, then, by June 1884, when Dimitris was pulling him in and out of railway carriages 'like a sack of hay'.

CHAPTER NINETEEN

THE DEATH OF
EDWARD

EDWARD had not exhibited in the Royal Academy since before his Indian expedition, the last one was his *Megaspelion* (1873). He sold pictures with a few exceptions exclusively to his old patrons and friends or at times to their friends, but almost always to people he had met. There was an air of the private and amateur that clung to water-colour painting in the 1880s: a woman who had seen his water-colours in his own house declared in shocked tones, 'Do you know, the man actually tried to *sell* me one!' In his last years he was trying very hard to finish his Tennysonian series. Tennyson still sent him new poems, Hallam and Lionel were his friends as well as Emily, and when he offered his house for Hallam and Audrey's honeymoon Hallam answered with a sonnet, thanking him for the invitation to come 'And find him in his labyrinthine maze Of orange, olive, myrtle . . .', which sounds as if he had seen a photograph or a garden sketch. The poem is printed in Lear's *Later Letters*.[1] It is odd how Lear's letters to that family came to revolve around flowers – 'today it is just the same as before the Fathers fell asleep, which is all sunshine and comfort' . . . in Maeldune 'I shouldn't mind living on the Silent Isle or the Isle of Flowers'.

The Tennysonian pictures of which he assured Hallam as late as 1880 that there would be 300, but of which 200 or 201 is the normal number, went through an egg, a caterpillar and a chrysalis stage. 'But I suppose everything will come right some day, as the caterpillar said when he saw all his legs fall off as he turned into a chrysalis.' In the season, both his house and his garden were crowded: it might be with the large Bishop of Sidney on the terrace, the small Bishop of Sierra Leone in the gallery, Lord Aberdare's children on a lower path, an organ-grinder somewhere, and the Welds arriving, so that it is amazing how he worked. He also became great friends with his doctor's wife, Mrs Hassall, who mothered him as he needed. Still, he had 'near completed' the 200 in December 1883, and when Alfred was made a peer, Edward wept all over his charming letter to Hallam.

The entire series was like a diary, somewhat jumbled up, of Edward's whole life, and was to be his equivalent to a *Liber Studiorum*, such as Turner, whose *Liber* he owned, and Claude had left. One full set is at Harvard, and another, which belonged to Lord Tennyson's family and was disgracefully dispersed by the Lincoln municipal authorities, was fortunately caught and photographed by Ruth Pitman for the Carcanet Press (1988), just a moment before it was scattered for ever. It was not singled out for this treatment: Lincoln tried to sell their *In Memoriam* manuscript at the same time. The pictures are therefore easily available, so I shall not need to praise them. Their tone is subtle, as becomes a *Liber Veritatis* or *Studiorum*. They do not add to the phrases of poetry that had caught Lear's attention in Tennyson's works: but they do illuminate the way in which words or poems can insinuate themselves into the way a painter sees. What you mumble and rumble to yourself over a lifetime becomes the substance of your mind. The Harvard series is darker, I think, and smaller, but thrillingly powerful, as if the artist was fighting for his life, or tearing at the lining of his brain or soul. The series of the Athos monasteries is uniquely complete, and now the only such record there is of those buildings before any of them was abandoned or ruined. Ruth Pitman offers an excellent introduction to the many forms these Tennyson pictures took.[2]

In 1981 the British Library bought Lear's fair copy of the poem written in April 1879, 'How pleasant to know Mr Lear'. He writes of it as 'My and Miss Bevan's verses', but it is highly doubtful whether that lady, who was the Vice-Consul's daughter of San Remo, contributed more than the title line. The poem is remarkable because of the balance it embodies between self-revelation and nonsense mythology: it goes with the long series of his self-caricatures. It has something in common with the mass of occasional verse he casually threw off to individuals in his letters, but it is formally strong and could not have been written without such mature, sad lyrics as the Yonghy-Bonghy-Bo, who of course is Lear, and Uncle Arly, who is also Lear. From these various ways of seeing himself one can learn a good deal about him. 'Some think him ill-tempered and queer' was only beginning to be true that year, it became truer after the quarrel over the new hotel. One of the best and truest sentences of all is 'his mind is concrete and fastidious'. As for singing, he still did it when Henry Strachey visited him years later: and he did sit in the parlour with hundreds of books on the wall, though he calls it a parlour only to rhyme with Marsala, which he did drink, though he switched about this time to Barolo. The stanza about his friends, his cat, his spherical body and his hat is a precise description of his self-caricatures. The self-revelation comes in the seventh stanza, 'He weeps by the side of the ocean, He weeps on the top of the hill . . .' The rest is concrete and fastidious, but the whole poem is masterly, and it properly found its way into the *Golden Treasury* in late editions. Can that be Tennyson's influence?

The rest of 1885 was stuffed full of work: in the summer Lubbock (Lord Avebury) bought a dozen sketches for £68, and Lady Reid a Corsican drawing. The Tozers came for Easter and Lear subscribed two guineas for a Holman Hunt print. At Easter Nikos Kokalis's two brothers began again their insistent begging letters, some quite nasty, and the chaos of their debts went on coming to light. But Ellen left Edward £500, and he taught Luigi to make proper mint sauce. His privet and his pines had grown up, so he began to cut his eucalyptus, which had the advantage in the early period of Villa Tennyson that it grew four feet a year, and screened him. Frank Lushington came out and cheered him beyond measure. It was an advantage that he was not in politics, because Edward was now finding it prudent to tear up his letters to Carlingford when they strayed on to that ground. He does not seem to have realized that he and Carlingford both longed to bring back Palmerston from the grave. He had had a sharp exchange even with Lord Northbrook when he suggested the Russians should be given Budrum because it would make them more responsible: why not give them Anglesey then, asked Northbrook, or the Isle of Wight? Lear went to Brianza and Barzano in June, well armed with Tennyson sketches. In Milan he looked again into lithography but he disliked his proofs: they lacked sharpness, they were woolly and soft. Meanwhile Northbrook and Frank Lushington agreed the prices of his big pictures should come down: from 400 to 150 guineas each.

Should he go to England and do the job himelf, or get Arny Congreve and Underhill to do it? Underhill agreed to do it if employed. At Brianza a typical lunch was quails and bacon, plain rice and sweet omelette. He got on well with Luigi and his other servants and began to feel better. 'O the quiet of Villa Figini at Barzano.' He drew the landscape and saw a threshing machine set up, and Luigi's father and sister called on him. Only the anniversary of the death of Giorgis was surrounded by days of stomach upset and of remorse. Old Penry Williams died, and the sale of his remaining pictures in London was a disaster: it is hard to know quite why. The main cause may have been that he lived abroad. Monkton Milnes died at Vichy at this time: another friend gone. The work Edward was doing was rather mechanical, so he brooded a good deal over things, and water-colour came to agonize him as only oil used to do. One day he was giddy, fainting and vomiting, but on 12 September he was back to San Remo and Foss and the two pigeons: Brianza may have poisoned him for a day, but it cured his lungs, and his garden delighted him again. The walk to the post and back was easy now. With passionate and gloomy anxiety he noted down every one of the changing, often lying stories he heard from Nikos's brothers. He decided to try photography for his pictures.

He was happy at his piano, and happy with his garden. The gardeners of Villa Figino sent him roots and seeds in October, and he ate a good dinner one night with Barolo, Marsala and a little cognac, and felt better for it, but in November Underhill sent a lithograph, 'deficient in force, very careful'. Edward meanwhile was just moving on from *Framley Parsonage* to the *Last Chronicles of Barset*. At the end of November Lord Carlingford arrived in a depressed mood, perhaps because he had broken with Gladstone and with political life. But he then caught cold and the San Remo doctor sent him to bed. The two of them were both unwell and elderly and cared more for each other than for themselves perhaps, and there was an element of farce in their extremely serious situation. 'Fell over Foss and hurt my nose.' Underhill's proofs were poor and feeble: 'Shall not proceed.' Edward bought three new Trollope books and played chess in the kitchen with Luigi. When he dined with Fortescue at his hotel, Luigi came for him and brought him home. He came across a portrait of himself done by Fowler of Amherst Island about 1835; it is now lost, alas.

In January 1886 he decided his two or three hours with Fortescue must avoid politics: 'Much talk, perhaps too much, of the Queen, John Brown, Bulgarian massacres etc.' A schoolmistress from Petersburg wrote to know what 'runcible' means. (My suggestion is that it meant marmalade, as that fits a hat, a bird, and a spoon.) He was now sending massive numbers of sketches where he was apparently still indebted:

some to Stratton to Lord Northbrook, some Ionian ones to Lord Aberdare, the 1849 Morea sketches to Lushington. He seems to have felt a relief about this, though it alarmed Lord Carlingford a little. Then on 22 February, as if it were part of the same process, a disposal of his intimate records more than the settlement of debts, he wrote out 'Uncle Arly'. It is, as I have said, possible or likely that this poem had been on the boil for many years, and he knew at once he would never write another like it. It was the intimate core of what he wanted to say. I do not know whether he realized that this or 'How pleasant to know Mr Lear' were in some sense great poems, startling and unforgettable and perhaps immortal. Probably not, but he would have done if someone else had written them, and he saw that the poem he sent to Marianne North, for example, and to Hallam, about packing or not packing a Tennyson in Milan that summer, was a slight thing, a private joke by comparison.

Uncle Arly squandered his money and went to the goldmines, the Tiniskoop Hills (tin was his word for money), lived as a tutor and sold pills like Mr Holloway. Here the mystery starts: he found a first-class railway ticket, and a cricket perched on his nose. It never left him and he loved it. For forty-three years he wandered until he came upon his old home; his shoes were worn to splinters, yet they were far too tight.

> On a little heap of Barley
> Died my aged uncle Arly,
>   And they buried him one night; –
> Close beside the leafy thicket; –
> There, – his hat and Railway-Ticket; –
> There, – his ever-faithful Cricket; –
> (But his shoes were far too tight).

The list of his complaints and adventures is swallowed up in comedy, it becomes mythical and arouses true wonder, the tragedy is almost too funny to be sad, except for that final, repeated grumble.

He sent Arnold Congreve the six volumes of Roberts on Palestine and Egypt, Lushington his Maltese and fourteen Ionian sketches, 'Uncle Arly' to a number of people from Carlingford to Ruskin. He calculated 130 sketches might be worth £260. He sent money to Dimitris, who seemed to be dying, and other sketches to Clowes and to Strachey. There can be no doubt that in the spring of 1886 he was disposing of things like a man on his deathbed, and on 23 April he signed a new will. In the middle of all this he heard that Lionel Tennyson had died in the

Red Sea and buried at sea off Aden; Lear himself was more seriously ill than one might discern from the diaries, but there was a sad exchange of letters. At this time someone (perhaps Hallam) was acquiring more of Lear's work: *Lugano* and *Pentedattylo* and I think others. He was not at all well at Barzano in June, though he tried telling himself his only trouble was asthma. 'The big magnolia flowers, also the nightingales and robins are a satisfaction – but his boots were far too tight, i.e. my chest oppression and cough are a sad set off.' He still thought of selling ground and building elsewhere, probably because of asthma. But the owner of the Villa Figini was asking £20,000 for his villa and 200 ruinous cottages, which would be an expense to pull down. He was seriously ill in July at Mendrisio. Even in October he could hardly walk. 'Got on a list shoe but left it off as it heated the foot.'

His only discernible comfort that October was *In Memoriam*, 'wonder-fuller the more one studies it'. In November 'no pain in left leg, great weakness all over'. Suddenly in December S. W. Clowes bought his *Ravenna* for £150. The Autotype Company were no good to him and 'must send back the two hundred', probably the Tennyson pictures now at Harvard. Lambis was in and out of prison and now squealed to be sent home to Corfu, but 'I have nothing more to do with it' (in Italian). And then, quite casually, he scribbles down this: 'Dec. 30th dined with Foss only, rather good mutton.

> Huntley and Palmer arose with the earlyful
> beams of the morning sun,
> Huntley a chop for his breakfast chose
> Palmer preferred a bun.'

His investments in his last two years of life do not alter much. On 20 April 1887 he was with Lady Emma Baring and her father Lord Northbrook. They composed another brief verse together: 'Below the high Cathedral Stairs Lie the remains of Agnes Pears: Her name was Wiggs it was not Pears, But Pears was put to rhyme with stairs'. When Edward heard from his old friend Wilkie Collins that 'Uncle Arly' was his best poem ever, he was so delighted that he sent the Rev. E. Carus Selwyn news that 'There is another pome about the same ingividgual begun – but shunted –

> Accidental, on his hat
> Once my Uncle Arly sat:
> Which he squeezed it wholly flat.

(Incomplete MSS – found in the brain of Mr Edward Lear on dissection of the same.)'³ Eighteen eighty-seven was not an easy year because Luigi left. Scott took away Edward's pictures to try photographing them: all these experiments that failed were financed with the £500 Ellen had left him. Foss was always with him, he was an old cat now who had been in the house fourteen years, and may have been two or three when he arrived, but in November he died, and he was buried in the garden, under the fig tree at the end of the terrace, with a memorial stone of his own. Edward was convinced he was thirty years old.

Lear spent most of that year until he became ill in August worrying about new photographic processes. Platinotype was an American invention that interested him; a Mr and Mrs Dana Estes came to see him about it. In May his fits or seizures returned after long absence, but only as a kind of physical irritation. 'There is a great relief in having ceased to believe it was what I formerly thought.' When he was bedridden his greatest pleasure was to watch the pigeons preening on his windowsill and playing in the warm air.

His last letter to the Tennysons was to Hallam (30 May 1887). It includes a note of the photographs of friends above his fireplace. (He had prints of Lord Tennyson and Lord Derby elsewhere.)

Lord	Earl	Carlingford	Emily	Dean	Lady	Vickers
Baring	Somers	3	Tennyson	Stanley	Emma	Boyle
1	2		4	5	Baring	7
					6	

Rev C.	Goddaughter	Mrs Hassall	J. Ware	Selwyn	Mrs Ed
Church	Gertrude	Doctor's	Edgar	Twin	Hornby
8	Lushington	wife	11	Children	13
	9	10		12	

Gussie	Earl of
Bethell	Northbrook
Parker	15
14	

'There! it ain't everybody as has such friends! Goodbye, E.L.'

Ruskin chose him as a nonsense-writer and poet first among his favourite books, and the *Spectator* wrote eloquently in praise of his *Nonsense*. Even Holman Hunt, writing in the *Contemporary Review* what later became his large book about the Pre-Raphaelites, had at least left Lear more or less out of his piece, and Lear was grateful. He mused over a Moore-like 'Song of Lady Charles Hornby'. 'Roses wonderful. Pigeons allegro.' Dimitris surprisingly settled down as a village schoolmaster in Paxos. Gussie came to San Remo and knitted Edward some socks and read him some Wordsworth, 'much beautiful poetry', he writes in a surprised tone. In July he saw 'the same goldengreen of the new terrace, the sparkle of pigeons' wings, the pulled blue of the sea breaking beyond'. He felt pigeons were the most beautiful of all birds. But as he had written in May a year before,'my own Aim and End in life must be topographic illustration'.

He dreamed one night that he was young again and riding wildly round the walls of Rome with Charles Knight. He woke at 6.20 from that dream and played the piano before going back to bed. He hated flies and at two one morning he records 'hours of flyflopping but it is laborious'. At last, after days of worrying about it, he got to Milan and bought himself twenty Bristol boards, and 'prepared a bit of charcoal for Tennyson trials'. He touched up 118 (*Athos*) and 150 (?*Nice*). He mused on Marsala in Sicily with Proby. In October he was greatly upset by the death of his nephew, Charles Street, in New Zealand. The last, isolated diary entry is for 5 December 1887: 'a beefsteak mascherato. Good in its way but nasty more. I should try to get some sleep if possible, but I have no light or life left in me. And the flies are as horrible as ever.'

Edward Lear died at about 2.20 in the morning on 29 January 1888. His last words to his Italian servant were: 'My dear Giuseppi, I feel I am dying. You will do me a sacred service with my friends if you tell them that my last thought was of them, specially the judge, and Lord Northbrook and Lord Carlingford. I can find no words sufficient to thank my good friends for all the good they have always done me. I haven't answered their letters because I couldn't write, because as soon as I picked up my pen I felt I was dying.' None of his English friends except Dr Hassall and his wife could come to his funeral.

The plants in Lear's garden

LISTED FRIDAY 17 FEBRUARY 1871.

Pinus cephaloica (seeds saved at Selborne)
Orange Lily
Malope toifida (annual)
Mixed sweet peas
Giant mignonette
Linum azureum (herbaceous)
Fraxinella (herbaceous)
Climber from Japan
Everlasting peas
Disteruma coccinea, a beautiful passionflower climber
　　to be placed in a warm aspect
Scarlet intermediate stock, to be grown *at once*
Blue larkspur (herbaceous)
Delphinium hendersonii (handsome, herbaceous)
Clematis mimertea
Convolvulus minor (annual)
Concopsis tinctoria (annual)
Phlox drummondii (herbaceous, handsome)

These seventeen sorts of plants from Selborne.

On the 19th he adds ten more sent by Sarah Street.

Paesonea given me by Sir G. Walker
Paesonia volk
Blue gum, New Zealand, 1870
Castor oil, New Zealand
White *Sinium* NZ

Clyanthus NZ
Kaureuai, large white clematis
Clyanthus dunedin
Crimson flax, NZ
African plant, NZ
American groundsel
Alonjea

25 January, 1881. Seeds of India.

Impomaea vilifolia and *caerulea*
Mixed convolvulus
Poinsettia coccina
Lophospermum
Antigonia
Leptospermum
Passiflora alba
Iponica disecta

APPENDIX B

Children of Jeremiah Lear and Ann Skerritt

Ann	Sarah	Mary	Henry	Eleanor
born 1791	4th child	born 1796	born 1798	born 1799
	m.	m.	USA (N)	m.
	Mr Street	Mr Boswell	4 children	Mr Newson
	born 1794			

Jane	Olivia	Harriet	Cordelia	Fred
		1802–40	born 1803	USA (S)
				10 children
				born 1805

Florence	Charles	Edward	Catherine 1813
born 1806	born 1808	born 1812	
	13 Nov.		

Dates of birth as registered in 1822, Dr Williams' Library

Notes and References

Works also listed in the bibliography are given here with a reference number; they are listed there under the author's name in date order.

INTRODUCTION

1. Royal Academy Exhibition Catalogue (1985), pp. 210–11.
2. Iona and Peter Opie (eds.), *Oxford Dictionary of Nursery Rhymes* (Oxford, 1951; rev. edn 1975).
3. Herbert Read (ed.), *Knapsack: a pocket-book of prose and verse* (London, 1939), n. 167.

ONE: BOYHOOD

1. Vivien Noakes [5].
2. Ray Murphy discusses it in the introduction to Edward Lear's *Indian Journal* (1953, an incomplete selection from the text Lear prepared for the press). The life and development of Gravesend and other relevant suburbs, including Holloway, is pungently discussed by John Collins in *The Two Forgers* (1992), pp. 57–72, because T. J. Wise was born there.
3. Peter Ackroyd, *Dickens* (London, 1990), pp. 69–76.
4. Angus Davidson, p. 5.
5. Ackroyd, pp. 115–23.
6. Edinburgh Ms. 3321, f. 18.
7. Ibid., November 1829, f. 26.
8. Ibid., f. 29.
9. Ibid., f. 31.
10. Royal Academy Exhibition Catalogue (1985), p. 77.

TWO: THE PAINTER OF BIRDS

1. Harvard Ms. Typ. 55.4
2. Royal Academy Exhibition Catalogue (1985), p. 78.

3. Vivien Noakes [5], p. 32.
4. Frances Smith, *Daniel Fowler: The Painter of Amherst Island*.
5. Noakes, [5], p. 33.
6. Ibid., pp. 34–5.
7. Susan Hyman, *Edward Lear's Birds* (London, 1980), p. 34.

THREE: THE LITHOGRAPHER

1. D. Porzio (ed.), trans. Camberwell, *Lithography* (London, 1983).
2. Aloys Sennefelder was born in Prague in 1771; his father, who was from Franconia, was an actor in royal theatres.
3. Porzio, illus. Goya: p. 50; Géricault: p. 59; Delacroix: pp. 20, 58.
4. Brian Reade [1], p. 28.
5. Royal Academy Exhibition Catalogue (1985).
6. Susan Hyman, p. 45.
7. Vivien Noakes [5], p. 40.
8. Royal Academy Exhibition Catalogue (1985), pp. 207–9.
9. Harvard Ms. Eng. 797.
10. Vivien Noakes (ed.) [4], pp. 19–20.

FOUR: INTIMATE INTERLUDES

1. Royal Academy Exhibition Catalogue (1985), p. 94, 13(b).
2. Ibid., p. 94.
3. Harvard, Ms. Typ. 55.14.
4. Arts Council Exhibition Catalogue (1958), no. 13.
5. Vivien Noakes [5], pp. 42–3; [2], p. 78.
6. Noakes [5], p. 32.
7. Lady Strachey [1], pp. xviii–xx.
8. Dated as 1821 by the Opies, 1823 by Noakes.
9. Much light is cast on this entire subject in the Introduction and various notes to the *Oxford Dictionary of Nursery Rhymes* (Oxford, 1951), and I pieced together this part of my story from that volume.
10. Royal Academy Exhibition Catalogue (1985).
11. Angus Davidson, p. 118f.
12. Royal Academy Exhibition Catalogue (1985), pp. 179–80.
13. Ibid., pp. 180–1.
14. Arts Council Exhibition Catalogue (1858), p. 34.
15. Royal Academy Exhibition Catalogue (1985), pp. 176, 84(a).
16. Ibid., p. 166.

FIVE: ITALY

1. Arts Council Exhibition Catalogue (1958), no. 13.
2. Royal Academy Exhibition Catalogue (1985), p. 20.
3. Ibid., p. 23.
4. Vivien Noakes [5], p. 44.
5. Ibid., p. 45.
6. Royal Academy Exhibition Catalogue (1985), p. 97; Noakes [4], pp. 9, 29.
7. Royal Academy Exhibition Catalogue (1985), plates 45, 47.
8. Ibid., plate 46.
9. Ibid., plate 44.
10. Noakes [5], p. 46.

SIX: SOUTHERN ITALY

1. Vivien Noakes [5], pp. 50–1.

SEVEN: A TASTE OF GREEK LANDS

1. Vivien Noakes [4], p. 66.
2. Lady Strachey [1], p. 127.
3. W. M. Thackeray, *Notes of a Journey from Cornhill to Grand Cairo* (1845; 3rd edn), p. 37.
4. Noakes [4], p. 86f.
5. Philip Hofer, pp. 30–1.
6. Royal Academy Exhibition Catalogue (1985), p. 190f.
7. Hofer, p. 38.
8. Ibid., pp. 39, 40.
9. Noakes [5], pp. 22, 58.
10. Ibid., p. 61.
11. Arts Council Exhibition Catalogue (1958), pp. 20–1; Hofer, p. 41.
12. Noakes [5], pp. 10, 11, 12, 57.

EIGHT: LEAR AT FORTY

1. Peter Ackroyd, *Dickens* (London, 1990), pp. 462f, 720.
2. W. Holman Hunt, *Memoirs*, vol. 2, p. 168f.
3. Judy Egerton, p. 10.
4. *Memoirs of the Life of Wilkie Collins*, by his son, London 1848.
5. Holman Hunt, *Memoirs*, p. 309.

6. 1845; published Tate Gallery, 1982.
7. *Memoirs* (1858), vol. 2, p. 273.
8. Vivien Noakes [7], p. 116.
9. Royal Academy Exhibition Catalogue (1985), pp. 131–2.
10. *Diaries, 1851–62*, ed. O. W. Hewett 'and Mr Fortescue'.
11. Noakes [4], p. 132.

NINE: CORFU

1. Edinburgh, Acc. 10089.
2. Lady Strachey [1], p. 68.
3. The disastrous trail of his affairs is plotted by Diana Holman Hunt in *My Grandfather, His Wives and Loves* (London, 1969).
4. Vivien Noakes [5], pp. 72–3.

TEN: THE DEATH OF ANN

1. Lady Strachey [1], pp. 124–5.
2. Vivien Noakes [5], p. 73.
3. Now in the Ashmolean Museum, Oxford.
4. Stevenson [1].
5. Byles [1].
6. Noakes [5], pp. 74–5.

ELEVEN: GREECE

1. Judy Egerton, p. 17.
2. Royal Academy Exhibition Catalogue (1985), pp. 169–70.

TWELVE: CRETE

1. *Cretan Journal*, ed. Rowena Fowler, Athens and Dedham, 1984, pp. 112–13.

THIRTEEN: SUCCESS

1. Vivien Noakes [5], p. 81.
2. Royal Academy Exhibition Catalogue (1985), p. 20.
3. Ibid., pp. 174, 171.
4. Iona and Peter Opie (eds.), *Oxford Dictionary of Nursery Rhymes* (Oxford, 1951), pp. 203–5.
5. Royal Academy Exhibition Catalogue (1985), p. 62; Noakes [4], p.89.

FOURTEEN: THE HOUSE AT SAN REMO

1. Royal Academy Exhibition Catalogue (1985), p. 118.
2. Vivien Noakes [4], p. 307n.
3. Royal Academy Exhibition Catalogue (1985), p. 155.
4. Robert Armin, *Fool Upon Fool, or a Nest of Ninnies.*
5. The mummers' plays were first studied a generation after the last possible moment by R. J. E. Tiddy who was killed in the 1914 war, and the texts of many are printed in his memoir (1923). 'The Mummers' Play' by Sir Ernest Chambers, in his *English Folk-play*, followed in 1933.
6. Royal Academy Exhibition Catalogue (1985), pp. 173–4.
7. Iona and Peter Opie (eds.), *Oxford Dictionary of Nursery Rhymes* (Oxford, 1951), pp. 162–3; Royal Academy Exhibition Catalogue (1985), p. 176; *Chatto Book of Cabbages and Kings*, p. 125; Tiddy, p. 231.

FIFTEEN: TO SEA IN A SIEVE

1. Vivien Noakes [5], p. 91.
2. Vivien Noakes [4], p. 239.
3. Ruth Pitman, p. 29; Noakes [3], p. 301 n. 239.

SIXTEEN: INDIA

1. Royal Academy Exhibition Catalogue (1985), pp. 155–6.
2. Vivien Noakes [5], pp. 92–3.
3. Philip Hofer, pp. 76–7.
4. Ibid., pp. 78–9.
5. Ibid., p. 83.
6. Arts Council Exhibition Catalogue (1958), plate 8.
7. Ruth Pitman, p. 205 n. 145.
8. Lady Strachey [2], p. 180.
9. R. Murphy (ed.), p. 35.
10. Lady Strachey [2], pp. 179–82.

SEVENTEEN: THE FALL OF A HOUSE OF CARDS

1. Vivien Noakes [4], p. 247.
2. Royal Academy Exhibition Catalogue (1985), p. 177.
3. Ibid., pp. 189–93.

EIGHTEEN: THE VILLA TENNYSON

1. Royal Academy Exhibition Catalogue (1985), p. 187.
2. Angus Davidson, pp. 247–8.

NINETEEN: THE DEATH OF EDWARD

1. Lady Strachey [2], p. 363.
2. Ruth Pitman, pp. 27–31.
3. Vivien Noakes [4], p. 280.

Bibliography

Note: for Lear's own original publications, see the Royal Academy Catalogue (Bibliography) 1985.

Agnews, *English Watercolours*, 1993

Byles, C. E., *R. S. Hawker*, London, 1906

Clay, Edith (ed.), *Sir William Gell in Italy, Letters to the Society of Dilettanti, 1831–1835*, London, 1976

Davidson, Angus (ed.), *Edward Lear, Landscape Painter and Nonsense Poet*, London, 1938

Durrell, Lawrence (ed.), *Lear's Corfu, an anthology drawn from the painter's letters and prefaced by L. Durrell*, Corfu, 1965

Egerton, Judy, *British Watercolours*, Tate Gallery, London, 1986

Fowler, Rowena (ed.), *Edward Lear, the Cretan Journal*, Athens and Dedham, 1984

Hofer, Philip, *Edward Lear as a Landscape Draughtsman*, Cambridge (Massachusetts), 1967

Holloway and Errington, *The Discovery of Scotland*, National Gallery of Scotland, 1978

Hunt, Diana Holman, *My Grandfather, His Wives and Loves*, London, 1969

Hyman, Susan, *Edward Lear's Birds*, London, 1980

Leger, *British Landscape Painting*, London, 1992

Murphy, Ray (ed.), *Edward Lear's Indian Journal*, London, 1953

Noakes, Vivien, *Edward Lear, the Life of a Wanderer*, London, 1968

The Discovery of the Lake District, Victoria and Albert Museum, London, 1984

(et al.), *Catalogue of the Royal Academy Exhibition of Edward Lear, 1811–88*, London, 1985

(ed.), *Selected Letters*, Oxford, 1988

The Painter Edward Lear, London, 1991

Pitman, Ruth, *Edward Lear's Tennyson*, Manchester, 1988

Read, Brian, *Aldeburgh Arts Council Catalogue*, 1958

(ed.), *Edward Lear's Parrots*, London, 1949

Sherrard, (ed.), *Edward Lear, the Corfu Years*, Athens and Dedham, 1988

Spanakis, *Guide to Crete* (2 vols., in Greek), Heraklion

Stevenson, Alan, *The Victorian Archbishops of Canterbury*, Rocket Press, 1991

Strachey, Lady (ed.), *Letters of Edward Lear to Chichester Fortescue, Lord Carling-ford, and Frances Countess Waldegrave*, London, 1902

    Later Letters of Edward Lear to Chichester Fortescue, Frances Countess Waldegrave, and others, London, 1911

Thackeray, William, *Notes of a Journey from Cornhill to Grand Cairo*, London, 1845

Van Thal, H. (ed.), *Lear's Journals, a selection*, London, 1952

Wilton and Lyles, *British Watercolours 1750–1880*, Royal Academy, London, 1993

Wordsworth, Dorothy, *Lakeland Journals*, London, 1987

Index